MEMOIRS

OF

JOSEPH JOHN GURNEY;

WITH

Selections from his Journal and Correspondence.

EDITED BY

JOSEPH BEVAN BRAITHWAITE.

Herein do I exercise myself, to have always a conscience void of offence toward God and toward men." Acts xxiv. 16.—*Motto selected by J. J. Gurney for some of the earlier volumes of his Journal.*

IN TWO VOLUMES.

VOL. I.

PHILADELPHIA:
LIPPINCOTT, GRAMBO & CO.
1854.

PREFACE.

WHEN, towards the close of the year 1849, I was requested by the widow and family of Joseph John Gurney to undertake the editing of a Memoir of his Life, I naturally shrank from so responsible a task. Little as I felt myself qualified successfully to pourtray the varied features of such a character, I could not but recollect that nearly three years had already elapsed since his decease; and that, with the very limited leisure which I could command, amidst the pressure of professional and other duties, my engaging in the work would necessarily postpone its appearance several years longer. Finding, however, that, notwithstanding these difficulties, it was still the decided wish of those most nearly connected with the subject of this Memoir that I should undertake the work, I finally concluded to engage in it, though under a deep sense of my own want of qualification. Since that time, (the beginning of the year 1850,) I have endeavoured to pursue this interesting object with as much assiduity as my limited intervals of leisure would admit; and I wish to take this opportunity of acknowledging my grateful sense of the large measure of warm and cordial encouragement and assistance, which I have, from time to time, received during the progress of the work from the various members of his family, and from other valued friends.

The materials which I have had before me have been rich and abundant. To say nothing of Joseph John Gurney's numerous published writings; the manuscript volume of Autobiography, written in the year 1837, whilst on his voyage to America, and which contains many passages of deep interest; the fifteen volumes of his private Journal, commenced in his eighteenth year, and continued, with but little interruption, until within a few days of his death; together with a large mass of papers, letters, and correspondence, have, altogether, furnished a repository in regard to which the task of judicious selection and arrangement has been the principal difficulty. In making the selection, the omission of much that was in itself deeply instructive has often appeared unavoidable. The continued reiteration of similar sentiments, however excellent, tends to weaken their force upon the mind, by impairing its relish for them. Impressed as I have been with the truth of this observation, it has not been without pain that many passages have been rejected, in themselves striking and interesting. And I may truly say that few parts of my labour have been attended with greater difficulty, or, at times, with less of confidence in the correctness of my own judgment.

No faithful portrait of Joseph John Gurney could represent him otherwise than as an earnest and consistent member of the Society of Friends. Being myself fully persuaded of the accordance of the principles of this Society with those of primitive Christianity, I have had no inclination, nor would it have been practicable, to throw into the shade his views and feelings in reference to these important subjects. It is not improbable that the peculiar tone which this circumstance necessarily imparts to the present work, may render it especially attractive to his fellow-members in the same religious society. And yet, in the recollection of his enlarged and Catholic spirit, and of his varied services in the universal Church, I venture to hope that there are those—and not a very few—among other denominations of Christians, who will feel some interest in tracing, in his experience, the "life, walk, and triumph" of the same precious faith, "once delivered to the saints." Even in the case of the more general reader, it is difficult to believe that any heart can be stirred up by highly-wrought recitals of feelings and actions wholly fictitious and imaginary, and yet not be touched by the simple and truthful records of a life devoted to the service of Christ, and to the welfare of man. And to the sincere-hearted Christian it can surely afford no uninstructive object of contemplation, to watch the growth of the intellectual, moral, and religious character of one who, in a position in which he was exposed, in no common degree, to the alluring blandishments of the world, was enabled, in so conspicuous a manner, to choose "the better part;" and, consistently with other duties and engagements of no ordinary interest, to maintain, above all, the important position of a Christian minister, called, qualified, and ordained, by the Great Head of the Church.

The ample materials before me have enabled me in general to introduce Joseph John Gurney as relating his own history, leaving me little else to perform, than to add such observations as appeared necessary for the due illustration and connexion of the narrative. Amidst the variety of transactions and sentiments which are here brought under review, it would be unreasonable to expect an entire harmony of feeling, in regard to each particular, amongst the readers of these pages. Into the region of controversy I have little disposition to enter. Such a life stands in need of no laboured vindication. And I feel assured that none can give to Joseph John Gurney's own statements a fair and candid perusal, without being satisfied that it was, at least, his earnest and continued desire so to act, in the varied, and often peculiar, circumstances in which he was placed, as to have always "a conscience void of offence toward God and toward men."

Far, indeed, is it from my desire to exalt the instrument. Few were more deeply sensible than he was, that, in so far as he had himself become "a partaker of Christ," or had been made, in any degree, a blessing to others, it was all of rich and unmerited mercy; truly not of himself, but of "*the grace of God.*" And, in holding out the language of affectionate exhortation to others, his frequent expression was, in accordance with the tenor of his whole life, "Follow me, *so far, and so far only*, as I have followed Christ." Greatly shall I rejoice if the perusal of these pages be made the means, under the

Divine blessing, of leading any to a more deep-felt sense of what lies at the very foundation of all true Christian experience, and to yet more earnest and steady endeavours after an humble, watchful, constant, and confiding walk with God.

Very sensible as I am of the deficiencies that abound in the present work, it is with sincere diffidence that I now venture to commend it to the candid perusal of the reader; and, above all, to the blessing of Him who can alone prosper any of our labours, and cause them to bring forth fruit to his praise.

J. B. Braithwaite.

Mornington Road,
Regent's Park, London,
5th month, 1854.

CONTENTS.

CHAPTER I.

Page

Birth; Family; the first John Gurney; his two Sons, John and Joseph; John Gurney of Earlham; his Wife; his Daughter Catherine; Description of Joseph John Gurney by one of his Sisters; Extracts from Autobiography; his Sister Catherine's Letter of Advice on his going to Oxford 11

CHAPTER II.

John Rogers; Extracts from Letters; Life at Oxford; Studies; "Rest Week;" Return Home; Settlement in the Norwich Bank; "Quarterly Review;" Death of his Brother John's Wife; Extract from the Journal; Edward Edwards; Friends' Week-day Meetings 29

CHAPTER III.

Studies; Butler's Analogy; his Literary Associations; Habit of Self-Examination; Quæstiones Nocturnæ; Extracts from his Journal and Letters; Death of his Father.................... 46

CHAPTER IV.

Reflections after his Father's Decease; Review of his Objects; Studies; his first Essay as an Author; Correspondence with Sir William Drummond; gradual Attraction towards Friends; attends the Yearly Meeting; Extracts from his Journal....... 55

CHAPTER V.

Page

Growing interest in the welfare of others; Lancasterian School; Establishment of the Norfolk and Norwich Auxiliary Bible Society; Parties at Earlham; Course on becoming more of a Friend. 79

CHAPTER VI.

His Review of his Progress up to 1815; his Uncle Joseph Gurney; Bristol; Letter to a Friend on his Marriage; Thomas Foster's Appeal; Death of his Brother John; his Cousins Joseph and Henry Gurney; Capital Punishments; Wilberforce; Retrospect from Autobiography.... 99

CHAPTER VII.

Extracts from Autobiography and Journal; Jonathan Hutchinson; Engagement in Marriage; first speaks as a Minister; his Marriage; Letter to William Forster; Chas. Simeon; Correspondence with Jonathan Hutchinson; Journey on the Continent; Visit to London; Visit of the Mayor and Corporation of Norwich to Earlham; he is acknowledged a Minister.... 127

CHAPTER VIII.

Earlham; Family Meetings; Position in Business and as a Christian Minister; Journey to Scotland and the North of England with his Sister Elizabeth Fry; Edinburgh; Glasgow; first "Public Meeting;" Visit to the Earl of Derby at Knowsley; Publishes his first Book; Notes upon Prisons; Letters from William Wilberforce; Correspondence with Edward Harbord; Exertions to save three Prisoners; Birth of his Son.... 146

CHAPTER IX.

Ackworth School; Joseph John Gurney's Labours there; Scriptural Instruction; Extracts from Letters and Autobiography; Extracts from Journal.... 175

CHAPTER X.

Page

Extracts from Journal and Letters; his first Day School; Journey to Bristol; William Forster's Departure for America; Yearly Meeting; Letters from Jonathan Hutchinson and William Wilberforce; Letter to Thomas Fowell Buxton; Illness and Death of Priscilla Gurney.......... 191

CHAPTER XI.

Extracts from Journal and Letters; Letter from William Wilberforce; Tract on the Authority, Importance, and Effect of Christianity; Illness and Death of his Wife.......... 209

CHAPTER XII.

Extracts from Letters and Journal; Commencement of Work on the Distinguishing Principles of Friends; Home Pursuits; Literary Journal; Anti-Slavery Movements; Religious Services in Essex and Suffolk; Hannah More; Religious Visit to Yarmouth..... 226

CHAPTER XIII.

Visit to Friends at Bury; Amelia Opie; Anti-Slavery Speech at Norwich; Publication of his Letter on the Authority of Christianity, and of his Work on the Distinguishing Views and Practices of Friends.......... 243

CHAPTER XIV.

Extracts from Journal and Letters; Journey to the North of England; Letters to Thomas Fowell Buxton and Lord Suffield; Return Home; Visit to Suffolk.......... 267

CHAPTER XV.

Extracts from Journal; Letter from William Wilberforce on his retirement from Parliament; Visit to Lincolnshire; Alfred Corder; Yearly Meeting; County Meeting on Slavery; Publication of his Essays on Christianity.......... 289

CHAPTER XVI.

Page

Panic in the Monetary and Commercial World; Engagement in Marriage with Mary Fowler; Journeys in the West of England and in the Midland Counties; Extracts from Journal and Letters; Prospect of a Visit to Ireland with his Sister Elizabeth Fry........ 309

CHAPTER XVII.

Departure for Ireland; Labours in Dublin; Visit to the Marquis Wellesley, the Lord Lieutenant; Prisons; Dr. Murray; Archbishop Magee; Archbishop of Tuam; Trim; Cootehill; Armagh; Lisburn; John Conran; Lurgan; Belfast; Londonderry...... 329

CHAPTER XVIII.

Route to Sligo; State of the Country; Hibernian Blunder; Galway; Illness of Elizabeth Fry; Clonmel; Carlow; Dr. Doyle; Ballitore; Yearly Meeting in Dublin; Final Visit to Lord Wellesley; Wicklow; Enniscorthy; Wexford; Waterford; Return to England........ 349

CHAPTER XIX.

Arrival in London; Alarming Illness of his Brother-in-law, Thomas Fowell Buxton; Marriage with Mary Fowler; his Sister Rachel Gurney's Illness and Death; Publication of Report on Ireland; Various Journeys; Extracts from Letters and Journal........ 367

CHAPTER XX.

Interest in Norwich Poor; Breakfast to Operatives at Earlham; Visits to Prison; John Stratford; the Bethel; Reconciling Letter; Visits of School Children to Earlham; Advice to a Young Friend on his Marriage; Giving and Receiving; Day upon a Stage-Coach; Household Discipline; Economy of Time; Youthful Recollections of Earlham........ 392

CHAPTER XXI.

Page

Visit to Friends in Suffolk; Letter to Sir James Mackintosh on Capital Punishment for Forgery; Yearly Meeting; Chalmers and Wilberforce; Journey in Scotland and Cumberland; Detention at Edinburgh; Chalmeriana; Southey; Carlisle; Penrith; Kendal; Manchester; Return Home; Death of his Uncle Joseph.......... 411

CHAPTER XXII.

Publication of the Biblical Notes and Dissertations; Letters respecting them; Work upon the Sabbath; Religious Engagements at Bristol; "Teaching" Meetings; Letter to his Son, describing an Evening at Cambridge and a Morning at Oxford. 439

CHAPTER XXIII.

Extracts from Letters and Journal; Essay on the Moral Character of Christ; Controversy in the Bible Society on the admission of Unitarians; Terms of Union; the Portable Evidence of Christianity; Religious Visits to Birmingham and Lancashire; Meetings in the Open Air; Address to the Mechanics of Manchester; Death of Joseph Kinghorn; Conference in London on the Revision of the "Book of Extracts.".......... 464

CHAPTER XXIV.

Anti-Slavery Proceedings; Meeting of Delegates; Passing of Emancipation Act; Election at Norwich; Petition against Bribery; Prospect of entering Parliament; Doubts respecting it; ultimate Decision; commencement of Visit to Friends in London and its Neighbourhood; Letter to a young Friend; Letter to his Children; Rachel Fowler; George Withy; William Wilberforce.......... 483

CHAPTER XXV.

Visit of Dr. Chalmers at Earlham; Conversations with him; Extracts from Journal; further Labours in the neighbourhood of London; Letters; Sermon at Devonshire House.......... 507

CHAPTER XXVI.

Page

Further Labours in London; Interview with Earl Grey and Edward G. Stanley; Extracts from Letters and Journal; Visit to Ackworth; Essay on Love to God; Conclusion of Labours in London; Death of Jonathan Hutchinson 532

APPENDIX.. 549

LIFE

OF

JOSEPH JOHN GURNEY.

CHAPTER I.

1788—1803. ÆT. 1—16.

BIRTH; FAMILY; THE FIRST JOHN GURNEY; HIS TWO SONS, JOHN AND JOSEPH; JOHN GURNEY OF EARLHAM; HIS WIFE; HIS DAUGHTER CATHERINE; DESCRIPTION OF JOSEPH JOHN GURNEY BY ONE OF HIS SISTERS; EXTRACTS FROM AUTOBIOGRAPHY; HIS SISTER CATHERINE'S LETTER OF ADVICE ON HIS GOING TO OXFORD.

JOSEPH JOHN GURNEY was born at Earlham Hall, near Norwich, on the 2nd of the 8th mo., 1788.* The family of Gurney, or Gournay, is said to have sprung from a house of Norman barons, who followed William the Conqueror into England, and obtained large estates in this country, chiefly in the county of Norfolk. From them descended a line of country gentlemen, who maintained themselves at Harpley and West Barsham in that county for many generations, and from a very early period

* It was not until he entered into active life that he assumed the lengthened name of Joseph *John* Gurney, to distinguish himself from his uncle Joseph Gurney, of Lakenham Grove, near Norwich, who had also, at that time, a son Joseph Gurney.

had one of their residences in the city of Norwich. The last of these dying without male issue, about the commencement of the reign of Charles the Second, the old family estates became, at that period, mostly dispersed among females. The name of Gurney was, however, honourably continued in Norfolk, through a descendant of one of the younger sons of an earlier generation—John Gurney, (or Gourney, as he usually spelled his name,) the ancestor of the present family. He was born in the year 1655, and, notwithstanding his family connexions, commenced life in Norwich in somewhat straitened circumstances. Devoting himself, in his youth, to the cause of religion, we find him in the year 1678, at the age of twenty-three, already connected with the then oppressed and persecuted Quakers. Richard Hubberthorn, from Yealand, in North Lancashire, and George Whitehead, from Westmoreland, (then a young man scarcely eighteen,) were among the first under that name who visited Norwich. There, about the year 1654, they were encouraged, amidst severe suffering, by finding some who were prepared to receive the truths which they were commissioned to declare;* and a meeting of Friends was then established which has been kept up to the present time. The family of John Gurney appear previously to have had some connexion with the Puritans. Henry Gurney, indeed, of West Barsham, the representative of the family in the early part of the 17th century, had a distaste for Puritanism, if, at least, we are to judge

* See George Whitehead's Christian Progress, pp. 23, 24, *et seq.*

from the insertion in his will, (proved in 1623,) of a special charge to his younger sons, "that none hould any fantasticall or erroneous opinions, so adjudged by our Bishop or civill Lawes." But Edmund Gurney, rector of Harpley, one of these younger sons, who was a person of influence, became known as a zealous Puritan; he declined wearing the surplice, and was probably among those who took the Covenant in 1643.* After him John Gurney successively named two of his children. Others of his connexions were also inclined to Puritanism, and some of them, like himself, joined the Society of Friends. In the case of the early Friends generally, their ultimate settlement in those gospel principles by which they became distinguished from others, was preceded by a state of much religious awakening and earnest seeking after God, in which they "searched the Scriptures daily, whether these things were so." Through what course of experience John Gurney arrived at his conviction, the scanty materials of his history do not inform us. Let it suffice us to know that what he became convinced of was precious to him as the truth, and that for it he was prepared to suffer. On the 29th of the 9th mo., (O. S.,) 1682, (so the records of Friends in Norwich inform us,) "Friends being kept out of their meeting house, met together in the street to wait upon the Lord;" and, being there, John Gurney and another Friend were violently pulled out from among the rest, "as if they had been malefactors," and carried before a Justice of the

* See Master's History of Corpus Christi College, Cambridge, p. 301.

Peace, by whom, as they declined giving, on such an account, the required bail, they were committed until the next Quarter Sessions. In the following year, 1683, he was again imprisoned* for refusing to take an oath; and continued in prison, under successive recommitments, nearly three years. He died in the year 1721, having greatly prospered in his temporal concerns; and, what is far more important, having, according to the testimony of those who knew him, taken "particular care in the religious education of all his children," and "continued faithful to the end."†

His two elder sons, John and Joseph, were both men of marked character. John was gifted with much natural eloquence, and obtained considerable reputation by the spirit and ability with which he successfully defended the Norwich trade before a Committee of the House of Lords, against some apprehended encroachments. He subsequently received from Sir Robert Walpole the offer of a seat in Parliament, which, however, he declined, as inconsistent with his religious principles in the then state of the law. Religion had early taken possession of his heart, and about the twenty-second year of his age, in obedience to the call of apprehended duty, he had yielded himself to the work of the public ministry of the Gospel, in which service he laboured diligently for many years; neither "the temptation of prosperity," nor "the kindness and esteem of great men of this

* See Besse's Sufferings of the People called Quakers, vol. 1, p. 515.

† See Collection of Testimonies concerning several Ministers of the Gospel among the People called Quakers, London, 1760, p. 134.

world," being, in the simple but forcible language of the memorial respecting him, "permitted to separate him from that truth which the Lord had eminently convinced him of."* Besides numerous other descendants, he was the grandfather of Martha Birkbeck, whose daughter Jane became, as will be seen, the first wife of Joseph John Gurney.

Joseph Gurney, his younger brother, who, towards the close of his life, fixed his residence at Keswick, near Norwich, also became a valued minister of the Gospel among Friends. His Christian profession was eminently adorned by a life of humility, benevolence, and moderation. He died in the year 1750, after a suffering illness, which he bore with exemplary resignation, giving a final evidence of the truth of what he then expressed—that it had been "the business of his whole life to be prepared for such a time."†

His eldest son, John Gurney, was a man of great activity and energy, and, notwithstanding his extensive engagements in business, devoted much of his time to the interests of his own religious Society, to the principles of which he was warmly attached. In the midst of a course of remarkable temporal prosperity, it is instructive to observe the fear which he expresses in one of his private memoranda, lest his increasing opulence should lead away his children from those religious habits and associations in which they had been educated. He left three sons, all of whom married and settled near

* See Collection of Testimonies, p. 139, and Life of Thomas Story, p. 617.

† See Collection of Testimonies, pp. 238—240.

Norwich.* Richard Gurney, the eldest, on his father's decease, in 1770, became the occupant of the family residence at Keswick. John Gurney, the second son, the father of the subject of this memoir, had, previously to Joseph John Gurney's birth, settled at Earlham. Joseph Gurney, the youngest, resided at Lakenham Grove. The three families were naturally much associated, and exercised an important influence upon each other. At a later period especially, the consistency with which Joseph Gurney, of the Grove, was enabled to maintain his position as a Friend and as a Christian minister, rendered his influence peculiarly valuable.

To those who have read the Memoirs of the late Elizabeth Fry and Sir Thomas Fowell Buxton, the character of John Gurney, of Earlham, cannot fail to be familiar. Generous, ardent, and warm-hearted, he abounded in kindness to all, uniting remarkable activity both in public and private business, with an acute intellect and extensive information. Though he did not in all respects strictly maintain the habits of a Friend, he was accustomed to treat Friends with the warmest respect, his house was ever open to receive their ministers, and he entertained, through life, a decided preference for their religious principles. His wife was Catherine Bell, a daughter of Daniel Bell, of Stamford Hill, near London, her mother being a grand-daughter of Robert Barclay, the

* The elder Joseph Gurney was also the grandfather of Priscilla Hannah Gurney, and Joseph Gurney Bevan, both highly esteemed members of the Society of Friends.

well-known author of the "Apology." She is described as a woman "of very superior mind, as well as personal charms, who in her latter years became a serious Christian and a decided Friend." An animated portraiture of her character is drawn in the memoirs of her highly gifted daughter.* Eminently fitted, as she appeared to be, for her responsible position, the stroke, by which she was so early removed from it, was not a little appalling. She died in the autumn of the year 1792, leaving her sorrowing husband the widowed parent of eleven children,† the youngest not yet two years old. The maternal mantle was, however, in a remarkable manner cast upon the elder sisters, more especially upon Catherine the eldest. Though scarcely seventeen at her mother's death, her capacities ripened into an early maturity, which admirably fitted her for the necessities of the occasion. In her were seen blended a judgment at once sound and comprehensive, a quiet firmness and promptitude in action, a sympathy quick to discern, and a noble

* Memoirs of Elizabeth Fry, vol. i, p. 3, &c.

† The following list of the names may be found useful:—

Catherine died unmarried, 1850.
Rachel died unmarried, 1827.
Elizabeth, married in 1800, to Joseph Fry, of London, died in 1845.
John died 1814.
Richenda, married in 1816, to Francis Cunningham.
Hannah, married in 1807, to Thomas Fowell Buxton.
Louisa, married in 1806, to Samuel Hoare, died in 1836.
Priscilla died unmarried, 1821.
Samuel.
Joseph [John] died in 1847.
Daniel.

disinterestedness, eager to supply the wants of those around her. All this, brought out and matured in her new situation, and, with increasing years, sanctified and enriched by divine grace, gave her a place in the hearts of her younger brothers and sisters, which few besides a mother could have filled. Her advice, usually the result of a conference with her father, occasionally assisted by her two sisters the next in age, became law, not so much by reason of any authority of her's, as that it was illustrated by her own conduct, and felt by the younger members of the family to be mingled with so much wisdom and sisterly love. Her system, if such it might be called, was marked by but little restraint. This was doubtless, in part, owing to the peculiarity of her position. As a sister she preferred the gentler influences of example and persuasion, and as her principles became gradually more decided, she above all sought to encourage a healthy self-control under the discipline of religion. Constant in her own course of duty, the more conspicuous services in which others of the family younger than herself were afterwards engaged, awakened no unhallowed feelings in her heart. She rejoiced in their faithfulness and in their fruits, and still sought to strengthen their hands, without forsaking her own more private path of usefulness.* Thus much seemed due to the memory of one, whose early influence upon her

* Interest in the welfare of young persons was throughout life a marked feature in Catherine Gurney's character. She delighted to attach herself to those of this class who visited Earlham, encouraging and directing them in useful pursuits, and frequently giving them important advice upon their course of reading, &c.

own family, and, not the least so, upon her brother Joseph, was so richly blessed. It will be seen that in later years they had to feel the trial of separation in outward religious communion. This, especially to a mind so susceptible as his, was not without its pain. But, through all, the harmony of their fellowship in essential truth continued unbroken. And as life advanced, the bond which more and more closely united them, was among the many tokens of a growing meetness for that glorious rest, where the redeemed "see eye to eye," and all their aspirations after a union of holiness and perfected love are satisfied for ever.

The state of mind and feeling which prevailed in this young and interesting family, under their altered circumstances, is so fully before the reader in the works already referred to, that it seems unnecessary to do more than briefly allude to it. The naturally grave and practical disposition of their sister Catherine hardly formed an exception to the general liveliness and gaiety which pervaded the circle, and rendered the members of it peculiarly liable to be led away by the various temptations to which they were exposed. Their earlier years were, in fact, distinguished by much which they afterwards felt to have partaken largely of the vanity of youth, but which was yet singularly mingled with not a little of an opposite character. The evening dance, with its whirl of mirth and merriment, the excitement of the youthful day-dream, gave place, in their turns, to days of industry and study, to concern for the poor, and at times to religious seriousness. The contrast was striking and not without promise.

In this large family, Joseph John Gurney, or Joseph as he was then called, was the tenth in order of age, there being but one brother younger than himself.

"My first recollections of our dearest brother," writes one of his sisters, "are those of a lovely boy, who, from his great beauty and sweetness of disposition and manner, was a very gratifying child to his mother. He was so quick that he learned French words almost as soon as he could speak at all; full of tender feeling, of love, and gentleness, and possessing a temper that nothing could irritate, or render fretful. After the death of his mother he became closely attached to his sisters, and very dependent upon us, choosing ever to unite with us, and to follow us in our gardening, building, and other projects.

"Joseph had been nursed by the gardener's wife, who lived in the park by the bridge. He was very fond of 'nurse Norman,' and, when five or six years' old, would escape to her cottage, and share with her children their usual homely fare. We would amuse ourselves by following him, and finding him seated at the little table with the poor family by the cottage window.

"He was always studious, and fond of reading, and had a real taste for his lessons, to which he applied with industry. Whether at school or at home, he bore the character of a boy of unsullied conduct, of fine disposition, and excellent talents.

"As he grew older, he became more and more delightful to his father, and brothers and sisters. He was fond of joining the latter in their schemes of benevolence, and frequently accompanied them in their visits to the poor. His return home at the vacation was always peculiarly agreeable. His life and playfulness, his spirit and zeal in every pursuit, rendered his company most enlivening. He spent his holidays with great method, allotting much time to study, reading Latin with Louisa, and books on serious subjects with Rachel, and would join our family circle in the evening in hearing amusing reading, while he drew."

Many years later, Joseph John Gurney, in his autobiography, thus recalls his own impressions of his early life.

"I remember that in the family order, my three eldest sisters, Catherine, Rachel, and Elizabeth, were classed together; after them came John, my eldest brother, who was succeeded by Richenda, Hannah, Louisa, and Priscilla, usually ranged together under the familiar name of "the four girls;" Samuel followed between Priscilla and me, and my youngest brother Daniel concluded the series. It was a material disadvantage to this circle of young people, that Norwich, soon after my mother's death, was remarkable as the residence of certain talented unbelievers; and these persons were the means of introducing occasional visitors, [at Earlham,] who united decided democracy in politics with very low sentiment on the subject of religion. * * * * But the God of all grace had better things in store for us. He did not permit us to be carried off into the cold regions of infidel speculation. Catherine, our eldest sister, was naturally of a sober mind, fond of reading, which had some approach at least to subjects of a serious import; and she gradually became the decided Christian. Her influence was soon found to be invaluable with her younger brothers and sisters. By degrees she became to them a check on the vanities of the world, a faithful guardian against loose and dangerous views of religion, and a cherisher of all that is good and valuable, whether intellectual or spiritual. * * *

"I do not look back upon my childhood with much comfort or satisfaction. * * * I was a very fearful, nervous child, not, I believe, fractious in temper, nor by any means destitute of a relish for enjoyment, but acutely alive to suffering of mind. Often in the night I was overtaken by an indescribable nervous agitation, as if the very walls were falling down upon me to crush me; and many a time did I spring from my bed, and seek refuge with some kind friend or sister, particularly my sister Elizabeth, who well understood me, and never failed, as occasion required, to pity and protect me.

"I was by no means insensible, in very early life, to religious considerations; being no stranger, from the first opening of my mental faculties, to those precious visitations of Divine love, which often draw the young mind to its Creator, and melt it into tenderness. If religion has indeed grown in me, (as I humbly believe it has, though amidst innumerable backslidings,) it has pretty much kept pace with the growth of my natural faculties; for I cannot now recall any decided turning point in this matter, except that which afterwards brought me to plain "Quakerism." Cases of this description are, in my opinion, in no degree at variance with the cardinal Christian doctrine of the necessity of conversion, and of the new birth unto righteousness. The work which effects the vital change from a state of nature to a state of grace, is doubtless often begun in very early childhood—nay, it may open on the soul, with the earliest opening of its rational faculties; and that its progress may sometimes be so gradual, as to preclude our perceiving any very distinct steps in it, we may learn from our blessed Lord's parable: 'So is the kingdom of God, as if a man should cast seed into the ground, and should sleep, and rise night and day, and the seed should spring and grow up, he knoweth not how; for the earth bringeth forth fruit of herself—first the blade, then the ear, after that the full corn in the ear.' I have no doubt that some seed was sown in my heart when I was little more than an infant, through the agency of my watchful mother; and afterwards *that* seed was sedulously watched and cultivated by my dearest sister Catherine. Yet I believe that much of the feeling into which my young mind was at times brought on the subject of religion, was the simple result of those gracious visitations, which are independent of all human agency, and like the wind which 'bloweth where it listeth.'

"My pursuits as a child were very far from being of the hardy order: I was fond of reading, often made verses, and loved to keep company with my sisters, rather than unite with my elder brother Samuel in manly games, and in following the farming men in their various pursuits, riding on the team to the hayfield, &c. * * *

"I was about twelve years old, when I rode on horseback from Earlham to Colne, in Essex, the residence of Fowell Buxton's mother, in company with her and her children, and spent some weeks in their society. It was a very wholesome change for me, and under the influence of my companions Fowell and [his brother] Charles, whom I heartily loved, I was trained to greater manliness of pursuit, and by their favourite attendant, Abraham Plaistow,* through a somewhat severe disciplinary method, I was taught to swim. Well do I remember plunging into a deep stream, with a rope round my body, and that when with a vast effort I had contrived to reach the opposite bank, my teacher pulled me back again, in a state of great exhaustion, to the bank from which I had made the leap. However, by the help of my comrades, I recovered my spirits, and soon mastered the art; which I am the more inclined just to mention, as it was, many years afterwards, the means of saving my life. * * * During this pleasant and useful visit at Colne, the strong foundation was laid of that warm friendship which I have always since maintained with Fowell Buxton, who afterwards married my sister Hannah. * * *

"It was when (as far as I remember) I was eight or nine years old, that my brother Samuel and I were sent to a boarding-school at Norwich, kept by Simon Browne, a person eminent for his penmanship; his son a respectable clergyman, superintending, with considerable ability, the classical department. The old gentleman died, and John Henry Browne, his son, removed after a time to Hingham, a country town, about twelve miles from Earlham, where I continued at school until I had nearly completed my fifteenth year. The classics and some other parts of literature, were well taught by our master, who had been one of Dr. Parr's scholars; and being much inclined to study, I made considerable progress under his care, filling up some of my leisure hours with English reading. * * It may be remarked, that in sending us to this school, our dear parent did not much protect our Quakerism.

* See Memoirs of Sir T. F. Buxton, ch. i, p. 6, first ed.

However, even this subject was not entirely forgotten; for he arranged with a Friend, who lived at a distance of about two miles, to convey us every First day to Wymondham Meeting. Many a pleasant drive have we enjoyed in this worthy farmer's cart, and seldom did we fail to partake of his generous hospitality on our return from Meeting."

In the autumn of 1803, soon after Joseph John Gurney had completed his fifteenth year, he was sent to Oxford, with his cousin Gurney Barclay, to pursue his studies under the care of John Rogers, a private tutor then resident there. His elder brother John had lately finished his education with the same tutor, and his ever watchful sister Catherine had prevailed upon her father to allow her brother Joseph a similar opportunity of improving himself. Previously to his leaving home, she addressed to him a letter of advice, from which a somewhat lengthened extract may be here given.

"That I may not quite lose my influence over thee, in thy absence, dear Joseph, I mean to give thee, in writing, some general principles of conduct, which it would be a great comfort for me to believe thou wouldst attend to. * * The next two or three years will be most important to thee; and on the right use of them thy future good will in great measure depend. * * Nothing but experience will fully convince thee of this, but I can now see it for thee; and will leave nothing undone that it is in my power to do, to satisfy my own conscience concerning thee, and to make thy path safe and easy. I wish thou mayst sometimes recollect what a friend thou hast in me, and that if I know my own heart, there is scarcely anything I would not sacrifice for thy sake.

"Whilst I have anxiously and affectionately thought over all that concerns thee, it has struck me that thy duties may be comprised under three principal divisions. Those of religion, those of social life, and those more particularly owing to thyself, or which relate to thy own objects and pursuits.

"First. — The duties of religion differ in their external form, according to the capacities and circumstances of the individual, though the internal principle must be the same in all, and this principle leads to a simple endeavour to make *acting right*, whatever may be our situation, our first object, and in order to do this, to make inclination and impulse *secondary* to conscience. * * * It requires little or no appearance of peculiar devotion, but it resides in the heart and manifests itself in the conduct. Something external is however necessary to confirm the internal principle of religion, and as thou wilt now be circumstanced, it will be more incumbent on thee, than it has before been, to attend to this; for the more external temptation there is, the more do we require to have that principle fortified which can alone stand against temptation. Thou art now about to enter upon a new era of life, in which thy own principle must be thy chief security, and hence whatever tends to confirm this is of far more importance to thee than ever. To require a peculiar degree of strictness, as to the externals of religion, at thy age, [is not my aim.] All I desire of thee is to *avoid* a few things, and to *do* a few things. Above all, I desire thee to avoid joking on religious subjects, a fault which is very common to young people. Whatever relates, either remotely or immediately to religion, I wish thou mayst be able to treat seriously, or say nothing about. Much depends on the habit of mind acquired by conversation and sympathy. And though I do not ask thee to stand forth as the champion of religion, yet shouldst thou hear the subject unworthily spoken of, I earnestly wish thee to avoid taking a part in what must corrupt thy heart, and is moreover a proof of a narrow, prejudiced, illiberal mind. And if the temptation be ever thrown in thy way, I also beg of thee to avoid reading books written against religion, of whatever kind, whether of argument or satire — at least till experience shall have fully confirmed thy own principles. As to what thou art to *do*, it is but little, but that little ought to be more conscientiously observed. Thou wilt, of course, always go to meeting on a Sunday, and perhaps sometimes to church also, and if it is only to oblige *me*, do not lay aside the distinction of Sundays from other days, in thy own mind, nor in thy pursuits. Taking it only in a moral point of view, but much more in a religious one, recollect how salutary an institution it is, and how much it is for the general interests of society, as well as for our own individual good, to set the day apart, as much as we can, for sober reflection on our own conduct, for reading the Scriptures, and any other reading of a moral or religious tendency. I believe thou hast too much principle, and good sense, as well as good taste, to pass the day in idleness, as so many loiterers do: I had far rather thou shouldst work hard at the common business of a week-day, than do so. * * * Do not fear being ridiculed for appearing religious. Amongst well-bred and judicious people, such as I trust thou wilt be with, there is no danger of it; on the contrary thou wouldst be the more respected for it. Thy father and I have so fully made known our sentiments, on these subjects, to Mr. and Mrs. Rogers, that they would rather expect, than be surprised at such an appearance. And when thou art reading the Scriptures, remember that there is much that thou must expect to find mysterious, and some passages perhaps to thee wholly unintelligible; but let not this shake thy confidence in their divine authority, nor thy belief in Christianity, nor lead thee into reasonings above thy understanding.

"Secondly.—With regard to thy social duties, I must entreat thee to beware of entering into any pleasures, or forming any connexions, of whatsoever kind, that thy conscience tells thee thy father or I would disapprove. This, till thou hast attained more experience, will be thy best and safest guide; and I earnestly hope thou wilt attend to this precept, as being one of the most important of any I shall give thee. * * And, dearest Joseph, cultivate a principle of true honour, which comprehends much. Though in different terms, it appears to me to be almost the same thing in spirit, as the Christian maxim of 'doing to others as we would they should do to us.' Beware of satirizing those who may not suit thy temper or thy taste; and endeavour to speak generously, as well as to feel benevolently, towards others. Be very cautious never to betray secrets, especially the affairs of thy own family, through inadvertency, for otherwise thou wouldst never do it. Recollect how important it is for our conversation to be well-timed. I need scarcely advise thee to be, as far as thou art able, the gentleman. Thy taste evidently leads thee to this, as well as to despise low and debasing pleasures and associations. Equally avoid low and debasing subjects of conversation, vulgar jokes, &c.; which, more than almost anything, undermine virtuous principle.

"Thirdly.—As to thy objects of pursuit, thou wilt be chiefly regulated by Mr. Rogers, and to him I wish thee to look, in the first instance, for every thing of the kind. * *

In thy leisure hours have a decided object, either of exercise and recreation, or of intellectual amusement; and if the choice of books depends at all on thyself, choose the best, and those of the most established repute of every kind; and if it is only from a principle of honour towards me, refrain, dear Joseph, from reading any that are said to have a licentious tendency.

"Whether or not it is Mr. Rogers' plan with his pupils for them to rise early, I recommend thee to keep to the practice of it. I have mentioned it to him as one of thy good qualities, and I have no doubt thou wilt find it more and more beneficial as thy employments increase upon thee. General temperance and sobriety of conduct I scarcely need mention; but I must observe, that as years increase, temptations increase; temptations to pleasure under various forms; and as temperance is the law which forbids all kinds of immoderate or unlawful pleasures, it becomes, as we advance in life, a most important duty to cultivate this principle in our hearts. * * All unnecessary indulgence degrades, while the reverse ennobles our nature.

"'My son, forget not my law; but let thy heart keep my commandments.' 'For length of days and long life and peace shall they add to thee.' 'Let not mercy and truth forsake thee; bind them about thy neck, write them upon the table of thine heart.' So shalt thou find favour and good understanding, in the sight of God and man:'" Prov. iii.

To this striking illustration of sisterly love, the following extract may be subjoined as an additional proof of the place which the young student had in the hearts of his sisters, at this critical period. It is from the journal of his sister Rachel:—

"*Evening*—walking and talking with Kitty of dear Joseph's going to Oxford. It is a trial to us both. I went to bed under the sweet influence of religious hope, and, therefore, with more comfort about him. I humbly endeavour to tranquillize my mind by committing him to the merciful care of the Searcher of all hearts, who alone knows our earnest desire for this dear boy."

Was this solicitude—were these prayers in vain?

CHAPTER II.

1803—1808. ÆT. 16—20.

JOHN ROGERS; EXTRACTS FROM LETTERS; LIFE AT OXFORD; STUDIES; "REST WEEK;" RETURN HOME; SETTLEMENT IN THE NORWICH BANK;" "QUARTERLY REVIEW;" DEATH OF HIS BROTHER JOHN'S WIFE; EXTRACT FROM THE JOURNAL; EDWARD EDWARDS; FRIENDS' WEEK-DAY MEETINGS.

JOSEPH JOHN GURNEY continued at Oxford two years, with the exception of the vacations, which he spent mostly at home. His tutor, though resident at Oxford, was not in that character connected with the university, or with any of the colleges. "He was," in the words of the autobiography, "a very worthy man, but in no small degree singular." His eccentricity had manifested itself early. "Born in the neighbourhood of London, he had been accustomed, when young, to ride about Epping Forest, standing on his horse, and spouting Homer as he went." Previously to the present period he had been the incumbent of a considerable living in Dorsetshire, which he had resigned from conscientious motives, but had again joined the Church of England, and besides his labours in private tuition, he was now the corrector of Greek for the Clarendon press.

"For him," writes Joseph John Gurney, "I soon felt a warm affection. He was an admirable tutor, taught us thoroughly, worked us hard, and gave us variety of study by way of recreation. We often read fourteen hours in the course of the day. The habits which he enjoined upon us corresponded with my taste. * * [Under him] I pursued my classical and other studies with a delightful relish, and was enabled to form the *habit* of persevering literary labour."

Whilst at Oxford Joseph John Gurney was accustomed to write a weekly account of his proceedings to one of his sisters. Most of these letters have been preserved. They are full of liveliness and good feeling, and as characteristic of the youthful student, a few extracts may be not unsuitably given. He highly prized the opportunities which his journeys to and from Oxford afforded him of more frequent intercourse with his sister Elizabeth, who had been married, three years before, to Joseph Fry, and was now settled at Mildred's Court, in London.* The decided change had already taken place which had been marked by her adoption of the principles and practices of Friends, but her example in this respect had not as yet been followed by any of her family.

Soon after his arrival he writes

TO HIS SISTER CATHERINE.

Oxford, Friday evening, Sept. 10th, 1803.

My examination took place this morning; I can hardly say what it was to me. Mr. Rogers put into my hands Cicero's Offices; I read and construed some lines to him. He then made me construe an ode of Horace. I got through with the Latin better than I expected; but I am

* See Life of Elizabeth Fry, ch. 5.

sure I should have been much better off, if I had not been in such a trepidation. Greek came next, a still harder trial. He gave me Xenophon's Memorabilia; I luckily construed three or four sentences without much hesitation, and with no mistakes. He then set me directly into a difficult part of Euripides, which I had never read; but by summoning up my fortitude, I got through as well with that as with Xenophon: afterwards he made me write Greek and Latin, in which I made no mistakes. As soon as this long and terrible examination was over, Mr. Rogers began quite a discourse: he said that he had never had a boy who had been so well taught, and thought I had made great progress under Mr. Browne's care, which he heard was aided by my own industry, &c. As I feel disposed to tell thee the real state of every thing, I thought I ought to put this in with other things, and I cannot say what a relief it was to me when his judgment was pronounced. As to Gurney, I begin to like him extremely; he is really clever, very agreeable, and is quite free in his conversation from too much joking. * * I was quite discouraged when I heard him talking of reading 1000 lines of a Greek Play in one morning, but as Mr. Rogers says that I am very nearly equal to him, I hope, by application, in time to be entirely so. * * As to my own feelings, I see no reason for being uncomfortable: but still the parting from you has had a great effect upon me. I am sure I feel all that you have done for me, though I was not able to express it. * * I value thy writing more than any thing I have, and shall often read it.

TO THE SAME.

Oxford, Friday, Sept. 17, 1803.

We began our regular studies on Monday. * * * Mr. Rogers has fixed seven o'clock to be the time of beginning before breakfast, but Gurney and I get up a little before six, and take some exercise in the public walks to fortify us against the literary fatigues of the day. We stay in the study till nine o'clock, which is our breakfast hour; the time is employed in algebra, geometry, writing, and ciphering in their turns; and we constantly read a chapter of [the] Greek Testament before we go up to breakfast. We are allowed an hour, from 9 to 10, for breakfasting and taking a run. We then go in and settle to Greek, &c., till one. At one we either take a walk, or go to bathe till two, when we settle to our studies till three, which is our dining time. The remaining two hours are taken from the afternoon, and much to my comfort, the evening is leisure. Perhaps eight hours may seem too little, but we are kept so close to study during these eight hours, that I seem to do more than I did at Mr. Browne's. * * There is not the least probability of my getting acquainted with any of the young collegians, so thee need have no anxiety on that head. * * I read thy writing over last Sunday, and intend to do it every week, as *nothing does me so much good*, and I shall endeavour as much as I can to keep to thy injunctions.

TO HIS FATHER.

Oxford, Sept. 25, 1803.

* * * Mr. Rogers is a very pleasant and learned gentleman; he makes us fag, but treats us very kindly and sociably. Altogether I like him extremely. * * We write copies every other morning, besides exercises and themes, which, according to thy injunctions, he makes me *write neatly*.† * * On Sunday we go to meeting about 11 o'clock. There is only one family besides Gurney and me, and we sit in a private room. The family is very respectable, and I see no reason for not having as good meetings there as any where else.

TO HIS SISTER CATHERINE.

Oxford, Sunday Morning, May 28th, 1804.

I often think that I never lived more pleasantly anywhere than I do here, for in such continued occupation, I have really no time to think of anything uncomfortable. We are going

† See the remarks on writing well, in the Thoughts on Habit, p. 123, 8vo. edition.

on better than ever in our different pursuits. In Latin we are wading through Tacitus, and have almost got to the end of Lucretius. * * What time I have to spare, which has been actually none for the last week or two, I employ in writing Latin.† * * In Greek we have read, this half year, a great

† He thus describes his daily habits in a Latin epistle, which he wrote about this time to his sister Louisa. As the production of a boy not yet sixteen, the extract may not be without its interest to some readers.

* * * * procedo semper iisdem
In studiis constans; tempusque volubile currit.
Cum primum Phœbus dispergit lumina grata,
Assiduus surgo; recipit me bibliotheca;
Lectito, vel scribo; cerebrum geometrica vexant.
Sobria post hæc solantur jentacula fessum;
Butyrum panisque novus cum lacte recenti.
* * * *
Mox iterum petimus Musis sacrata sacella,
Ac modo Thucydides, Sophocles modo conterit horas.
Cum vero Phœbus,—namque is mensura diei,—
Cœruleam cœli curru jam transiet arcem,
Et declinat equos, libros dimittimus; atque
Aut animum recreant corpusque, virentia rura,
Aut apud Oxonii collegia sancta vagamur.
* * * *
Ad libros tandem redimus; doctrinaque rursum
Gaudia, sudores præbet. Mox advenit hora
Lætarum dapium, mensæque struuntur opimæ.
Vescimur; atque focum pransi circumdamus omnes,
Dulci colloquio major pars tum fugit horæ.
Jam Rogera sales, jam nunc Gurneius edit
Germanus noster; Rogerus et ipse relaxat.
* * * *
Cætera pars studiis solitis devota diei;
Annales Taciti legimus, Carumque profundum,
Aut Popius noster delectat carmine mentem.
Adveniunt tandem tenebrosæ tempora noctis,
Tempora defessis, credas, gratissima nobis!
* * * *

deal of Thucydides and Sophocles. What we do least of is Mathematics. * * We attend a good deal more to the different kinds of Philosophy, Law, and History. * * I have finished reading Ecclesiasticus on Sundays; I like it very much, but not nearly so well as the New Testament.

TO THE SAME.

Oxford, June 11th, 1804.

I have not spent my time quite so pleasantly since I last wrote; for our tedious "rest week" pursuits have, as usual, thrown a gloom over our party, particularly over poor Gurney, who is certainly liable entirely to lose his spirits, by being too much fagged. To explain this to thee in the most concise manner:—we have been reading aloud constantly every day to Mr. Rogers, and writing down sheet after sheet of what he has dictated to us, from about seven before breakfast till nine or half-past nine at night, at least with but few intermissions. Thee may imagine how tedious this must be.

The following extract from the Autobiography will throw further light upon this singular misnomer.

Sometimes the eccentricities of my preceptor puzzled me not a little. I well remember that when we were reading Livy together, he insisted on our writing down the patriotic harangues which he poured forth at every lesson, in defence of the People, *versus* the Patricians. It was an unprofitable task, until I bethought myself of writing down in Latin the effusions which my teacher spouted in English. This impromptu translation was of course extremely inaccurate, but it gave me a facility in writing Latin, of which I find myself even now not wholly destitute. I observed that Rogers allured us into industry, by frequently varying our lessons. One exception to this rule, however, fell to our lot during the closing week of the half year, which went by the name of "rest week," when he insisted on our re-construing to him the whole of the Latin or Greek which we had been reading for months previously. Never, while memory lasts, shall I forget our thus translating to him the whole of Longinus in a single day. I knew the book pretty well, and went on glibly enough with the work, but my companion stumbled sadly, and at last lost his temper and half kicked down the table at which we were sitting, but it was all in vain; our master was peremptory, and the task was finished before we retired to bed.

TO HIS SISTER CATHERINE.

Oxford, 8th July, 1804.

I had kept my learning Italian a secret, in order to surprise Priscilla with a letter in that language. I like it extremely, and am reading Davila and Tasso. * *

He thus notices his holiday pursuits in a letter to his future brother-in-law Thomas Fowell Buxton, then a student at the University of Dublin,* who had recently returned thither after spending his vacation at Earlham.

5th September, 1804.

I have passed another very pleasant month with my sisters. Dan came home from Cromer, and I was appointed his master in classical studies; but this, though pleasant, was but a poor substitute for reading Xenophon's Memorabilia with you. With Priscilla I continued to study Italian during the course of the morning, and in the afternoon the whole party used generally to assemble in the dressing room and listen to some interesting work. My father headed these parties and seemed highly to enjoy them. * * We continued our nightly wanders in the garden, but really their spirit had well nigh fled away with you to Ireland. * * I stayed at Earlham over the 1st of September, carried my gun, and shot—nothing. How I long to borrow a little of your power in that line!

*See Life of Sir T. F. Buxton, chap. 2.

TO HIS SISTER CATHERINE.

Oxford, Sunday, 10th February, 1805.

We began on Tuesday with putting all our things in order, after which I once more commenced fagging. I walked a good deal about the town in order to find one of Dr. Kidd's advertisements, but as I saw none, in any hole or corner, all good judges considered it as a proof that he had not begun his lectures, and therefore, by their advice, I staid quietly at home, employing myself chiefly with Greek and Hebrew. * * On Thursday evening, the next lecture night, I sent the boy to the Cellar, as it is called, in order to make myself quite certain that Dr. Kidd had not yet begun, when, to my surprise and mortification, he brought me word that he had seen a light and heard a voice. I flew directly to the place, and, sure enough, found the Dr. in the midst of his harangue. I was really disappointed to find I had missed *three* lectures upon the Nitric, Muriatic, and Carbonic Acids ; but have partly made up for my loss, by studying an account of them in chemical books.

TO HIS SISTER RACHEL.

Oxford, 23rd February, 1805.

My studies go on in rather a flourishing way. I have read this week almost half through one of Æschylus' plays, a great deal of Thucydides and Josephus, two or three acts of Plautus, a great part of Caligula's reign in Suetonius, four cantos of Dante, and a proportionate quantity of Davila; a tolerable number of verses in the Hebrew Bible, some Euclid, and a great deal of algebra; a crowd of German grammarians, with portions of Locke, Gregory, and Ferguson. Besides these things, I have been employed by exercises of all kinds, Latin verses, chemical lectures, and, to conclude the whole, the composition of a long dissertation in Greek:—rather a good week's work.

TO HIS BROTHER DANIEL.

Oxford, 9th July, 1805.

I am truly glad to hear of the very satisfactory manner in which you are now going on with your studies. Never despair; fag on, and you will soon have your reward. I know I have not made much proficiency myself in different languages; yet little as I may have made, there is not one of them that does not now afford me real pleasure. Learning Greek is so arduous an undertaking, that I should not wonder if you now and then felt a little damped about it. Never imagine yourself more backward than you really are. I hope Mr. —— does not follow ——'s method of not laying sufficient stress upon the grammar. Unless you know *that* perfectly, you will always find Greek difficult. * * *Never let a word pass without knowing every circumstance belonging to it.* You will find this method tedious at first, but it will, I assure you, soon smooth down your difficulties.

He was scarcely seventeen when he was removed from the care of John Rogers, in the 8th month, 1805. He had become attached to his tutor and to his studies, and quitted the place with regret; but there was brightness in the thought of settling at home.

"In three months I shall be with you," he wrote to one of his sisters, "What a delightful prospect! I have set my mind upon cutting some figure in business!"

The bank, in which his father was a partner, had been established in Norwich, in the year 1770. Since that time the concern had been considerably extended, and several branch banks, at Lynn, Fakenham, Yarmouth, and other places, were now connected with it. His elder brother John had been placed in the establishment at Lynn. His brother Samuel had been sent up to London, where he finally became the head of a distinct concern; so that circumstances had prepared the way for that which Joseph John Gurney had himself all along desired,—a place in the bank at Norwich. Here, in the enjoyment of daily communication with his father, and a home at Earlham with his sisters, the ensuing three years passed in what then appeared to him almost uninterrupted happiness. The family circle was, for some time, but little broken in upon. Of his sisters, Elizabeth only was married. The two elder ones continued to watch over the progress of his mind, and the gradual formation of his character, with an almost maternal solicitude. All were ardent in their thirst for knowledge, and anxious for self-improvement, and their society was at once delightful and stimulating to their younger brother.

In the year 1806 he accompanied his father, and a large family party, in the tour through Scotland, and the English Lakes. Several important changes in the family circle quickly followed. His sister Louisa became the wife of Samuel Hoare, of Hampstead and his sister Hannah was soon afterwards married to Thomas Fowell Buxton. A warm friendship had long subsisted between himself and his new brothers-in-law, which more frequent association and closer intimacy served only continually to strengthen as they advanced in life. Bright, indeed, appeared these days of his early manhood. Happy in his family circle, the world around seemed to him to partake of its loveliness. His fondness for music and dancing gave an additional fascination to some of the more specious allurements of pleasure, and whilst the duties of business were not neglected, and his studies were pursued with unremitting eagerness, he became at this period a frequent visitor at balls and other similar entertainments, where his engaging manners and person, and varied accomplishments rendered him an object of general attraction. It is plain, however, from his private memoranda, that Divine Grace was through all secretly working in his heart. He had early accustomed himself to the habit of self-examination, and soon after his return from Oxford he commenced the practice of periodically reviewing his conduct upon paper. The following are from the earliest that have been preserved of these "Quarterly Reviews," as he called them:—

22nd February, 1807. * * Alas! I am still a prey to evil desires. But thanks be to God, his grace has visited me at seasons. I do feel and know my own great weakness, and have been enabled at times to pray fervently to the Lord of our salvation for his gracious assistance. * * * He knoweth the frailty of our natures, and I am humbly led to hope that the spiritual light with which he has lately favoured his sinful servant may be the beginning of his work on my heart, and may fortify me in time against the many temptations that surround me. O may a continual watchfulness and unshaken perseverance on my part bring down upon me the increase of his grace and prepare me for the more constant influence of his Holy Spirit. * * * * My studies have been subject to family interruptions. But since the marriages have been completed, and a few of us have been left at home in delightful quiet, I have accomplished a great deal, and that with much satisfaction to myself. I have not yet by any means perfected myself in the habit of digesting, and reasoning upon what I read. I am, however, improved in this respect, and am more than ever sensible of its importance. As to my *manners;* would that I could stamp that doctrine more firmly on my heart, of preferring others in all things little and great to ourselves. This, I have often thought, is the true spring of politeness. Another consideration which has lately occupied much of my attention is this, whether or no I should give up the amusement of field sports. I have often taken great delight in the pursuit of them, but am in my heart convinced that they are morally wrong. I have this day come to my determination, and have solemnly renounced them for ever. May the Spirit of the Lord support me in this, as in all other good resolutions, for of myself I am nothing.

December 20th, 1807. * * * It is impossible for me to express how deeply I feel that the *grace* of God has been exercised towards me. I ascribe to myself no merit. The Saviour of the world, and the Lord of Light has been my comfort and my cure. O that my gratitude may be commensurate with his *gift.* O that I may continue to be conscious in deep humility of my own entire insufficiency, and of the excellence and necessity of his redeeming grace. * * From the experience which I have now had, I am sure that if I do really humble myself before my gracious Creator he will continue to protect me, and that all my failings will be expelled, at last, by the power of his grace. * * For if our nature were not capable of perfection, Jesus would never have commanded us to be perfect, even as our Father which is in heaven is perfect. But how impossible for us to attain to such a state without the merits of our Redeemer and the grace of our God.

March 20th, 1808. * * * It has struck me most forcibly this day how constantly the thoughts of all mankind are occupied about their worldly business, and though many may believe in Christ, yet how little they think of him. O that our souls could be enlightened, so that we might not only believe, but know, not only know but feel that we are now existing in a state of trial, that it signifies little whether we are rich or poor, fortunate or unfortunate, that the period of this life is but as a *speck in eternity*, and that if we continue to be thoughtless through that little life we lose our chance of happiness for EVER. O think what these words imply.

O Father all—merciful, be thou pleased to lighten our darkness so that we may be convinced that the things of this world are as a flower that withereth, as a shadow that fleeth away. Be pleased to make us careful of our eternal welfare, and so to order our lives that we may walk in thy way, and through Christ obtain thy mercy. Establish us upon the rock of thy faith, that when the floods beat, and the winds blow, we may stand fast, and be thine for evermore!

It was not long before an event occurred which was made the means of effectually confirming these impressions. His sister-in-law Elizabeth, the lovely and accomplished wife of his eldest brother John, the daughter of his uncle Richard Gurney, and the favourite of the whole circle, sank into a rapid decline, and died about a year after her marriage, on the 12th of the 5th mo. 1808.

"This," he writes in the Autobiography, "was our first grand draught of family affliction, since my mother's death—a draught, which, in the bitterness and dismay of our spirits, we all drank together to the very dregs. Never, I believe, shall I forget the solemn summer evening, when our sister's remains arrived at Earlham, the hearse slowly advancing to the house through the avenue of lime trees. Never shall I forget the overwhelming woe of our beloved brother. His bodily health was dangerously affected by his long watching and nursing; but, thanks be to the Author of all good, the affliction was blessed to his soul, and was the means of bringing him, in repentance and humiliation of spirit, to the Saviour's feet. There he found his home, for this world, and I humbly trust for that which is to come."

Joseph John Gurney's "Quarterly Review," written soon after this event, records in a striking manner the state of his mind at this period.

June 19*th*, 1808. Many things have conduced to render this last quarter deeply interesting. In March, I was in London, attending a brother's wedding;* in May, how different was the scene produced by a sister's death! I pray God that the impression of this last sad event may never be lost on the minds of any of us; at least that the effects of it may last for ever. I may truly say, it has left upon me a comfortable impression. While it has convinced me by bitter experience of the instability of every human thing, it has led me to look forward, at times, in deep humility, to that eternal rest, which is awarded to the righteous by "the Father of lights," and which ought to be the constant object of our desires and our energies.

O may this blessed prospect incite me and all of us, not only to call Lord, Lord! but to do the will of our Father which is in heaven. Indeed I have strongly felt lately that it is not by word alone, not by making profession, but in acting up to the precepts of a Saviour in all humility, that we must expect salvation. We have the comfort to think that the mind of our dear departed Elizabeth had long been influenced by the religion of life: we may reasonably hope, therefore, that she is blessed in the sight of God; and if we also strive in the same good cause, we may trust through the grace of God that we shall be reunited to her, and that in bliss; not in this motley, passing, and unsatisfying scene, but in the purity of heaven, and the everlasting presence of our Lord.

How light is affliction, if Christ be our refuge—"Come unto me, all ye that labour and are heavy laden, and I will give you rest; for my yoke is easy, and my burden is light."

But I must turn to the review of myself. It is discouraging, amidst such lessons, to find myself still a prey to many

* The marriage of his brother Samuel Gurney.

imperfections: — but I am improved. I have been less addicted to my various faults this quarter than I was before: may I not say that I have been more devoted to Jesus my Saviour? May I be patient, therefore, under all my discouragements till the Lord shall have perfected his work. My principal faults I have enumerated in my nightly questions;* they are still with me, but I trust they are diminished in substance, though not in number. They arise from my nature, which is very weak, far weaker, I believe, than that of my neighbours. Thence it is that I do not always boldly adhere to the plain unaltered truth — thence that I am immoderate in my diet or unseemly in my thoughts—thence that I am personally vain—thence that I am ever afraid of the rebukes and accidents of life. In proportion as I become in any degree more devoted to religion, I find these defects decrease; which convinces me that religion and only *that*, affords a remedy; and that in religion I may finally experience a *complete* remedy. It remaineth, then, that I should more and more fervently pray for the assistance of my Saviour—more and more earnestly endeavour to do his will.

Almighty and everlasting Father! I thank thee that thou hast been pleased to chastise me, because I know that thou chastisest him whom thou lovest. I thank thee that thou hast vouchsafed to draw me one step nearer to thee; to wean me in some measure from the transitory scenes of this life; and, O Lord, I entreat thee to perfect the work which thou hast begun, to make me daily more humble, more pure, more godly; and not me only, but all those whom I tenderly love; that in union of spirit we may serve thee here, and together partake hereafter of thy rest eternal in the heavens!

Business.—I have but little to say on business. It has gone on much as usual. I am not sufficiently diligent. In a late instance I fear I have exulted in the misfortunes of others. This must not be.

Studies.—On a review of my studies, I find that they have

* See *infra*, p. 51.

been much interrupted by my journey to London, my sad sojourn at Lynn, and other succeeding circumstances; but they have, at times, unusually prospered, and on the average, have been very fairly getting on. I hope I begin to learn not to consider study, that is to say, literature, my first object. May I more and more keep the first of all objects in view, through this and all other of my pursuits. I have felt great satisfaction lately in many of my studies, themselves conducing to the furtherance of the great cause in my own heart.

As a consequence of the above event, his brother John was brought into an intimate acquaintance with Edward Edwards, of Lynn, a pious minister of the Church of England, the friend of Charles Simeon and of Henry Venn, who became a principal means of drawing him, together with his sister Catherine, and several other members of the family, into a more decided religious course in connexion with the Church of England. Joseph John Gurney's own course, however, continued for some time undecided, though every year strengthened the hold of religion upon his mind.

"Daily prayer," says he in his Autobiography, "was, I believe, my unfailing practice at this time. Possibly," he adds, "it might sometimes be too much in my own strength; but I am thoroughly convinced that the duty of private devotion demands, on our part, a real diligence; and that very great care is requisite, that, under the plea of our natural inability to seek the Lord, we do not, in this primary concern, fall into neglect and indolence. The promise remains to be sure, "Ask and ye shall receive, seek and ye shall find, knock and it shall be opened unto you."

Further on he remarks, in allusion to his attendance of the Meetings of Friends,—

In the retrospect of the period now alluded to, and, indeed of my whole life since my return home from Oxford, I can with truth acknowledge that no greater means of usefulness and happiness have fallen in my way, than our week-day meetings. These I have regularly attended from my seventeenth year to the present time. Deeply am I responsible for the refreshment and edification which I have often derived from them. Their quietness, the seriousness of those Friends who were in the regular habit of attending them, the sweet feeling of unity in our worship, and the liveliness of the ministry sometimes uttered on these occasions, are all hallowed in my mind and feelings; and were I asked, what has been the happiest portion of my life, I believe I should not be far wrong in replying, the hours abstracted from the common business of the world for the purpose of public worship. The sacrifice is greater than that which we have to make on the First Day of the week, when all business ceases; and the reward graciously bestowed has been to me, and I believe to many others, great in proportion. May none of my young friends and relations, who belong to the Society, ever throw themselves out of the way of so precious a privilege.*

* On this subject, see also his remarks in the Thoughts on Habit and Discipline, p. 210, 8vo. edition, a work which can hardly be too strongly recommended to the youthful reader.

CHAPTER III.

1808—1809. ÆT. 20—21.

STUDIES; BUTLER'S ANALOGY; HIS LITERARY ASSOCIATIONS; HABIT OF SELF-EXAMINATION; QUÆSTIONES NOCTURNÆ; EXTRACTS FROM HIS JOURNAL AND LETTERS; DEATH OF HIS FATHER.

NOTWITHSTANDING his regular attendance at the Bank, and his other frequent interruptions, the first few years after Joseph John Gurney's return from Oxford had been characterised by considerable literary effort. "I do not know," he writes in his Autobiography, "that I ever exerted myself in this way more than during the first two years of my residence at home." Whilst maintaining his acquaintance with the Greek and Latin poets, his attention appears to have been at the same time steadily directed to the ancient historians, most of whose works he carefully perused in the original.

"The course of Greek History," he remarks, writing to a young friend many years later,* "which I adopted for myself, and which I went through with great pleasure, was nearly, if not exactly, as follows:—Diodorus Siculus, up to the time at which Herodotus commences; Herodotus, Thucydides, Xenophon's Hellenics, Xenophon's Anabasis, Polybius, Diodorus Siculus again, filling up all the gaps with him. He is a delightful historian. * * I forgot to mention Josephus, the latter part of whose work ought to be read."

* Under date 3rd mo. 17th, 1820.

Gradually, however, his attention became increasingly devoted to Biblical literature, which continued for many years to absorb much of his leisure. To an enlarged knowledge of the Old and New Testaments in the original languages, he added a diligent study of Jewish history and antiquities, and a critical acquaintance with the ancient translations of the Scriptures, more particularly with the Septuagint and the Syriac version of the New Testament. His ardour in these pursuits led him to the study of the Chaldee Targums, and of the works of Philo and Maimonides and parts of the Talmud; and to the careful perusal of most of the extant monuments of the early Christian Church. The writings of Justin Martyr, Clement of Alexandria, Irenæus, Tertullian, Origen, Eusebius, and Athanasius, with the Commentaries of Chrysostom and Theophylact, may be named among those with which he became more or less familiar. These, however, were the labours of maturer years. The picture of him at the present time, given by Edward Edwards, who was introduced to him soon after the decease of his sister-in-law, is that of "an extraordinary young man, about twenty, actively employed in the bank at Norwich, yet in the habit of devoting so much time to study early in the morning, as to have read nearly the whole of the Old Testament in the original Hebrew."

His habits of study were eminently methodical, exemplifying his favourite maxim, which he was afterwards accustomed strongly to inculcate upon his young friends, "Be a whole man to one thing at a time." The facility at composition which characterised him in later years, was doubtless, mainly the result of the severe training to which he thus early disciplined his mind. Among the works of English authors, few, perhaps, impressed him more deeply at this period than those of Bishop Butler. He was introduced to them by his sister Catherine, who had long known their worth.

"My first recollection of this valuable old book," (to use the words of a memorandum written by her in the fly-leaf of her copy of the 'Analogy,') "is seeing my mother reading it in her early morning walks on the Earlham lawn. I do not remember that she ever mentioned or recommended it to me, but several years afterwards, when she was no more, and I was groping my way to find the truth, I read many books in search of it, and being greatly perplexed by 'philosophy and vain deceit,' I was led to take up Butler, which immediately fastened me. My inquiring mind was met by his just and comprehensive view of the truth of religion. I was fully convinced, and my future course became decided. * * I read Butler over and over again, and always with profit, so that I have ever considered it as one of the marked providences of my life that I was first instructed by so sound and comprehensive a writer. From my recommendation, the other members of the family took to it, especially Louisa and Joseph. The latter profited greatly by it, and infused much of its spirit into some of his own writings, the Portable Evidences in particular."

His position and tastes introduced him to the highly cultivated society for which Norwich was at that time remarkable. At the house of his cousin Hudson Gurney, in particular, he was accustomed to meet many persons eminent for their parts and learning.

Among these, he writes in the Autobiography, were "the late Dr. Sayer, the poet; Dr. Middleton, afterwards the first Bishop of Calcutta; Walpole, the author of 'a Tour in Greece'; Wm. Taylor, abounding in learning, but very unsound in sentiment; Pitchford, a pious and well-informed Roman Catholic, and several others. After I became a decided Friend I lost my interest in this kind of society, and it soon ceased of itself. Dr. Sayer, the brightest and the wittiest of the circle, died. Middleton and Walpole left Norwich; Taylor's infidelity became intolerable to me; and Pitchford settled in the neighbourhood of London. Thus the whole affair passed away just after my own change had given a new turn to my thoughts and feelings."

He had early become a favourite with Dr. Bathurst, then Bishop of Norwich; and their intercourse gradually ripened into a warm friendship, which was maintained unbroken until the Bishop's decease in 1837, at the advanced age of 93.

"He was a man," remarks Joseph John Gurney, writing soon after his decease, "of singular liberality of mind, an orthodox Christian, and friendly to the cause of religion; a staunch advocate of the Bible Society, over which, in Norfolk, he presided; remarkable for a tenacious memory, a great quoter, much read in the ancient classics, and general 'belles lettres,' full of anecdote respecting olden times, and one of the most amiable and gentlemanlike persons, with whom I have ever communicated. His memory will always be dear to me."

Whilst at Oxford, and for some time after his return, Joseph John Gurney's motives for study were not unconnected with literary ambition. But religion failed not to bring with it humbler views,

Writing to one of his sisters, under date "December 1st, 1809," he says:—

"I once thought of establishing a learned name. I now see I have no chance of doing any thing more than very partially to instruct myself. But I often think that fifty years hence, and perhaps far less, it will signify nothing."

From the time of his sister-in-law's decease his periodical reviews of his religious and literary progress become more instructive.

"This practice of self examination," he writes in his Autobiography, "was, I think, useful to me, and afterwards resulted in my keeping a regular journal, the writing of a perpetual letter to myself for my own private use. Thoroughly as I am aware of my own deficiencies, I may venture warmly to recommend to all my young friends, the two practices to which I thus early habituated myself;—the reading of the Scriptures in the original languages, especially the New Testament, and the keeping of a private journal chiefly with a view of close self-examination before Him who 'searcheth the reins and the heart;' and who will render to every one of us according to our works."

The most remarkable feature of his private memoranda at this period consists in the anxiety which they manifest, that whilst study is pursued with regularity and diligence, the culture of the heart and the formation of moral and religious habits may ever be the first object of desire. With this view we find him accustomed to test himself by a series of heart-searching questions, often recording with humiliation a variety of faults, and at other times thankfully noting apparent improvement. The following will illustrate the general character of the questions. They are from an isolated page of the Journal, headed

QUÆSTIONES NOCTURNÆ.

Have I this day been guarded in all my conversation, saying not one thing inconsistent with truth, purity, or charity?

Have I felt the love towards my neighbour?

Have I done my part towards my own family?

Have I been temperate in all respects, free from unlawful desires, habits, and anxieties?

Have I been diligent in business? Have I given full time to effectual study?

Have I admitted any other fear than that of God?

Have I passed through the day in deep humility, depending constantly upon, and earnestly aspiring after divine assistance?

And have I in every thing acted to the best of my knowledge according to the will of God?

Have I worshipped him morning and evening?

It is possible that in the early stages of his experience, there may have been, in the habitual use of these questions, somewhat of a bondage to form; but the honest diligence and earnestness which they manifest are highly instructive. Gradual as, from his own description,* the work of conversion in his case appears to have been, his Journal affords convincing evidence of its reality and depth. Faith and holiness are here every where spoken of in their mutual and essential connexion. No less

* See *supra*, p. 22.

emphatic is the testimony borne to the absolute necessity of the inward and immediate operations of the Spirit of God. With no object in view but his own improvement, and not knowing the things which should befall him in later years, he here speaks with plainness and simplicity of what he himself had heard and seen and handled of the Word of Life. High indeed is the standard of moral excellence which is set before us in the Gospel. And in proportion as the mind is raised to it, so does the judgment upon the thoughts, words, and actions, become more and more severe. This may in part account for the depression that appears predominant in some of the following extracts; yet it is instructive to observe how hope breathes through all, still cheering onwards in the path of faith and holiness. Doubtless there is something, may it not be said, of sacredness, belonging to such communings of the soul with itself, and with its Maker, and it is right that this should be felt. The sense of it is calculated to awaken that seriousness in which alone we can profit by their perusal. And happy will it be for the reader if he be thereby stimulated to seek with equal diligence, that through the power of the same Spirit his mind and heart may become as effectually disciplined to "the habitual exercise of love to God."

July 8th, 1808. It is really wonderful, after even the little experience I have had in a Christian course, that I should be in the state I now am. * * I feel no longer; believe no longer; remember no longer; I seem entirely a prey to the weak and wicked inclinations of my own self;

and as my spiritual, so my temporal concerns—all go on badly; late in the morning; lazy in the afternoon; little study, and no relish for that little; and an inattention to all that is good. I put myself down upon paper that I may see my deformity more clearly. I feel as if I could not look for the divine help, because I do not deserve it. Indeed I do not deserve it; yet whither else can I fly? O cleanse my foul heart, Lord! that it may [be] rendered a fit vessel to receive thy mercy. I can indeed say with the publican, "have mercy upon me, a miserable sinner."

I feel a spring within me at this moment, as if I could return to the right path; may the blessing of the Lord attend it, and I shall prosper once more.

August 8th. I often think of that passage in the [New] Testament, "not those who say unto me Lord! Lord! but those who do the will of my Father which is in heaven, shall enter the kingdom." To do my duty surely is to do his will; and what is my duty? My duty appears to be threefold —to myself, to my neighbour, and to my God.

My duty to myself is to keep myself pure, avoiding every thought that cometh of evil, and keeping my spirit fixed upon the one simple and principal thing. It is also a part of my duty to myself to attend diligently to my studies and private pursuits, inasmuch as they clearly tend to enlighten and improve me.

Secondly. My duty to my neighbour. To fulfil this, let me be diligent in business, and careful of the interests of those under whom I act; let me attend to social claims, by cheering my father, and being constantly yielding, obliging, and polite, in my family circle: let this extend in the proper proportion to other relations and friends. Above all let me become more and more active in serving the distressed and poor; and let me, on all occasions, prefer others to myself; walking with all humility in the sight of my fellow creatures.

In my duties to God, are included all that I have classed under the [other] two heads; but my devotional duties are those peculiarly due to Him. To fulfil these I must study the Scriptures diligently; pray every morning and evening with a fervent and honest spirit, adding the tribute of thanksgiving and praise to the Almighty. Moreover, I must constantly humble myself before him, acknowledging my weakness and sinfulness, and giving glory to my Redeemer, through whom I hope for pardon. I must bear a steady testimony to the truth in this world, I must bow with perfect resignation to the will of my God in all temporal and spiritual trials. In short I must draw near unto Christ, and if need be, take up my cross to follow him.

The hymn which immediately follows the above extract, although subsequently published, is too characteristic of his present feelings to be here omitted.

HYMN.

Whilst, lost in universal dream,
  The giddy crowd is hurl'd
Along the gaily eddying stream
  Of this deceitful world;

Jesus, in secret still to thee
  O! point my holier way;
Bid me from each gay chain be free
  To own a Saviour's sway:

Bid me, beneath thy parent wing,
  Still, Lord, in peace remain;
That every charm the world can bring
  May tempt my soul in vain.

So shall that soul to heaven above,
  To thee in heaven aspire;
And thy celestial light and love
  Be all that soul's desire.

August 19th, 1808.

He thus alludes to the progress of his studies in a

letter to his brother-in-law, Thomas Fowell Buxton, under date

September 4th, 1808.

* * * My time is occupied by the minor prophets, Greek poetry in Sophocles and Brunck's Analecta, some Italian reading, Josephus, Livy, and the Eastern Travellers. Besides these, I am endeavouring thoroughly to study the Greek Testament, writing notes and making extracts as I go along. I sincerely hope you will not absolutely give up Greek, if it be only that you may read the New Testament in the original. Schleusner's Lexicon of the Greek Testament is a book I have just bought, and find of the greatest use. * * I do not go on with Arabic, which is a work of fifteen years; but have enough of it to be of considerable use to me. * *

Notwithstanding this apparent diligence, he writes in his Journal:—

September 22nd. I was to have passed September in the most industrious, steady manner; alas! how frail are all our resolutions. I have done scarcely anything for the last three weeks. * * I will endeavour, if possible, for the remaining week, to make a great exertion, be up at four every morning, doing at least a chapter of Hebrew, one of Luke, and then Josephus till breakfast; beginning in the afternoon at five, Livy till half-past six, Josephus till half-past eight, and Sandys till bed time; endeavour not to go out once, and to be extremely temperate all the while, which will render the effort easier.

The memorandum appended is instructive.

Not done, nor anything like it. O, the folly of an extravagant resolution!

September 25th. * * I have felt not only an indifference, but an antipathy to religion. I have been disposed to look in a gloomy point of view upon that which at this moment I feel to be the source of all light and comfort, and joy and peace.

Now that my eyes are more open to the truth, I see that there is nothing in the Christian religion which warrants either gloom or discontent. * * If therefore I have looked upon revelation with a gloomy mind, it must be, because that mind has been misled by the temptation of worldly and sinful pleasures. This is the explanation and the fact. I have [been] in a worldly state, and when in such a state, it is impossible to look upon religion, which condemns it, but in a gloomy point of view. Religion has no comforts for the unrepenting sinner. It is to this worldly spirit, which has been unusually predominant in my mind, that I trace all the evils of the past quarter. I speak it with sorrow — I am not improved; I am gone backward. I mean more particularly in those duties which respect myself; in that duty, I should say, for the whole may be comprised in one word, "*Temperance.*"* O the blessing, the beauty of temperance! how ardently do I desire it, and how constantly, through the weakness of my soul, do I fail from the attainment of my object. I have been intemperate in my love of worldly dissipation. I believe and hope that it is not our duty to give up general society. We are made to live in it; but we should enter into it with pure hearts and clean hands, with all the caution of careful Christians, lest it should, at any time, steal away our hearts from that which ought to be our primary, nay, only object.

THOMAS FOWELL BUXTON.

December 1st, 1808.

* * * * I am obliged to attend at the Bank at nine o'clock every morning, which cuts off a good hour from my

* The comprehensive meaning attached by Joseph John Gurney to the word *temperance*, may be best illustrated by the following extract from his Thoughts on Habit and Discipline. "The 'temperate' man of the New Testament," says he, "is ἐγκρατής, which means, 'the man who has power *in* himself *over* himself.' Hence it follows that the temperance (ἐγκράτεια) of Scripture is a most comprehensive virtue, embracing the whole scope of that internal government, which, under grace, it is our duty to exercise over our own propensities." 8vo. edition, p. 182.

time before breakfast, and tends not a little to prevent my getting on with anything. Whatever be the cause, I am sorry to inform you I get on with nothing. It is well that learning is not absolutely essential, for I begin to discover I shall never be learned. * * Nor am I conscious of being really improving in my moral capacity, which fills me at this moment with rather despondent feelings, but I trust in time I shall be enabled to make a little progression. Of one thing I am certain, that I much require it. I am reading Butler, whom, as far as I now know him, I exceedingly admire.

January 1*st*, 1809. I sit down in a weak state of mind to perform a duty, which would only become heavier by being deferred. It is the first day of the new year. This is to me a most serious consideration. I wish I could feel it more than I do. But as it is, it imperiously demands of me to think where I am, what I have been doing, and what I am going to do—whether I am advancing or going backwards in that path which alone leads to eternal life. * * *

During the last three months, my external temptations have been such nothings, that there is little excuse for my not having conducted myself *entirely* to the approbation of my conscience. I have at many times had deep religious feelings; I have felt faith in the Saviour of the world; true love to God, and the things of God; and have often prayed to him fervently, that he would vouchsafe to visit me with his Spirit, that I might in all things be obedient to his will. But then, O how wonderful it is, that in the time of trial I stand no longer with the Lord. I have in several instances yielded to present temptations, and have been so blinded as not to see during those seasons of probation, how infinitely preferable is the light and purity of a Christian soul to the foul deceitfulness of sin. O how hateful is sin in its nature, yet how does it tempt us and carry us away.

It is a consideration of the utmost importance, that sin, independently of the punishments which are due to it from the justice of God, must, in its nature, unfit us for heaven. A sinful man, a sensual man, must be incapable of heaven. * * May he who is powerful, vouchsafe to supply my weakness. May he do that, which I can never do myself—renew a right spirit within me, and so regenerate my foul heart, as to render it truly incapable of sin.

Who shall say that we may not be perfect, even in this world? We may, by the divine grace, or otherwise we should never have been commanded to "be perfect, even as our Father, which is in heaven, is perfect."

I proceed with the order of my nightly queries.* Have I, in honesty of heart, constantly adhered to the truth? Not entirely. I have at times fallen into equivocation. I am not straightforward enough; I am not, in this respect, like Edwards, John, Hudson, my uncle Joseph. Let me propose them to myself, as examples on this head.

Have I been charitable? This query embraces much—very much. * * I observe a want of politeness; a want of activity, in exerting myself, in very little things, in the service of others. * * My calling prevents my making exertions for the poor, which I should otherwise wish to make. I fear I have not sufficiently counteracted this effect of business. As to the widest notion of charity, I am not Christian enough to be always charitable. I am still incautious in my manner of speaking of other people; and surely my feelings towards them have been, very often, far other than brotherly. Yet is not this one of my heaviest trials, because my temper is smooth, and very little teased by others. * *

Have I been free from vanity and worldly pride? Far from it. The more I think on this subject, the more I see that Christianity is the only remedy for the evils in question. Christian humility is indeed rarely attained to, yet, doubtless, absolutely necessary to prepare us for the blessings of heaven. May the Lord abase me to the very earth; show me, with full light, what an insignificant, corrupt, worthless creature I am. Then may I, indeed, become ripe for exaltation—for the true honour, which cometh from God only. * *

*See *supra*, p. 51.

I begin this year with an earnest desire to be, throughout its course, careful in business, diligent in study, straightforward in speaking the truth, careful to perform my social duties, moderate in my diet, temperate in all things, charitable to all men, without fearfulness and without vanity, trusting in the Lord, obedient to his will, and full of his Spirit; and whenever he is pleased to call me away from this transient scene, may I be ready to give up all for him.

TO HIS SISTER HANNAH BUXTON.

January 27th, 1809.

* * * I do not know when I have felt more easy and happy. * * I am reading Daniel, the Greek Testament, Apollonius Rhodius, Prideaux, (an excellent book in its way,) Livy, and Ariosto. I have lately finished Butler, from whom I hope I have derived real advantage. His comprehensive and clear view of religion, and his unanswerable arguments are very confirming to me as far as they go. Though at the same time I deeply feel the extremely superior importance of the religion of the heart, over the religion of the head, and that, after all, the doctrines of religion are of importance to us now, *only* as they affect practice. But then I fully see of how much practical importance these doctrines are, because the relations which, according to them, exist between the Deity and us, have the most positive duties annexed to them.—But Fowell will kindly tell me I am stealing out of Butler. So farewell my dearest H.

The practical tendency of his mind, indicated in the foregoing letter, is also instructively apparent, notwithstanding some obscurity of conception, in the following extract from his Journal. His published writings abundantly manifest the increased clearness, though not less practical character of his views in later years, on the points more particularly adverted to in the first paragraph.

April 2nd, 1809. I believe I am prejudiced against that set of people who call themselves Evangelical. But independently of all prejudice, I certainly clearly differ from them in some points. I differ from them in their favourite doctrine of the *inefficacy* of good works; though my opinions may bear towards the same point. St. Paul frequently tells us that no man is saved by his works, and why? not because good works are inefficacious to salvation, but because no man has good works sufficient for salvation. * * *

As to prejudice, it is a sin, and I pray that I may be delivered from it. Pain I certainly have felt, in the inclination of our family towards Calvinism and Calvinists. At the same time, I deeply feel, that as long as the grand thing—practical Christianity—is kept in view by us all, we have no reason to be discontented at differing from one another on secondary points. * *

This is now the time for reviewing my own conduct during the last quarter. How inexpressibly do I long for a manly spirit, that I may fear nothing but God, and for a heart so pure, as to be incapable of corruption. I can, at this moment, say that I am humbled under the sense of my own sins and weakness. At what an infinite distance am I from doing *all* that Christ has commanded. May the Lord bring it home to my heart that of myself I am *nothing*. This is the first step towards confidence in him, towards that faith whereby I may be saved.

TO HIS SISTER HANNAH BUXTON.

Earlham, Sunday, April 30th, 1809.

I rather think the family have given up their old habit of writing letters on a Sunday, but I confess I do not feel alive to the impropriety of the practice, especially if our letters are made the means of our communication on those subjects which are of infinitely greater importance than any thing else. I was very much struck at Meeting an hour ago, by the extreme injudiciousness which there is in our not communicating more freely with one another on those points which I trust we all feel to be our chief concern. How plainly is it a matter of importance that we should endeavour to help one another along in our spiritual path, or at least, that we should be open and intimate on the subject! If it does not lie in this, in what does lie our intimacy and brotherly love? I was induced to write to you, my dearest brother and sister, by reading a sermon of Paley's with John this morning, which is most strikingly applicable to me, and to you, Fowell, and to all of us as men of business. It is that in which he lays down in such clear colours, the danger there is lest men of business should be brought by a continued round of temporal interests and occupations, to a state of religious indifference. * * * John and I both agreed that it was absolutely essential to us all, that we should, while engaged in business, even at the most hurried times, abstract the mind from the cares of this world, if it were only for a few moments, to think of those of the next. Forgetfulness and torpor are the evils which of all others, we are in the most danger of incurring.—I am ready to make an apology, even to you for writing on these subjects, yet I am sure this is a false feeling. It appears to me to be a crust which it is our positive duty to break through; only you must not imagine me from this to be much advanced in my own spiritual course. * * I am fully conscious of the need I stand in of improvement, and that my own endeavours are not alone sufficient; I may also say that I do look for help to him from whom cometh every good and perfect work.

My father is certainly better, and much more comfortable, though I believe him to be still fully persuaded that he is in great danger. This idea is most groundless, according to all the best opinions, but it is impossible to root it out of his mind. Priscilla is thoroughly engaged by her poor, the school, and her bible. As for myself, I am, as you know, rather an unsteady reed, but have seldom been more comfortable in all respects than at present. My studies really flourish very tolerably, though I give up the idea of being a colossus in learning. I wish to say before I conclude, that I am far from approving the practice of never writing to each other without filling our letters with religion; but when our minds are alive to the subject, I do not see why we should not communicate on our highest, as well as on our lowest interests.

On the 2nd of the 8th month, Joseph John Gurney completed his 21st year. A few days afterwards he writes:—

August 6th. * * It has been forcibly brought to my mind this morning, that my manifold transgressions and defects, though known only to myself and my Maker, are sufficient to weigh me down for ever, had I not a merciful Saviour to whom to look for support. I deeply feel that I have no power in myself, to extricate me from my present imperfect state, but that there is a Spirit, and a Comforter, who will lead me in time, if I put a humble reliance in his mercy, through a pure path to eternal rest; who will dissipate these dark clouds of indifference and insensibility, and fill my soul with light. * * Certain it is that much of our dissatisfaction on religious points, much of our impious doubting, is owing to our not sufficiently yielding up our reason and our souls to the *word* and to the *will* of God. * * * *

I have not yet learnt to keep strictly on every little occasion to the straight-forward path of truth. I feel as if I possessed integrity, yet in very little things, and in a hurry, without thinking, I sometimes exaggerate or equivocate. This is mean and pitiful, a disgrace to the religion I profess, and to myself; it arises entirely from the fear I have of other people. This fear is, I think, subsiding. May the grace of God so strengthen me, that in future I may totally banish it.

I am improved with respect to the manner in which I speak of others. The tongue is, indeed, the sign of our faith. Nothing can be more unlike a Christian than to blab the faults of others, and [it] is infallibly joined to forgetfulness of our own.

Worldly pride and vanity, I trust, have not been increasing in my mind. I see their folly, and earnestly pray that I may indeed become a *humble* follower of him who humbled himself for us.

I am often uncomfortable, when I think how little I do for the distressed. I have only one or two objects under my care. Yet I trust I have not lost what opportunities I have had of doing good to others, and I am comforted when I think [that] every man does good by filling up his own station in life, as he feels to be, each day, his duty. * *

I am just come of age. I feel it a striking period, and am thankful to the Almighty giver of all good things, that he has vouchsafed to bring me into it, through a path of peace and prosperity.

Most merciful Father, succour thou the weak-hearted. Help me, for I know that I am a sinner, and that of myself I cannot stand. I thank thee for all the spiritual blessings wherein thou hast mercifully vouchsafed to lead me unto this age, and I pray thee that they may daily increase, so that I may be truly born again of thy Spirit, that I may become, in all things, devoted unto thee, as a little child, in simplicity and submission of soul; that no impurity may lead me away from thy paths, which only are the paths of pleasantness and peace; but that I, and all of us, in union of spirit, may receive the one faith, and hold it fast, and so walk in activity and watchfulness, that we may be ready, at thy call, to consign ourselves into thy hands, that we may live the life and die the death of the righteous; even in Christ Jesus the Lord.

In the autumn of this year he was deprived of his beloved father, who sank under the effects of a surgical operation, on the 28th of the 10th month. The whole family assembled at Earlham on the occasion of his funeral, which was rendered additionally touching by the few words of solemn thanksgiving, which his daughter Elizabeth Fry, was strengthened to utter at the side of his grave;

being her first public offering in the ministry.* To this Joseph John Gurney alludes in a memorandum penned a few days after the funeral.

Sunday, November 5th. "Marvellous are thy works, O God, most merciful, thou King of Saints! Accept thou the thanksgiving of our hearts." May I be enabled heartily to join in this prayer, which was pronounced by dear Elizabeth, at my father's grave! Is it not indeed marvellous? He who was my greatest pleasure, and greatest stimulus in life, the constant object of every day, whom I fondly hoped to have retained with us yet many years, is gone for ever.

On Tuesday, the 10th October, he submitted to the operation. It was too much for his nervous system — he was thrown into spasms, and on Saturday, the 28th, he died. While he was on his death-bed I was seized with the scarlet fever, which, though not severe, has thrown my feelings into a distressing maze, from which they are only now beginning to recover. Yet shall I ever look back with joy, to Wednesday, the 25th, the day before I was ill, and during which I attended him constantly. It was a day of joy. His mind, which has passed through the deepest contrition, on that day rested in the assurance of hope, rested on the mercy of God through Jesus Christ.

How unspeakably great has been thy mercy O God, in thus preparing his soul for the last stroke of thy providence. May we also be mercifully led to an end as blessed, through lives of purity, charity, and peace!

* See Life of Elizabeth Fry, vol. i, p. 144.

CHAPTER IV.

1809—1811. ÆT. 22—23.

REFLECTIONS AFTER HIS FATHER'S DECEASE; REVIEW OF HIS OBJECTS; STUDIES HIS FIRST ESSAY AS AN AUTHOR; CORRESPONDENCE WITH SIR WILLIAM DRUMMOND; GRADUAL ATTRACTION TOWARDS FRIENDS; ATTENDS THE YEARLY MEETING; EXTRACTS FROM HIS JOURNAL.

Joseph John Gurney was but just 21, when, as one of his father's executors, as a partner in the Bank, and his father's representative at Earlham, new and grave responsibilities devolved upon him. That he felt the blow most keenly, is sufficiently evident from his Journal. But religion had already instructed him to seek relief, not in "nursing his sorrow," but in zealously turning his mind to the performance of duty. His father upon his death-bed, had exhorted him "to persevere," and nobly did he strive to respond to the exhortation.

Thus he writes two days after the funeral:—

Now that the funeral is over, and every earthly trace of my beloved father is gone for ever, I begin most painfully and deeply to feel the void that is left. It is indeed a wide void, and God alone can supply it. But, under all circumstances, I feel it my duty to enter with spirit, once more, into the engagements of life. To begin to-morrow, at an early hour, and re-commence my studies, to attend carefully and with activity to the gloomy offices of an executor, and resolutely to apply to business.

An extract from a letter addressed to his sister Hannah Buxton, dated "December 1st, 1809," will introduce the reader to the family party at Earlham under their altered circumstances.

We are going on remarkably comfortably; Catherine, Rachel, Richenda, Priscilla, and I, form so harmonious a party, and are so entirely united in all our cares, pleasures, and pursuits. * * I am extremely busy, having my time and mind quite crammed with the variety of my pursuits. The executors' accounts, banking, and study, are alternately uppermost. In the last item, I go on as usual, sometimes flourishing, more often thwarted and unsuccessful. * * Last week I was interrupted every day. * * We had a delightful visit from Edwards. I never enjoyed his company so much before, and never felt so much at ease with him. I strongly feel how invaluable a blessing it is, to have such friends, now we are so bereft. The loss of one hold makes one cling to the supports which are left behind. I am sure the afflicting event has had a powerful effect in bringing us more closely together.* *

His objects in life are thus reviewed in his Journal:—

November 19th, 1809. Launching afresh into life, as I now am, under totally new circumstances, and in a situation wherein I shall always be obliged to act for myself, I feel the various objects of my life crowding upon me so thickly, as to render it absolutely necessary to make a proper and strict arrangement of time.

My objects are these:—

1st. Prayer, reflection, and waiting upon God.

2ndly. My studies.

3rdly. The bank.

4thly. The business devolving on us by my father's decease.

5thly. The poor.

6thly. Bodily exercises.

7thly. Recreation and social pleasures.

Let the regular time allotted for the first head, be when I first rise in the morning, and last before I lie down to sleep. Also the time of public worship, on a Sunday and a Tuesday,* which I desire more and more to prize and turn to account. Let me also throughout the day, wherever I am, and whatever I am doing, be mindful of the Lord, and from time to time, silently turn my soul to him in prayer, doing all in the name of the Lord Jesus. * * *

January 7th, 1810. * * In reviewing myself during the last quarter, I humbly trust that the deeply affecting scenes it has presented, and carried away for ever, have left somewhat of a right impression upon my soul—have in some measure brought me nearer to the fountain of light and life. Yet many have been the imperfections in my conduct during that period. It is not only in particular actions, but in the *spirit* of every action, great or small, that I want and desire an improvement. To wear in all things the spirit of Christ Jesus; and to do all in his name. In this general *spiritual* manner of acting, which is something I know but cannot describe, I desire to make dear Elizabeth my example. * *

April 1st. O Thou, that art light in our darkness, grant me a single and enlightened eye, that I may see and know thy truth; and an obedient and courageous spirit, that I may be enabled to follow its precepts. Grant, O Father! that my will may more and more be subjected unto thine; that I may not fear to make sacrifices for thy sake. Whatever be the temptations and trials which assail me, be pleased to uphold me with thy right hand, and finally to bring me to thine everlasting kingdom, for the sake and merits of thine only Son, my Lord Jesus Christ.

April 22nd.—Sunday after meeting. * * * I do indeed live amongst those who are faithful to the Lord Jesus—whose conduct is regulated by the principles of Christian

* The day on which the meeting for worship of Friends at Norwich, during the week, was usually held.

truth. A most affecting and striking instance I have had of this in one of my beloved sisters* this morning. May I be enabled to follow her example; may I, like her, walk through this world without selfishness; willing to bear the burthens of our neighbours, for the Lord's sake; and, without fear, willing to risk anything in the cause of duty, and humbly walking in the liberty of the children of God. * * * I thank God that he has given me many objects in life; and I pray that he may be pleased to enable me so to give them my diligent attention that my course may not be run in vain; at the same time that I may always remember, it is but a short course, that eternity is at hand; that all I do here, is, or ought to be but a preparation for what follows: that I may do all, therefore, in the name of the Lord Jesus.

May 20th. I thank my Almighty and All-merciful Father that he has been pleased to preserve me through this past week in the path wherein I should tread. My nightly catechisms, with one or two small exceptions, have been satisfactorily answered. I have been uniformly diligent, and I humbly trust, generally speaking, under the wing of the Lord. I, indeed, know that it is he that worketh in us both to will and to do of his good pleasure. * * I desire to humble myself more and more before him, that he may be willing more and more to exalt me with that true honour which cometh from God only.

The ardour with which, amidst the other numerous engagements now pressing upon him, he continued to pursue his varied studies at this period, is evident from many passages in the Journal. The following may suffice as an example. It is under date

January 7th, 1810. I wish to complete the Psalms, attending a little to Syriac and Chaldee as I go along. After that,

* Elizabeth Fry, then on a visit at Norwich.

to read Solomon, then Job again; to make myself master of the Jewish laws, and translate the "Yad Hachazekah," of Maimonides; to study the New Testament critically, and with a particular view to the great doctrines of the Trinity and the atonement; to finish Ancient History in Plutarch, Sallust, Cicero, Cæsar, &c., after that to read Tacitus, then Gibbon; to read every afternoon a hundred lines of Greek Poetry, and go on with Pindar. After I finish Michaelis I shall launch into English History, and follow it up, if possible, with English Law.

It was at this period, when he was little more than 22, that he made his first essay as an author, in an article published in the Classical Journal, in the 9th month, (September,) 1810, under the title of a Critical Notice of Sir William Drummond's Dissertations in the Herculanensia. The late Sir William Drummond, a name well known in literary circles, was for some years the representative of the British Government at the Court of Naples, and had long cherished the idea of editing the Herculanean Manuscripts, and with that view he had published the dissertations, which thus became the object of Joseph John Gurney's animadversion. It was the first and the last time that the latter appeared in the character of a critic. The article extends over twenty-three octavo pages, and contains an elaborate exposure of Sir William Drummond's mistakes and shortcomings, which are detected with great acuteness. The comments upon them are pungent, and at times severe; displaying on the part of the youthful critic no common acquaintance with Latin, Greek, and Hebrew learning, and with the remains which had then been discovered of the old Etruscan. His numerous references and quotations, made apparently without effort, evince a surprising familiarity not only with the great writers of antiquity, but also with those whose works are, by ordinary students, but little read or consulted, such as Apuleius, Macrobius, Aulus Gellius, Maximus Tyrius, Pausanias, &c. Whilst regretting the small degree of attention paid in England to the cultivation of Hebrew, he will not admit this as any justification of Sir William Drummond's errors; observing, with some warmth, "Nor are the boldness of his assertions, or the inaccuracy of his quotations, the less to be lamented, because they are characteristic of the age." He even ventures severely to criticise Sir William's Arabic, producing several quotations to show that "it is still more extraordinary than his Hebrew." The whole is written in a style at once forcible and graceful, neat and easy, devoid of mannerism, clear, and very pleasing. Though not in its spirit and object what in his calmer judgment he even then fully approved, the effort may be regarded as some index of what he might have accomplished, had he yielded to the fascination of a mere literary ambition.* In consequence of the ability which the article displayed, Sir William Drummond was induced to submit for Joseph John Gurney's perusal an essay which he had subsequently prepared for publication.

* The article is in the Classical Journal, Vol. II, No. 3, p. 524. Having been myself unable to procure a copy of it, I am indebted for the substance of the above account to my friend James Grant, of the Middle Temple, barrister-at-law.

SIR WILLIAM DRUMMOND TO JOSEPH JOHN GURNEY.

No. 47, Harley Street, London,
September 29th, 1810.

SIR—I take advantage of the liberty which you gave me to send you the proof sheets of my essay. I flatter myself that you will have the goodness to correct any errors which may strike you. * * *

Upon coming to town I looked over some of my notes, which prove to me beyond a doubt, that some of the errors which you have pointed out have resulted from errors of the press, to which I did not sufficiently attend, when I transmitted the printed sheets from Palermo. * * In your *critique* upon my "dissertations" you have been more fortunate in a printer. You made a mistake, however, about that same Arabic word for which you have given me so sharp a reprimand. When I was with Mr. Valpy, yesterday, I told him of the error. He informed me that it had been already corrected; *but not by you.* Do not suppose, however, that I shall not do justice to your acuteness and learning, of which I really think very highly. I have not yet had time to consult my books, nor do my notes furnish me with means by which I can account for some of the misquotations which I have made; but with respect to some particular words I have found some of my papers which have, in some measure, explained the causes of the mistakes. * * In deference, however, to your opinion, I mean to cancel the 109th page of my present *opusculum.* I am afraid you will think that my suggestions concerning Hannibal, in my letter to Lord Aberdeen, (prefixed to the Essay,) are too bold. I think them so myself, but some of my friends have encouraged me so much as to make me leave the statement as I first drew it out.

When you have a little leisure I shall be happy to hear from you.

I remain, Sir, your most faithful,
humble servant,
W. DRUMMOND.

Sir William Drummond subsequently writes, under date

October 5th, 1810.

* * * I feel that I have taken a great liberty in troubling you with my work in its present state, and in begging you to examine and correct it. I cannot conceive that much of it goes beyond the sphere of your learning, unless it be that part which relates to the Ethiopian. Of the inscription you are quite competent to judge.

Gratifying as these expressions must have been to a young man, Joseph John Gurney could afterwards thankfully acknowledge that the restraining hand was near to preserve him from being allured out of his own proper field of labour into one more flowery, perhaps, but far less usefully productive. In his Journal under date "September 2nd, 1810," he thus adverts to the subject:—

During this time, besides business, the school, and somewhat of my usual studies, I have been much employed in finishing my *critique* on Sir W. Drummond. In this I am apprehensive I have not strictly followed the light that was given me. I now sincerely wish I had never engaged in it, for it has not been a work of *Christian love.* I have offered to withdraw it: whether it is too late or not I do not yet know, but I am resolved, if it please the Lord, never more to engage in a similar undertaking, unless it be in the simple service of God and religion.

His mind was now becoming increasingly drawn towards the principles of the Society of Friends, and many of his allusions to his feelings on this subject are peculiarly interesting and instructive. "My course in religion," he writes, in his Journal,*

* Under date "July 14th, 1811."

"is a matter of great weight to me. It is my indispensable duty to stir myself up to greater diligence, to more earnest investigation. Above all," he emphatically adds, "may I never fail to *watch and pray*. For I believe he will guide us, if we look to him as the Shepherd of the flock."

The example of his sister Elizabeth Fry, as well as of his sister Priscilla, who, like her, became a decided Friend and a minister of the gospel, strengthened his growing convictions. But the influence of the other members of the family who resided at Earlham, as well as of many other estimable persons with whom he was intimately associated, tended in an opposite direction. This peculiarity of his position should not be overlooked by those who would trace the gradual course of his mind. The change was to him emphatically a work of conviction and of faith.

July 1st, 1810. During the last week I have derived some spiritual advantage, by God's grace, from the preaching and influence of Friends, particularly Priscilla Hannah Gurney, and Ann Crowley. I attended the Quarterly Meeting throughout, with much satisfaction and peace of mind; and I trust I am more and more desirous of subjecting my will to that of my heavenly Father. At the same time I am not yet a believer in the peculiar pretensions of Friends; nor has anything which I have witnessed this week, tended to make me so. Yet if it be the will of God, to bring me more nearly to them, I earnestly pray that no countervailing dispositions of my own may stand in his way. This day I am going to London. Most merciful Father! grant me thy protection during this journey; that I may, in no one thing, disobey thy heavenly will; but that I may cautiously and diligently keep in the path, wherein thou wouldst that I should walk.

September 2nd. "Shew me thy ways, O Lord! teach me thy paths! lead me in thy truth and teach me, for thou art the God of my salvation."

"The secret of the Lord is with them that fear him, and he will shew them his covenant."

That I may experimentally know the ways of the Lord, his truth, his teaching, his secret, and his covenant, I may say is the desire of my soul. Shall I not know them if I fear him, that is if I so fear him as to become humble in his sight, and subjected to his holy will? * *

The last four months contain a motley history. From April 22nd to July 1st, I was much employed. At home I made some progress in my studies; abroad, I was much occupied with business of all sorts. In June, Ann Crowley, and other Friends were at Norwich. Their preaching animated and affected me; but I am apprehensive that I, in measure, deceived myself into throwing off the effect, by entering soon after, into gay and dissipated scenes, at Oxford and Cheltenham. I think I have had experience enough to shew, that this sort of dissipation improves not the heart, but rather, that it forcibly turns it away from things of infinitely greater importance.

* * I have been a good deal under the influence of Friends; and am more aware of their opinions, and better understand their system than before. I have also great doubts about the sacraments; and am at this moment perfectly uncertain, whether it will, or will not, be required of me to become more of a Friend. It would indeed be difficult to the outward man. It is [the] path of [the] cross. I humbly desire that the Lord may be willing to help me through all external and spiritual conflicts, with which it may please him to visit me,—that I may become victorious over myself, in whatever way it may be required of me, through the Spirit and grace of Christ.

Dost thou desire to have eternal life? Then must thou do the commandments; thou must take up the cross, and follow the Lord Jesus, *denying thyself.* St. John says, "And I looked and lo, a Lamb stood on the Mount Zion, and with him an hundred and forty and four thousand, having his Father's name written on their foreheads. And I heard a voice from heaven ;—These are they which follow the Lamb *whithersoever he leadeth them.*"

September 9th. In the first part of this week, which has been spent undisturbedly at home, except one day's company, I was blessed with the presiding wing of divine Providence sensibly protecting, enlightening, and comforting my soul. I have, I believe, endeavoured, throughout the week, to pray for divine aid, and to follow divine guidance; yet I certainly mark a relaxation in the last three days. O how deeply does it impress me with the knowledge of my own weakness, that I cànnot, even for one week, persevere in holiness unbroken, before God! That, at the very moment after earnest prayer, and eager desires after righteousness, I should be ready to sink into indifference and false rest. This false rest is the greatest danger to which I am exposed. I long to have my soul more alive to the infinite peril of doing wrong, or forgetting the Lord. The natural and infallible consequence of continued sin is death. There is but one means of escape, —justification through the blessed Saviour. And in this justification we have no part if we are not sanctified by his Holy Spirit, and *always* walk in obedience to his will.

January 6th, 1811. * * I believe I may say that my desire to live under subjection to the only safe Guide is increased. May He be pleased to render this desire effectual. I have had some powerful doubts on my mind, whether or not it was my duty to adopt the phraseology of Friends; whether in not doing it, I was not paying something like a false tribute to other people. I desire that I may not drive away these, or any other scruples, and yet that I may be favoured with a clear discernment of what is really my duty. At present, as such a step would involve large consequences, and as the thing itself is not now very forcibly on my mind, I believe I may rest, till I have more closely investigated the differences which exist between Friends and others. For this purpose I wish, (D. V.) to read Barclay and Hooker, and to renew a diligent search into the Scriptures. But in this research, I know how important it is, not to lean to my own powers of understanding, nor to suffer in my own mind anything like sophism, but to be willing to be moulded, even as the Lord would mould me. * * I pray that I may be quite independent of all the world, doing simply that which is RIGHT.

March 4th. For the last few weeks, I believe I may say, I have striven against my sins and imperfections. But I still labour under the same want of feeling and want of power. In keeping to my resolution, [as to early rising] I have found it necessary to be pretty firm, and I desire to have a renewed care this week about it, and to guard myself if possible against discouragement. O for more of the life, and the spirit, and the faith! Gird me, O Lord, to a diligent and watchful conduct throughout this week, that in all my works begun, continued, and ended in thee, I may have peace.

May 19th. I am this day going to London, chiefly for the purpose of attending the Yearly Meeting of Friends; also with much business on my hands.

It is my earnest desire, that I may keep myself alive, whilst I am there, to a humble, religious, and diligent state; that I may remember, that I am only an inquirer, and that I may conduct my inquiry under the wing and protection of Almighty God. Above all, I desire that nothing human may influence my judgment, that my eyes may be open to the truth, my heart sensible of the life of the gospel, and my whole soul brought under subjection to the Author of all good; and may he be pleased, graciously to regard the extreme weakness of his servant, to lighten his eyes, confirm his steps, and finally accept him, for the sake of his ever blessed Redeemer!

June 25th. I came down this morning [at] a quarter past seven, after having determined to be down always at a quarter past six. I am sensible this is a transgression, an act of disobedience to the Spirit of light within, and I desire to impress upon myself the necessity of obeying that call more punctually in these little things, (which in themselves, however, are to me of great importance,) lest the Spirit be grieved and my strength impaired.

July 14*th*. It is now more than half a year since I regularly reviewed myself on paper. It has been a half year full of business of many sorts, and, I trust, not entirely unproductive of good. * * At *some* times during this period I have known what it is to live, as it were, in the presence of the Beloved; and O may that blessed and only satisfying lot become, through faith and patience, more my constant portion! * * * I believe that if I do more humbly and more sedulously endeavour to observe and to follow the will of my Great Master, he will in his own good time give me more power and more light. In the meantime let me humble myself in his presence, acknowledging, with contrition of spirit, that *of myself I can do nothing;* and let me come unto Jesus, as a little child, desirous, in simplicity of heart and eye, to know and to do his will.

In May, I went to the Yearly Meeting of Friends. It was an interesting time, and I think wholesome to me in many ways. In the first place it afforded me a fresh stimulus, on general grounds, to seek the Lord with all my heart; and secondly, it introduced me to a more particular acquaintance with the Society. I thought, some time since, I was advancing to a greater agreement with this most excellent religious body; but I now feel a little thrown back;—but this is at a time of general weakness.

I can, in theory, agree with them in much of their doctrine of spiritual guidance; but I fear greatly that my practice is contrary to the precepts they build upon it. If it be true, that there is this living power which will direct us, under all circumstances, in the sure path which leadeth to life, O what a happiness to know it; and what a misery to be without it! O that the Lord would be pleased to give me this holy gift in larger measure, and to bestow upon me a heart to follow and obey him.

I also think, that Friends have reason on their side with respect to the ministry; because I can hardly conceive any other authority for the ministry, than the direct gift of the Spirit. * * Their testimonies about oaths and war, put them, I think, upon a very high ground; and their ecclesiastical discipline is very admirable. I also think there is some reason in their minor testimonies, about plainness of speech and dress. Indeed, I have felt so much about the former, that I have adopted their modes in some degree. How far the reason of the thing will bear me out I know not; but my having made such a change, should induce a state of watchfulness and prayer, in a far greater degree than is at present my portion. If it be the Lord's pleasure that I should adopt these things, may I be enabled to do so with all Christian boldness. Let me not be afraid of approaching my Saviour in solemn waiting to know his will. With respect to the sacraments, I own they are matters of great doubt; may I use all my efforts to discover the divine will respecting them!

O blessed Lord and Saviour, who willest not the death of a sinner, but rather that he should turn from his wickedness and live, redeem me by thy holy power and Spirit from the lusts, cares, and affections of this life; and be thou pleased, O Lord, to centre my soul on thee, the eternal rock of salvation; that I may, with fuller purpose of heart, dedicate myself to thy service, which is perfect freedom.

CHAPTER V.

1811—1812. ÆT. 24—25.

GROWING INTEREST IN THE WELFARE OF OTHERS; LANCASTERIAN SCHOOL; ESTABLISHMENT OF THE NORFOLK AND NORWICH AUXILIARY BIBLE SOCIETY; PARTIES AT EARLHAM; COURSE ON BECOMING MORE OF A FRIEND.

WHILST Joseph John Gurney's religious convictions were thus gradually drawing him into a narrower path in connexion with the Society of Friends, his heart was becoming increasingly enlarged in Christian concern for the welfare of others. He had already warmly interested himself in the formation of a Lancasterian School in Norwich, an institution which long continued to have his effective support. The establishment of an Auxiliary Bible Society in that city, was an object into which he now entered with youthful ardour. The General Meeting for its formation was held on the 11th of the 9th mo., 1811.

"We had a rare day indeed on Wednesday," he writes, two days afterwards, to his Aunt Jane Gurney; "nothing could pass off more pleasantly than our Bible Society Meeting. Understanding that considerable numbers would attend, we were obliged to transfer ourselves from the Market Hall to the Hall of St. Andrew's. Every thing was prepared; a scaffolding for the speakers, and seats for the company, which was most respectable, unexpectedly clerical, and mustered about six hundred in number. John Owen and myself contrived the order of business with the Bishop in the morning. * * The Bishop first harangued, and admirably well, upon the excellence of the British and Foreign Bible Society, its objects, constitution, and effects. He then introduced the Secretaries. Steinkopff, a most interesting German and Lutheran, and (as far as I can judge from an acquaintance of three days) a remarkably simple and devoted character, first came forward. He told the tale of what the society had done in Germany and other parts of Europe, in broken but good English; and by degrees warmed the meeting into enthusiasm. He was followed by Hughes, the Baptist Secretary, an eloquent, solid, and convincing orator. The company was now ready for the resolutions. The Bishop proposed them, I seconded them; and after I had given a little of their history and purport, they were carried with acclamation. Fellowes moved thanks to the Bishop; Kinghorn seconded, with some excellent remarks upon the Bishop's liberality. The Bishop replied, and said some fine things of Kinghorn. It was really delightful to hear an old Puritan, and a modern Bishop, saying every thing that was kind and Christian-like of each other. The Bishop's heart seemed quite full, and primitive Kinghorn, when the Bishop spoke of him so warmly, seemed ready to sink into the earth with surprise and terrified modesty. Owen closed the meeting, with an unnecessarily splendid, but most effective address. More than £700 was collected, before the company left the Hall. * * *

FROM JOHN TALWIN SHEWELL TO A FRIEND.

Ipswich, 9th mo. 13th, 1811.

* * The opening of the Auxiliary Bible Society at Norwich has been delightful and most satisfactory in every respect, and we have returned much encouraged to try and do likewise. * * * * The union of all denominations of Christians, in this great and glorious work, was very interesting; and has left an impression upon the minds of most present, not likely to be soon effaced. At five we adjourned to Earlham Hall to dinner, where we sat down to a bountiful

entertainment, thirty-three or thirty-four in number, a mixture of different sects and persuasions, eminent for their parts, their piety, and their virtue. Words cannot adequately express the delightful feeling that reigned; so pure in its nature and object, it seemed somewhat like a foretaste of that blessed communion which the just of all generations shall finally partake of. Soon after the cloth was removed, our dear friend, Elizabeth Fry, knelt down in supplication, in a most sweet and impressive manner imploring the divine blessing upon the present company, upon the peculiar labours of the day, and for the general promotion of truth upon the earth. On her rising, the Secretary, Joseph Hughes, observed in a solemn manner—"Now, of a truth, I perceive that God is no respecter of persons, but that in every age and nation, those who fear him and work righteousness, are accepted of him"—and the conversation becoming more general, flowed on in so pleasing and edifying a strain, as surely "had less of earth in it than heaven." The wine and dessert were kept back, and the servants dismissed for half an hour, that nothing might interrupt the soul-refreshing current. The like was never witnessed by most of us before,

"For this was converse, such as it behoves
Man to maintain, and such as heaven approves."

After tea, most of the company still remaining, we again assembled, and that chapter of Isaiah being read which begins, "Arise! shine, for thy light is come, and the glory of the Lord is risen upon thee," the Foreign Secretary, C. F. Steinkopff, in his usual affectionate and simple manner, knelt down in extempore supplication, and we all retired to rest. Amongst the family present on this occasion, were Samuel and Louisa Hoare, Joseph and Elizabeth Fry, and Catherine, Rachel, Priscilla, and Joseph John Gurney. Of Priscilla I had known a little previously, but she appears to more advantage, if possible, at home than abroad. She is the nearest to Hannah More's Lucilla, of any one I ever saw, in person and manners, in benevolence and piety. We left this interesting and peculiar group with feelings of regret, mingled with a belief, that he who is guiding them in different ways, no doubt for purposes of his own glory, will conduct them to peace and happiness, as his wisdom sees best, for although they do not "walk by the same rule," they "mind the same thing," and appear all equally earnest to follow their Guide and Pattern in all simplicity and lowliness of mind.

The simplicity and deep Christian importance of the objects of the Bible Society attached Joseph John Gurney warmly to it, and henceforward it ranked amongst the objects nearest to his heart. He was appointed one of the Secretaries of the infant Association, and for many years he was accustomed to devote the principal part of several weeks in each year, to visiting, on its behalf, various places in his own county, besides not unfrequently, as occasion offered, advocating the cause in other parts. The anniversaries at Norwich became connected with Earlham by associations which imparted to them a peculiar interest. The large dining room at the Hall, which had been built by a former occupier for electioneering purposes, was now, to use Joseph John Gurney's words, "devoted to the friends of Christ and his precious cause." Here, for a full quarter of a century,* a large company of Christians of various denominations, the party sometimes amounting to

* These meetings at Earlham were continued from the year 1811 to 1836 inclusive, when they were given up during Joseph John Gurney's lengthened absence in America. In the latter years of his life, after his return, he usually invited large companies of the friends of the cause to breakfast at Earlham previously to the Annual Meeting.

eighty persons, were accustomed to meet on the day of the anniversary, many of them remaining as guests in the house for several days, to attend other meetings usually held about the same time. His beloved daughter, in a short sketch written during the brief interval between his decease and her own, thus vividly recalls her impressions of these anniversaries:—

"From the time that my dearest father put me as a little child on the table at dessert to look at a party of 90, (the largest we ever had,) until they were discontinued, I looked forward to them as a great treat. But they were, for better reasons, occasions of extreme interest, and I have no doubt were the means of great good in uniting many in Christian fellowship, who would otherwise have known each other only by name.

Though my father steadily maintained his own views as a Friend, he was always ready to give a warm welcome to the individuals who came down to attend the meetings of the Missionary and Jews Societies; which were held in the same week with that of the Bible Society. He treated the missionaries and agents with the greatest kindness, and helped them in those parts of their objects in which he could do so consistently with his principles, especially in the distribution of the Hebrew Scriptures to the Jews, and in the schools of the missionaries. He certainly had a remarkable power of showing love and friendship towards his fellow-christians, while he always openly acknowledged and maintained his own opinions on particular points. A more complete illustration of this part of his character there could not be, than in his mode of conducting the very large parties at Earlham of which I am speaking. There were always three dinner parties on the 3d, 4th, and 5th days of the week of the meetings. His brothers-in-law (my uncle Buxton and my uncle Cunningham) were generally his helpers on such occasions, and invited whom they pleased; and certainly the dining room filled on those days was no common sight. There were persons of all denominations; among the rest, many of the Norwich Friends, most of them indeed, on one of the three days. It was so different from a party called together for mere amusement; so fine a feeling pervaded the whole, while he, as master, was wonderfully enabled to keep up the tone of conversation, so that I should think it never sank to a mere chit-chat level. My impression is that while he greatly felt the responsibility of these occasions, he most truly enjoyed them, having often around him those whose conversation was a feast to him, such as Wilberforce, Simeon, Legh Richmond, John Cunningham, and many others. I never saw my dearest father look more beautiful, than he did at the bottom of those long tables. As soon as the cloth was removed, he would extract from his guests their varied stores of information in the most happy manner.* Thus the time was turned to account, and I have no doubt these days were often very profitable to many, as it was his most earnest desire they should be. He was careful to be attentive to guests of every degree, and was particularly kind to those whom, from their position in life or otherwise, he thought liable to be overlooked."

His watchful endeavours to maintain, with steady consistency, his own religious principles was not the least striking feature of these anniversary meetings. To this they doubtless owed no small measure of their peculiar interest, and many who have been privileged to meet there can recur with genuine satisfaction to the sweet and tranquillizing influence

* "I recall one day," writes one of his nieces who was frequently present, "when the sitting at the breakfast table was prolonged half the morning, by a deeply interesting conversation, and comparing of notes between him and the present Bishop of Calcutta, on the important subject of the Christian ministry, the late Sir Fowell Buxton also taking a lively part, and pointing out the defects to which he considered the delivery of the message the most liable."

that has appeared to preside over the large and varied party, when the liveliness of conversation has been succeeded by the calm of an impressive silence; and they have been permitted to feel, amidst all outward separations, something of that communion which subsists between the members of the "one fold," under the "one Shepherd." "Very sweet and solemn," he writes in his Autobiography, "have the family readings and other religious opportunities been found at these times. It has been a rallying point, a point of union to many, in this world of uncertainty and dispute." Rare indeed were the circumstances in which so many individuals, separated by so many differences of character and position, could be thus drawn together as to a common centre. Rarer still was that peculiar combination of learning, talent, and refinement, dignified by the graces of the humble Christian, and exercised under the powerful influence of Christian love, which was required in the host who could give the tone to so varied an assemblage, making the occasion of their meeting at once delightful and instructive.

To turn once more to the Journal:—

November 10th, 1811. I am now in my twenty-fourth year, and surely it behoves me to delay no longer coming into the fold of my Saviour, there to remain in his service established for evermore. * * I feel deeply the weakness of my nature, which is constantly retarding all my efforts to enter in at the narrow gate. I labour, and may say, mourn, at this moment, under a sense of deplorable indolence and want of power; of a sluggish inability to receive and dwell on the sacred truths, upon which are founded all my hopes. I grievously fear lest the foundation I have laid should at length be found sandy. My principles want clearness, strength, and depth. I long for that well-grounded undeviating faith, which will produce a persevering and unalterable course of righteousness, and bear [me] up beyond all the trials of this world and death itself. "This is life eternal, to know thee, the only true God, and Jesus Christ whom thou hast sent." To have an experimental knowledge of God our Saviour, to feel that we are kept by his power, and thus solidly to trust in his living grace and the multitude of his tender mercies—this is indeed life eternal; this is that joy which the world can neither give nor take away. O the entanglements of the world! I have many pursuits; many cares; and though these cares are generally of a nature pertaining to the duty of a Christian, yet in these very things I fall from the Lord. * * "My spirit cleaveth unto the dust; quicken thou me according to thy word. My soul melteth for heaviness; strengthen thou me according unto thy word." How can we walk in peace on the waves of this troubled sea; this sea of hopes, and fears, and cares; unless we have faith in him upon whom help is laid? * * O thou, in whose presence is fulness of joy, merciful Redeemer, thou Lamb without blemish and without spot, may it please thee to purify thy servant. Burn up the chaff, O Lord. Let not thine hand spare, nor thine eye pity, till thou hast made me that which thou wouldst have me to be: that when this world and all its vain cares and lusts are passed away for ever, thou mayest still be my Light, my Lord, my present Saviour, and my God.

In allusion to the meeting of the Bible Society, at Norwich, he says:—

It was a profitable thing to be thrown into the company of so many good and zealous persons; though I fear I did not reap that benefit from it which some experienced. During the whole of this period my dear sister Fry's example and ministry were affecting to me, and I hope useful. But how is every earthly help in a religious life apt to become of no avail, unless the mind is thoroughly awake to receive the gift!

His convictions in favour of the principles of Friends were now gradually deepening, though it was his lot for some time longer to struggle with many conflicting feelings. It is instructive to mark how strongly he continued to feel the discovery of the truth to be chiefly, or indeed only important, as it affected his practice; how the earnest disciplining of his heart in righteousness appears, through all, as his primary object.

November 10*th*. * * When I wrote my last review,* I had been under strong impressions from Friends; these impressions were increased by all that passed about the time of my uncle's funeral.† Henry Hull, Ann Burgess, and Elizabeth Robson, were in Norwich. The first a most excellent simple-hearted American, was, I think, very deep in his religious experience; wonderfully devoted to his Master's service, and embracing a large and orthodox view of religion; but, for my own part, I was chiefly impressed by the ministry of Ann Burgess, which, on one Tuesday morning, in particular, was delightfully encouraging to me, when I was in a state of doubt about my religious course. I was now plainer in my dress and using Friends' language in part. The month of August I spent with John at Yarmouth and Aldborough. Priscilla, with Louisa and her children, joined us at Aldborough. I read some of Butler's Analogy with Louisa, and had many opportunities of becoming more nearly acquainted with the sweetness and greatness of her character. During this time the impression from Friends, certainly, I believe, through my own weakness subsided.

December 15*th*, *Sunday*. The present day has been passed satisfactorily. * * The burden of it has been the necessity of regeneration; of the knowledge which is from the Spirit; and

* See extract, *supra* p. 77. † His uncle Richard Gurney.

of more complete dedication of heart to the service of Jesus Christ my Lord. O may I be enabled to pass the coming week in the presence and fear of the Lord. May it be my only pleasure and object to do his will; and, aided by his Spirit, to apply myself effectually to the different departments of my business in life; still looking forwards to the city not built with hands, eternal in the heavens.

January 3rd, [1812.] [On] Thursday, [26th December,] to Lynn. Spent a week there with John and Daniel: a pleasant and satisfactory time. At church on Sunday afternoon, where E. Edwards preached a striking sermon on the shortness of life. On Tuesday night, the 31st, Edwards with us; the last hour or two of the old year introduced an interesting conversation and prayer from E. Edwards.

TO JOHN TALWIN SHEWELL.

Lynn, 1st January, 1812.

When we were strolling together last summer upon Aldborough shingle, we little expected that we should so soon see two flourishing Bible Associations in Norfolk and Suffolk. The important work has prospered under our hands more than we could have hoped for, and in a manner which ought to lead us humbly to return thanks to him from whom cometh "every good and perfect gift." You appear to have managed your concerns better than we did. You are evidently right in having at once set to work to increase your funds by personal applications, and the establishment of minor associations. I trust *we* shall ultimately effect the same thing. The committee at Norwich, has been lately occupied by the subject of home distribution, which it has at last determined to effect through the subscribers. We began with Norwich where there were more than 1500 families containing readers, entirely without the Scriptures. Many of these have already been supplied by the Society for Promoting Christian Knowledge, and I hope that when our distribution is effected, no great deficiency will remain. Our school at Norwich has taken up still more of my time than the Bible Society. It is already brought into excellent order, and I am at last pretty confident of its ultimate success.

I heartily unite with thee in the sincere desire, that while we are looking to the good of others, we may not be neglecting ourselves. May we all be advancing in obedience to the will of God, and in the knowledge of his Son, Jesus Christ: —the latter is the consequence of the former. "He that hath my commandments and keepeth them, he it is that loveth me; and he that loveth me, shall be loved of my Father, and I will love him, and will *manifest myself to him.*" This text affords great consolation to those who are very sensible, as I own I am, of the darkness which surrounds us here. If we humbly endeavour to do our Master's will, he will *manifest himself* to us. I humbly hope and pray, that this new year may bring us both nearer to the Fountain of living waters. I write it with a deep impression of my own instability; but may we, through divine assistance, not be "of them who draw back unto perdition, but of them that believe to the saving of the soul."

The following are from his Journal: —

Sunday, 5th January. The new year is now before me, and I can truly say, that I earnestly desire it may be spent more to the glory of God, and more to my own peace, than the year which is gone by. My objects are numerous and important. O may I not fail from my duty in any of them, and may my heart be so fixed on my Maker, that all things may be carried on in subjection to his Holy Spirit, and with a view to serving him.

The Bible Society lies pretty easy upon me. The school will require constant attention; so will the Bank; so will the cultivation of my own mind. * * Before breakfast I purpose to employ myself with quotations;* [the] critical study of the New Testament; and Tomline's refutation of Calvinism.

* This refers to the comparison with the Hebrew original of the quotations from the Old Testament occurring in the New, in which he was now engaged. See *infra*, p. 114.

For the present, to be at the Bank regularly at nine; to visit the school daily; to fill up my leisure every afternoon with English History and Greek. I deeply feel how uncertain it is whether my life and health will enable me to execute my plans. Truly I hold everything at the hand of my God; he giveth, and if he taketh away, blessed be his name.

Sunday, 19th January. Read with Rachel before breakfast; attended at the Sunday school, where I tasted pure pleasure; a striking visit after Meeting to an insane person; at Kinghorn's chapel in the afternoon, tedious but striking sermon upon Isaiah liv. 13: "All thy children shall be taught of the Lord."

Saturday, 8th February. * * I have great doubts whether I have not disregarded Quaker scruples to my hurt. May I be enabled simply to perform the Lord's will in this and all other respects; and may it please thee, O Lord, to strengthen me in that which is right, and to shine once more upon my wandering mind. Let me remember, that it is the very purpose of multiplied trials, whether little or great, to loosen our hold of this world, and to fix our prospects upon the world which is to come.

Sunday, 21st March. To-day twice at Meeting. Beautiful testimony borne by dear Elizabeth to the power and offices of our Saviour; — reading satisfactory. Next week must be a busy one. Improved exertion will be necessary before breakfast; let me never enter upon the day without the due preparation. The Bible Society, the school, the Bank, Friends, my studies, will I hope find respectively their right places. May I, by a closer walk with God, enjoy in all things a sweet communion with him; and that direction, safe and clear, which is given to all who seek it in sincerity. Let my watchwords be temperance, diligence, watchfulness, prayer.

April 12th, Sunday. * * To-day has through mercy been peaceful and refreshing. Read life of Penington with Priscilla before breakfast; walked to Norwich; two very reviving meetings. * * May the good impressions given this day continue with me for my benefit during the week to come. 17th. [After alluding to a religious visit from his uncle Joseph Gurney and another friend, he remarks,] I have felt that if ever I go forth in the Lord's service, I must first pass through tribulation and deep trials of faith. * * I am conscious of my own manifold past transgressions; I am conscious of the instances in which, I believe, I have fought against the Lord's Spirit; and am truly conscious of my present weakness and ignorance. I believe, I may add, that I feel a simple and sincere desire to be actuated by his grace in the heart, to bow before him and to do his will, whithersoever he may be pleased to lead me.

O Lord, enable me to be faithful unto thee; try me not with greater temptation than I can bear. Give me the knowledge of thy holy truth, and finally accept us all, for the sake of thy beloved Son Jesus Christ.

May 3rd. Since I wrote, it has been, I fear, a dark and unfruitful time in my own mind. The Edwardses here from Monday the 20th, to Tuesday, the 28th of April. Their visit very delightful, and I trust not unprofitable, though I fear my soul was very barren. On Sunday, the 26th April, Edwards preached in the afternoon on forgetfulness of God, and pronounced a very striking comment in the evening, upon the 3rd chapter of John. Priscilla, Rachel, he, and I, read his and dear Elizabeth's correspondence upon the doctrinal faith of Friends. May the Lord graciously enable me, in my course with them, to hold fast to Jesus Christ crucified, the only hope of glory. * * Tuesday, parted with E. E., after a solemn prayer from him. O the vail, the phlegm, the poverty of my spirit, which prevented my reaping more benefit from the society of this dear friend.

May 17th. [After alluding to a Bible meeting at Fakenham.] There is great danger lest self should be exalted in these public matters. I desire to be preserved from this danger. May the Lord be pleased yet to guide me, though I have, indeed, to confess myself a poor wandering sheep.

To-morrow I intend going to the Yearly Meeting. * * My wish is—1st. To stand fast, on fundamentals, in general Christianity. 2nd. To conform to Friends wherever it may appear my duty. 3rd. To seize this opportunity of laying my heart open to God; to get upon good ground; to expose my chaff to the fire.

O thou Saviour who changest not, be pleased to comfort and restore thy servant. Do with him as thou wilt; enable him on this occasion to do his duty; cleanse him from all impurity; teach him thy ways; clothe him, gracious Lord, in the robe of thy righteousness; give him faith, and present him spotless in holiness to the throne of grace.

June 6th. Returned this day from London, where I have passed eighteen busy and interesting days. The Yearly Meeting, which engrossed me almost entirely, has been interesting, and I hope profitable. I have been enabled to unite with Friends in their spirituality, and have thought I had reason to be satisfied with their mode of spiritual worship. The first few days were to me a season of humiliation and peace; little communication with particular individuals, but great satisfaction in observing generally the striking manner in which the character of Christ, and the doctrine of the cross, were frequently brought forward.

July 12th, Sunday. * * * I desire to thank my God for his unmerited blessings this day; during which I have experienced the necessity of humiliation and watchfulness; a willingness to obey the Lord, and a humble desire to be led about and instructed by him. The principal point in my mind, the necessity of greater and more complete integrity. A questioning, whether it may not soon be right for me to conform, in other little matters, to the habits of Friends.

Sunday, July 26th. Another week passed in considerable indolence, the effect of visiting far from profitable; very little done, and this morning my mind very low. Yesterday I went to ——'s, and doubted whether it was not my duty to go into the room with my hat on. I did not do it, and believe it was not absolutely required of me; still I was afraid of trusting the impression on my mind. Be pleased, O great God, to deliver this poor worm from the workings and scruples of his own creation, but graciously enable him, by thy mighty power, to do whatsoever *thou* wilt; yea, Lord, create an honest and an upright heart within me, and deliver me, for thou art God: this I pray, for the sake of thy beloved Son Jesus Christ.

TO ONE OF HIS SISTERS.

Cromer, Sunday Afternoon, July 26th.

I am just arrived at this place on a visit to the Grove family. While part of the family are walking, Jane and I are seated by a window looking upon the sea, and I thought I might as well employ myself by sending thee a few lines. * * Every day's experience serves to prove that the Lord leads his children by different ways to the same end. For my own part, though just now faint and discouraged, and feeling with more than common force the obstructions which my nature is opposing to divine grace, yet I believe I am moving on slowly, and in a line somewhat diverging from thine. Far as our external paths may diverge, if we each can but be faithful to the light given us, I believe our hearts and our religious sympathies will always remain strong and near.

I am much and increasingly under the power of some of the minor difficulties which Friends have to bear; my judgment is also increasingly accordant with them on some very important points, particularly about ministry. I have been engaged lately in reading the Bible, with the desire of forming a scriptural view of the mode of the influence of the Holy Spirit, and I must own that, whether it be a warped mind, or whether it be the truth, the result of my researches is much in favour of the opinion of Friends. At the same time I do not mean to say that I have not many doubts. I only wish that I more watchfully and completely acted up to the knowledge given.

The entry in the Journal which follows, written upon his 25th birthday, a few days after he had penned the foregoing letter, is the first which is dated according to the usage of Friends.

First day, 8*th mo.*, 2*nd*, 1812. I believe I may rejoice in having had the assistance of the Lord in the past week. On sixth day, on my return from Cromer, I made up my mind, I humbly trust, with the divine blessing, to conform more entirely with Friends in plainness of speech and apparel. Another little difficulty, which I mentioned last week, (great in prospect to so poor a creature, but surmounted at ——'s on sixth day, I believe for the best,) has been the only thing which has caused me much pain, though my mind, throughout the week, has been a good deal oppressed. I now feel thankful and at ease, and I trust the experience of the last week has been confirming, through mercy, to my general faith. I do humbly desire to be enabled to look to Christ, as a precious Saviour, who has shed his blood for my justification, and giveth his Spirit for my sanctification. I desire to love and obey him without reserve; conscious, however, that nothing can be done in my own strength.

Many years later, in his Autobiography, he thus reviews this important period of his life:—

I am not sure of the precise time, but I think it was very soon after my father's decease, and after a visit from my dearest sister Fry to our family and meeting, that as I lay in bed one night, light from above seemed to beam upon me and point out in a very explicit manner, the duty of submitting to decided Quakerism, more particularly to the humbling sacrifice of "plainness of speech, behaviour, and apparel." The visitation was strong, but my will was stronger; I would not, I did not comply; putting off what appeared to me almost unbearable, to a more "convenient season." I was then rather more than twenty-one years old, and the morning sacrifice was not bound to the horns of the Lord's altar with the integrity, boldness, and simplicity, which the case required. Many persons might say that, taking into view the danger of imagination in such measures, I did well in resisting this call. After a space of nearly thirty years, full of a variety of experience, I am not of this judgment; for I believe that nothing is more profitable than the ready obedience of faith, and nothing more dangerous than the contrary. In my own case, the effect of irresolution was a painful state of spiritual weakness; and when at last I made the sacrifice, it was but lamely done, and under circumstances of still greater humiliation to the pride and vanity of my own heart than it would have been at first. In the mean time I enjoyed some very precious religious privileges, two of which deserve to be particularly recorded. The first was a visit to our meeting from our friend Ann Jones, (then Ann Burgess.) I was powerfully affected and subdued under her ministry, almost, if not quite constrained to surrender at discretion by the love of Christ. The second was an attendance at the Yearly Meeting, to which, in despite of my youth and lapelled coat, I was appointed representative. I well remember insisting in our Quarterly Meeting, on the reading of the advice of the Yearly Meeting respecting what ought to be the character of representatives, by way of showing myself unfit, but the Friends prevailed. * * The Yearly Meeting was to me, in this as in other years, an occasion of inexpressible solemnity—I hope of edification.

Soon after my return home, I was engaged to a dinner party at the house of one of our first county gentlemen. Three weeks before the time was I engaged, and three weeks was my young mind in agitation, from the apprehension, of which I could not dispossess myself, that I must enter his drawing room with my hat on. From this sacrifice, strange and unaccountable as it may appear, I could not escape. In a Friend's attire, and with my hat on, I entered the drawing room at the dreaded moment, shook hands with the mistress of the house, went back into the hall, deposited my hat, spent a rather comfortable evening, and returned home in some degree of peace. I had afterwards the same thing to do at the Bishop's; the result was, that I found myself the decided Quaker, was perfectly understood to have assumed that character, and to dinner parties, except in the family circle, was asked no more.

To some readers such an incident may appear almost inexplicable. That true religion leads into no wayward eccentricities may be readily admitted. Yet if there be, as every believer in the New Testament must acknowledge, a reality in the being and guidance of the Holy Spirit, it cannot surely be denied that, under such a guidance, adapted as it is to all the varieties of individual character and circumstances, there may be cases in which the awakened soul is constrained to do or to leave undone, things which, at other times, and under other circumstances, may be felt to be matters of indifference. The workings of imagination, leading into the ever varying forms of "will worship, and voluntarily humility," have been doubtless, at times, mistaken for divine illumination. But it is not imagination—it is the work of the Holy Spirit alone—which, whilst calling for the sacrifice, humbles the soul, draws it from evil, and establishes it in holiness; which, apart from all excitement, can inspire living faith in Christ, true love to God, and simple resignation to his will in all things. And shall the errors of a misguided fancy, or the mistakes even of good men, lead any to doubt the truth or the safety of his heavenly direction when so evidenced. To the religious mind the view here presented of the young disciple, but a few years before conspicuous for his elegant accomplishments in the ball room, now made willing, in obedience to the call of apprehended duty, to "become a fool" amongst his former acquaintance for the sake of his Divine Master, cannot fail to furnish matter for profitable reflection.

"The wearing of the hat in the house," continues Joseph John Gurney, "is not my practice. I have no wish to repeat what then happened; but I dare not regret a circumstance which was, under the Divine blessing, made the means of fully deciding my course, and thus of facilitating my future progress. Here I would observe that when scruples on points of a religious and practical nature are well founded, they abide the test of time and experience. This has been completely the case with me, as it relates to plainness. Never have I regretted the change which I then made; never have I doubted, that in that direction precisely, lay my appointed course of religious duty. I might have taken a more dazzling course in the world, or even in the "religious world;" but I believe that, in proportion to my willingness to be circumscribed within these somewhat humiliating boundaries, has been, in fact, the scope both for usefulness and happiness. Let it always be remembered, that the restraints of the Spirit are most abundantly recompensed by its blessed liberty."

The passage in the Journal under date 8th month, 2nd, after recording his decision as above noticed, closes with the following reflections:*—

In thus entering more completely into a small society of Christians, I feel satisfied on the ground of believing that they hold the doctrine of Christ, in many respects, more in its original purity than any other sect. At the same time, my judgment differs from them about some particulars; I think I may say, it does about the sacraments; and I *seem* to see how much Friends would be improved, by a more extensive knowledge and profession of the great offices of a Saviour's love. I also think, that there is a danger in the Society of laying too great a stress upon trifles. Thus impressed, I earnestly hope I shall ever be able to stand upon a broad basis, whereon I can heartily unite with all Christians.

* The extract given at p. 93 *supra*, with that here inserted, constitute the whole of this important entry. It is hardly necessary to add that it is printed *verbatim* as it stands in the Journal.

I desire a catholic spirit; a truly humble and dependent mind; an increase of faith, hope, watchfulness, and knowledge of Scriptural truth.

This day completes my 24th year. I can with sincerity return my humble and hearty thanks to the Author of all good, that he has been pleased graciously to look upon one who has greatly sinned. May he still preserve me upright and free from error. May he lead me and all of us in the way of life everlasting.

They who have accompanied Joseph John Gurney thus far, conversing with his most retired thoughts, may have been not unfrequently reminded, how gradual is often the growth of conviction, how varied are the phases which the mind assumes during its progress; and that even after the judgment has ripened on some points, there may be others, hardly less important, which remain to be matured under the influence of increased light and experience. In further illustration of this remark, it may not perhaps be unfitting to close the present chapter with a striking passage of the journal, written many years later,* where he thus sums up the convictions of maturer years:—

"I own no priesthood, but the priesthood of Christ; no supper in worship, but in spiritual communion with him and his followers at his own table in his kingdom; no baptism, as an introduction to the hopes and citizenship of the Christian believer, but that of the Holy Ghost;" adding emphatically; "I heartily crave and pray that the blessed principle in me of light and life and love, (even the perceptible operative influence of the Spirit of Christ,) may consummate its victory."

* Under date 8th month, 1st, 1840.

CHAPTER VI.

1812—1817. ÆT. 25—29.

HIS REVIEW OF HIS PROGRESS UP TO 1815; HIS UNCLE JOSEPH GURNEY; BRISTOL; LETTER TO A FRIEND ON HIS MARRIAGE; THOMAS FOSTER'S APPEAL; DEATH OF HIS BROTHER JOHN; HIS COUSINS JOSEPH AND HENRY GURNEY; CAPITAL PUNISHMENTS; WILBERFORCE; RETROSPECT FROM AUTOBIOGRAPHY.

THE following reflections from Joseph John Gurney's Journal, written in his twenty-seventh year, may form an appropriate introduction to the present chapter:—

2nd mo., 27th, 1815. * * Occupied several hours since yesterday afternoon in perusing my Journals up to this period. I could hardly read them without pitying myself. When a mere lad, from 18 to 19½, I appear to have been much the prey of some evil habits and passions, to my own distress; in some degree open to the utility and charm of the truth; but still yielding, yielding; and never established on a sufficiently firm foundation. From the time of my father's death, in the 10th mo., 1809, to the present, many relapses, and very many uncomfortable seasons of weakness and non-performance of duty are noted; but with increasing stability as to practice, in later years, which is some encouragement to me. In the autumn of 1810, I was forcibly impressed with its being my duty to use the language of Friends. I resisted this impression, which was graciously repeated about seven months afterwards, when I yielded to it; and since that time I have been drawn pretty close to the Society in religious sentiment and habit. I believe that this resistance has been one of my great errors in life; and that want of timely obedience to clear manifestations [of duty] has probably been one cause of my vision having been so long and so much obscured. The years 1810, 11, 12, 13, and 14, have been marked with a constant tide of employment, which has brought with it an unfixed and ineffective condition of mind, to my frequent trial and distress. Greater steadiness and quietness have of late, in some measure, arisen; and I am inclined to hope that, after much stormy weather, my gracious Master will indulge me with a little calm. In my sense of religion I am somewhat clouded; and I still feel the power of silent waiting to be a principal, if not *the* principal desideratum. Nevertheless I hope to remember that I am a traveller; that heaven is the object of my journey; and that my Saviour is my master, leader, and counsellor. The objects which life presents are the duties in which I have to seek to know and execute his will. These objects are much the same as formerly, though a little varied and altered in their proportions. I shall consider it an unspeakable favour if the Lord will enable me to eye him in all that I do; and if he will graciously keep me more abased in my own eyes than my proud heart would have me be. * * [May] the practical result of my restrospection be a deeper feeling that I deserve nothing; and a more constant, and ardent, and faithful aspiration, for the grace which availeth to sanctification, redemption, and eternal life!

His pursuits and engagements during this period, numerous as they were, and calling for close attention, do not present much variety of incident, though the register of them in the Journal affords abundant evidence of his steady diligence. Without fatiguing the reader by too minute a detail, the following selection may perhaps sufficiently indicate the course of his mind, and the more important circumstances.

9th mo., 21st, [1812.] The stream of life has been full and rapid. Bible Society; school; banking; Richard Phillips; the Buxtons; Hoares; much pleasure; much business. Yesterday (first day) was, I trust, not without its blessings. Thomas Clarke at the afternoon meeting. His sermon came home to me: addressed to those who were labouring under a sense of not being able to reach divine things. God is faithful who promises; these feelings and difficulties are not his work; the deficiency is all on our side; the true way to meet it is to humble ourselves, and become poor in spirit:—"Blessed are the poor in spirit, for theirs is the kingdom of heaven."

4th mo., 25th, 1813, *First day evening.* This day has been, I trust, in some measure, filled with the things of God. In the morning meeting I was enabled to take a clear view of my sins, of my hope in Christ, and of the necessity of clinging to the rock of my salvation. The afternoon meeting very solemn; a deep feeling of the terrors of the Lord, and something of an aching anxiety for the preservation of every individual in our family. Powerful testimony borne, both by my uncle Joseph and my dear sister Fry, to the sinner's hope of salvation in Jesus Christ.

There were, perhaps, few among his immediate connexions by whom he was, at this period, more cheered and assisted in his religious course than his uncle Joseph Gurney, his father's younger brother, and a minister in the Society of Friends. "He had," says Joseph John Gurney in his Autobiography, "as much of native charm of character about him as any person I have ever known; and was a man of original thought, always prepared to look at the 'other side of the question,' when any point was presented to him, and particularly when it was strongly urged. We lived on the most easy and happy terms together, and I was in the uniform practice of dining with him at least once a week.

He was lively in his ministry, though seldom treading any beaten path; sometimes a little obscure, but always interesting, and increasingly evangelical as he advanced in years and experience."

6th mo., 26th. My uncle Joseph desired me to give him in twelve lines, the account of my faith with respect to the Atonement. I have written the following:—

Under some sense of my own poverty, and a desire not to handle deep doctrines without divine help, I trust I may safely make the following confession of faith.

Had I been during the whole course of my life, perfectly obedient to the Divine law, I should still be an unprofitable servant, without surplus of merit. But since, on the contrary, I have grievously offended in many particulars, I not only deserve no favour, but have become subject to God's just wrath. Under the effects of this just wrath, I believe I must have fallen, had not God provided for me a way of escape in his own free pardoning grace, through the sufferings, death, and sacrifice of his son Jesus Christ.

I believe that God hath appointed this sacrifice, in its nature propitiatory, as the means of atonement or reconciliation, and that he hath therein at once displayed his mercy to the sinner and his judgment upon sin. This pardoning of sinners, for Christ's sake, is what I understand by the term "justification."

In order to partake of these mercies, I believe I must possess a living faith, which shall lead me, first, to place my whole hope of acceptance with God in the merits of my Redeemer; and, secondly, to obey the dictates of the Holy Spirit, whom Christ has sent to bring me to repentance, to purge me from all sin, and to guide me in the way to life eternal. This work of the Spirit, by which we become freed from sin, born again, new creatures, is what I understand by the term "sanctification."

These two, justification and sanctification, I believe to be necessary and sufficient for the salvation of my soul—the first, the cause—the second the condition; both the result of the grace of God, in Christ Jesus my Lord.

8th mo., 8th. * * This day has been very peaceful and quiet, and I hope profitable. At the morning meeting I endeavoured to examine my conduct in life a little more methodically than I have for some time been accustomed to do, and have several things to note.

In the sight of him, who calleth thee to be holy as he is holy, and whom without holiness it is impossible to please, take care never to entertain an impure idea. Dismiss it, the instant it occurs to thee. Endeavour to be, in this respect, as an infant; knowing nothing and thinking no evil.

Be strong in the Lord. Cultivate a close dependence both on the providence and promises of God. Then, if thou art blessed with a deep sense that the Lord governeth all things for good, and with a certain expectation that "whosoever liveth and believeth in him shall never die," thou wilt live in quietness and hope, and fear no evil.

Never act from motives of fear, contrary to thy judgment. When thou art anxious on any subject, do not magnify evil in anticipation, and learn to expect good rather than evil. Let the presence of the Lord restrain and counsel thee in thy choice of employment; and, having found thy right place, whatsoever thou doest, do it heartily, as unto the Lord and not unto man.

Give thy mind to one thing at a time; nevertheless, in all things maintain thy recollection of heaven. For this purpose allow thyself, during the hours of business, occasional short pauses for devotional meditation. Take care also, not to suffer thy time for recreation to be disturbed by the thoughts and cares of business.

Whatsoever is committed to thy care demands thy attention. Be watchful, therefore, not to forget thy lesser memoranda. But load not the mind with memoranda; rather execute without delay whatsoever can be effected as well at the present as at a future moment. Nevertheless, think twice about everything, and in all thy concerns endeavour to dwell under the direction of the best Guide.

Keep thy secrets carefully; and, in conducting business with any one, be sure to speak no more words than the case requires. Above all things, be strictly honest and upright in all thy dealings. Rigidly adhere to the truth on little as well as great occasions.

If thou art careful never to act except upon good grounds, thou wilt afterwards have no temptation to be otherwise than candid, fair, and open in thy communications with others. Let thy light shine therefore; be transparent; let thy neighbour see through thee, that there is no evil way in thee.

"Let thy moderation be known unto all men. The Lord is at hand." Present thy body "a living sacrifice, holy and acceptable unto God." Sleep and food are mercifully bestowed on thee for the preservation of thy health. Enjoy them, as far as they are required for that purpose; no further. Judge not, lest thou be judged. Never expose the faults and infirmities of others, except for a decidedly good purpose. Let it be thy general rule, never to mention what is amiss in thy neighbour to a third person, until thou hast been faithful in communicating thy sentiments to the individual himself.

Be in love and charity with all. Love "thinketh no evil," and speaketh no evil, "is not puffed up and is kind." Be kind in sentiment, kind in manner, kind in action; yet away with all ostentation. Take care that thy left hand knoweth not what thy right hand doeth. In all things let self be abased. Be willing to suffer for Jesus Christ's sake. His word will be "a lamp unto thy feet and a light unto thy path." Watch for his guidance, follow it with a firm and manly step; dwell deep in the power of his love; live not to thyself, but live as Christ liveth in thee.

The increasing illness of his brother John now called him to Clifton. After his return he writes:—

1st mo., 23rd, 1814. * * * I continued with my dear

brother at Clifton till fourth day, the 12th of this month, a highly interesting three weeks. When in his company, we were chiefly employed in reading together, Pascal, Fox's History, Plato, Greek Testament, Milner.

I was glad to know Bristol. It is a noble place, full of zeal, of almsgiving, and of good works. It was pleasant to form an acquaintance with many individuals—John Hilton, Richard Reynolds, William Lewis, John Waring, &c. Of Mary Ann Schimmelpennink we saw much, and with real pleasure. With our cousin Priscilla Hannah Gurney, who was staying at Richard Reynolds's, we had much intimate communication. * * Upon the whole, I trust, that my sojourn at Clifton has been attended with some spiritual edification. It was a time of leisure, and my mind had, in every way, opportunity for religious progress. I have strongly felt the necessity of having all that belongs to the creature, humbled and laid prostrate at the footstool of the Creator. Yet I have too truly found the great difficulty of being really set free from self-love. I would, it seems, be somebody of importance in the Church, and can hardly reconcile myself to the idea of being kept in the back-ground. I do, notwithstanding, heartily pray that I may be made willing to do and to be that and that only which seemeth right to him "who seeth not as man seeth."

2nd mo., 6th. * * I have been of late in the practice of waiting, morning and evening, in silent attempts at worship. Though sensible of much weakness in it, I have experienced some beneficial result, and desire to persevere in this important duty. * * In my many communications with my beloved uncle, I have lately remarked the weight of sound and real sense to be observed in all he says. O for that true wisdom profitable for this world, as well as for that which is to come.

2nd mo., 12th. * * My endeavours to wait on God in silence have increased. I desire that they may increase and that in patience I may possess my soul. I have felt this afternoon a willingness to fill any station, however low, in religious society; but to fill any, to be in any degree the servant of Christ, I must fairly bear the cross and the yoke. How often have I flinched from bearing it! May I be led therein, by the power of the Lord my God.

TO A FRIEND UPON HIS MARRIAGE.

Yarmouth, 3rd mo., 18th, 1814.

* * One thing I am convinced of, that your happiness, my dear friend, in married life, will depend much less upon external circumstances, than upon your uniting "in the fear of the Lord, and in walking in his ways." * * I often think of the blessing which David pronounces upon the man who walks "in the fear of God." (See Psalm 128th.) Few things are so likely to afford comfort to persons setting off in life under a right influence, (as I believe you are now doing,) as a just view of the doctrine of providence, which is beautifully unfolded in the psalm I have mentioned. With the Jews, the moral government of God, as it relates to this life only, was, perhaps, carried into more exact fulfilment, than is the case under the present dispensation. With them, definite sins, both national and individual, appear to have been punished, by definite, temporal calamities. Although our views are more exclusively directed to reward and punishment in a world to come, I believe we cannot too firmly trust in that providence which cares for us here as well as hereafter. I give literal credit to David's declaration "that he never saw the righteous forsaken, nor his seed begging bread;" and that the saying is in as great a degree, at least, applicable to our times, as it was to his. Neither of us, to be sure, have lived very long, but I question whether we have ever seen an instance of real misery which may not be traced to some deficiency of principle. * * No doubt the most righteous have to bear affliction, but it is the affliction, not of punishment, but of discipline, and can only be intended to promote their more essential happiness. * *

3rd mo., 27th. * * This week I have been favoured with a portion of the Lord's sweet presence. Yet I have to acknowledge the weakness and doubtfulness, the clouds, the indifference which still beset me. I still find it very, perhaps increasingly, difficult not to seek my own glory. Lord! what am I, that I should thus be mindful of myself? Do thou so display unto me my real self, that I may be bowed at thy footstool, as in dust and ashes; to live only as Christ liveth in me.

First day morning, 4th mo., 17th. * * The day has been comfortable. After meeting held satisfactory counsel about a school for men. I desired a blessing upon our undertaking. May the instrument in all things be kept low.

4th mo., 24th. I long to be so ordered by the prevailing influence of the Divine Spirit, that the tendency to creaturely activity and self exaltation which is still strong in my mind may be utterly destroyed. * * How acceptable would it be to me, how like a shower of rain to dry ground, were I enabled truly to wait on God, were I enabled to reach that deeply internal principle which can alone hold communion with the Author of life and light! Until this point is attained, I can never be fit to serve God in his temple.

5th mo., 1st. * * My expedition to Yarmouth is worth remembering. As I rode thither on the outside of the coach, reading parts of Romans vii, and 1 Corinthians xiii, I was favoured with more insight into the truth, than is often my lot. The depravity of human nature, the purpose of redemption, and the extent and tendency of love, were in some degree opened to my view, and sweetly impressed on my mind. The latter part of the 7th of Romans appeared to me, contrary to my former opinion, to describe a state of one not without grace, and I felt it clearly applicable to my own condition. O may I be delivered by the prevalence of the true principle of divine life, even in Christ Jesus, my Lord.

In the 5th month of this year, he attended the Yearly Meeting in London; where he took part in a deeply interesting deliberation upon a case involving the important question whether Friends, as a body, could sanction the promulgation of Unitarian doctrine. The case will be best understood from his own account written a few years later.

"In the year 1814, Thomas Foster, a man of talent and education, was disowned by the Monthly Meeting of Ratcliffe, for subscribing to the Unitarian Book Society. He had long been supposed to entertain low views of the person of Christ; and had he kept those views to himself, he would probably have been left by Friends to pursue his own course. But no sooner did he publicly assist in the diffusion of them, than he became, from this overt act, a proper object of the discipline of the Society, and accordingly lost his membership. The Monthly Meeting among Friends sometimes acts in a judicial capacity, from the decision of which the appeal lies to the Quarterly Meeting as the superior body, and from that to the general assembly of Friends at the Yearly Meeting.

Thomas Foster appealed to the Quarterly Meeting of London and Middlesex, which confirmed his disownment; but, still dissatisfied, he carried forward his appeal to the Yearly Meeting, at which I had the privilege of being present. Such cases come, in the first instance, before the Committee of Appeals, which is composed of one of the representatives of each Quarterly Meeting, the Quarterly Meeting appealed against alone excepted. I was appointed for Norfolk and Norwich, and acted as clerk to the committee. After hearing a long speech from Thomas Foster, and the answer of the respondents from the Quarterly Meeting of London and Middlesex, we were left to make our decision. I drew up a plain series of resolutions, which terminated with one, confirming the disownment. The resolutions were read *seriatim* to the committee. Each in its turn met their unanimous approbation; and never, I trust, shall I forget the feeling of unity of mind with which, during a most solemn pause, we all gave our silent assent to the concluding resolution. We were twenty-seven in number, collected out of every part of the kingdom, and previously but little acquainted with each other's sentiments; but it was as if we were moulded together into one man. At length the silence was broken by Jonathan Hutchinson, who expressed, in a few pointed words, his entire concurrence with the decision of the committee. "I do not know," he added, "what may have been the experience of my brethren, but for myself I can truly say, that without Christ I should be of all men most miserable." Our unanimity being ascertained by the signatures of the whole committee, our report, confirming the disownment, was presented to the Yearly Meeting.

Against our decision, Thomas Foster, as in right entitled to do, made his final appeal to the body at large, consisting of about 1200 men Friends, of various ages and conditions, without any written creed, and without any human president. Then, indeed, came on the trial of the Society's faith, the great question being immediately before us, whether orthodox Christianity or Unitarianism was the belief of Friends. The appellant's speech was long and insinuating, calculated to amuse the young and perplex the old. The reply of the respondents was plain and luminous, and accompanied by abundant evidence, selected from the writings of the early Friends, of the uniform adherence of the Society to the doctrines of the Deity and Atonement of Christ. These extracts were compared with the notes of the Unitarian New Testament, and it soon appeared that the contrast between them was as palpable as between day and night. After the appellant had replied, both parties withdrew, and our large assembly was left to form its decision on the vital and all-important question. A solemn silence overspread the whole meeting, and continued for a considerable time uninterrupted. At length William Grover arose; an elderly man, as remarkable for his clearness of mind, as he was striking from his pleasing and venerable appearance. In a single expressive sentence he pronounced his judgment against the appellant. After him our elder Friends rose one after another, all with the same sentiment in their mouths; then Friends in the middle stages of life, then the young, the more and the less serious, the plain, and those whom we somewhat technically call the gay. I never heard so many, or so various Friends speak to any point in our annual assembly; and, blessed be the name of him whom alone we acknowledge to be our Saviour and our Head, all were of one accord. I am almost ready to question whether 1200 men, gathered together without previous concert, from so many different places; persons of such various ages, circumstances, and characters, were ever before known to manifest, on a theological subject, so perfect an unanimity.*

Soon after his return from the Yearly Meeting, he thus briefly notices his first public effort on the subject of slavery.

7th mo., *4th.* The latter part of the week, especially sixth day, has been occupied by the slave trade business.† The petition is now signing largely, and on sixth day morning, we were favoured with complete success, after much opposition, at the public meeting. I pleaded for the cause very earnestly, but have since had to understand, with too much "posture," and probably too little simplicity. * * O that the quieting, humbling spirit of divine love may be permitted to guide me safely, through the troubles, cares, and occupations of the present week.

7th mo., *31st.* On Fourth day to Holt with Brereton. The meeting of the Bible Society not at all elevating to myself. I had to reproach myself for too hastily using, in my speech, the name of the Almighty. May I henceforward never pronounce or write that name, without awe and reverence.

8th mo., *21st.* * * On the 9th I left home, and was occupied on the 10th, 11th, and 12th by the arbitration in the case of ——. Francis Gibson was my able and exemplary

* See Chalmeriana, pp. 51—55. The Journal contains only a reference to a "paper," which probably contained the account of these proceedings, but which has not been found.

† See Life of William Allen, vol. i, p. 192.

coadjutor. The business, through the divine blessing, ended in the restoration of harmony. On the evening of the 12th to Brampton, [Lady Olivia Sparrow's.] There I staid till First day morning, the 14th, among many of the great of this world; not I trust, excluding the next. This peep at high life was curious and instructive, and I hope not hurtful in the main, though it set me a little afloat.

His brother John, whose declining state of health had been for some time an occasion of much solicitude, breathed his last on the 8th of the 9th mo. He had never recovered from the effect of his anxious watching and nursing during his wife's illness. Partial paralysis soon began to appear, which was accompanied by a general state of bodily feebleness. Notwithstanding his increasing infirmity he successfully applied himself to recover his knowledge of Greek, with a view to reading the New Testament in the original; the study of which, together with the perusal of the ancient Greek historians and poets, became an object of deep interest to him during his protracted illness.

"We were occasionally," says Joseph John Gurney, in his Autobiography, "united very pleasantly in these pursuits. The last few months of his life," he continues, "though humbling to the view of his friends, were to him without a thorn. Obscured as his fine intellect now was on all other topics, it was clearer and brighter than ever on the subject of religion. The part that was to live for ever shone with a mellowed lustre like the setting sun. As the day of his death approached, his happiness increased. Everything was beautiful in his eyes; the hymn sung by one sister, and the prayer uttered by another, were to him, in his childlike condition, like the orisons of angels. * * I loved him dearly, but the cup of sorrow was mingled to us all with hope and peace and joy."

A few days after the funeral he thus writes in his Journal:—

9th mo., 12th. * * * The event, which has just occurred, is a precious talent, of which I have much use to make. First: let me consider it as affording an evidence of the truth of religion.

What is practical religion? Is it not the work of God's Spirit upon the soul of man, bringing it to a spiritual knowledge of the Saviour, and redeeming it from all sin? Has it not been marvellous to observe this work carried on, and, humanly speaking, perfected in my dear brother, at a time when his merely rational faculties were so decayed? Does it not evince that, independently of the rational faculties, there is a soul capable of being filled with faith, and hope, and love? Does it not also evince that there is an influence, which works upon the soul, which sows the seed, and rears the plant, and produces the fruit? Our dear brother afforded us a striking instance of the assurance which the Spirit of God gives of the things of God. He was truly brought to the simplicity of a child. In that simplicity he saw the things of God, not clouded and perplexed as we see them, through a maze of fleshly feelings and worldly cares, but clearly, and in their real brightness. He doubted not. He appeared to have that sort of evidence about the truth that the eye gives us of things visible. * * Another great point, which has been particularly manifested in his case, is, that "the blood of Jesus Christ taketh away all sin." He knew it! May I be permitted to know it more and more! * *

Referring to his own position, he adds,—

My worldly situation is altered. I am become the master of Earlham and have received some addition to my old stock of *curanda.* I am very sensible of the importance of order, and true economy of mind and time, rather than of money, in all my concerns. What can I say, but that I desire direction?

10th mo., 10th. On fifth day went to the Yarmouth Bible Society Meeting, with —— and ——. Nothing could be less successful than my attempt as it regarded myself. Otherwise I trust it answered some purpose. Their company was interesting, though I am sorry to find them such Calvinists. * * Is there not a predestination *according to foreknowledge?* And does this affect the freedom of man's will? Surely not.

11th mo., 21st. * * I exceedingly desire to grow every day in the knowledge of the truth. May I live this week with renewed care and watchfulness, remembering that every day ought to make me one degree fitter for heaven; as it brings me, I trust, one step nearer to it.

First day, 12th mo., 18th. * * I hope I am, in some degree, brought to a willingness to be little — to be nothing, if it be the will of God. There is at the bottom of my heart a lurking desire to obtain the praise of man. It certainly is so; it is a drying, limiting, paltry feeling. It is a great enemy, and one which adheres closely to me; but may I not yet encourage a hope that my Lord and Master hath power even over the inmost evils of my soul?

TO ONE OF HIS SISTERS.

Norwich, 1st month, 14, 1815.

* * What are we to say to this full and rapid stream of worldly employment which hurries us along so quickly that we cannot even stop for a minute to speak to one another? I am half ashamed of saying that I have as much on my hands as ever, perhaps more; and were it not for being favoured, just now, with a tolerably quiet mind, I think I should be quite swallowed up. I hope and believe that I am more able than I used to be to give my undivided self to one thing at once. This is a lesson which we shall all do well to learn. And if we can, at the same time, attain the habit of more constantly looking forward to the end of our journey, we may pass through life pleasantly and profitably, even amidst multitudinous worldly cares. I have often felt lately

that I do not sufficiently bear in mind the true object of a religious course, namely, the attainment of a heavenly reward. Religious progress *itself* is too apt to be, as it were, the final object of my wishes. * *

O what a fine thing it would be really to get rid of self, and of self dependence, and self seeking. We may talk a great deal about atonement, and yet secretly and in the centre of our hearts, entertain a feeling, if not a notion, of *merit*. We may talk of humiliation in the presence of God to the exclusion of all human pride, and yet secretly desire our own glory. We may talk of our dependence upon the guidance of our Lord, and yet allow our own imagination and understanding privately to hold the rudder. So it is at times with me; perhaps always; and yet I do not wish to complain, hoping that there is that, which, if sought, will more and more deliver from the bondage of corruption.

His continued diligence in study, amidst the pressure of his varied engagements, is remarkable.

"Our business being extensive," he writes, in the Autobiography, in allusion to this portion of his life, "and requiring great care, and public objects of a philanthropic kind pressing upon me a good deal, my literary leisure was more curtailed than I could have wished; but study was not altogether neglected; and at the period of which I am now speaking, and for a few years afterwards, I read and wrote much, and continued to be greatly interested in my biblical pursuits. One object which I pursued with some industry was to compare the quotations from the Old Testament, contained in the Gospels and Epistles, with the present text of the Hebrew Original, and of the Septuagint; and to show what are the collateral evidences which confirm the evangelical use made of many of these passages in the New Testament. I have by me some rather long manuscripts on this subject; but they were the work of a young student, and, though useful to myself, quite unfit for publication."

"Now is the time," he writes in the Journal,* "for whole mindedness and industry. The Old Testament; the New Testament with quotations; Herodotus, and Bacon's Novum Organum, after Clarendon is finished, I intend shall be my intellectual pursuits."

"I wish to push Justin Martyr," is his observation a few months later.

The spirit in which he studied is admirably indicated in the following sentences from a work ascribed to the last mentioned author, which he copied, in the original, on the cover of one of the early volumes of his Journal.

Οὐδὲ γὰρ ζωὴ ἄνευ γνώσεως, οὐδὲ γνῶσις ἀσφαλὴς ἄνευ ζωῆς ἀληθοῦς. Ὁ γὰρ νομίζων εἰδέναι τι, ἄνευ γνώσεως ἀληθοῦς καὶ μαρτυρουμένης ὑπὸ τῆς ζωῆς, οὐκ ἔγνω· ὑπὸ τοῦ ὄφεως πλανᾶται.

Epistle to Diognetus, c. xii.

"For neither is there life without knowledge, nor is there any sure knowledge without the true life."

"For he that thinketh that he knoweth any thing without the knowledge that is true, and borne witness to by the life, knoweth not, but is deceived by the serpent."†

He thus notices his "designs," under date—

6th mo., 11th, 1814. [After alluding to the Banks.]

Public objects.—Bible Society—Norwich Association; Branch Meetings; School; the Scriptures with the Boys; Adult school twice a week; Benevolent Society—to raise a

*Under date 10th mo. 31st, 1813.

† It has been lately suggested, with some appearance of probability, that the conclusion of this Epistle, in which the foregoing passages occur, formed part of a Treatise of Hippolytus. Sec. 1, Bunsen's Hippolytus, 186—195.

fund; Coals for the winter; Provident Society; Public Houses.

Literature.—To press on in "the Quotations" and in the Hebrew Bible, with particular reference to the subject of the Spirit; Texts regularly; Family reading as before; Robertson to be studied; Œdipus Tyrannus; Demosthenes de Coronâ; Lucretius.

He characteristically adds,—

And what does this castle in the air signify, if I do not hold the *foundation?*

In addition to these objects, it had been of late one of his recreations, to assist his uncle Joseph Gurney's two sons, Joseph and Henry, who were now growing up to manhood, in the further improvement of their minds. Referring to a visit of his two cousins at Earlham, he writes

TO HIS AUNT JANE GURNEY.

Norwich, 11th mo., 18th, 1814.

* * Thou wilt think me a preceptor of some influence, when I tell thee that I have induced them every morning to exchange their beds in pretty good time, for my study fireside, and the Epistle to the Corinthians. This Epistle, of which we have read about half, has occupied us before breakfast; and I have been agreeably surprised to find Joseph so much at home in his Greek. Harry's scholarship I did not doubt, and he has it evidently in his power to become thoroughly accomplished in classical literature. * * In the afternoon we have been reading Cicero's orations, and Juvenal. In the evening Richenda assumes the character of drawing mistress, and something is read aloud for general edification. It is pretty clear from my account that we have not been fagging very hard; but it is something to encourage a taste for intellectual pursuits. This, indeed, is my chief desire in

reading with them, because I see that it is the chief thing wanted. * * No employment is more gratifying to me, and I feel it quite a relief, after Bible Society speeches, banking journeys, &c. Daniel has been with us for a few days, which was the highest delight to the boys, though it was not without the effect of throwing me and my books into somewhat distant background. * *

Upon the whole, I am sure they find the Earlham atmosphere cheerful, though a little inclined to be serious. Not that Joseph objects to seriousness in its place, for he has volunteered several sentiments which have given me real pleasure, and which prove that his mind is a good deal directed to the most important objects; and I trust the same may be fairly believed of Harry. * *

Dressing Room, alone at home, 2nd mo., 27th, 1815.

The Lord has been pleased to throw a gloom over our family, by an event scarcely exceeded in melancholy by any that had before taken place amongst us. On the very day* when I last wrote in this book, my beloved cousin Henry died. We were summoned to the Grove after breakfast, and found him completely overcome by a violent apoplectic attack, and in the strift of death. The scene was overwhelming. The anguish of our spirits, as we surrounded his bed side, was relieved, at length, by earnest and deeply impressive prayer from Priscilla. Then indeed was the time to know the value of a Saviour! About half an hour afterwards, he quietly and almost imperceptibly breathed his last, leaving us all with a sweet impression, that his spirit was returned to the bosom of the Father, and centred in the presence of the everlasting Shepherd. * * The stroke came home to my tenderest affections. I, too, have lost an object which I fondly and dearly cherished.

During the spring of this year, his friend William Forster visited Norwich in the character of a

*2nd mo., 10th, 1815.

minister of the gospel amongst Friends, and held many religious meetings in that city and its neighbourhood. The mind of Joseph John Gurney was powerfully impressed, and he afterwards spent several weeks as William Forster's companion in a journey through parts of Lincolnshire, Cambridgeshire, and the Eastern Counties, an engagement which laid the foundation of a warm and lasting friendship between them, and was the means of deepening his attachment to the principles and practices of Friends. A few days after his return from this journey, he writes,

7th mo., 3rd, 1815. * * My excursion has greatly refreshed me. * * I have felt an increase of faith in Christ; more inclination and ability to stay myself upon his merits and mercy. Τὸ ἐπαναπαύεσθαι τῷ Χριστῷ, is I trust a desire increasing in me. This is a great favour.

The year 1816 opens with the following entry in his Journal:—

1st mo., 3rd, 1816. I desire not to commence a new year without some effort at self-examination. With regard to my religious state, if I were not so insensible to everything, I think I should be sensible of more alarm about it. It is, in fact, alarming, not to attain to more of the life and reality of religion; and not a little so, that the habit of a wandering mind continues to impede, almost constantly, that spiritual communion with God, which I feel to be essential to my true interest. Sometimes, indeed, I have felt a good deal alarmed, and the prayers of my perturbed spirit have been permitted to bring the blessing of peace: on the whole, I have just now a good hope, that, notwithstanding the many discouragements which I have so long felt, I may yet, through abundant mercy, be amongst the few who shall be led by the narrow way to everlasting life. * * If I have, with any degree of right vision, seen the guidance of Providence respecting me, I certainly have reason to believe that *the Lord cast my lot among Friends*, and it is on this account that I may well feel discouraged at my peculiar infirmities. More simplicity! Oh, for more simplicity! I believe that if I did but dwell more as a little child, I should more find and feel my right place in the church. * * Lord draw me nearer to thyself, and keep me from evil. Make me sensible that my only safe position of soul, is that of complete prostration before thee. Grant that in this humiliation I may so be permitted to depend livingly upon thy mercy, that my joy in thee may more and more abound. Once more I entreat thee to set my heart upon the kingdom of thine everlasting rest and glory, and mayest thou be pleased so to deal with me during my pilgrimage here, that I may accomplish that whereunto thou sendest me; and continue to ascribe unto thy holy name all honour, praise, and thanksgiving, for ever and ever.

On his return from a short visit to London at the beginning of the year, he passed a few days at the house of Lord Calthorpe. From thence he writes—

Ampton, 1st mo., 23d, 1816.

* * Though I could not kneel at their prayers, I was really cheered by the seriousness and simplicity with which this duty was performed; and by the apparent order of the household. May we, whilst we display our nonconformity, ever remember to what a holy conversation, to what a spirit of love, meekness, and watchfulness, our profession calls us. If we were but sufficiently alive to this call, I think our little peculiarities would be merged, as it relates to others, in the savour of our spirits, so that they would offend no one; and as for ourselves, they certainly help to keep us humble, if rightly adopted; for they are very mortifying to the natural man.

Whilst at home during the preceding autumn he had entered upon the composition of a work, which, though never published in its original form, afterwards furnished the material for several important chapters in the Essays on Christianity and the Biblical Notes.

"It was," to use his own words, "the history of our Lord Jesus Christ, in its largest character and bearings, as set forth in Scripture. It consisted of three parts: Christ in his pre-existence; during his abode on earth; and in his reign of glory. Each part was divided into chapters, and illustrated by copious notes. This work formed the principal object of my literary attention for some years, and led into no small extent of collateral investigation and study. My chief aim in it was, clearly to set forth the scriptural proofs of the glorious doctrine of our Saviour's proper Deity; and I can truly say, the more I scrutinised the evidence, the more largely I collected, compared, and assorted it, the more complete became my own convictions of this blessed truth. The manuscript of the work was long, and completed with great care; but had I published it, it would, I doubt not, have betrayed, in various points of view, the inexperience of a young writer."

TO HIS SISTER-IN-LAW ELIZABETH GURNEY.

Norwich, 3d mo., 5th, 1816.

* * I am deeply interested in my book, which however proceeds slowly. * * A large field is opening before me; the undertaking is truly an arduous one. * * May I have my dependence rightly placed with respect to it. * *

The subject of Capital Punishments had already claimed much of his serious attention, and ever afterwards continued to be a matter of deep and painful interest to him. Under date 4th mo., 8th, 1816, he particularly alludes to his attendance "on poor Lea," a convict, before his execution, and later in the year he felt it his duty to make a vigorous effort to save the life of a prisoner under sentence of death for burglary. Gunton, the prisoner in question, had been convicted on the evidence of a young woman, who had lived as servant in the house which had been robbed, and some circumstances transpired, which led to the belief that her evidence had been misapprehended either by the court or by the jury. A re-consideration of the case appeared to be most important, but this could not be obtained, unless the witness could be brought before the proper authorities. In the mean time the period for the execution was approaching; immediate exertions were necessary, but the young woman, after whom inquiry had been made in every direction, could not be found. The case now appeared hopeless. At length, however, the witness was traced, and Joseph John Gurney took her to London, travelling with all practicable speed through the night. He quickly obtained a respite, which was immediately forwarded to the sheriffs at Norwich; and on the following morning he himself arrived, bringing with him a reprieve; and Gunton's sentence was commuted to transportation for life. But though his efforts in this case were happily successful, three other prisoners were left under sentence of death. On the day of their execution he thus addressed his fellow citizens in a letter published in the Norwich Mercury :—

Norwich, 8th mo., 31st, 1816.

I have observed vast flocks of people—men, women, and children, apparently of various conditions, but chiefly of the lower orders, passing through the streets, crowding with eagerness, and, as it seemed to me, not without feelings of a pleasurable nature, to witness a scene the most dreadful and melancholy, when properly considered, that the mind of man can conceive! They are now returning in large numbers. What is the sight which they have been beholding? Three poor victims of folly, vice, and crime, put to a cruel and untimely death.

It is by such sights, and by *the repetition of them*, that we become callous to the woes and torments of our fellow creatures! The momentary compassion which they excite, is soon exchanged for a feeling of pleasure in the excitement itself, and a most stupid indifference to the sufferings of others! Thus that hard heart, which is the source of every crime, becomes harder and harder still; and, therefore, yet more productive of the same results. The deterring influence of the "example" is seldom felt by obdurate sinners. At any rate, it becomes weaker and weaker by repetition; and were it even much stronger than it is, would be little in point of real effect, in comparison with the contrary tendency of a spectacle which strengthens criminality *in its root!*

Let us, as Christians, look at the facts of these cases. Men who have immortal, accountable souls, are suddenly transferred from their only state of probation to their eternal, unalterable state, by the hands of other men. These sufferers are generally persons of depraved character; and as the tree falls it must lie. The facts, therefore, involve doubts and probabilities of most tremendous magnitude. And is poor frail man to take the responsibility of these doubts upon himself? Is he to throw the die by which the awful question is decided? Are there any considerations of a merely temporal nature, relating either to individuals or to nations, which can possibly justify it, especially in a Christian country? The religion which teaches us, that the eternal allotment of one soul is of greater importance than the temporal prosperity of a whole nation, prohibits us, by its very principles, from taking upon ourselves the responsibility of that allotment, for any purposes which terminate on this side of the grave.

To return to the Journal: —

6th mo., 7th. * * [After spending a few days in London.] The Yearly Meeting was refreshing, confirming, and comforting to my spirit. Let me record my full belief, that the affairs of the society have been conducted, under the weight and power and in the spirit of divine truth. Love and unity have been the portion of the body. I am, I trust, thankful for this renewed evidence of having found my right place in the Christian church. May the Lord be pleased to preserve the savour of divine truth on my mind. How do I desire to be, indeed, one of his servants and children; in all my life to magnify and glorify his holy name.

8th mo., 17th. * * My own experience, which has certainly of late partaken considerably of pain, is sufficient to prove that there is no peace in placing our dependence upon the world, no peace whatever but in a living faith in God, and in a real participation of his promises in Christ Jesus. * * Oh, there is no safety but in the lowest spot. When our own plans, which seem to be the right plans, are unexpectedly overturned, it is a trial of faith and patience. *Then we must get lower.* Lord do all things according to thy will! Help thy children and thy servants. Be pleased to extend the wing of thy pity over us! Relieve the pressure which we are not able to bear! Above all, grant us, we beseech thee, such a sense of thy truth, that, whether in heights or in depths, in prosperity or in trouble, we may ever rejoice in thy love, which is in Christ Jesus our Lord.

The ninth month of this year was rendered memorable to him by a visit which laid the foundation of an intercourse, that was, at intervals, in after years, the source of much lively interest and pleasure. The circumstance is thus graphically related in a Familiar Sketch of the late William Wilberforce, which he subsequently published.

"I was introduced to Wilberforce," writes Joseph John Gurney, "in the autumn of 1816. He was staying with his family by the seaside at Lowestoft, in Suffolk. I well remember going over from Earlham, partly for the purpose of seeing so great a man, and partly for that of persuading him to join our party at the time of the approaching anniversaries of the Norfolk Bible and Church Missionary Societies. I was then young, but he bore my intrusion with the utmost kindness and good humour; and I was much delighted with the affability of his manners, as well as with the fluency and brightness of his conversation. Happily he acceded to my solicitations, nor could I hesitate in accepting his only condition, that I should take into my house not only himself, but his whole family group, consisting of his amiable lady and several of their children, two clergymen who acted in the capacity of tutors, his private secretary, servants, &c. We were, indeed, to be quite full of guests, independently of this accession; but what house would not prove elastic in order to receive the abolisher of the Slave Trade? In point of fact, by dint of various contrivances, we managed the affair with tolerable facility. It was a large party, composed of persons of several denominations, who were all anxious to promote the extension of the kingdom of their Redeemer; and Wilberforce was the star and life of our circle."*

A few days after this visit, he writes in the Journal:—

9th mo., 30th. The last has indeed been an eventful and interesting week. We have had a vast party in the house. Francis and Richenda,† Samuel Hoare, Fowell and Hannah, the Carrs, John Cunningham, the Wilberforce Family, Langton, Rolleston, G. Kett, &c. No society could have been much more pleasant, and I hope it has also been profitable. The Bible Society Meeting on fifth day passed off delightfully; Wilberforce's speaking most interesting; about sixty at dinner, at Earlham. Since that time, we have been almost entirely occupied by the Wilberforces; his mind is indeed rich, and

* See Minor Works, vol. ii., p, 228. See also Life of Wilberforce, vol. iv., p. 298.

† His sister Richenda had been recently married to Francis Cunningham.

varied, and elevated. It is equally pleasant and instructive to enjoy his company.

I hope I have not materially departed from my testimonies during this week. O, I desire to see clearly what and where I am, and though the heavens have, at times, felt around me as brass, impenetrable and inaccessible, I still hope that the Lord will help me. Sure I am, that an attentive inspection of my own great infirmities is sufficient to prevent all pride or vain glory. O Lord, sanctify me I pray thee with thy truth, that my inmost corruptions may be reached by the cleansing efficacy of thy Spirit. Create in me, I beseech thee, more of a willingness to give up, for thy sake, whatsoever thou mayest require at my hands.

His cousin Joseph, the only surviving son of his uncle Joseph Gurney, had been in declining health since his brother Henry's death. Joseph John Gurney writes—

12th mo., 2nd, 1816. The past week has been rendered deeply interesting by the last scenes of dear Joseph's life. He died on sixth day evening, as the clock was striking nine, in great peace and perfect quietude, after a day of much suffering. What heart-rending scenes are we called upon from time to time to witness! To day we are immersed in all the cares, the pleasures, and the business of life; to-morrow we are dead: and, what is still more wonderful, the survivors go on nearly as before, the wheel never stops! How watchful, how diligent, are we called upon to be, by the uncertainty of our tenure!

His review of this and the preceding period of his life, written many years later in the autobiography, may properly close the present chapter.

My spiritual condition from my twenty-second to my twenty-ninth year was by no means a high one,—generally very much the contrary. Notwithstanding all the advantages of my situation I often went mourning on my way, athirst for the waters of eternal life. Many disconsolate hours after this sort used to fall to my lot, and in looking back upon this period of my course, I have frequently compared it to a journey in the wilderness after passing through the Red Sea. I ascribe this state of things to two causes; first, my own unwatchfulness; for the enemy too often prevailed over me with his secret temptations, so that as a convert, I trust, to the truth, yet not far advanced towards "the measure of the stature of the fulness of Christ," I could apply to myself the plaintive language of the apostle, "I delight in the law of God after the inward man, but I see another law in my members, bringing me into captivity. O wretched man that I am, who shall deliver me from the body of this death!"* But secondly, I doubt not that this dispensation was allotted me for the trial of my faith and patience, and for my further humiliation, by way of preparation for future service.

Nor can I deny that my gracious Lord and Master was at times pleased to speak comfortably to me. "I will allure her (the church) into the wilderness, and will speak comfortably to her, and will give her her vineyards from thence, and the valley of Achor for a door of hope."† The valley of my soul's humiliation was, at times, made a door of hope to me; and although I was very weak and wandering, a poor struggler after worship at many or most of our meetings, they were, at times, seasons of great refreshment to me. The ministry of Friends affected me greatly, and was often a means of comfort and strength. I never suffered myself to criticise it, but acted on the uniform principle of endeavouring to obtain from what I heard all the edification which it afforded. This is a principle which I would warmly recommend to my young friends in the present day; for nothing can be more mischievous than for learners to turn teachers, and young hearers, critics. I am persuaded, that it is often the means of drying up the waters of life in the soul; and sure I am, that an exact method of weighing words and balancing doctrines, in what we hear, is a miserable exchange for tenderness of spirit, and for the dews of heaven.

* Rom. vii, 22, 24.

† Hos. ii, 14, 15.

CHAPTER VII.

1817—1818. ÆT. 29—30.

EXTRACTS FROM AUTOBIOGRAPHY AND JOURNAL; JONATHAN HUTCHINSON; ENGAGEMENT IN MARRIAGE; FIRST SPEAKS AS A MINISTER; HIS MARRIAGE; LETTER TO WILLIAM FORSTER; CHARLES SIMEON; CORRESPONDENCE WITH JONATHAN HUTCHINSON; JOURNEY ON THE CONTINENT; VISIT TO LONDON; VISIT OF THE MAYOR AND CORPORATION OF NORWICH TO EARLHAM; HE IS ACKNOWLEDGED A MINISTER.

"THE year 1817," writes Joseph John Gurney in his Autobiography, "was one of great importance to me — my 29th year. The early part of it was characterized by no small measure of mental weakness and lowness; but the Lord who saw me in my adversity, had two precious gifts in store, both of which were freely and bountifully bestowed upon me in the course of that year; a faithful partner of my joys and sorrows, and a part in the ministry of the glorious gospel of our Lord and Saviour Jesus Christ. The two things were connected in a manner which might appear very singular to those who have not been accustomed to watch the harmonious workings of external providence and inward grace. But 'whoso is wise and will observe these things, even they shall understand the loving kindness of the Lord.'" The course of his mind is thus exhibited in the Journal.

1st mo., 7th, [1817.] * * To-day I leave home on a banking expedition to Halesworth and Yarmouth. How beautiful is that text, "The Lord shall preserve thee in thy going out and in thy coming in, from henceforth and even for evermore."

1st mo., 13*th*. Second and third days and part of fourth, Lord Gosford here; very pleasant party in the house; afternoons swallowed up by it. * * Most earnestly [do I] desire to be preserved and redeemed from all evil, and to be clothed with that pure spirit of faith and love, which will be ever seeking heaven supremely, and which leadeth a man to seek also another man's weal, rather than his own. But, indeed, I have found myself painfully immersed in the world and the flesh, and at a distance from the Lord. O this unstable heart! this wandering imagination! I have no other plea, O Lord God Almighty, for approaching thy holy presence, but this plea: that thou willest not the death of a sinner, but rather that he should tnrn from his wickedness and live. "Turn me O Lord and I shall be turned; heal me and I shall be healed."

2nd mo., 16*th*. [Last] Third day morning meeting, and the Monthly Meeting were favoured and consoling opportunities. That afternoon I passed an interesting time with poor Aram Mackie on his deathbed. I did not feel easy without commending him to the grace of our Lord Jesus Christ; and afterwards found, to my encouragement, (having been depressed on the subject,) that my visit was acceptable to him. He died the next morning, and I trust is at rest.

Second day morning, [*2nd mo.*, 24*th*.] Yesterday on the whole satisfactory. Rather an unusual concern felt for the body [of Friends]; a doubt on my mind, whether, notwithstanding all my sins and infirmities, it may not lead to speaking in meeting. I have felt this morning an earnest desire that my life henceforward may be to Christ, and not to the world.

The name of Jonathan Hutchinson has been already mentioned. The close intimacy which so long subsisted between him and Joseph John Gurney, seems to claim for him a little further notice in this memoir. Though he had been for many years the friend and correspondent of his uncle Joseph Gurney, and they had previously met more than once in London, it was whilst travelling in Lincolnshire, with William Forster, in the course of the preceding year, that Joseph John Gurney had been first brought to a nearer acquaintance with the sterling worth of his character. Born at Gedney, in the fens of Lincolnshire, a respectable yeoman in station, he was a man under whose remarkably simple and unadorned appearance lay concealed a thoughtful and well-cultured mind, and a heart subdued and chastened by the power of divine grace. Though a skilful practical grazier, and carefully attentive to the business by which he maintained his family, he had read much and variously, and thought deeply and largely on many subjects; and his lively imagination was no stranger to the walks of poetry. As a minister of the gospel amongst Friends his communications were usually short, but full, pertinent, and lively; his prayers fervent, simple, and emphatic. He had known what it is to doubt, and almost to despair, and was prepared by a somewhat peculiar and severe course of discipline to sympathise with others. "Our close agreement," says Joseph John Gurney,* "on all points of a religious nature, and on many of a merely intellectual character, was the means of bringing us into a near and easy friendship, which I shall, I believe, always look back upon as one of the choicest privileges of my life."

* In a Short Tribute to the Memory of Jonathan Hutchinson; prefixed to a volume of his letters, published in 1841. London: Harvey and Darton.

FROM JONATHAN HUTCHINSON.

Gedney, 3rd mo., 17th, 1817.

* * Thy letter confirmed me in a thought, at which perhaps I hinted in my last, that, however different in some things we may be,—in age this difference is doubtless great,—yet that there are certain experiences common to each of us, and certain sentiments wherein we are agreed; and that thus it should be, with travellers on the same road, and with the same object in view, need not surprise us. I was so far from thinking thee "too open," that, on the contrary, I really have considered myself benefited by those very passages in thy letter, wherein thou seemed to apprehend some danger of being thus thought. There is, though one can hardly tell why, as thy dear deceased relation, Joseph Gurney Bevan, in a letter once said to me, a "kind of consolation in finding that others are no better off than ourselves," especially if we have imagined very differently; and I truly felt something of this, on discovering, by thy affecting complaints, that I had at least one companion in a way wherein I have been often ready to consider myself alone. * * Well, "be of good cheer," for I believe the Master has called, and is calling thee, and whatever difficulties thou mayest meet with in endeavouring to obey his call, yet as thou art concerned to follow him in simplicity, and as *entire dedication* is thy only aim; as thus thou perseverest, thou shalt ultimately witness that "overcoming" to which so many precious promises are annexed. * *

To continue the Journal:—

3rd mo., 24th. My corrupt nature has again suffered violent temptation. Thence has arisen the deepest depression. I have felt unable to help myself, and have cried out, "The enemy hath smitten my life down to the very ground." * * During this painful season I fear I have been too ready to complain. What little hope I have had has, I trust, been directed to Jesus Christ and him crucified. This morning I feel more hopefnl, and I earnestly pray that the hand of discipline may bring me into a state of greater holiness and nearness to God. May he condescend yet to purify, help, and guide me.

4th mo., 6th. Visited two poor lads, who are to be executed for highway robbery. How awful and afflicting do I feel their doom to be, and how inconsistent with the tenor of Christian humanity!

He had long cherished a warm regard for Jane Birkbeck, daughter of John Birkbeck, of Lynn. The bond of a somewhat distant relationship had been strengthened by frequent intercourse.

"We had known each other," to use his own words in his autobiography, "from early childhood; our pursuits were similar, and she, like myself, had become a decided Friend from conviction. In some other respects [our characters] were different. Generous, steadfast, and lively, she had one of those hardier souls, on which weakness is prone to lean, but her feelings were nevertheless warm and acute. She knew and adored her Saviour, and remarkably walked by that rule, 'Whatsoever ye do in word or deed, do all in the name of the Lord Jesus, giving thanks unto God and the Father by him.'"

Her father was now deceased, and she was residing with her widowed mother, Martha Birkbeck, when she accepted Joseph John Gurney's proposals of marriage in the 5th month of this year. He afterwards writes:—

6th mo., 7th. How extraordinary is the change wrought in my circumstances, and in my mind, since I last wrote! How beautifully has the atmosphere cleared! and after some of the deepest conflicts, which I have ever yet gone through, how delightful a calm am I introduced into! How do I desire to be bowed down in thankfulness to the God of my life, for his abundant blessings! How do I desire to receive from him renewed ability to love and serve him with my whole heart! Ah! may I never prefer the creature to the Creator, nor any earthly delight, to the cause of the crucified Jesus!

I left home about the 20th of 4th month; arrived at Runcton very unwell; remained a full fortnight, my mind deeply absorbed by the subject of marriage. Inexpressibly deep were the conflicts, and as great the happiness and peace, which were my allotment during that memorable fortnight; I believe the Lord was with me, and laid his hand upon me, in a remarkable manner. Never have I so experienced and known the reality and the power of the religious principles which I had adopted. After acute suffering, I had to rejoice as in the presence of my God. I hope I shall never forget the sweet peace and genuine happiness I enjoyed at Hunstanton,* in the society of one, who is now likely to be brought into such near union with me. This step seems to have been closely connected with something like a change for the better in my spiritual course; something of a clearer atmosphere and brighter view; more of the liberty of the gospel of Christ; less, I hope, of the intolerable impertinence of self.

He adds,

I think it right to record that my mouth has been several times opened in ministry.

On the third day evening, at Hunstanton, after I had been wonderfully delivered from conflict, I expressed, in dear Rachel's room, two or three sentences of thanksgiving; the next morning in our little meeting in the summer house, I

* The country residence of Martha Birkbeck, on the sea coast of Norfolk.

had something to say on the searching of heart, which we had all gone through, and of my confidence that the Lord would rightly direct us, did we put our whole trust in him. The following first day afternoon, at the Lynn Meeting, I simply said, "I cannot feel satisfied to leave this little gathering, without expressing the affectionate salutation of my heart; grace be with you all that love the Lord Jesus Christ in sincerity." Whether this is likely to go on, I know not. I feel it will be to my encouragement if it do; but I heartily desire to commit my way unto the Lord. * * My chief fear is, lest I should not, on this head, be sufficiently simple; but may I watch and pray, lest I enter into temptation.

Often did he afterwards recur to his feelings in the Meeting at Lynn above noticed; the first in which he was publicly engaged as a minister of the gospel. "O the delightful flow of quiet happiness," is his exclamation many years later in reference to it, "which continued to be my portion, through the whole of that day. No words can adequately set it forth; and the savour of it is even now fresh in my remembrance. Few such days have I yet spent on earth. Similar feelings," he adds, "though not in so high a degree, followed the further exercise of the gift; and the Lord led me gently forward in his work, giving me to feel the sweetness of obedience to his commands, and of a surrender of soul to his service."

6th mo., 15th. Last first day was interesting. * * In the afternoon I had to encourage the faithful to closer dedication. * * It was very difficult. I afterwards rejoiced that I did not bring my burden away. On fifth day I had something on my mind at meeting, but did not feel obliged to express it. Yesterday, before dinner, at the foundry, I fear I was not ready for the service, and have painfully felt the deficiency since. But I trust, unworthy and unwilling as I am, I shall not be cast off.

8th mo., 15th. * * My ministerial gift, which I have felt very precious to me, though it is attended by its conflicts and crosses, has continued to show itself. It is wonderful to me, to find myself actually under such an influence. Truly it is "as the wind that bloweth where it listeth." So far the work has been attended by a deeper feeling than I ever before experienced, of my own unworthiness, incompetency, and nothingness; and of the power, love, and present wisdom of the Almighty. Wonderful, indeed, is his condescension to us and care for us!

From Ackworth, where he was engaged on one of those visits the results of which will be hereafter noticed, he wrote to his sister Hannah Buxton, who, with her husband, was then deeply feeling the recent death of their brother Charles Buxton.*

Ackworth, 8th mo., 1st, 1817.

MY DEAREST HANNAH,

* * * For thee, for Fowell, for dear Martha, and for all who have more immediately entered into this deep cloud of suffering, I feel most sincerely, and earnestly desire that it may be the means of bringing you individually into a closer dependence upon Israel's everlasting Shepherd. * * I am deeply convinced that nothing will do, that nothing will stand us in stead, but yielding ourselves wholly to the guidance and protection of our heavenly Master. And when we consider how greatly we have all sinned and come short of the glory of God, may we not acknowledge that his love in shedding his precious blood for us, in redeeming us from sin by the influence of his Spirit, in dealing with us and disciplining us after the tenderest mercy, and in speaking peace to us from time to time, in the midst of the necessary conflicts, and finally in

* See Life of Sir T. F. Buxton, chap. v, p. 66.

preparing for us an everlasting inheritance, where the joys of the righteous are far above all that hath yet entered into our hearts; can we not acknowledge that such love is indeed marvellous; and ought we not individually to enter into solemn covenant to serve him with simplicity and godly sincerity in all our ways? * *

As regards myself, my experience during the last few months has been a little out of the usual course, or at least *my* usual course. I wish to say it in reverence, but I seem to have got out of a thick wood, into a verdant and beautiful plain, where the riches of the Lord's bounty are displaying themselves on every side. Deeply and totally unworthy am I of such a favour. I have indeed cause for thankfulness under the sense which is just now permitted me, of my clouded atmosphere being cleared, of my loins being more girt up; of a light within me, not of my own creating, being commanded to burn a little for my spiritual improvement and consolation. I may add to the list of divine mercies, my near prospect of a settlement in life, after my own heart's desire. Yet I have had my conflicts to pass through as well as my joys. May we all abide in true humiliation, and when the sunshine becomes overcast, (for its being so occasionally is, I doubt not, necessary for us all,) may patience equal to the day be afforded. * * I have several times felt it my indispensable duty to break the silence of our meetings, and the work appears more likely to proceed than to wither away, if I am faithful to its requisitions. But my gift is at present very small; and perhaps thou art little aware how entirely it appears to be out of my power to choose for myself [in it.] I may acknowledge that I find it not only a deeply interesting, but a *purifying* work. That it is one calling for peculiar dedication, and submission, must be fully admitted. I feel that I must wholly resign myself to the Spirit which "bloweth where it listeth," and if it be not given me to know "whence it cometh or whither it goeth," I must be content. * * *

On the 10th of the 9th mo., he was married to Jane Birbeck. He was scarcely settled at Earlham after the event, before other interests crowded upon him.

TO WILLIAM FORSTER.

Norwich, 9th mo., 30th, 1817.

* * Strange and new things have indeed happened to me; and I am but just finding my footing on the new-found land of married life and ministerial duty. It makes me feel as if I could not understand myself; but I trust that thankfulness is the prevailing feeling of my heart. I know that I have been greatly helped, blessed, and comforted; and I know also, from having passed through depths unknown before, that I have needed the help, the blessing, and the consolation which I have received.

But to proceed to more historical information, I am married, happily and satisfactorily married. The event took place, as was intended, at Wells Meeting, on the 10th of this month. The meeting and the day were I think highly favoured by the owning and cheering presence of the Master whom I desire to serve. The former was very solemn. * * I was constrained by a most sweet influence to supplicate that we might be enabled, on that solemn occasion, to enter into covenant with God, to serve, honour, and obey him in all our ways; and that, in things temporal and things spiritual, in heights and in depths, we might be more and more taught to place an unqualified dependence upon his mercy in the Lord Jesus Christ. We lodged at a nice country inn about seven miles from Hunstanton, and arrived at Earlham to dinner on the following day. The sun shone sweetly upon us, and that dear place received us with open doors in all its brightest colours. There we spent some quiet days of solitude before our friends came in upon us. For the last week we have had the house full, a delightful party of brothers and sisters, my mother-in-law, and some interesting friends of the Bible Society, especially Charles Simeon, of Cambridge, a man eminent for talent, for piety, and for singularity. This is a brief sketch of our external history: with regard to the *esoteric* part of it, it has been deeply interesting, and I think

I may add, affecting to me. The change is so great, so important, the union so close, so heart-tendering.

After alluding to his part in the work of the ministry, he proceeds,—

I believe the baptisms I have had to pass through have been intended to prepare me for this work, but they have not taken the shape of discouragement about the work itself: yet indeed I know and have felt its humiliations. How does it behove me to be watchful and dedicated to the Lord's will. I do indeed feel the awfulness of my profession.

The following are from his Journal.

9th mo., 15th. [After briefly describing his marriage]—and now I may record the thankfulness I have felt, and do feel, to the Author of every blessing, for the marvellous manner in which he has first suffered my faith to be tried, and then delivered me from conflict, and set my foot upon the rock. In my wife he has been pleased to bestow upon me a most precious treasure, exactly suited to my need, and I feel his presiding wing mercifully extended over us.

9th mo., 23rd. It has been our Quarterly Meeting. The meeting for worship was highly favoured by the divine presence. It was upon me to pray at considerable length, and under a very solemn influence, which continued after my prayer was finished. What a blessing,—how high a privilege is the spirit of prayer!

FROM JONATHAN HUTCHINSON.

Gedney, 9th mo., 29th, 1817.

* * With an affection and a solicitude which are as foreign to mere compliment as *it* is a stranger to them, I now congratulate you on a union which has so much of mind in it, as well as of outward advantages, as to promise the greatest share of temporal felicity. And yet I would apprize you that even

these satisfactions and privileges should be enjoyed in reference and subordination to the Giver of "every good and perfect gift;" that they ought frequently to be offered in sacrifice at his footstool; and that whilst you admit no inferior competitor into your hearts, he, the Creator of the heart, must reign unrivalled there. I would also apprize you, that, without any fault of ours, the sweetest, the most innocent earthly enjoyment, is liable to frequent and unexpected interruptions. In this *ordeal*, this prison of the soul, many things combine against our present happiness. The war of elements, the more fierce and cruel war of men's passions, prejudices, and interests, all aggravated by the malice of an unwearied and potent enemy, will one or other of them be frequently reminding the most prosperous and the most happy that this world affords not the ultimate rest of an immortal spirit,—that earth is not its final home. Of these things, beloved pair, though you knew them before, I have thought it might not be amiss, even in the zenith of your allowable enjoyment, to put you again in remembrance. But there is another thing, which perhaps you may not so readily admit, or so easily credit, but which I think it may be at least safe for me to communicate, and that is a belief which has attended me, particularly since your marriage, that the way cast up for you is rather an arduous than an easy one; and whilst I hope it will have many roses in it, I am apprehensive it will also have its thorns;—amidst other causes, on this especial and scriptural ground, that "they who will live godly in Christ Jesus, shall suffer persecution;"—for though racks and other torments of the body are, for the present, excluded our favoured land, yet there remain in it, in pretty full play, two small but powerful engines of mental disquietude, the tongue and the pen. The former of these, in certain heads, and under a certain direction, is strongly characterized by the Psalmist and the apostle James; and the latter, as perhaps some of us think, is not, when serving the same Master, either less mischievous or poignant.

Sixth day morniny, 10*th mo.*, 10*th*. Yesterday was a happy day. In the morning meeting I believed it my duty to pray in the following words:—

"We reverently thank thee, O Lord God Almighty, * * because thou art healing all our diseases, forgiving all our iniquities; because thou art redeeming our life from destruction, and crowning us with loving kindness and tender mercies. We beseech thee, O Lord, so to impress upon our spirits, a sense of thine abundant loving kindness in Christ Jesus, that we may be constrained by his love, to enter in at the strait gate; to walk in the narrow way; to take up our daily cross in simplicity and godly sincerity; and to follow the Lamb whithersoever he goeth. Thus, O Lord, though we are indeed unworthy in thy sight, suffer thine own works to praise thee; and whilst thou art making us sensible that of ourselves we can do nothing, enable us to acknowledge, that great and marvellous are thy works, Lord God Almighty, just and true are all thy ways, thou King of Saints."

I felt it a privilege thus to be brought to the sense, and to the expression of thanksgiving; but I have since felt in the midst of our large and pleasant party, and abounding luxuries, and indolent tendencies, a fear lest the narrow path should be forgotten. May this never be the case. I do feel a genuine desire that all may be kept in true and right order, by the Spirit and power of my Lord and Master.

TO JONATHAN HUTCHINSON.

Norwich, 10th mo., 11th, 1817.

How is the Christian's faith, at times, permitted to be tried, even to a hair's breadth, and after these seasons of probation, how wonderfully is relief afforded, when perhaps least expected, from the presence of the Lord! I am writing to one who knows far more of these things than I do, but I believe thou mayest receive me, if thou wilt, as a fellow traveller in suffering, as well as in rejoicing. To open my mouth in public ministry, is a duty which I have had deep reason to believe has been required at my hands not unfrequently. It has seemed to me impossible to do otherwise, consistently with my own peace, than to go straight forward in it, without much looking to the judgment of others. What others think of me

I know not, but I heartily desire to live more simply in this and everything else, to the Lord, and not to man.

Towards the close of the year, in company with his wife, his brother Samuel Gurney, his brother and sister Buxton and Francis and Richenda Cunningham, he took a short tour upon the continent of Europe, their principal objects being to establish a Branch Bible Society in Paris, and to procure information as to the systems of prison discipline adopted in the jails of Antwerp and Ghent. In crossing over to Calais they were surrounded by a dense fog, in which they drifted about for two days and nights, and narrowly escaped running the vessel ashore. Joseph John Gurney's own account of this journey has not been preserved, but the reader will find several interesting details respecting it, in the life of Sir Thomas Fowell Buxton.* Having accomplished their objects, they returned home after an absence of about a month.

TO HIS SISTER-IN-LAW ELIZABETH GURNEY.

Norwich, 12th mo., 9th, 1817.

* * We arrived late on seventh day evening. A hearty welcome, and a warm, bright house awaited us; dear Catherine and Priscilla looking charmingly, and all the household in good order. What a blessing is there in such an arrival at home!

* * It was very comfortable yesterday to find ourselves once more seated in Goat Lane.† Our morning meeting was solemn. The afternoon meeting was also comfortable, and a satisfactory reading at Earlham, and cheerful evening over the great parlour fire, concluded the day. Yesterday brought the

* See Life of Sir T. F. Buxton, chap. v.

† One of the Meeting-houses of Friends, in Norwich.

usual round of banking, writing, reading, &c. How pleasant is the settlement into regular domestic life!

My wife and I spend our evenings alone together. I do not think our dear sisters will be the least interruption to us. * *

The occasions on which he felt called to speak as a minister were now more frequent, "though often," as he says,* "attended with unusual conflict, and much in the cross and fear." "How vain," he remarks in another place,† "would be my own efforts to minister without the command!"

Early in the year 1818, private business called him to London. His sister Elizabeth Fry had previously entered upon her important labours for the benefit of the prisoners in Newgate, and for the improvement of prison discipline generally. Joseph John Gurney warmly entered into his sister's views, accompanied her to the Committee of the House of Commons on the occasion of her giving her evidence, and afterwards to Lord Sidmouth, then Secretary of State for the Home Department.‡ On his return, he thus briefly alludes to his visit.

3d mo., 9th, 1818. The [last] fortnight has been a very interesting one. After two busy days of preparation, we left home on fourth day, (the 25th ult.) by day coach, and arrived that night at Upton. * *

Sixth day, to London, to the Committee of the House of Commons, with dear Elizabeth; afterwards to dine with W. Smith, M. P., where we met Wilberforce and Sir S. Romilly. A very interesting time.

* Journal under date 2nd mo., 1st, 1818.

† Under date 2nd mo., 11th, 1818.

‡ See Life of Elizabeth Fry, vol. i, p. 292—313.

Seventh day, breakfasted with William Smith; corrected my sister's evidence; returned with her in the evening to Upton.

First day began in lowness, followed by deep exercise of spirit, and a great flow in the ministry at Plaistow: in the morning, on giving up the world to come to Christ; "who hath believed our report?" &c., with prayer for the different states in the meeting: in the afternoon, comfort and advice to the discouraged, and prayer for them. * *

Second day, interesting visit to Newgate; solemn meeting there. * *

Third day with my sister to Lord Sidmouth.

Fourth day, breakfasted with Wilberforce; met Lord Rocksavage. * *

His visit to London, and the pamphlet on Prison Discipline, soon afterwards published by his brother-in-law, Thomas Fowell Buxton, tended to deepen in his own mind a sense of the importance of that subject; and an opportunity soon occurred for endeavouring to influence the authorities at Norwich to some exertion respecting it. The Mayor and Corporation, attended by the Sheriffs and other citizens, whilst perambulating the boundaries of the county of the city, were, by his desire, invited to partake of refreshment in passing by the hall at Earlham. Besides those immediately connected with the magistracy, many others assembled, the whole company consisting of about 800 persons. On this occasion, Joseph John Gurney, in an address to the Mayor and Corporation, urged the erection of a new jail, and its establishment on better principles, with a view to the employment of the prisoners and the improvement of their morals;

enforcing his appeal by a reference to the extraordinary change that had then recently taken place in Newgate through the exertions of a committee of ladies, and concluding by offering a donation of £100 towards the object. The effort was not without fruit, though the result was not immediately apparent.

In the spring of 1818, a dissolution of Parliament took place, which was followed by a general election. Upon religious and philanthropic grounds he had long desired to see his brother-in-law, Thomas Fowell Buxton, in Parliament, and now rejoiced with him in his success at Weymouth. His letter to him on the occasion, which is already before the public,* is sufficiently expressive of the hopes which he indulged as to his parliamentary career, hopes not of political distinction, but of the powerful and successful advocacy of the cause of righteousness and love. As regarded himself, he was called into a different sphere. His advocacy of this cause was to be elsewhere than in the House of Commons. Much, however, as he disliked the strife of politics, he was involved in some effort at the election at Norwich, in consequence of the illness of a near relative, who was one of the candidates. "It was my endeavour," he writes in his Journal, "not to yield myself up to the interests of the election, but being called upon, I made one speech to the electors, in which I communicated my whole mind on the subject before us, and endeavoured to raise their minds to something higher than mere politics.

* See Life of Sir T. F. Buxton, chap. vi, p. 78.

The whole effect," he adds, "has been rather lowering to the best things." "When we look, on the one hand," is his subsequent reflection in the Autobiography, in allusion to this incident, "to the party spirit, the dissipation, and corruption which attend these political strifes, and, on the other hand, to the meekness, quietness, impartiality, and purity, which ought to mark the character of Christians, we can scarcely avoid the conclusion that the less we have to do with such affairs the better; at the same time we are not to forget our character as citizens of the state, and ought neither to despise our rights, nor neglect our duties in that capacity. 'Let all things be done decently and in order.'"

It was in the sixth month of this year, that the Monthly Meeting of Friends in Norwich recognized him as a Minister of the Gospel, called to the work by the Great Head of the Church. Referring to this and to his previous attendance of the Yearly Meeting in London, he writes in his Journal:—

6th mo., 20th. * * The Yearly Meeting was exceedingly interesting, and, in most respects, quite satisfactory. To me it was a period of much religious exercise; I had frequently to speak, and both to open and conclude the Yearly Meeting in supplication. I met with much kind encouragement and some useful warnings. * * On fifth day, the 11th, at our Monthly Meeting, I was acknowledged a minister; much was felt, and the unity of Friends appeared complete. This has been a consolation to me. I feel the necessity of being very, very watchful, that my practice may not linger behind my high profession.

First day morning, [*6th mo.,* 21*st.*] I feel a good deal at sitting [as a minister] in the gallery, not being to my own apprehension, adequately spiritual; but I believe help will be afforded. May I be enabled to enter afresh into covenant with my Redeemer, to renounce the whole spirit of the world, and to serve him faithfully!

Night. I feel thankful for the day's experience. In the afternoon I uttered a few sentences in supplication; the first time of opening my mouth in ministry, in my new situation. It has afforded me relief.

CHAPTER VIII.

1818—1819. ÆT. 31.

EARLHAM; FAMILY MEETINGS; POSITION IN BUSINESS AND AS A CHRISTIAN MINISTER; JOURNEY TO SCOTLAND AND THE NORTH OF ENGLAND WITH HIS SISTER ELIZABETH FRY; EDINBURGH; GLASGOW; FIRST "PUBLIC MEETING;" VISIT TO THE EARL OF DERBY AT KNOWSLEY; PUBLISHES HIS FIRST BOOK; "NOTES UPON PRISONS;" LETTERS FROM WILLIAM WILBERFORCE; CORRESPONDENCE WITH EDWARD HARBORD; EXERTIONS TO SAVE THREE PRISONERS; BIRTH OF HIS SON.

AFTER his marriage Joseph John Gurney continued at Earlham, and the hall where his father had resided, and in which he had himself lived from his birth, may be henceforth regarded as his settled residence. To this place, "with its lovely lawn, nested among large trees," possessing within itself those ample accommodations which it was his enjoyment to share with his friends, and combining a convenient proximity to a large and important city, with great quietness and retirement, he was strongly attached. And they who knew him there can still picture him in his study among his books; or in his drawing room amongst his friends, his countenance beaming with love and intelligence, the life of the whole circle; or in his garden amongst his flowers with his Greek Testament in his hand, still drawing from the books "of nature and of grace" that lay open before him, new motives to raise the heart to the Author of all his blessings.

Placed by circumstances, though not the elder brother, in the position which his father had occupied in Norfolk, as master of Earlham and a partner in the Bank, it was his delight as far as possible, to continue Earlham as the family house. Even after his marriage, his sisters Catherine, Rachel, and Priscilla continued to live with him, occupying their own apartments; and it was the custom of the other members of the family frequently to meet there as under a common roof. "How often," (is his characteristic exclamation,) "has the large family circle assembled there; and how often have we found occasion when so collected to acknowledge the loving kindness of the Shepherd of Israel!" Up to the period of his brother John's decease, and for some time afterwards, it was the habit of his brothers and himself, with their brothers-in-law Thomas Fowell Buxton and Samuel Hoare, to improve these occasions by a mutual impartial examination of their conduct, in which each, with brotherly openness, stated what he conceived to be the others' faults. Happy indeed was such an intercourse between such minds. "It has inspired me," remarks Joseph John Gurney, in allusion to it on one occasion,* (and his Journal contains many similar allusions,) "with a fresh desire to be bold, resolute, honest, straightforward."

Beside this, to him, delightful band of brothers and sisters, his house was, as must have been already apparent to the reader, freely opened to a large circle. Whilst every year strengthened his conviction of the soundness and importance of the Christian princi-

* Journal, under date 10th mo., 25th, 1812.

ples which he professed, he rejoiced in "that liberty wherewith Christ" had made him "free" to embrace as brethren all those in whom he thought he could discern traces of his heavenly image. His natural character doubtless led him to dwell rather on the points of union than of difference with those around him. With his expansive feelings, it was to him peculiarly painful to be separated in outward religious fellowship from some whom he much loved, from many whom he highly valued, and from the great bulk of his fellow professors of the Christian name. Nothing, it may be said with truth, but a deep sense of duty, an absolute necessity laid upon him, would have reconciled him to such a separation. It is in this point of view that his decision is entitled to the greater weight; and, under his circumstances, the degree in which his natural sensitiveness, almost amounting to timidity, was gradually overcome, the courage and firmness with which he was, on various occasions, enabled to act out his convictions, were not the least striking evidences of the work of divine grace upon his heart.

Whatever may be the advantages of smaller circles, it may be a question whether these advantages have not been sometimes overrated. To the tender plant they are often highly serviceable, if not absolutely essential. But are there not instances in which, if there has been less to obstruct the formation of the character, there has been, on the other hand, less to develope and invigorate it, where, instead of growing up to a healthful maturity, it has been either permanently crippled, or what is equally disastrous, permanently deformed; one limb or member growing out of its due place or proportion, to the prejudice of the rest. They who have been accustomed always to associate with those of similar opinions, and who are acquainted only with the habits and modes of thought of their own particular circles, are naturally but ill prepared to understand and sympathize with the difficulties of others. That which is known is, in far too many cases, all that exists, to them that know nothing beyond. Ignorance is thus apt to beget exclusiveness, and the mind and the heart become contracted together. And, even assuming the educational opinions of such individuals to be strictly correct, it may well be doubted whether the discipline, or rather the absence of discipline, through which these opinions have been imbibed, has led them to so deep an understanding and heartfelt an appreciation of them as he possesses who has "bought the truth" at the price of much inward and outward conflict, and has had to contest, as it were, every inch of the ground on which he stands.

The reader has now to view Joseph John Gurney not only in the varied relations of private life, but in the important character of a Christian minister. The work of the ministry of the gospel is one of the most serious and responsible in which man can be engaged. In Joseph John Gurney's mind the sense of its importance was not diminished by the peculiarity of his position. He was well aware that it was not his learning or his talents that had qualified him for such a service. He had received no ordination from human authority, nor any "call" or appointment from the congregation. The "acknowledgment" of his friends, was simply a *recognition* of the *gift* which both he and they felt to be altogether dependent upon the free and unrestrained mercy of the glorified Head of the Church, bestowed through the agency of that Spirit who "divideth severally to every man as he will," and for the due exercise of which the steward entrusted with it must give a strict account. His course of life bears witness to the earnestness of his desire to be found faithful in this stewardship. His labours were extensive and abundant; yet he did not esteem the duties in which he became on this account involved, incompatible with those of his ordinary calling. And whilst his secular occupations led him into a closer intercourse with others, and made him better acquainted with the difficulties and conflicts of ordinary life, thereby enlarging his heart to a more extended sympathy with those among whom he was called to labour, they tended at the same time to refresh and invigorate his mind and affections, by the very diversion of them from the contemplative to the more practical parts of religion. As a man of business he was exact and methodical. Promptness and dispatch equally characterized him. It was his endeavour, through that assistance without which he felt himself weak even in these things, to act out the scriptural maxim, "whatsoever thy hand findeth to do, do it with thy might." Whilst this strikingly marked his conduct in the ordinary duties of business, it became especially apparent in times of difficulty and danger. And on more than one occasion of great commercial distress and anxiety, the quiet firmness and effective decision which he was enabled to evince, afforded practical evidence, of no mean value, of the reality and power of his Christian principles. Deeply was he impressed with the responsibilities of his position. Deeply did he feel that to perform duties so various as those of a man of business, and of a Christian minister, requires (may it not be said) a double portion of divine wisdom and grace. But in his example, as in that of many others, there is encouraging evidence, that the right combination of these services, so far from tending to dim the lustre of the Christian's armour, serves rather to brighten his weapons, and to nerve his limbs the more effectively to wield them. His comparative affluence doubtless materially facilitated the carrying out of his views, and relieved him from those corroding cares which are so apt to absorb or wear down the mind; but it placed him, at the same time, within the reach of other and not less dangerous temptations. Solemn indeed is the language, "How hardly shall they that have riches, enter into the kingdom of heaven!" And whilst the assurance that "with God it is possible," ought to prevent any from being dismayed, it should never be forgotten that the power of divine grace is peculiarly exemplified in the character of those who, amidst the allurements of ease and pleasure, and the temptations of worldly ambition, have been enabled, through unmerited mercy, "to fight the good fight of faith, and to lay hold on eternal life."

In the 8th and 9th months of this year, (1818,) in company with his wife, his sister Elizabeth Fry, and one of her daughters, he took a journey into Scotland, visiting many of the prisons both there and in the north of England, besides attending many of the meetings of Friends. On this occasion, in conformity with the Christian order established in the Society of Friends, he was furnished with a minute or testimonial expressing the concurrence of the Friends of his own "Monthly Meeting" in his prospects of religious service. They proceeded through Darlington and Newcastle to Edinburgh and Dundee, and thence by Montrose to Aberdeen, where they attended the General Meeting of Friends in Scotland. Returning by way of Perth, after having visited the families of Friends at Kilmuck, the first service of this kind in which he was engaged, and which he describes as "humbling and difficult," —they proceeded to Edinburgh, and thence to Glasgow, where, amidst a pressure of other duties, he held his first "public meeting." After attending the meetings of Friends in Cumberland and at Kendal, they came to Liverpool, from which place they visited the Earl of Derby and his family at Knowsley Park. Proceeding homeward by way of York, they arrived at Earlham in the early part of the 10th month. The particulars of this journey are already so fully before the public in the Memoirs of Elizabeth Fry,* and through the work upon prisons published by Joseph John Gurney, that it seems unnecessary to give more than the following extracts from his Journal.

Stonehaven, 8th mo., 28th, 1818. Our day's journey has been remarkably agreeable. We crossed the ferry to Dundee after an early breakfast; a very pleasant sail of two miles; a fresh gale blowing, and the morning delightful. The mouth of the Tay makes a noble harbour, and Dundee is a place of much trade; the number of its inhabitants 35,000. The return for salmon there is £100,000 per annum, and they manufac-

* Memoirs of Elizabeth Fry, vol. i, p. 328.

ture brown linen in great quantities. We called upon two of the magistrates. One of them showed us the jail, which like other Scotch jails, is quite defective. It contains no criminals at this time. It is a rare thing to have a criminal in this jail, which serves not only for this populous town, but for a large district of the county of Forfar. The scarcity of crime in Scotland, which is very striking to an English observer, must be attributed to the early and religious education of the whole people. The population appears in a healthy state of morals. Would it were so with us!

The road hither from Dundee by Aberbrothock, or Arbroath, Montrose, and Bervie, runs along the coast of Forfar, and presents a delightful variety of sea views. The towns are pleasant and prettily situated. At Arbroath we visited the jail, very dirty, though not an old building, and with the usual accommodations of Scotch jails, and nothing more. *Not a single criminal in it.*

At Montrose we were shown the prison by Provost Barclay, a distant relation of the Ury family, strongly resembling some of the Barclays in person. Like every other Scotchman in authority whom we have yet met with, he was extremely civil. There is a real readiness to serve amongst the Scotch, and they often expect no pay for many of the little things with which they furnish us.

The drive between Montrose and Bervie is beautiful, especially on account of the sea views, and the little villages of Johnshaven and Gordon situated at the foot of lofty hills, and on the rocky shore of the sea, quite sheltered from the world but apparently populous. There is also a highly beautiful deep and richly wooded ravine, through which a mountain stream runs over the dark rocks into the sea, in one place forming a cataract seventy or eighty feet in height. There is nothing remarkable between the little town of Bervie and Stonehaven, except the approach down the side of a steep hill to the latter place, which is beautifully situated round a natural basin of the sea.

9th mo., 5th. We left Perth at noon and were three hours on our road to Kinross. Our way lay through some beautiful scenery. On leaving Perth for Edinburgh, the traveller ascends a hill from which there is a delightful view of the town, the bridge, the mountains, and the river Tay. The hill called Kinnoul on the right of the town is particularly beautiful, finely cultivated, and adorned with pretty white houses on one side, and, on the other, a precipitous barren rock. About eight miles from Perth we came to the beautiful rocky and wooded glen of Nairn through which the road winds for about a mile. On our approach to Kinross we had a fine view of Lochleven, and the old castle where Queen Mary was confined. The jail of Kinross, and a dinner upon Lochleven trout, detained us not an hour, and we reached the North Queen's Ferry by half-past six, we crossed the Firth in about an hour, the wind being contrary, but the evening delightful, and did not reach our hospitable quarters [at Alexander Cruickshank's, Edinburgh] before half-past ten.

9th mo., 12th. First, second, and part of third day were spent at Edinburgh. Second day was one of great labour and religious exercise. We spent an hour pleasantly at the "deaf and dumb asylum," where the interesting company of intelligent children struck us very much. There is a *naiveté* and cleverness about them which is delightful. They are excellently taught to read, write, cypher, &c.; and had evidently received good religious instruction. Here we were met by Erskine of Mar, a generous old man, a great supporter of public charities and very cordial to us. Ten or eleven family visits occupied the remainder of the day. In the evening returned to supper at Alexander Cruickshank's, where we were met by John Wigham, jun., Thomas Allan, Leonard Horner, &c., and having got well through the labours of the day, we passed the first watch of the night very pleasantly together. On third day morning a fine party collected at breakfast, Leonard Horner, Archibald Constable and family, my friend Andrew Hamilton, Henderson, an active dissenting minister, Sir George and Lady Grey, with their son and daughter. I very much enjoyed their society, and before we parted my dear sister Fry was solemnly engaged in prayer.

First day morning, [*9th mo.*, 14*th.*] In allusion to the public meeting at Glasgow held the preceding fifth day. The class who met us were of the thinking, and rather superior kind. We were both engaged in preaching and in prayer. My text was, "Search the scriptures, for they are they which testify of me." It was a solemn, quiet, and I trust edifying time; and there seemed much openness and cordiality amongst the people. * * I may truly say that this public meeting, and many other occasions since I left home, have been abundantly sufficient to convince me how near the Lord is to help us if we place our trust in him. I have, from time to time, been made sensible of my own entire poverty; but have never been disappointed when I have gone, with full purpose of heart, to the only true source of help. * * [Last] fifth day was the anniversary of my marriage, and was also marked by my first public meeting. On looking back upon the past twelve months, I have indeed much cause for thankfulness. How have I been blessed and comforted in [my] union; and though we have met with one affliction,* how much cause have I, even for this, to praise him who has thus been mercifully with us, both in prosperity and adversity, in heights and in depths. My gift in the ministry has been very much enlarged, and I humbly trust there may have been some spiritual progress accompanying it; yet on looking into myself impartially, I seem to find nothing but cause for repentance. How often am I brought to feel the necessity of leaving that which is behind, and of clinging to him who can save!

9*th mo.*, 19*th* [Referring to the decease of a devoted servant of Christ.] The account we heard of her mental sufferings in her last days, was affecting; and shows that even the most devoted of the Lord's servants are, at times, permitted to know a deep cloud when they pass through the valley of the shadow of death. Too much stress ought not to be laid on death-bed scenes, nor ought the expectation to be too much fixed on sunshine in that awful hour; though it is sometimes my prayer, that sunshine may be my portion in it.

* In allusion to his wife's confinement, and the death of the infant.

9th mo., 26th. * * We have more than once been cheered in the course of this journey by meeting with dear friends green in old age, alive in the truth, and evidently fast ripening for the garner. Such instances strongly confirm the truth of religion, and, as I think, more particularly so, when they are attended by a decay of intellectual powers. * *

——— breakfasted with us, and afterwards met us at the prison, and to dinner. I was much pleased with him. He is evidently a man of remarkable amiability, uncommon cultivation, and very considerable talent. His company and conversation afforded me real pleasure; but it grieved me to think that he never attends any place of worship, and is probably not thoroughly convinced of Christianity. Such characters may do much harm. Here is a man, presenting many charms, with a life of excellent morals, and yet not publicly professing Christianity, and perhaps, not believing in it. There may be, and I believe there is, a deception of the enemy in this pleasant picture!

Referring to their visit at Knowsley, Joseph John Gurney writes:—

Lord and Lady Derby, with others of the family, met us at the door, and received us most heartily. Lord Derby is an elderly man, remarkably kind and attentive, and without anything of manner to make one feel his rank. Lady Derby is somewhat younger; a very interesting and pleasing woman; her mind much too great for affectation or pride; her disinterestedness conspicuous in the little occurrences of the day; and her conversation attractive from the force of her mind, which is evidently under the power of religion. She lost her only son about a year ago; a chastisement which appears to have had much effect upon her. They were surrounded by a large patriarchal family party, consisting chiefly of the Stanleys, and Hornbys. The most conspicuous individuals were Lord Stanley, his daughter Charlotte, and his son Edward;* Lady Mary, Lady Derby's only remaining child; the mother of the Hornbys, Lord Derby's sister;

* The present Earl.

surrounded by several pleasing daughters, besides sons and sons' wives. There were also some agreeable guests in the house; the whole party about thirty-five in number, exclusive of many children. I have seldom, if ever, seen so much love and harmony prevailing without any form, over a large family circle. Lord and Lady Derby took a walk with us before dinner, and showed us the pictures and the house. The afternoon and evening were agreeably spent in not trifling conversation. A crowd thronged around my sister, whose tales were thoroughly relished. I passed part of the evening in a very interesting conversation with Lady Derby on religious subjects. * * Before breakfast next morning, the ladies Mary and Charlotte took us in the carriage to see their girls' schools, which are in excellent order. They seem to take great pains with their poor neighbours. Lord Derby gives prizes annually to those of his cottagers who most excel in neatness, propriety, &c. After breakfast we ventured to propose that the whole family might be assembled. My dear sister had felt a strong concern for this object, and I was ready to bear her burthen with her. The proposal was readily acceded to, and nearly the whole party, including the servants, about seventy persons in all, assembled in the dining room. After a short pause, I began by reading the third chapter of John. The religious opportunity which followed lasted nearly an hour, and was truly solemn. I have scarcely ever known a time of such apparent baptism of the Spirit. My sister prayed almost as soon as I had concluded reading; much power attending her. I afterwards felt unusual liberty in preaching the gospel to this interesting party, from one of the verses we had been reading; "As Moses lifted up the serpent in the wilderness," &c. My sister afterwards spoke, and I was enabled to pray in conclusion. We may thankfully acknowledge that our blessed Master was pleased on this occasion to send us "help from the sanctuary." Almost all present, both old and young, appeared to be brought to tears; some to many tears. I felt thankful for having so favoured an opportunity of plainly declaring the truths of Christianity to the family of a great nobleman, and as the ground was evidently prepared, I trust the seed did not fall into it in vain. I think we read of circumstances very much resembling this visit, in the journals of the earliest Friends. May all the praise be attributed where alone it is due! We left Knowsley about twelve o'clock on sixth day morning, and dined at Warrington with two dear old friends, John and Elizabeth Bludwick. They seemed to be ripe for eternity! With them also we were sweetly engaged in waiting and prayer.*

10th mo., 5th. Fourth day [at York] was devoted to the Quarterly Meeting, which was large, but not so large as I expected. The day was very interesting to me. The meeting for worship was marked principally by the ministry of Benjamin White, from America, and Ann Alexander. The meeting for business appeared to me remarkably well conducted. The afternoon sitting was chiefly taken up by considering the best mode of distributing and using the Yearly Meeting's address on the subject of the religious instruction of children. It was peculiarly gratifying to me to find in this Quarterly Meeting so great an unanimity, and such an uncommon weight of exercise on this great point of religious instruction. It was agreed that a committee of men and women Friends should be appointed in each of the Monthly Meetings to read the address, and communicate advice on the subject, in the families of Friends. * *

On fifth day morning, 10th mo., 1st. we all breakfasted at Samuel Tuke's, where a large party of Friends and others met us, including J. Graham, a very active evangelical clergyman. He seemed much satisfied with a religious opportunity, which took place before we parted. [The meeting for worship, which followed,] was largely attended, principally by Friends. The ministry lay entirely on my dear sister, Jonathan Hutchin-

* In his autobiography, Joseph John Gurney adds, "I afterwards carried on a correspondence with Lady Derby, and some of the young people. I had recommended their searching out texts on particular subjects in the Bible, as a useful exercise. This became their regular weekly practice; and, at the close of the week, some one of the party was appointed judge of the selection, and expressed his decision in writing, in the form of a brief essay."

son, and myself; and I think that very many were truly baptized that day into one body. It was a great consolation after our heart sinkings, and low feelings, in Scotland and Cumberland, to be brought amongst so many, who appeared settled and established in the blessed truth. After my sister had been engaged very beautifully in supplication, Jonathan Hutchinson preached in a peculiarly touching manner, on the case of those who had at one time been enabled to testify, "Behold the Lamb of God," and were afterwards induced to inquire "Is this the Christ, or look we for another?"—also of those who were *almost* persuaded to be Christians. After he sat down I felt much liberty in speaking on the apostle's exhortation: "I beseech you therefore, brethren, that ye walk worthy of the vocation wherewith ye are called." It was a time of real feeling, and love seemed to flow like a river. It was truly comforting, thus to finish our course with the warm sympathy and concurrence of our friends. We left York immediately after the meeting, and proceeded to the Archbishop's palace. There we were kindly received by the Archbishop, and Lady Ann Vernon, his wife, with their son and daughter. He is a fine dignified looking man, and very polite. He entered cordially into the prison cause, and Lady Ann is to preside over the York ladies' committee.

We arrived at Lynn after a comfortable and quiet journey, on seventh day, the 3d. There I left my sister and my dear wife, and reached Earlham to breakfast yesterday morning. I feel like a vessel which has been filled, but is now empty; quiet and not uncomfortable, thankful in my small measure for the help and preservation experienced in the course of our long travel, and desirous to resume my home duties with vigour, as "unto the Lord, and not unto men."

10th mo., 17th. This week our party [has been] almost entirely confined to our own family. I have felt it no small privilege thus to renew my old affection for my brothers and sisters, and to find these affections living with unabated force. I am indeed remarkably and most undeservedly favoured by a gracious Master and Saviour; a spiritual course open before me in a manner which at one time I little expected, and to which I was altogether a stranger, and old fears and sorrows, best known to myself, completely done away. "O for a closer walk with God."

11*th mo.*, 8*th.* To Hunstanton on second day; my ride in part, at least, profitable by reading and reflection. I thought very intently for some time on the subject of religious instruction—perhaps the seed of a future pamphlet. Whilst there, I wrote a good quantity in my prison book. Fifth day; Lynn meeting; a comfortable time, after much feeling of lowness. I went to meeting impressed with the sad account of Sir Samuel Romilly's death, and preached on the evils of the world, and on the only remedy. I afterwards prayed for all in affliction, and particularly for the king and queen, in which I felt much satisfaction. Home on sixth day: delightful to be there again; Fowell, Hannah, and Priscilla, our almost constant companions. I felt burthened this morning with business, but am now very much relieved. May grace govern me through the day. Second day morning; I may acknowledge that this was in a degree, my case yesterday, for I was drawn out of *cares* into *duties* to my own consolation.

TO JONATHAN HUTCHINSON.

Earlham, 12th mo., 3rd, 1818.

* * It is now more than two months since we reached home, and very swift and full has been the stream which during that period has been carrying us along. Almost the first object was the Bible Society, and a large meeting, not only of our own family, but of several religious and agreeable guests at Earlham. This was attended by some exertion, but the scene passed off very pleasantly, not without real edification. * * Amongst our guests was the Countess of G——, a lady who, through many sufferings, internal and external, has been brought to a deep, and at length, a consoliug sense of religion. Our large party has been for some time dispersed, except that Fowell Buxton and his wife are living for a few months at Earlham lodge—a house which was occupied when thou wast last here by Charles Brereton. I wish thou knew something of Fowell. He has one of those noble and excelling minds with which it is very useful and stimulating to come

into contact. He is rather a singular instance of a person going into parliament for the simple purpose of doing as much good as he can. * *

Notwithstanding all my weaknesses, I have frequently felt the privilege of being united in the bonds of love with many righteous servants; and more especially have I prized my connexion with our own Society; which though it may be in a very low state, certainly contains much substantial worth, and does not yet fail in supplying our minds with a home, in which we are often permitted to experience true rest. Whether it be declining or not, I know not—I hope the contrary,—in most parts of the kingdom. With *us* certainly, there does not at present, appear a very bright prospect; our young people are so estranged from the simplicity which ought to distinguish them, and seem to have so little of an ear open, that one hardly sees what is to become of us, when the support of our church will come to depend externally upon this rising generation. But let us not encourage a shortness of faith. "The husbandman waiteth for the precious fruit of the earth, and hath long patience for it, until he receive the early and the latter rain." This is a good example for Christian ministers, who are sometimes led to suppose, by external appearance, that their labour of love is nothing availing.

"On my return home," he writes in his Autobiography, after alluding to his northern journey, "I published my *first book*,—Notes of a Visit made to some of the Prisons of Scotland, and the North of England, in company with Elizabeth Fry, with some general remarks on the subject of prison discipline. Buxton had published his extraordinary pamphlet on prison discipline the year before, which had met with a warm and very general reception; my little work was regarded in the light of a supplement to his, and three thousand copies of it were sold. I trust it might be useful in calling the further attention of the public to a subject of much practical importance, but some of the local managers of the prisons whom I had not spared, were angry enough. This was of little consequence, and I believe in some cases, they were shamed into reformation."*

2nd mo., *1st*, 1819. I have been troubled about the Norwich jail, but having done what I could, I must leave it to Him, in whose hands are the hearts of all men. The idea of being the object of a sort of sour grumbling feeling with some of my fellow citizens, is somewhat depressing; but I desire afresh to live near the source of quietude and true peace, that I may be clothed, far more than I am, in the righteousness of Christ.

TO HIS SISTER ELIZABETH FRY.

Earlham, 1st mo., 19th, 1819.

My dearest Betsy,

"He that giveth, let him do it with simplicity." In the desire to fulfil this precept, I may state that I have, on the settlement of my accounts, £500 to spare; and after some consideration, believe it my duty to apply it to the oiling of thy wheels. I therefore put it into Samuel's hands, to whom thou mayest apply for the money, as wanted. My intention is, that it should be a little stock in hand, to meet thy private and personal exigencies. My condition is, that thou wilt not say a word about it to any one. Of course I take no refusal, and can admit but very little gratitude. I finished correcting my press last fifth day, and am wishing to know whether the book is published. I have ordered copies to John Smith, Wilberforce, and the Derby family.

In haste, thy very affectionate Brother,

J. J. Gurney.

P.S.—I shall consider myself very ill used, if thou art ever detected in walking, when it is better for thy health that thou shouldst ride, or if thou art ever denying thyself any of the comforts of life, which are needful for thee.

* An edition in 8vo. was published in 1847, uniform with Joseph John Gurney's other works.

FROM WILLIAM WILBERFORCE,

(who had, three days before, presented a petition from the Society of Friends, against the severe enactment of the penal code.*)

London, February 12th, 1819.

MY DEAR FRIEND,

Your affectionate letter, just now perused, calls forth a feeling which must have vent.

The subject of our criminal laws, (more especially as it regards capital punishments,) has long occupied my mind, and I own, I think, the just principles on that subject are clearly ascertained. But [on presenting the petition] I sincerely, as well as explicitly, disclaimed all idea of bringing any proposition forward myself; and I called on the House, not without a previous anticipation that Sir James Mackintosh would answer the summons. He has many of the requisites for such a task; though it is to be regretted that he is so much a party man. I believe *we* never have discussed that question of party. I own I have a strong sense that when pushed to any extent, (for of course occasional co-operation and concert, among those who concur in sentiment, is advisable and even necessary;) the political, and not less the moral evils of party, are very great. Shall I confess to you what I assure [you] is the honest truth, that I do not recollect a single occasion of any kind of importance, in which I was so dissatisfied with my own performance, as on that of presenting the petition; and my surprise was as great as my pleasure, when I found that Mr. Samuel Gurney, and one or two others, had been pleased. The fact is, that the House, before I got up, had been very inattentive and noisy. It grew latish, and it appeared to me that everybody was in haste to get to dinner. Under this impression, though I had ideas and principles sufficient, I did not at all put them together, or arrange them in my mind, but got up wholly unprepared, as I may say, meaning to utter but a very few words. But when I had begun, I found

* See Life of Wilberforce, vol v, pp. 12—14.

a very attentive, and, contrary to my expectation, a very sympathising audience. So that then, if I could have collected myself sufficiently, I would have gone somewhat into the *rationale* of the subject. But like a general, whose troops were scattered, I could not at once call them into order, so that I was fain merely to pour forth what was uppermost. This happened to be what interested my own feelings deeply, and when that is the case, we often interest the feelings of others.

Though I have rather *felt* than *seen* my way along my paper, my eyes feel overdone, and I must say farewell;—begging you to continue your prayers for me and mine, and to believe me,

Ever your sincere and affectionate friend,

William Wilberforce.

It was about this period that Joseph John Gurney became acquainted with Edward Harbord, afterwards Lord Suffield, an acquaintance which soon ripened into friendship, and was maintained at intervals, until the death of the latter in 1835. "Connected as he was by family ties, and by the predilections of education, with the high party in church and state," writes Joseph John Gurney, in allusion to the period when Edward Harbord first offered himself, in 1818, as a candidate to serve in parliament for the city of Norwich, "the internal struggle of liberal principles had made great way in his mind. He was already a friend to public improvement, especially adverse to all kinds of warfare, opposed to capital punishment, and zealous for the administration of prison discipline. These common interests presently united us. In company with his wife, (a daughter of the late Lord Vernon's) he visited us at Earlham, and we commenced a correspondence which lasted for many years."

The shameless system of bribery which then unhappily disgraced the municipal elections at Norwich, had called forth a public remonstrance from Joseph John Gurney. This at once excited the attention of Edward Harbord, who immediately wrote

TO JOSEPH JOHN GURNEY.*

March 20th, 1819.

DEAR SIR,

I have this instant read in the Norwich paper, with the sincerest pleasure, your note, or postscript, relative to certain ward elections. I willingly surrender to you the glory of having struck the first blow, but as the field is yet open, I must beg leave to put in my claim as an ally and coadjutor, not of the past, but of your future efforts, in a scheme which I hope I may now say *we* have in view. * * I formed my determination while I was last at Norwich, and was once on the point of communicating my purpose to you; but contemplating it as a work of difficulty, and one in which the concurrent exertion of two hostile parties, is indispensable, I deemed it prudent to deliberate a few days upon the best mode of opening the campaign, before I hoisted my standard. I will tell you candidly the course I thought of pursuing. * * If you should be disposed to favour me with any suggestions, you may draw upon me to any amount of caution, for the attainment of our mutual object. There shall be no more "cooping." * *

JOSEPH JOHN GURNEY TO EDWARD HARBORD.

Earlham, 3d mo., 22nd, 1819.

* * The corrupting effects of our ward elections I have not painted in too strong language. Nothing can exceed them.

* For this correspondence I am indebted to the interesting unpublished memoir of Lord Suffield, by Richard Mackenzie Bacon See pp. 71–81.

Independently of the utter annihilation, by dint of bribery of all right political motives in the minds of the poor men, the dissipation, drunkenness, and confusion produced by this annual battle are excessive. Husbands are taken from their families, kept in a state of intoxication for two or three weeks, and then returned upon them wholly unfitted for the duties of domestic life. Young men not yet settled in life, are plunged into scenes of dissipation, from the effects of which they never recover. And young and old are wrought up into that state of violent excitement and enmity one towards another, which keeps the whole town in almost constant fermentation; and all this really for NOTHING—the object being one perfectly unimportant as it regards the general elections.

I fear that nothing now can prevent the "cooping" and the bribery of this season; for it is already begun, and I believe each side is already provided with a purse. On this subject, however, I mean to make some further inquiries in the course of to-day. With regard to the future, perhaps a public declaration, signed by everybody of any importance in the two interests, might prevent it. If both sides would agree not to open a single public house, and not to spend one farthing, the object might be effected. Why should not the poor men go quietly up to the hall and vote, and then go back again to their homes? * * I conceive, however, that it would not be thy wish to confine thy views to the *ward elections*. Let us get rid, if we can, of the whole system; for at present, our general elections bring with them an immense mass of corruption. Perhaps thou art hardly aware to what extent "cooping" is carried on on these occasions also. * * *

EDWARD HARBORD TO JOSEPH JOHN GURNEY.

Park Place, March 23d, 1819.

MY DEAR SIR,

I received your very obliging letter this morning, and shall gladly avail myself of your suggestion. Our sentiments are in perfect unison on the subject of elections. A declaration signed by principals on both sides, may be, and certainly is desirable, but we must have better security than *that* will afford, I fear, to accomplish our purpose. Impossible as it has been for any man of character to defend or justify the proceedings alluded to, each party has hitherto reconciled itself to the system, under the necessity of keeping pace with the measures of its opposite. Each charges the other with its origin, and both console themselves with the belief that good will be the result, however bad the means.

Our endeavour must be to invert and transpose this mode of reasoning. First, if the law will enable us, we must make it the object of both parties to detect the other in a breach of covenant; and to punish it when detected;—in this measure the lamentable hostility which prevails, will leave us little to perform. Secondly, we must endeavour to inculcate the errors of the principle at present acted upon; and persuade our friends that, however good the object aimed at, the means used in its attainment should not be bad; that, however bright the gem laboured for, its lustre may be tarnished by the instruments employed in procuring it. * * *

Some months elapsed before Joseph John Gurney again wrote upon the subject.

TO EDWARD HARBORD.

Hunstanton, 8th mo., 18th, 1819.

My dear Friend,

I suppose thou wilt deem it a proof of some neglect, that I have not sooner reported our proceedings, in the matter of the Norwich elections. I can, however, assure thee that, in the midst of many engagements, and with the interruption of a journey into the North, our joint important concern has not been laid aside. I have no objection to the allowance of a little *time* in the case. There is a great deal of labour connected with it, and as far as I am concerned, this labour must be brought to bear gradually. I also think that the difficulties which we now have with several individuals, will be surmounted by patient perseverance; and that the *determined* guilty ones will be at length effectually *blockaded.* I am inclined to hope that the mere step of getting the declaration generally signed, and the subsequent publication of it with the names attached, will be sufficient to give a deadly blow to these corrupt practices. But this hope will not prevent our forming in *due time* a committee of management to draw up certain regulations; and in the end to carry forward the necessary prosecutions.

* * * * * *

I am now going to perform the office of a true friend, and to find a little fault with thee. Thy heart is remarkably set upon a variety of benevolent objects; and I can truly say, *Euge frater, i, secundis afflatus zephyris;* but it has appeared to me, (and I have heard it remarked by others,) that thou art too much in the habit of making these matters the subject of conversation. Thou wilt perhaps think me heretical, but it does not suit my notions about these things that they should much intrude themselves into the intercourse of private life. I would not entirely exclude them, but I feel that these things are our *business,* our *labour;* and that the intellectual and social intercourse between friends is our recreation, our refreshment, our *play.* I very often have to communicate with others on these subjects, and when this is the case, I endeavour to take a suitable opportunity of saying "my say" rather as a matter of business and duty than anything else, and the "say" if necessary can be repeated, and then there is probably an end of it. I do not find it answer with others (nor do I like it for myself) to make these things very prominently the subjects of what may be called social intercourse. I know not whether thou wilt quite understand me, for I find it difficult to express my meaning clearly; but I am confident thou wilt bear with me, and we can talk more about it when we meet.

* * * * * *

Believe me with affectionate regard,

Thy sincere friend,

J. J. GURNEY.

TO THE SAME.

Norwich, 9th mo., 11th, 1819.

MY DEAR FRIEND,

The exceeding pressure of many engagements must be my apology for not proceeding quite so quickly as we should both wish. I must acknowledge that my hopes are somewhat dashed by the kind of suspicious and determinately prejudiced feeling, which appears to prevail against the object amongst the decided party men; but we must do our best, and leave the result to him, in whose hands are the ends of it. I have kept back the idea of *prosecution* because I find it *very* unpopular. We pledge ourselves in the declaration to no particular method, and I have simply stated our intention of calling together those who sign it, and of then considering the mode to be adopted. On the other hand several have expressed their opinion that prosecution is the best mode, and I have not hesitated to state, *when called upon*, that this is my *own* view.

I suppose that the anonymous letters in our papers on the subject of prison discipline are thine. I like them exceedingly, and have no doubt they will do real good. I truly rejoice in thy thus being enabled to employ thy time, talents, and influence in the cause of humanity, and may I not say Christianity? Most heartily do I wish thee well on thy way, and may the preserving power of the Lord be with thee to protect, bless, and sanctify all thy proceedings, and thy whole self, in body, soul, and spirit!

Notwithstanding these efforts, the elections at Norwich still continued to present disgraceful scenes of bribery and corruption. Joseph John Gurney was more successful in his exertions, in connexion with the same zealous coadjutor, to save the lives of three men who had been convicted of burglary in the spring of this year. In allusion to this effort he writes in his Journal:—

4th mo., 11*th*. A busy, broken, and rather troubled fortnight; the chief interest in it, the case of the three men left for execution, which took me to Bury to see Judge Graham on fourth day week. The case alluded to has cost me much labour of head and heart, and, amongst other things, led me into a remarkably interesting correspondence with Edward Harbord. Two of the three [are] saved, the third [Belsham] suffered yesterday.

JOSEPH JOHN GURNEY TO EDWARD HARBORD.

Norwich, 4th mo., 10th, 1819.

I spent some little time with poor Belsham yesterday afternoon, and was much comforted by my visit. I was engaged with him in prayer. * * He wept much, but in the midst of his weeping, he displayed a quietness and a steadiness which will, I believe, go far to disarm death of its terrors. * * May God have mercy upon him, through Jesus Christ.

I cannot conclude without saying, how much I have rejoiced for thy sake, and the sake of many others, in the zeal, energy, judgment, and feeling, which thou hast manifested on this occasion. To flatter thee is very far from my wish, but I must say two things on the subject. The first is, that after what is past, it is impossible not to feel a warm personal interest in thee. The second is, that such a heart and mind, are talents to be employed in thy Master's service.

TO HIS SISTER ELIZABETH FRY.

Norwich, 4th mo., 30th, 1819.

* * With regard to the attacks made upon our prison book, they are of no importance, and do not now trouble me. I have ascertained my correctness in all the cases. The Yorkshire magistrates are already answered.* I am right in every point

* This answer will be found printed at the end of the last edition, published in 1847, of the Notes on Prisons.

between us, and they have made me appear wrong, only by stating the improvements made since our visit, as if they had existed at the time when we made it. I quite think with thee that there is as much inclination to set us down as to raise us up, but if our motives are pure, our dependence rightly placed, and our conduct correct, neither praise nor blame will hurt us.

I was much interested at Yarmouth a day or two since, by a mantua-maker, who has been induced to give up the time and earnings of one day in every week, in order to visit the wretched prisons in that place. She has surmounted many difficulties and has produced great effects.*

TO JONATHAN HUTCHINSON.

Norwich, 5th mo., 8th, 1819.

* * I cannot think that my business claims a very inferior share of my attention, for it is extensive, and multifarious, and, if not attended to sedulously, would soon bring me and all my profession into disrepute. Yet why should I be so circumstanced? Is it right for one who feels called upon to preach Christianity to occupy such a station in life? Indeed, my dear friend, I must leave it to thee, to answer these questions. I can only say, that such is the situation in which my predecessors placed me, in which I have long continued, in which I now am, and from which, as far as I now see, I cannot extricate myself. On the other hand I must acknowledge, that if business were less prevalent with me, I should probably have more both of time and mind, to serve the Lord and his people. On the whole, I believe it to be best quietly to wait, and to watch the divine dispensation towards me. Perhaps the day will come, when circumstances will, at least in part, relieve me of my burthen. In the mean time let me be thankful for all the blessings both temporal and spiritual with which, though thoroughly unworthy, I continue to be so bountifully supplied! * * *

* See the brief but interesting sketch of the life of the late Sarah Martin, of Yarmouth, published there in 1844.

First day evening, 5th mo., 16th. Began this day with several uncomfortable impressions, thoughts and feelings not to be admitted; but through silent, though earnest, prayer I found my rest in God. The day has been spent leisurely, for I have so far done very little but attend the two meetings. I have felt "waiting on the Lord" to be my main duty, connected with a watchfulness to fulfil the calls of my ministry.

5th mo., 25th. [Last] third day, the 18th, my plans of quietude interrupted by a summons to attend the Parliamentary Committee on Jails.* I determined to go, though I felt real difficulty in leaving my wife. After a hot, restless journey, I arrived on sixth day morning at Plashet; [thence] to Gracechurch Street meeting, which was very comfortable and restoring. From meeting, rapidly to the House of Commons; met by Buxton, Bennett, and others. My examination before the Committee lasted about two hours, and was on the whole satisfactory. I found it very much so, on the correction of my evidence. Pleasaut interview with Wilberforce, F. Calthorpe, &c.

TO JOHN HODGKIN, JUN.

Earlham, 7th mo., 11th, 1819.

* * * During my very short stay in London, my time was chiefly occupied by the Parliamentary Committees, and I had not that room left for friends which I should so much have liked to enjoy. I was quite pleased to get even a peep of thee, and should have been truly so to have obtained more of thy company. But the world is full of *vortices*, and amidst the variety of circumstances which hurry every one of us separately down *our own* stream of life, it is well for those who love each other, to have their friendship grounded on that rock, which will abide when the world, with all its interests and casualties, shall vanish from our view. I have no very important intelligence to communicate respecting myself. My time is fully occupied with the usual variety of business

* See Life of Sir T. F. Buxton, chap. vi, p. 87.

meetings, public objects, study, and home delights. In the last particular I believe I spend a great deal more time than would be consistent with thy elevated standard of *perennial industry*. But thou knowest how I fail in this respect, and whether it be owing to the mental occupation which my avocations in life occasion me, or to bodily constitution, *I cannot help it*. * * A certain portion of time after breakfast is, however, devoted to my book* almost daily. I have written the dissertation on the Hebrews again, on a new construction, and with emendations; and have since been employed chiefly by the other notes, which I find must, with little exception, be written over again. Just now I am engaged by a very laborious critical discussion of the reading θεὸς ὃς and ὃ, in 1 Tim. iii, 16. I hope that some good may arise out of this engagement, and I am resolved, *if possible*, to persevere.

Now for ——s manuscript. It would have been shameful had I refused to look it over for *thee*. I think it interesting, and there is something very attractive and engaging in the mind which produced it. With regard to the principles laid down in the essay, this is the only part in which I do not fully unite. I cannot accede to the proposition that a nation must be civilized before the gospel ought to be introduced to its attention. The two things ought, in my opinion, to go hand in hand. I cannot at all understand how those who *know* the value of *Christ* can settle amongst comparatively savage tribes and continue with them for years, and yet make no effort to communicate that knowledge.

6th mo., 24th. I have again to acknowledge some experience of the redeeming and preserving love of God, and I trust that as I am enabled to maintain humility and watchfulness, I shall continue to find safety. * * Joseph Wood and his companion breakfasted with us. After breakfast I accompanied them as guide, they in their wicker cart, and

* The allusion here is to the unpublished work mentioned *supra*, p. 120.

I on horseback, first to Attleborough, and then back to Wymondham; a small public meeting at Attleborough, and a larger one in the evening at Wymondham; both highly favoured. Returned home in much peace about ten o'clock, leaving the dear friends, with whom I felt closely united, at Wymondham. Joseph Wood is a deep and able minister, a thoroughly honest, innocent man. Ah! what, in point of effect, is to be compared to the forming hand of the Lord *willingly* and *completely* submitted to.

In the early part of the 7th month, his domestic happiness was crowned by the birth of a son.

"May I be preserved," is his remark in allusion to this event, "in a humble and thankful frame of spirit. What can I render?"

CHAPTER IX.

1813—1819. ÆT. 25—32.

ACKWORTH SCHOOL; JOSEPH JOHN GURNEY'S LABOURS THERE; SCRIPTURAL INSTRUCTION; EXTRACTS FROM LETTERS AND AUTOBIOGRAPHY; EXTRACTS FROM JOURNAL.

In the retired village of Ackworth near Pontefract, in Yorkshire, stands a large and commodious building, erected for a branch establishment of the London Foundling Hospital, but now, and for many years past, occupied as a school for the children of Friends not in affluent circumstances. This latter institution was founded about the year 1778, at the suggestion of the late Dr. Fothergill, whose efforts were warmly supported by the great body of Friends, among whom, David Barclay, a grandson of the "Apologist," and the late William Tuke, of York, were two of his earliest and most efficient coadjutors. In this school, at a very moderate charge, in most instances much below the real cost, about 300 children of both sexes are educated. It is under the care of a committee annually appointed by a "General Meeting" composed of Friends from various parts of the nation, which every year reports upon the state of the school to the Yearly Meeting in London. The object of the founders of this institution was to impart a sound literary and religious education in accordance with the principles of Friends; and, from its first establishment, great care was exercised to shield the children from evil example, and to train them in moral and religious habits, in the fear of the Lord.* When Joseph John Gurney commenced his labours at Ackworth, it was the practice to read the Scriptures at least daily, to the children; short Scripture passages illustrative of particular truths, were required to be committed to memory; a few Bibles were placed in a library to which the pupils had access on the morning of the first day of the week; and a copy was presented to each child on leaving the school. No arrangement, however, existed for ascertaining the extent of the children's acquaintance with the inspired volume on first coming to school, or for supplying each child with the Scriptures during his stay there; and it was manifest from the examination which Joseph John Gurney instituted, that something more was required than the existing provision for imparting scriptural knowledge.

In addition to the regular supervision exercised by the managing committee, it was the custom, once a year, at the time of the General Meeting, to examine the children more publicly in the various branches of their learning. It was to attend this meeting in the year 1813, that Joseph John Gurney first visited Ackworth, in company with his sister Priscilla. In his Journal he describes the meeting

* An interesting narrative of the proceedings in relation to the establishment of Ackworth School, is to be found in Part 3 of the papers published by the Friends' Educational Society, "On the past proceedings and experience of the Society of Friends in connexion with the education of Youth."

as "very interesting;" and his visits were subsequently repeated, but without resulting in any particular effort until the year 1816. In that year, he again attended the General Meeting, and, upon examining the children as to their knowledge of the Holy Scriptures, he found among them not a little ignorance. Impressed with the great importance of the subject, he suggested that, instead of the plan then acted upon, of giving a Bible to each scholar on leaving the school, every child should be furnished with a copy of the sacred volume immediately on entering the institution; a suggestion which was at once cordially agreed to. He then proposed to the children that they should study the scriptures during the ensuing year with particular reference to several important subjects which he pointed out to them,* offering to examine them himself at the close of the year, and to reward them according to their proficiency and good conduct.†

On his return from the General Meeting, he thus unfolded his views to Robert Whitaker, then superintendent of the establishment.

Lynn, 9th mo., 3rd, 1816.

Whilst I feel deeply convinced that the religious improvement of the children is a subject of essential importance to

* These subjects were embodied in the form of a "proposition," which was circulated among the children. It had reference to the books of the Bible, their order, authors, contents, &c.; to the history from Genesis to the book of Acts; to the Prophecies concerning our Saviour, and their accomplishment as shown in the New Testament; to the doctrines and moral precepts; and to the evidence from Scripture confirmatory of the views of Friends.

† On this and other occasions the rewards usually consisted of books selected by himself or the teachers.

the well-being of the school and of our religious society, I am sensible that great difficulties attend it. What is the thing wanted? To speak freely with thee, I am of opinion that the minds of the boys are not properly *cultivated* on the subject of religion. They are remarkably sheltered from evil; but do not appear to me to be positively enough led to good. The common round of reading, grammar, writing and ciphering, does little for the improvement of the mind; and a pursuit which would draw forth their powers of thought and reflection, and, at the same time, operate in forming and strengthening their religious principles, would be of incalculable advantage to them. Such a pursuit appears to me to be the study of the Bible. It is a duty devolving on those who have the care of youth, to give them religious knowledge and form their religious principles; and though I am well aware that God alone can give the increase, yet Paul must plant and Apollos must water; and this truth is peculiarly evident as it relates to the education of children.

This is a duty, a religious one indeed, but widely differing in its mode from that of the Christian ministry. It calls into action different powers, and a different gift; and must be performed as a simple duty, in the liberty of that Gospel which commands us to bring up our children "in the nurture and admonition of the Lord." Now if it be a simple duty to enlighten and cultivate the minds of children, concerning the one thing needful, it will surely be allowed that the Scriptures, which contain the authorised account of the whole matter, present us with the most important means of doing so. Forms, catechisms, and compendiums of doctrine may probably be useful, when nothing better is to be obtained; but this is clearly an *inferior* mode of giving religious instruction. It is besides open to some strong objections. It is dry and unedifying. It exercises the powers of memory, whilst it leaves those of reflection untouched. It flattens the study of the Bible, from which it selects the most precious texts, and presenting them, in a dry form, side by side, as mere proofs of propositions, it takes away half their value; and renders the Bible itself far less interesting, by forestalling its chief beauties. Children should be taught to search in the original mines, to find these jewels for themselves, and then they would know how to value them. In short, I long to have the children *taught the Scriptures*. If they are left entirely to themselves in this study, something may come of it, but not much: not enough, in my opinion, to justify you in laying aside your compendiums, however disadvantageous they may be in some respects. They must be led to the study of the Bible; and helped in it by those who have the care of them. If *thou* couldest give up an hour every morning to the religious instruction of the boys, much might be done. I should have them all together, and all with their Bibles in their hands. I should read the Bible through with them; omitting such parts as appeared unsuitable for very young persons; yet *not much*. I should make remarks as I went along, explaining what was difficult, impressing what was important, and comparing, all the way through, such passages, from other parts of the Bible, as might throw additional light on any occurring subject. When I compared another passage with one before me, I would make all the boys turn to it and mark it. The last quarter of the time, or more, should be employed in thoroughly questioning the children on the lesson of the day. This would ensure habits of general attention; and give a life to the object which no other mode of instruction will impart.

Such a plan would give thee, or any truly religious Friend, abundant opportunity of fixing the best principles on the children's minds, and more especially of unfolding to them the scriptural grounds on which we build our faith. There are one or two other points I should endeavour to introduce. Instead of compendiums, the boys might occasionally get by heart from the Bible itself. Many of the most striking Psalms and chapters of Isaiah; many of the most pithy parts of the New Testament, might thus be made to form in their memories a store from which much good would afterwards be derived. They ought to be encouraged to private devotional duties, morning and evening; to read small portions of scripture by themselves, and to lift up their hearts in prayer for the blessing which can alone preserve them day and night. Whether this point can be accomplished more than is now the case, I know not; but it is surely of importance to bring up children in this particular habit. Thou art aware by what I have already written, that I do not mean common-place, formal, dry tuition. I mean the instruction which every Christian parent is bound in conscience to give to his child; "the nurture and admonition of the Lord."

Thus encouraged, the superintendent and teachers warmly seconded his views. The interest awakened in the minds of the children was remarkable. "They received," says Joseph John Gurney in his Autobiography, "every one a copy of the Bible, and well thumbed was that copy, in a great plurality of instances, in the course of the appointed time. The children took their Bibles to bed with them, read them by the early morning light, pored over them at leisure hours during the day, and especially on first days. The teachers rendered them their best assistance; knowledge of the subject rapidly increased, and with it good; and when I visited them, at the close of twelve months, the whole aspect of affairs was changed."

The result is thus noticed in a letter

TO HIS SISTER HANNAH BUXTON.

Ackworth, 8th mo., 1st, 1817.

* * * My journey has been one involving both labour and difficulty, but has been crowned, in rather a remarkable manner, with success and peace. A few seeds which I was the means of sowing here last year with respect to religious instruction, have unexpectedly and abundantly brought forth fruit. The children have made great progress in the knowledge of Scripture, and many of them seem under a very serious influence. Their general deportment is already

changed by it. I have hardly ever been sensible of so sweet a spiritual influence as during the last week in this place. It seems to accompany us on all occasions; in meetings; in the schools, and at table. It has brought to my mind more of the communion of saints than I have ever felt before, unless perhaps in a few instances.

He now issued a second "proposition," to a number of the more forward boys, which formed the basis of the useful manual, which he subsequently published, under the title of Guide to the Instruction of Young Persons in the Holy Scriptures; including the Lock and Key, or passages of the Old Testament which testify of Jesus Christ, explained by others in the New Testament.

From this time forward the Scripture examinations were continued with great regularity after each General Meeting; and were for some years principally conducted by Joseph John Gurney himself. Gradually, however, the subject was brought under the care and control of the school committee, after which his visits were occasionally intermitted, though seldom for more than two years.

"Many precious seasons," he writes in his Autobiography, "of reverent waiting on the Lord, and of true religious comfort and edification, have I enjoyed with my beloved Friends, in that favoured spot. Many a time have we rejoiced together in that Saviour who redeemed us with his precious blood. Yet natural cheerfulness always had its play amongst us; and with the children especially I endeavoured to maintain it. Much may be done in this way for their benefit; and I know of no line of service, secondary as it may appear, which has yielded me more satisfaction in the result."

The pleasure which these opportunities seem to have afforded himself, was largely shared by his young friends.

"The kind and engaging manners of our dear Friend," writes one of the masters at Ackworth,* the hearty and innocent cheerfulness of his intercourse with the scholars during their play hours endeared him to us all, and prepared our minds to benefit by his more serious engagements amongst us. Constantly did we watch for his arrival, and greet his entrance on the play-ground by a rush of earnest congratulation. And ever during his leisure moments, did we love to cluster around him to listen to his cherished conversation; which from the most lively familiarity was always rising to a higher tone, carrying up our youthful thoughts to "whatsoever things were lovely and of good report." How often, amidst groups of eager and happy listeners, would he comment on the importance of good manners and good habits, and the acquisition of useful knowledge; frequently referring to George Fox's enlightened desire that youth might be taught "all things civil and useful in the creation," and not forgetting to inculcate his own favourite maxim, "Be a whole man to one thing at a time." The wonderful structure of the human body was a theme on which he loved to dwell; and his last visit to Ackworth, very shortly before his death, was distinguished by a familiar but beautifully lucid description of the wise and curious provision made by the Creator, in the formation of the eye. His great aim was to expand the thoughts of the children, to excite the love of knowledge and the play of the intellect, as subservient to the great ends of man's being, and to an enlightened appreciation of religious truth; that the young mind might rise from the wonders of creative wisdom, to the marvels of redeeming grace. His Scripture questionings were uniformly made occasions for illustrating the grounds of Friends' princi-

* John Newby, in a letter to the Editor.

ples, and the nature of Christian truth generally; by the sacred history itself, by selected texts, by the prophecies that spoke before of the better covenant, and by the preaching of Christ, and the writings of his apostles. The excellence of the Christian character, and the beauty of Christian consistency were forcibly exhibited; and often did the examination melt away into religious silence, when the solemn prayer arose, or the fervent exhortation sank into hearts softened to receive the seed of the kingdom. The remembrance of the heavenly influence which overshadowed us on some of these occasions is very precious; and particularly do I recall one very solemn meeting with the boys, which closed the religious engagements of a full week, in which the beautiful parable of Christ the vine was enlarged upon, and the necessity and blessedness of abiding in him."

Joseph John Gurney was convinced from the depths of his own experience, that to render the knowledge of scriptural truth availing to the progress of the work of religion in the soul, it must be accompanied by an humble subjection of the heart and understanding to the immediate operations of the spirit of God. He was anxious that religious instruction, to use his own words in the Autobiography, "should, as far as possible, be made a pleasure rather than a task; that a taste for Scripture should be cultivated, and, above all, that the practical nature and issue of true religion should ever be held up to view, and a reverent dependence inculcated on that blessed influence of the Holy Spirit, without which knowledge is vanity, and the profession of the truth mere hypocrisy."

The anxiety thus manifested by Joseph John Gurney for the religious education of youth was no new thing in the Society of Friends. The Yearly

Meeting had frequently issued pertinent advice upon the subject,* and it was one of the circumstances especially marking the wisdom with which the mind of George Fox had been imbued, that he had so earnestly and pointedly pressed this subject upon the attention of his friends. So early as 1656 he thus writes to them, who, it must be remembered, had many of them been brought up as Puritans, accustomed diligently to instruct and catechise their children :—

> Dear Friends, exhort all your families at times and seasons, whether they be servants or children, that they may be informed in the truth. For when ye were professors, many of you did exhort and instruct them in the form, when ye had not the power, and therefore now, being brought into the truth, ye should be more diligent to exhort, admonish, and instruct them.†

So far was he from thinking that increased spirituality led to a neglect of these duties; in his view, it rather led to the more punctual and diligent performance of them. Robert Barclay, as is well known, had compiled a catechism expressly to assist in the instruction of children, and his work is especially remarkable as carefully stating each answer in the very words of Holy Scripture. Joseph John Gurney might therefore well feel that in urging his views on the importance of religious

* See the interesting paper, published as Part 2 of "Past proceedings and experience of the Society of Friends in connexion with the education of Youth."

† See the valuable Selection from the Epistles of George Fox, published by Samuel Tuke, p. 50. See also pp. 126, 210, 211, 247, 249, 265.

instruction, he was only enforcing that which had been desired from the very foundation of the Society. So far as it had been neglected, it had been neglected, not upon principle, but through weakness, and he desired that that weakness should be removed, in simple dependence upon the all sufficient grace of the Lord Jesus. It was not, as will have been observed, formal or systematic doctrinal teaching, but simple *scriptural* instruction that he sought to encourage. The Holy Scriptures, "given by the inspiration of God," formed, in his opinion, a manual for religious instruction, better adapted to the object, and more in accordance with "the mind of the Spirit" than any mere catechism or compendium of doctrine. He accepted them, as above all other books, "profitable for doctrine, for reproof, for correction, and for instruction in righteousness," being fully persuaded that, "through faith which is in Christ Jesus," they are "able to make wise unto salvation." But there were those, some of them, at that time, young in years and in religious experience, who from a fear (and doubtless it was a sincere one) of these engagements being entered upon in a merely formal manner, were not prepared at once to co-operate with him so cordially as he could have desired. With as great a dread of a formal and lifeless religion as they could have, he felt anxious that no mistaken impression as to his views should hinder the work that had been so happily begun. On this point he writes

TO HIS BROTHER SAMUEL GURNEY.

Earlham, 12th mo., 7th, 1818.

"I am inclined to think that there exists in some individuals considerable misunderstanding of our views. I go the whole length with them in believing and in feeling that no efforts or labours of ours can produce religion in the minds of children; but surely we may, and we ought, in dependence on divine help, to prepare the ground, "to plant and to water." I believe that such labours are simple Christian duties, that if we neglect these duties, we are not making use of the talents committed to us for the Master's use; and I also believe that he who can alone give the increase will give it. These general principles must, I think, be allowed on all hands. Differences of opinion may arise as to the mode. I agree with those who think catechetical forms, &c., an undesirable mode, and that it is better to lead children to search the Scriptures for themselves. The plan of questioning them on what they have read is peculiarly important, simply because it habituates them to read attentively; nor can I see the advantage of doing anything superficially.

The duty of giving religious instruction can only be performed well by those who are alive themselves to the subject of religion. When it is done by such, and is attended by a real exercise of mind for the spiritual welfare of the children, its benefits seldom fail to be known by its fruits. But though these only are rightly qualified, I would exhort all who have the care of children to the work, as I would exhort them to any other Christian duty. If they want a heart and ability for its right execution, let them seek help where alone it is to be found.

In allusion to the same subject, he writes in his Journal, under date,

7th mo., 23rd, 1819. It is my desire to dwell deeply in the root of life, and to be preserved in that spirit of true love, which judgeth not. There are two or three considerations which it is well for me to advert to. First, that such is the weakness and corruption of man, that the religious world, in this scene of being, is in a very imperfect state; which is manifested by nothing more than by this, that those who truly love the Lord Jesus Christ are nevertheless so frequently attached and subjected to a portion of error and prejudice. Look at the high Calvinist on the one side. On the other side look at those who pervert their dependence on universal and sensible grace, to the almost total rejection of those outward means, which God has provided for our help. Such is the constitution of things, and often must it occasion, to every sincere inquirer, deep exercise of mind; and he may well put the question to himself, is it not in some point or other so with me? In the mean time, let him be willing to "bear all things."

Secondly, that the duty of studying the Scriptures, and of leading our children to study them, rests upon the direct authority of our divine Master, and is, therefore, to be maintained by me perseveringly and unhesitatingly, whatever be the consequences.

Thirdly, that there is every reason to believe there is a mass of good feeling and good sense in our society, which will, in the end, be found sufficient to uphold this principle.

Fourthly, that my dependence ought not to be placed on any one Christian community, but simply on Him, who is the head of the whole body, and who careth for all its members.

The result has shown the value and importance of Joseph John Gurney's efforts. "All the doubts and scruples," (says the superintendent, in a letter to him under date 20th of 10th mo., 1825,) "which were raised at first to our examination plan, have gradually subsided, and we now hear nothing from any quarter, respecting our endeavours, but approbation and encouragement." The first "proposition" became the basis of the Ackworth course of scriptural instruction, and the system thus introduced was gradually adopted in all the public schools of the Society of Friends.

To return to the Journal: —

Earlham, 8th mo., 8th, [1819.] Last second day, after a quiet morning at home, I set off in the mail [towards

Ackworth.] * * My visit [there] was peculiarly interesting, and has afforded me fresh cause for thankfulness. In the sub-committee the task of examining the children was laborious, and I hardly knew how to enter into it. Samuel met me and worked with me, which was a real delight and consolation.

Fifth day; finished the examination of our class most comfortably with the Scriptures; a sweet feeling over us; and afterwards took the evidence of two of the masters. Of the eight sub-committees, seven examined in the Scriptures, and brought in highly satisfactory reports. Josiah Forster drew up a general report to the same effect; light and truth eminently prevailed, and the concluding meeting was truly a very favoured one. Seventh day was one of peculiar exertion; the girls in the morning, and the boys in the afternoon; reading and examination. The time with the girls was spent sweetly, the *life* flowed, and words had access. In the afternoon, (probably from the hot weather and other external circumstances,) it was a time of difficult labour, and I left off discouraged. * * * I passed the night partly in deep conflict of spirit, and was so entirely cast down, that I little thought I should rise again soon. First day, however, was, through mercy, one of complete restoration. The victory over the adversary was given in the power of Christ. The ministry flowed irresistibly; first, with the teachers at their breakfast table; then, very openly at meeting; with the girls at parting; and with the boys after dinner in the family. All little difficulties and great discouragements were alike removed, and I finally left Ackworth about three o'clock with full satisfaction. What cause for thankfulness!

In the afternoon Hannah Kilham, Henry Brady, and myself proceeded to Pontefract, where I was engaged to unite with Ann Alexander in a public meeting, at five o'clock, in the Town Hall. The meeting was eminently favoured. Ann Alexander finely explained our views relative to Water Baptism and the Supper. All well at home on my arrival on third day evening. * * *

I have been a little frightened during this late rapid course of my ministry, lest my own personal progress in grace and salvation should be neglected. I feel a renewed call to watchfulness and prayer.

10th mo., 4th. Whilst at Upton my sister Priscilla cautioned me against length in ministry, and quoting many passages of Scripture towards the conclusion, led on by their beauty rather than *the life*. *Nota Bene.*

TO JONATHAN HUTCHINSON.

Norwich, 10th mo., 2nd, 1819.

I have felt shocked by some instances, lately under my notice, of the miserably low moral standard prevailing in the world. It makes me cling to the remedial, redeeming, reforming principle. O that all would come to it! O that all could be brought to the reverent acknowledgment that "the Lord reigneth."

TO EDWARD HARBORD.

Norwich, 11th mo., 19th, 1819.

* * * I am grieved at hearing of thy being involved, by thy late manly conduct, in any personal and private difficulties, but yet I can truly rejoice in thy having publicly asserted the unalienable right of man TO THINK FOR HIMSELF. What a capital thing in life is it to be *tenax propositi*. I know of nothing more important, and when the character is applied to religion, it is certainly *all-important*. In thy situation in life, thou hast, of course, some *political* duties, and these to a religious man become religious duties. Whilst this is the case, all is right. But I am decidedly of opinion that if in politics, as in other things, our *first* motive be not to serve God, we shall soon become involved in a most dangerous vortex.

Earlham, 10th mo., 18th. My uncle, on fifth day morning, spoke on the case of Dives and Lazarus; and it was brought home to my serious and anxious consideration, whether I am not, as Dives, faring sumptuously every day. I trust it is not in the spirit of Dives. Earlham is certainly kept up, after the old sort, freely and handsomely. There are two or three points connected with the subject, which strike me. Spending money is better and less injurious to the spirit, than saving it unduly; nevertheless, Christian moderation, in mode of living, furniture, &c., is called for by my profession. I wish the establishment to be liberally conducted, with this principle always in view. I am living according to the mode of life, in which those with whom I associate are accustomed to live. How far, in doing this, and in aiming at a generous system, I exceed Christian moderation, I doubt. But on the whole my uneasiness on the subject does not dwell deeply with me.

11*th mo.*, 21*st.* Proceeded in our family visits; a service attended by great exercise of mind, and whether or no attended by fruits, I cannot judge. I have been discouraged by observing the appearance of the contrary in particular cases; and yet I trust it was right.*

12*th mo.*, 17*th.* Read the accounts of Jesse Cadbury, and Charles Coleby—highly instructive. Surely such are blessed, in being removed from temptation to security, from doubt to certainty, from trouble to peace.

* These visits were undertaken in company with a few other Friends, with a view to the distribution among Friends at Norwich, of the advices that had been issued by the late Yearly Meeting on the subject of the attendance of meetings.

CHAPTER X.

1820—1821. ÆT. 32—33.

EXTRACTS FROM JOURNAL AND LETTERS; HIS FIRST DAY SCHOOL; JOURNEY TO BRISTOL; WILLIAM FORSTER'S DEPARTURE FOR AMERICA; YEARLY MEETING; LETTERS FROM JONATHAN HUTCHINSON AND WILLIAM WILBERFORCE; LETTER TO THOMAS FOWELL BUXTON; ILLNESS AND DEATH OF PRISCILLA GURNEY.

TO JONATHAN HUTCHINSON.

12th of 1st mo., 1820. [At the Bank, seventh day.]

* * Though so busy that my mind has hardly time to turn itself round, yet I may acknowledge that I am permitted to experience something of the *staying* principle, even in the midst of the whirlwind, to which my occupations on this day may well be compared. How beautiful is the idea, and how comforting the experience of "staying" ourselves "upon God!" What a privilege for those who feel their own utter weakness, and their perpetual liability to fall, to have the divine arm of love to lean upon! What should we do or be without it? Certain it is that I know something of the "plague of my own heart;" and that I can adopt the words which, on a memorable occasion, (the conclusion of the labours of the committee on Thomas Foster's case,) I once heard thee use in ministry, "Without Christ I am of all men most miserable."

2nd mo., 28th. Public events in a high degree striking: the assassination of the Duc de Berri, and the horrible plot so providentially detected in London, which would otherwise, in all probability, have proved fatal to many of our governors. Notwithstanding all, it is my belief that good will prevail.

In the prospect of the election at Weymouth, he writes,

TO HIS SISTER HANNAH BUXTON.

Earlham, 2nd mo., 29th, 1820.

I am of course much interested about thy dear husband; and heartily wish him in again, from a belief that his parliamentary career is of real importance to the cause of humanity and Christianity. At the same time, we are, even the wisest of us, miserable judges and counsellors; and it ought to be our chief, our only desire, that the government may be upon the shoulders of Him, who is worthy to reign over us, and who will arrange all things for the ultimate good of those who love and fear Him. I rejoice in my confidence that Fowell is one of these, and that neither disappointment nor success will be permitted to harm him, if he do but abide in his Saviour.

I have been exceedingly busy ever since you left us, sometimes depressed and sometimes encouraged, but on the whole dwelling a little too much on the gloomy side of things. There is something in the fearful aspect of public affairs which strongly induces this state of mind. But it is our duty to wash and anoint, that we appear not unto men to fast. We serve an Almighty Redeemer, who in his own good time will triumph over all.

First day night, 3rd mo., 12th. This morning my uncle Joseph Gurney [in the prospect of leaving home,] gave us a warm and affectionate parting exhortation. Towards the close of the meeting I found relief and fresh strength in prayer, especially commending the travellers to Him whom they go forth to serve. The school comfortable and edifying. The afternoon meeting a time of outpouring: I know not when I have been enabled so to commit the flock to its Shepherd. I trust I am humbled and not exalted by the mercies of the day. The creature can have nothing to glory in; all that he has is not his own, but another's. The Creator alone is worthy. How clearly have I seen this truth to-day.

His frequent notice of his attendance at the first day school, even after his marriage, and notwithstanding the numerous other claims upon his time and attention, cannot fail to be encouraging to those who are engaged in similar services. How often is the unobserved path of laborious duty, the way of fullest comfort.

TO HENRY BRADY.*

Norwich, 3rd mo., 17th, 1820.

I have had increasing satisfaction in my little first day school at Norwich, from the real approach to seriousness in some of my pupils, and I think more particularly in our Norwich new Girls' School, where the same work is going forward under the auspices of a friend of admirable character.

With regard to the right mixture of cheerfulness and seriousness in teaching the Scriptures, I would say, "Be natural," let the mind have its play. I should never fear *thy* undertaking such an office otherwise than on serious grounds, and with a secret breathing for divine help; and, this being my confidence, I have the less fear in repeating my precept, "Be natural."

Some objection having been made to Joseph John Gurney's attendance at a public meeting held at Norwich, on the subject of the severe measures, attended with bloodshed and loss of life, which had been re-

* Henry Brady was one of the principal teachers at Ackworth school, "a young man," says Joseph John Gurney, "of rare worth, piety, and talents. He long superintended the religious instruction there with great effect and ability, and was very successful in other departments, especially the Latin class. We carried on an intimate correspondence; and inexpressibly affecting it was to me when he caught the typhus fever, which had been raging in the school, and died, I think, in 1828. He had just before come forth with brightness in the ministry; but the Lord had higher services for him than any to be found on earth, and took him home to himself."

sorted to by the soldiery at Manchester, in the dispersion of the vast assemblage of upwards of 60,000 persons congregated there, under the leadership of the notorious Hunt, in the 8th mo., 1819, he thus continues:—

Thou wilt be pleased to inform all inquirers—1st, That it was no *radical* meeting at all: it was certainly called for a political object, but that object was unexceptionable, being simply to ask for inquiry into the transactions at Manchester. It was a meeting summoned and presided over by the high Sheriff, and procured and conducted by a large number of the most respectable gentlemen in Norfolk.

2nd, That I attended the meeting simply as an observer, and without the slightest intention of speaking. Against my attendance I felt no scruple, but on the contrary do still believe it to be the duty of moderate men, who happen to have considerable local influence, to attend such meetings.

3rd, That, being there, I found that it was in my power to be of use in promoting a spirit of peace and good will, and in fixing the assembly in a marked disapprobation of radical irreligion. For this purpose I spoke. I presume my speech was misreported in the London papers. But it nevertheless succeeded, and I accomplished the objects, (Christian objects I hope I may call them,) which I had in view.

No persons mistake me more than those who suppose I feel the slightest interest in party politics: I dislike, as much as I disapprove, both the spirit and the principle of party; and I quite admit, that religious people, whether Friends or others, ought to be exceedingly careful how they meddle with politics in any shape. Nevertheless, there are matters in politics which religious people ought to concern themselves in; and where humanity, justice, virtue, and moral and religious improvement, are concerned, I, for one, am more than willing to be concerned also.

3rd mo., 25th. Yesterday I was much affected by discovering that two poor fellows are left for execution. This seems again to involve me in labour, and exercise both inward and outward, almost to sickness of heart. Alas, that these afflicting calamities should be renewed amongst us every half year! I hardly know how to bear it, but I desire to commit the cause to the Lord.

His retirement at home during the spring of this year was interrupted by a journey to Bristol for the purpose of taking leave of his friend William Forster, then about to sail from that port on a religious visit to Friends in America. From Bristol he writes,

TO HIS UNCLE JOSEPH GURNEY.

Bristol, 4th mo., 10th, 1820.

When I heard that William Forster had determined to sail so speedily, I could not be at all satisfied without seeing him and attending him on his departure. As soon therefore as circumstances admitted, I set off, and on arriving at Bristol on second day morning, found him and his wife at John Waring's, and very heartily pleased we were to meet. They are wonderfully supported; calm, strong, and happy in the Lord; appearing to reap something of the hundred-fold, even before the sacrifice has been completed. This state has, I believe, succeeded one of very sore conflict and natural distress. The lesson is peculiarly instructive.

In the latter part of the fifth month he attended the Yearly Meeting.

6th mo., 17*th*. We reached Upton on the 20th of the 5th month. Never has a visit to my dear brother been more acceptable and delightful to both parties. The Yearly Meeting for Ministers and Elders on second day, interesting chiefly on account of Stephen Grellett, and William Allen, who rendered their short, lively, and humble account of what the Lord had done for them on their journey.* Third day; the Prison

* See Life of William Allen, chapters x—xiv.

Discipline Meeting, which was extraordinary, as to the vastly mixed attendance; and on the whole very interesting and stimulating.

The Yearly Meeting opened on the fourth day morning. I was appointed assistant clerk, which office I performed without much difficulty, and felt in my right place. From that day to second day morning the 6th instant, the Yearly Meeting continued, and I was at last thoroughly engrossed and occupied by its concerns. The points which were most interesting were—1st, The subject of rightly conducting our meetings for Discipline. 2nd, The Appeal of Gracechurch Street Monthly Meeting, and the manner in which it was happily disposed of. 3rd, The history of Stephen Grellett and William Allen's journey. 4th, The law of appeals to Quarterly Meetings; in discussing which we finally succeeded in establishing a very important principle to our great relief. The business of the meeting was conducted in great harmony. Some of the meetings for worship were worthy of being remembered; particularly that on sixth day at Gracechurch Street; Edward Harbord there. Sarah Grubb preached an admirable gospel sermon, with clearness and authority. The meeting of Ministers and Elders, held on the second day afternoon after the conclusion of the Yearly Meeting, was exercising, and solemn. Some of the hints given as to ministry that day were very excellent.

1. Not too much of "Friends"—"dear Friends," &c.
2. Not to rise immediately after another sits down.
3. *To be faithful in preaching Christ crucified.*
4. To avoid as much as possible, the mixture of human with divine, matter of our own with that suggested of the Lord; a mixture to which our Society is much more exposed, than to absolutely spurious ministry. With this view always keep within rather than exceed the feeling.

6th mo., 21st. [After alluding to a successful effort on behalf of the Bible Society.] How necessary is it that a day in which so much of the divine blessing has been experienced should in no way elevate self. What have I, that I have not received?

In the 8th month, he again visited Ackworth, and, besides his usual engagements at the school, was occupied by holding several religious meetings there and in the neighbourhood.

FROM JONATHAN HUTCHINSON.

Gedney, 8th mo., 18th, 1820.

* * * There are some who make a difficulty of discharging duty from a hope of reward, as being unworthy and imperfect in its motives; but I am not sure whether this nicety does not savour more of the pride of the natural man, than of the humility of a regenerated Christian. For my own part, sheltered by the example of him who, "for the joy set before him, endured the cross, despising the shame," I am not aware of aspiring after, or acting upon any higher principle. Indeed I very much question its being either a required or a practicable duty for us, poor creatures of an hour as we are, to be divested of all self love—and with such a sentiment, the injunction to love our neighbour as ourselves, appears to me, to be so far from interfering, that I think it rather sanctions it.

Ah! 'tis humility—and by whatever means we may be brought to it—it is deep and still deeper humility that we want; and that must be the cure, if ever they are cured, of our many diseases whether general or particular.

FROM WILLIAM WILBERFORCE.

Bath, Oct. 23rd. 1820.

MY DEAR FRIEND,

I can truly assure you that you cannot wish more than I do, that we could again partake of your Earlham hospitalities, and I scarcely need say that I here include those of the mind; all the kindness; all the interchange of thought and feeling. I should delight to see you with your little one in your arms. But it just occurs to me to tell you that you should have imitated my example, and have published your book * before you married. Seriously—how and why is it so

* Joseph John Gurney was still engaged upon the unpublished work, mentioned *supra*, p. 120.

long delayed?—All this time that hateful subject, (for I really think we may deem it a fit object of hatred,) of the Queen's business has been presenting itself to my mind, and pressing for discussion. Yet I must resist the impulse; I have not time or eyesight to state my sentiments sufficiently to insure my not being misunderstood. In one particular I am sure we should agree—in thinking we may recognise in our present situation the chastening hand. * * *

First day evening, 10*th mo.*, 22*nd.* Enabled this afternoon to speak for a short time on gifts and grace, the transitory nature of the former, and the permanence of the latter. We must be careful not to deceive ourselves, even in our humiliations, by mistaking the disuse of our talents for a paucity of talents.

Second day morning, 11*th mo.*, 6*th.* Yesterday, a day of silence and internal humiliation. Such days I feel to be profitable, perhaps more so than those when the work and the word flow. My prayer is that, through the power of divine grace, I may be delivered from sin in deed, word, thought, and imagination. O that I may drink daily of the living water; ὕδωρ ζῶν, ἀναβλύζον, ἀναπηδῶν ἀεὶ κινούμενον.*

Theophylact, [in Joann: iv, 10.]

12*th mo.*, 22*nd.* Yesterday, about two o'clock, I received the delightful intelligence of the birth of my little girl, and the well doing of her mother. * * This morning, after having been enabled to return thanks with my family circle, I feel unusually peaceful and happy. How undeservedly, is known only to the Searcher of hearts.

The year closes with a visit to Ipswich, respecting which he remarks:—

* "Living water, bubbling up, springing up, ever moving." The passage of Theophylact from which this quotation is extracted, seems to have been a favourite one. In one of his memorandum books Joseph John Gurney refers to it as "singularly clear and instructive;" it is quoted at length in a note at the close of the first section of the Essay on Love to God.

I can acknowledge with thankfulness and even joy that much help was afforded me in the various services which attended (it). * * My heart flows with love toward those whom I have been visiting, and I feel it a cause for thankfulness, that the last day of the year should have been a day peculiarly devoted to my divine Master.

1st mo., 8th, 1821. We are apt to imagine that the trials of business are almost unbearable, and that even religion does not come in to aid them; but religion will apply itself to these as well as to all other trials, and submission to the will of God and confidence in his love, will help us through everything.

1st mo., 29th. The last twenty days have been replete with interest and occupation. The first of the three weeks spent industriously at home, till sixth day, when I went to Cromer. Memorable, indeed, to me was my visit there, chiefly on account of our dearest Priscilla, to whom I was enabled to devote myself, and whose state of mind is in the greatest degree satisfactory and instructive.

Her decline appears rapid, but her sky cloudless. On first day morning our family party assembled in her room. Fowell and Hannah, Catherine, Rachel, and myself. It was a season of close exercise of spirit and of true baptism. Seldom have I been so drawn out into supplication, particularly for every member of our family successively, for the church, for the poor Africans, for the world at large. Priscilla beautifully addressed Fowell. It was altogether a time of peculiar favour.

On second day I returned home, and the same afternoon went off by mail to London. There I spent a highly interesting fortnight: saw many interesting people;—the Duc de Cazes, Wilberforce, Brougham, &c., and delightfully partook of the society of all my brothers and sisters, in and about London. Business was at times sorrowfully perplexing; yet hope and strength were, from time to time, afforded. The spiritual blessings of these two weeks were great; and from day to day I experienced something of the "word of Christ" dwelling in me "richly."

2nd mo., 11th. Dearest Priscilla's state [continues to] engross much attention, and to excite near feeling and sympathy. Two days last week I passed at Cromer, and found her greatly sunk. Whilst I cannot but weep over the mortal decay of a most beloved sister, let me remember my blessings and my joys. First of all, the blessing of an assured belief, that the spirit of our sister is washed white in the blood of the Lamb, is purified for heaven, ready to ascend into the society of the angelic host. O the mercy of the Lord! O the call for thankfulness and joy! And next let me look at home. Have I not cause to be very thankful? And why should I be so very careful? Why should I so often go as one burthened on my way? Unto thee, most dear, and honoured, and gracious Master, I desire to commit myself, my wife, my children, my brothers and sisters, my loved ones of every description, my goods and estate, my body, soul, and spirit. Do with me as thou seest meet. Enable me quietly to cast every care upon thee. Comfort me with the hourly remembrance that thou art my Saviour, my Shepherd, my King, and my Friend; yea, that thou art thyself touched with a feeling of my infirmities. Raise me, I beseech thee, above every mortal fear, every worldly entanglement; deepen and enliven my faith, and plant my affections in that celestial region of love and peace, where they will ever flourish to thy praise, and yield sweet fruits of honour, service, and thanksgiving, acceptable unto thee, my God.

Whilst thus watching the gradual decline of his sister, another affecting event unexpectedly occurred. In the third month of the preceding year, his brother-in-law Henry Birkbeck had married his cousin Jane, the daughter of his uncle Joseph Gurney. On the 21st of the 2nd mo. of this year she breathed her last, a few days after the birth of her only child.

2nd mo., 26th. Alas! where are we? Truly, sorrow and dismay have been our allotment. Second day was the last day of hope respecting dearest Jane. On the following morning we were greatly alarmed by the return of her symptoms; no strength was left to bear the application of remedies, and she breathed her last early on fourth day morning. * * Third day was one of exceedingly great affliction. This was heightened to me by the absence of my dear wife, who was then at Cromer. In the evening my mother and I went to the Grove together, and it must be acknowledged, that in the very heat of the fiery trial, there was to be felt there, that evening, a sweet peace and great tranquillity. It was evident that divine support was near at hand to help the afflicted party. The beloved invalid was at first disappointed at hearing from the medical attendant that there was no longer any hope; and I believe she passed through deep humiliation and conflict, in the apprehension of her unfitness for the awful change. But her religion was pure, just, and genuine, and her faith gradually arose, so that she was enabled to throw herself, just as she was, on the bosom of a merciful Saviour. Her messages to her friends were instructive and full of love; her mind clear and very bright, to the last. Her sufferings were not great, and her end comparatively easy; truly and richly blessed, we may thankfully believe!

Under the same date he continues:—

On sixth day morning I settled some affairs; wrote a little in my book; visited the Grove; looked in at the prison; and then proceeded to Cromer, where I found another party of mourners. I stayed there until first day afternoon, and was much with dearest Priscilla. * * Sweet is the influence which accompanies and surrounds her, and truly lovely and desirable is her frame of mind. She lies most quietly, and her calm appears to be unbroken. Several times she spoke in ministry, and her whole state seems to indicate heaven at hand. It is peculiarly soothing to be with her, and an unspeakable mercy that she is so favoured with comparative outward ease, and with such eminent inward tranquillity, and true peace. Not a doubt appears to perplex her path. Her soul is centered in God.

Three weeks later he writes to his brother-in-law Thomas Fowell Buxton, who was then in London, attending upon his duties in Parliament: —

Cromer, 3d mo., 17th, 1821.

* * In thinking of thee, I feel entire satisfaction in thy having quitted for a time, thy retirement, and again launched thy vessel upon the world's ocean. Thy situation is undoubtedly one of great importance, and thy character is likely to obtain the more influence, because thy zeal for life, liberty, and truth, will move along in straight lines, and be disfigured by no *canting* or *whining*. Let no vain glory, no worldly lusts, no confidence in thy own strength, pollute its fair colours. Dwell low and deep in the humility which preserves, and mind what our dearest Priscilla said to thee when she exhorted thee to receive the Lord Jesus Christ in the fulness of his love, light, and power, not only as thy Redeemer, but as thy Governor, and thy Guide. Thy fond brethren may praise, perhaps flatter thee, but thy Master will ever be found an "unflattering witness." He will show thee where thou art, and what thou art. The denial of self, the bearing of the cross of Jesus, the arduous stepping on in the strait and narrow path, the reduction of the creature's will to its proper nothingness, will all be set before thee, and must all be accepted with submission. Yet, through all, will the smile of alluring mercy, of everlasting loving-kindness, of free redeeming grace, gladden and brighten every prospect, and teach the disconsolate pilgrim that all the ways of the Lord are "pleasantness, and all his paths peace." * * *

I have had great comfort in being here. Dearest Priscilla's state is to me increasingly consoling. Her sufferings appear to be considerably alleviated, and her spirit is like that of a little child. She has felt, thought, acted, and known as much as many, and manfully has she sustained the great cause of righteousness and truth. Now all is hushed; brought into rest and stillness; and, as I said before, her soul is like a weaned child. Nothing, in my apprehension, can be more lovely or beautiful than such a state. There is in it such an absence of enthusiasm, such freedom from all false colouring, such true fitness for an entrance through the pearl gates into the city of God!

3rd mo., 31*st*. * * On fourth day morning, the 21st, as we were sitting at breakfast, we received a note from Dalrymple, to inform us that he had been to visit Priscilla, that he found her near death, and that he recommended my setting off without delay. I felt undisturbed by this intelligence; and having completed what required attention at home, we left Earlham, and arrived at Cromer before dinner time, where we continued until last fifth day morning, the 29th. On our introduction to dear Priscilla, we found her greatly sunk. Much of the time, whilst she was awake, was passed in reading the Bible, hymns, Friends' books — chiefly Samuel Scott's Diary, and the History of the Moravian Missions. Every now and then, sweet openings of the living spring, and opportunities for short verbal ministry.

Seventh day was indeed a memorable one. She was evidently herself during the whole day; seemed to enter into what was read to her, and received the ministry of her brothers and sisters, especially that of Fowell. The 13th of 1st Corinthians was read, and the enduring nature of true love dwelt upon. She in vain endeavoured to address Fowell, but could not speak. She offered her hand to different individuals repeatedly, in token of love; to me sweetly, amongst the rest. About half-past nine in the evening, we were all summoned into the room, as there were increased appearances of approaching death. Solemn and sweet was the time we then passed together. Prayer and thanksgiving were offered. Our dear sister Fry, wonderfully strengthened in faith, and empowered of the Spirit, addressed the dying beloved one, in a strain of confident and assured encouragement; as it were, helping her over the waters of Jordan. In the course of the opportunity, Priscilla clearly smiled; and repeatedly and distinctly expressed the word, "Farewell." * * I sat up with her during the night. It was a night of dying; and early in the morning I was exceedingly overcome. About nine, we were all again assembled with her, and whilst our sister Fry was in the act of commending her into the hands of her God and Father, one gentle sigh closed the awful, yet peaceful scene! I repeated the words from a hymn: —

"One gentle sigh her fetters breaks;
We scarce can say she's gone,
Before the willing spirit takes
Her mansion near the throne.!'

Great and delightful was the flow of peace which after much deep distress, ensued to my own mind, for about half an hour.

Thus early was Priscilla Gurney called to rest from those labours which had promised a career of so much usefulness. Though the youngest sister, she was the first that was taken away, giving in the quiet assurance of her Christian hope, a sweet foretaste to those who were left behind, of the all-sufficiency of his grace who had thus loved her, and washed her from her sins in his own blood. She was born in the year 1785, and quickly became a conspicuous ornament of that bright and lively family circle, of which a sketch has already been given. Partaking, like the rest, of the gaiety of youth, she was with them also made a partaker of the gracious visitations of redeeming love. In the year 1810, she was led to unite herself more closely to the Society of Friends, and after passing through deep mental conflict, she felt it her duty, some years later, to speak as a minister in their religious meetings.

"Of all the ministry I was accustomed to hear," writes Joseph John Gurney in his Autobiography, "none perhaps was so beneficial to me, as that of my beloved sister Priscilla. It was generally in good authority, well expressed, lucid, and scriptural; and to me rendered much the more effectual by her life and conversation, which afforded me a pattern of no mean value. The language of her whole conduct, to her younger brother in the truth, was, "Follow me, as I follow Christ."*

After having been engaged in various religious labours among Friends in her native county, she accompanied her cousin Rachel Gurney, whose health was then rapidly declining, and several other members of the family, to the South of France in the year 1816, and spent some time in religious service among the few who profess the principles of Friends in those parts. Whilst absent upon this journey, she wrote

TO HER BROTHER JOSEPH JOHN GURNEY.

Nice, 12th mo., 26th, 1816.

There are few passages in Scripture that have been more animating or comforting to me than the promises in the Revelation to those who overcome. I have dwelt on them with peculiar interest and with a renewed desire for us that

* One feature of her private character may be particularly noticed —her assiduous attention to the wants of the distressed and poor. "You had more opportunity," writes Thomas Fowell Buxton, to one of her sisters, "of knowing the extent to which she was devoted to their service, and how many of the days in every week she was employed exclusively in visiting the sick and distressed. I can only speak of the manner in which she was prepared, as soon as breakfast was over, to proceed to her task, her basket in readiness, filled with such little presents as she thought might be useful or acceptable to those who were suffering from disease. * * Within a short period of her death, she said to me, that she had no wish to recover, but if there was anything which recalled her to life, it was the desire to be more diligent in attending to the sick; adding, 'I have been well nursed, admirably nursed; but, after all, sickness to me is a sore thing; and what must it be to those who want every thing?'"

we may with more faith, more humility, and more entire and simple obedience, enlist under the banner of the Captain of our salvation; that we may follow him whithersoever he leadeth us. It is the prayer of my heart, my dearest Joseph, that thou mayest be encouraged and enabled yet to go on, yet to press forward in every religious, domestic, and public duty, in quietness and humility, "not slothful in business," "fervent in spirit, serving the Lord." When the curtain drops and the scene closes here, how is then every sacrifice in the cause of religion, how is every act of faith and obedience to be prized; how inestimable do they become as evidences of that grace by which alone we are saved!

On her return to Earlham in the summer of 1817, she again became the warm and affectionate helper and counsellor of her brother in his various engagements, taking an especial interest in his efforts in favour of scriptural instruction. With his assistance she compiled the valuable selection of Hymns for Young Persons, which was soon afterwards published, and has since passed through many editions in England and America.

Towards the close of the year 1817, she was engaged in a short journey amongst Friends in Cambridgeshire and Huntingdonshire, and in the following spring, in company with Anna Forster, she paid a general visit to Friends in Ireland. Soon after her return from Ireland, her health began to give way, and with a view to its amendment, she was induced to pass some months on the southern shore of the Isle of Wight. The change appeared, for a time, to produce the desired effect, and in the 4th month of 1820 she again resumed her position at Earlham. There, however, her strength gradually declined, and in the 8th month of that year she finally removed to the house of her brother-in-law, Thomas Fowell Buxton, near Cromer, where she died on the 25th of the 3rd month, 1821.

Among many other letters received on the occasion of her decease, that to one of her sisters, written by the late Charles Simeon, and published in his Memoirs,* as well as the sketch given of her character by her brother-in-law Thomas Fowell Buxton,† are sufficient evidences of the deep impression which she had made upon those with whom she was associated. But among them all, there were few, if any, who more deeply felt her loss than her brother Joseph John Gurney. Having lived together under a common roof; a sister not only in natural affection, but as he was wont to say, "in the unchangeable truth," it was a dispensation under which he bowed in reverent submission, but which he ceased not deeply to mourn.

"Exceedingly precious to many," are his words in allusion to her many years later in his Autobiography, "is the recollection of her sweetness and delicacy, and at the same time, strength and clearness of mind; of her unreserved dedication of heart to the Saviour whom she loved; and of her instructive offerings in prayer and preaching, both in public and in private. Her image comes before me at this moment with uncommon sweetness!"

The funeral took place on the 2nd of the 4th month, and was very largely attended.

* See p. 551.

† See Memoirs of Sir T. F. Buxton, pp. 100, 101.

"There was something with us," says Joseph John Gurney, "of which words might be the channel, but which was far better than words. We may acknowledge, that we have been greatly favoured by the divine love and presence, ever since our sister's death, and we cannot be too thankful for this renewed extension of heavenly favour; but, alas! how mournfully have I at times felt the depth, height, length, and breadth of my loss! Priscilla was, indeed, a most valued and cherished sister!"

CHAPTER XI.

1821—1822. ÆT. 33—34.

EXTRACTS FROM JOURNAL AND LETTERS: LETTER FROM WILLIAM WILBERFORCE; TRACT ON THE AUTHORITY, IMPORTANCE, AND EFFECT OF CHRISTIANITY; ILLNESS AND DEATH OF HIS WIFE.

DEEPLY sorrowing, yet not as those who are without hope, Joseph John Gurney thus prepares for again engaging in his ordinary duties.

Fourth mo., 6th, 1821. I prayed this morning for ability to recommence my common duties in the fear of the Lord, and with a diligent spirit. This work is, I hope, begun. I have been visiting poor William Anderson on his death bed. A sudden illness, and as fatal as sudden! How awful is such a summons. I was strengthened to pray for him, and to direct his attention to a crucified Jesus.

Fourth mo., 16th. On fifth day at the Monthly Meeting, I proposed a public meeting [at Norwich] for last first day night. I felt much peace, and even joy, in consequence; something resembling the feeling which was permitted me when I first spoke in the ministry; but lowness and apprehension were at times prevalent. The meeting was full and very relieving. I experienced much power working in my weakness, enabling me to preach the gospel of my Lord and Saviour.

Fifth mo., 8th. Returned last night from London; the week spent there marked chiefly by the meeting of the Bible Society, and Fowell's parliamentary dinner party; the latter entertaining, the former highly interesting. Being invited to speak, I took the opportunity of discussing the right method of conducting public meetings, and bore a strong and generally, though I believe not universally, acceptable testimony against want of simplicity, votes of thanks, flattery, &c. As usual, though my speech was against *self*, I found *self* too busy, too eager after some satisfaction, when the effort was over.

The passage of his speech to which he here refers, is reported as follows.*

"I long to see the day when the General Meetings of the Bible Society shall be conducted with perfect simplicity, and when we shall studiously avoid everything like panegyric or eulogy. This line of conduct we have adopted at Norwich, and it appears to me to have greatly increased the success of the Bible Society there. We have always endeavoured to have as few resolutions as possible; and to make them all as much as possible of a practical nature. My heart went along with my friend from North Britain, when he was speaking of the evils of panegyric. We do not come here to panegyrize, but to acknowledge the unmerited mercies of our God and Saviour. We come to acknowledge, as in the dust, that we have all sinned and come short of his glory; and that so far from having any degree of merit for what we have done, we have cause to lament that we have done so little. I am fully sensible how much benefit this Society has derived from its president, from its secretaries, and from its committee; and one reason why I wish to promote the distribution of the Scriptures is because, while they teach us to fear God, they teach us also to give honour where honour is due, tribute to whom tribute is due, respect where respect is due. But when I remember that our object is a religious one; that we come together as the unworthy subjects and servants of our Lord Jesus Christ, I feel that we should not take that opportunity of bestowing praise on each other."

* See the Monthly Extracts from the correspondence, &c. of the British and Foreign Bible Society of that period.

Second day 5th mo., 4th. Yesterday brought with it some edification. The ministry was exercised shortly in both the meetings; considerably in the cross to myself. In the morning I spoke of the advantage of our mode of worship, as leading to the experience that we can of ourselves do very little to help or instruct one another, that there are times when the tongue of the teacher languisheth, and when the voice of the preacher is scarcely heard; and how profitable these times might be made to us, if they induced us to make God our only refuge, and to draw near to the true minister of the sanctuary, whose sacred touch can make the heart to glow, and whose anointing "teacheth of all things, and is truth and no lie." In the afternoon, I quoted the words of Isaiah, "How beautiful on the mountain," &c., and spoke to the case of those who, being to a certain degree awakened, were ready to acknowledge the goodness of the tidings, and the beauty of the feet of the messengers; but who were nevertheless unwilling to pay the price, to sell all that they have, and to present their whole selves an acceptable sacrifice. How desirable that I should take these lessons home to myself; that my body and heart be kept under true subjection, so that "having preached to others," I may not myself become "a castaway!"

Sixth mo., 24th. My dearest wife and I left home on the third day preceding the Yearly Meeting, and have been absent four weeks. This very interesting period was occupied first by Fowell and his criminal code debate;* secondly, by the Yearly Meeting; thirdly, by my own religious duties; holding various meetings, some in the neighbourhood of London, and some on my way home. Deeply interesting have been these successive objects. I have seen great talents devoted to the Lord's service and glory; I have seen a large body of persons deliberating for many days, under what I truly believe to be the immediate influences of the Lord's Spirit; I have seen produced these precious fruits of the Spirit, love, quietness, and great solemnity, which have evinced the solidity and substantial truth of our religious principles; and in the various

* See Life of Sir T. F. Buxton, p. 108.

public and other meetings, in which I have been myself engaged, I have had to acknowledge both the power and the love of God, manifested in renewed visitations to his unworthy servants and to their hearers. Surely then I ought to be animated by this fresh cloud of witnesses, "to lay aside every weight," and to press forward.

In allusion to a Friend's having "hinted at disunity with his gift" in the ministry, he remarks:—

Had it not been for this circumstance, I believe I should have returned home not only peaceful, but, in my measure, rejoicing in the Lord. It is well, however, to be brought into yet deeper searching of heart, and into truer silence of soul; and I believe this dispensation will be made profitable to me. It is my desire to get rid of that secret pride and presumption, which would arrogate to myself the right in this matter; and to humble myself more and more before God and man; and yet I believe it needful, that I should not take too much heed to any human judgment, but rather with simplicity and firmness follow my God.

The following are some of his reflections upon a review of his objects in life at this period.

7th mo., 8th. I suppose my leading outward object in life, may be said to be the bank. It sometimes startles me to find my leading object of such a nature, and now and then I doubt whether it is quite consistent with my religious pursuits and duties. I remember, however, that it has been the allotment of providence; that I was introduced into the business in obedience to my father, in early life; that my religious pursuits have found me in this situation; and that hitherto, the two things have not proved incompatible. It is, however, a very serious thing, to be so largely engaged in the cares and transactions of money matters. It calls for real watchfulness against avarice, against a careful spirit, and against worldliness in various forms. It is much my desire, that should it be the will of my gracious leader and commander entirely to divert my attention at any time from this object, that will may be made known to me, and some opening for escape given. While I am a banker, the bank must be attended to. It is obviously the religious duty of a trustee to so large an amount, to be diligent in watching his trust. It appears to me, on the whole, that our concern was never better watched or conducted in its several ramifications, and I trust it may please a gracious providence to preserve us from very rough waters. * * Public charitable objects are, in this age, numerous. With respect to myself, they are brought into far better order than formerly, and by no means occupy a great proportion of time, with the single exception of the Bible Society, which I continue to feel one of my most important objects in life. The school is pretty regularly visited, and goes on well. The prison I have not visited since my return; but intend to resume my operations there. The mendicity office, vaccination, and dispensary, occasionally claim attention.

My religious duties, or those which may be more peculiarly called so, alone remain to be noticed. My "overseership"* in Norwich meeting; my ministry; both are interesting to me. It is a great comfort, inexpressibly so, that this ministry is not at my own command; that it comes and goes; that I can neither stop it, nor set it going. O there is sweet rest in this. At present I am brought to an unusual feeling of nothingness, and it is my desire more and more to lie low under the mighty hand of God. My stock of faith, and spiritual grace seems often very low, yet hope springs up from time to time; and I do not forget that the "blood of Jesus Christ cleanseth from all sin."

I have been picturing to myself my outward history. My soul, however, is the thing to be chiefly watched. It is well

* "Overseers," are officers in the Society of Friends appointed, as the name implies, to watch over their fellow-members, and to give such Christian advice and counsel as may appear needful. The office is by no means confined to those, whose call to the ministry has been recognised by the body.

to have before me an orderly arrangement, a coloured map of things to be done outwardly; but the great lesson is to dwell deeply with the fountain of life, more earnestly to seek God, more thoroughly to cleave to the Lamb immaculate, who commands me to follow him. As this is the case, I need not greatly burden myself with my outward cares, but I shall receive ability, day by day, to move forwards with a meek and quiet spirit, towards the "final rest." My beloved wife and children are treasures inexpressibly precious. May my duties towards them never be neglected. So happily and completely are these duties interwoven with everyday's course, that I would almost hope that the neglect of them may be impossible.

"How differently from our expectations," he writes in the entry which immediately follows the above, "are sometimes ordered the ways of providence! The preceding analysis says much of business, and varied occupation of mind and body; the ways of providence have brought with them the command, 'be still.'

"I think it was about the 18th of the 7th mo., that, after a severe attack of indisposition, which had confined me about two weeks, my dearest wife and I, with our children, left home to spend a few quiet, restorative days at Cromer Hall. Those few days were extended to two weeks, which were succeeded by three weeks at Hunstanton, and these by five weeks of journeying through Derbyshire, Warwickshire, &c., which have at last brought us back to our beloved and long-left home. I could have but one excuse for such a mode of passing ten weeks of precious time;—the restoration of health."

Announcing his arrival at Hunstanton, he writes:—

8th mo., 1st, 1821.

* * On our way hither, my fancy was greatly caught by the wild flowers which bloomed in the hedges between Cromer and Holt, and of which I counted in blossom more than seventy species. How profuse and variegated are the results of the wisdom and goodness of God!

TO HENRY BRADY.

Matlock, 9th mo., 2nd, 1821.

Thou well knowest how warm and heartfelt an affection I have for thee, and for other dear friends at Ackworth, and how deeply interested I am in your welfare, and that of the institution over which you are presiding. May you be encouraged and helped by the Author of all our sure mercies, faithfully to perform your arduous duties, and more and more diligently to lead the lambs of the fold to their only true Shepherd. Who knows but that the language of "cease from your labours" may be proclaimed to some of *you*, and how desirable, in such a moment, to look back with peace upon a stewardship duly executed. I have been quite a wanderer, absent from home about two months. How good it is for me to be thus (after a manner somewhat novel to me,) convinced of my insignificance and powerlessness! May it be my own prayer, and that of my friends, that in all things I may be found truly subject to the will of Him, who loved us and gave himself for us.

10th mo., 9th. * * The societies, and the annual gatherings at Earlham, appear to have gone on well in our absence, which is a true satisfaction; and it has been much of a pleasure to open my doors wide, though not myself a partaker. I know, however, that there is no security in these things, unless they arise from a simple and unsophisticated desire to "honour the Lord with our substance, and with the first fruits of all our increase." May this honouring of the Lord be increasingly my only aim! There still dwells deeply in my heart a tendency to many and various evils, which I have long endeavoured to investigate and correct; but the work is by no means completed. How clearly do I perceive that the Christian weapons of watchfulness, prayer, and earnest seeking after God, can never cease to be necessary whilst we are in this state of being! Though there is no limit to the work of grace; and though the standard held out to us and closely enjoined, is nothing short of the standard of perfection, yet must we expect that the contest will continue to the end.

12th mo., 10th. The whole of yesterday, which was a low yet edifying sabbath, I felt real satisfaction in being silent. * * How invaluable is the liberty of the Spirit, as professed and enjoyed by Friends! In the afternoon meeting my mind was peculiarly drawn in near love and unity to our own society; and the desolate heritages were commended in secret prayer to Him who, I feel persuaded, has called us forth to bear peculiar yet living testimonies; and thus to answer, in his church universal, a specific purpose. Would that that purpose were more fully accomplished in us and by us; but, alas! the backwardness, waywardness, and carelessness of fallen man!

First day morning, 12th mo., 23rd. At home from meeting this morning in great quietness and retirement. I have felt enabled to pour out my heart in prayer for myself, my wife, my children, and many others, for the church, and for the cause of truth. It is indeed a solemn and awful thing thus to draw near in spirit to the Most High; and what an unspeakable privilege not to be separated from him by a state of sin; what a paramount blessing to know an access unto him by that new and living way which he hath himself revealed!

FROM WILLIAM WILBERFORCE.

(Written a few days after the decease of his eldest daughter.*)

Marden Park, January 15th, 1822.

* * We yesterday returned to the house in which our dear child had passed a few days of comparative health and bodily enjoyment, and many weeks of languor and pain. My wife was naturally much affected at first; but her grand cordial is of an efficacy as unlimited in point of place, as of time and circumstance. It is the assured persuasion that our dear child is gone to a better world. I own I had wished, and, with submission I trust, had prayed, that it might please God to grant her a measure of joy as well as peace in believing—

* See Life of Wilberforce, vol. v, pp. 109—113.

some of that holy exultation of which we so often read in the last hours of the dying people of God; and yet, except in some few particular instances, I know not but that the humble, but sure though trembling hope of a contrite heart, often approves itself to the judgment as a still more stable and solid ground for consolation. And it is observable, that though joy be sometimes held forth as a privilege, and even commanded as that to which, as Christians, we have a right, yet there are no promises made to it as an evidence. But, "the Lord is nigh unto them that be of a contrite heart, and will save such as be of an humble spirit." Joy needs no consolatory assurances, as does the humble, trembling penitent. To him that exquisitely beautiful assurance is given, the Lord delighteth in mercy; not merely kindness, but *mercy;* kindness to those who deserve punishment. O, how often are we reminded that God is love! Though a tender mother cannot but feel deeply, yet she can rejoice too; and blessed be God, while tears are transient as an April shower, the joy will be immortal as the light of heaven, as the glory of God, and the light of the Lamb. * * O my friend, what a world of glories does Christianity pour forth upon us when we, ἀφορῶντες, fix on it our steady and warm regards! What a gloomy—what a November evening prospect would present itself to the mind's eye of a man like myself, advancing into the vale of years, but for this blessed flood of light and love which flow forth from the throne of God and of the Lamb! My dear friend, pray for us, that what has passed, may not have merely a transient effect, but a deep and lasting, aye, everlasting influence; that it may impress us with a disposition to be more diligent, that we may be "found of him in peace without spot and blameless."

It was about this time, as appears from a memorandum in his literary Journal,* that Joseph John Gurney wrote the original of the tract which he

* Under date 4th mo., 8th, to 4th mo., 22nd, 1822; see the note p. 233, *infra.*

published in a revised and enlarged form towards the beginning of the year 1824, under the title of, A Letter to a Friend on the Authority, Purpose, and Effects of Christianity, and especially on the Doctrine of Redemption. In this letter he gives a condensed but clear and forcible statement of the evidences of the Christian religion; thence proceeding, at somewhat greater length, with the arguments drawn from Scripture in proof of the great doctrines of Christian redemption, particularly dwelling upon the efficacy of the atoning sacrifice of Christ, and the necessity and reality of the operations of the Holy Spirit, as the awakener of the world, the witness for Christ, and the comforter and sanctifier of the believer.

The friend to whom the letter was addressed had long been known to the family at Earlham. Distinguished by learning, talent, and intelligence, his heart was enlarged by a widely extended benevolence, and for a long series of years, his doors, during certain hours of each day, had been regularly opened to the distressed poor, and his time freely devoted to the alleviation of their sufferings and wants. But, with all his excellencies, one thing was wanting, without which his mind could not rest. He was yet a stranger to the joy and the peace which spring from a settled faith in the Lord Jesus Christ. He was now far advanced in years, and had known Joseph John Gurney from his childhood, and his position and character, coupled with the long familiarity of friendship, made the prospect of a religious visit to him not a little formidable.

"So weak was my faith," writes Joseph John Gurney, "that it seemed impossible, and I did not yield to the impression for a full month. Finding no peace, however, on any other terms, I at length called upon him, and induced him to allow me to sit down with him in silence. He was very restless, and my ministration as weak as possible. However, in broken terms, I expressed my sense of the unutterable importance of simple faith in Christ."

"Some considerable time afterwards, he was exposed to great personal danger on his way home from London, in consequence of the horses in the coach running away. He was alarmed. The Lord applied that alarm to the highest purposes; and he awoke to a painful solicitude respecting the state of his immortal soul. In this condition he applied to me for a selection of passages from scripture on the subject of the atonement. (O! the importance of that only refuge for the awakened soul.) Most willingly did I avail myself of the opportunity, and, without delay, I sat down and wrote the original of my Letter to a Friend on the Authority, Importance, and Effects of Christianity. * * I anxiously awaited the result, and soon found to my great joy, that it was well received. He placed the letter under the cushion of his arm-chair, and for several weeks read it daily. The Bible was read to him from time to time, and in the course of a few weeks his mind was changed. It was the Lord's doing, and was marvellous in our eyes. He was much afflicted by a painful disease, which he bore with exemplary patience. On calling upon him one day, I expressed a desire for his preservation in the truth. "I do assure you," he replied, "I have not one sceptical feeling left," and he allowed me to take away the following prayer which he had just been writing, and which I found lying on his table.

"Almighty God, and most merciful Father! I humbly beseech thee to ease my pain, increase my patience, and lay upon me no more than I am able to bear, although I have deserved it all; and grant, that when my soul is released from this prison of my body, it may be admitted into that rest which is appointed for all such as repent, amend, and believe; as, I trust, does this thy unworthy servant, who now lies prostrate before thee, in humble reliance on the atoning merits of thy beloved Son, who suffered death that we might enjoy life eternal, and to whom be all honour, dominion, and power, for ever and ever. Amen."

He continued stedfast in the faith until his death, which took place about two years afterwards. Though unhesitating in his belief, he was often in conflict respecting himself, but evidently kept his hold of the Lord Jesus. Standing by his bedside, two or three days before his end, I said, addressing him, "Ah, what a comfort it is, that the blood of Christ cleanseth from all sin." "Yes!" he replied with intense feeling, "if it were not for that, I know not what would become of me!"

Since its first publication, the Letter on Christianity has been widely circulated, several hundred thousand copies having been distributed through various channels. "For such a result," says Joseph John Gurney, at the conclusion of the above narrative, "I ought to be very thankful, and humbly trust that it may have been blessed to many. If so, the Lord alone be praised."

An event was now approaching which put his principles to their severest test. Little as he appears himself to have anticipated it, the following entry in the journal, written a few weeks previously, possesses a peculiar interest.

5th mo., 4th, 1822. Why are we so much surprised and discouraged at the afflictions of the righteous? Are they not appointed for good, in whatever shape they appear? And are they not, in comparison with eternal things, of almost momentary duration? O for an increase of true and lively, and reposing faith in God, with reference to those things which are invisible, and for ever.

A few days later he writes:—

TO HIS SISTER HANNAH BUXTON.

* * How in circumstances of trial, I should practise, I know not. One thing I know, that my nature most sensibly shrinks from pain and trial, and that a true and cheerful submission will never be displayed by me, unless I am immediately helped by him whose grace is sufficient, however deep the thorn, however torn and wounded the flesh.

Still later he writes in his Journal:—

5th mo., 26th. First day. I have been more than usually engaged in ministry to-day. This afternoon, on the nature of Christian fidelity; "Be thou faithful unto death;" and upon the particulars unfolded in Scripture, respecting the heavenly state; "And I will give thee a crown of life." How earnestly do I desire that my practice may not fall short of my public profession, that my life and conversation may, far more than they now do, "adorn the doctrine!" It is affecting to me to consider that I seem, for the most part, to dwell at such a distance from heavenly things; but, I trust, the Master whom I desire to serve, will bring me, and all of us, nearer to himself.

The next entry thus continues his history:—

6th mo., 19th. This great purpose has, I trust, in measure, been effected, by the awful and most afflicting dispensation, which has been permitted to overtake me. On the 10th instant, my tenderly beloved wife was removed from this mortal scene, to one, as I have every reason to believe, of infinitely greater happiness and joy.

I will endeavour, for my own comfort and benefit, and that of my beloved family, to record the circumstances.

A considerable cold and cough induced my dear wife to take more than usual care of herself, during the week before last. On first day morning, the 2nd instant, however, she was well enough to attend the morning meeting, and, indeed, seemed quite well. She remained at home in the afternoon, not being strong enough for a further effort, and when I came back, she requested me to take her a drive in the pony chair. The evening was bright and pleasant, and our minds were calm and united; but it is probable that the north wind, which then blew upon us, was made the cause of her death.

On fifth day afternoon, speaking of her illness, she said, "I have no wish that it should be otherwise. I have prayed that something might bring me to a livelier sense of religion;" and again, turning to me with great sweetness, she observed, "this is to bring down the high places." On sixth day night, my sisters, Rachel and Richenda, came with me into her room. We found her asleep: when she awoke, the Spirit of the Lord, (a spirit of humiliation, yet confidence,) appeared to be with her; and it was with great power that she addressed us, "How," said she, "has the love of God been opened to my soul lately!" adding, "I look upon this to be an awful and sudden call out of the world, and from all things that are in it." She emphatically described herself as a sinner; declared that she was deeply prostrated, and at the same time spoke with fulness of the good hope and sweet consolation, which had attended her through this illness. Soon after my sisters left the room, she said, "Give my kind regards to the servants, and tell them how much I have desired that they might be brought under the influence of *vital religion.*"

* * * * * *

On first day morning her mind became less occupied with painful, and more with pleasurable emotions. Sweet smiles dwelt on her countenance, and her delirium, for the most part, was that of a person who felt at once innocent and easy. This was an inexpressible relief to me, and the sorrow which I had to experience through this sabbath day, though deep and poignant, was a quiet sorrow, unruffled by the storm of the enemy. It was that of giving up unto death my tenderly beloved one; and whilst under the influence of this sorrow, the future assumed the appearance of dark melancholy. I, nevertheless, experienced true peace in recommitting her to her God and Father. In the afternoon, a painful struggle was excited, by the suggestion of a hope of recovery, and it was only in the full resignation of that hope that I again felt peace. I retired to rest on first day night, and obtained some hours of refreshing sleep.

About half-past four o'clock, Rachel called me, and informed me that there were marked appearances of the approaching change. I was soon again with my beloved wife. I was agitated, fearful, and nervous, but after some time, I was strengthened to kneel down, and a song of prayer and praise broke forth spontaneously from me, nearly in the following words:—"And now, O Lord, cut short the work in righteousness. Thou hast washed her in the blood of the Lamb; thou hast regenerated her by thy Holy Spirit; thou hast clothed her with thy salvation. Thou art about to receive her into thy kingdom, where her sun shall no more go down, neither her moon withdraw itself; for thou, O Lord, shalt be her everlasting light—her God—her glory!" As the last breath trembled on her lips, (and gentle was that breath,) the power of the Lord again came over me, and I cried out, with a spirit not my own, "The work, the glorious work is finished, to his praise, to her eternal happiness, and to my peace."

My dearest wife died on second day morning, the 10th of the 6th month, exactly four years and nine months after our happy marriage day. A sense of holy and elevated calm, was the immediate effect of this touching, solemn, and blessed scene. Here for the present I leave my history. The change wrought in my condition is wonderful. The mighty hand of the Lord's discipline and dealing has been upon me, and his Comforter is now with me; at his feet I feel sweet unbroken peace. There let me ever dwell, O Lord my God!

TO THE BISHOP OF NORWICH.

Earlham, 6th mo., 10th, 1822.

"I have this morning parted with my dearest earthly treasure, and have bid her God speed to the heavenly regions, where Christ dwelleth in his glory. One short week has marred my fond and pleasant pictures. My dearest wife on this day week was attacked with violent pleurisy, and is now numbered with the dead; may I not rather say with the *living;* with those who, like her, have placed a firm trust in their omnipotent Redeemer, and who have faithfully endeavoured to serve him; "*therefore* are they before the throne of God." It has been to me a period of the deepest anguish, and conflict of mind; but, at times, the storms have all been hushed by that divine power, of which I have indeed experienced the healing virtue, and on which it will, I humbly trust, be my endeavour to wait all my life long."

A few days after the funeral, he thus writes in his journal: —

6th mo., 21*st*. * * As I lay down last night, I endeavoured to console and strengthen myself with the following considerations: —

It has been our true, however feeble endeavour, to live together in the fear of God, and in the faith and love of Christ. And on this ground, I am persuaded, that we have been, as two individuals, and as one pair, under the special dealing of our heavenly Father; and this dealing has been displayed with power, in the awful dispensation which has brought our delightful outward union to a close. * * I have also assuredly to believe, that there is in this awful dispensation, mercy to me, as well as to her. The shaft has been directed of the Lord to my spiritual benefit. My dependence on earthly things required to be shaken. I was in need of something to dislocate me from things visible; and to bring me to a nearer and more satisfactory apprehension of the heavenly inheritance. Now my attractions to heaven are strengthened; those towards the earth proportionably weakened. The very great suffering which has been allotted me, was, I believe, needful for settling me more deeply in the truth. I hope I shall be permitted, by degrees, to rise out of it with fresh and profitable experience; better fitted than before to minister to others; and much strengthened, I humbly trust, for the working out of my own salvation. And yet truly I am nothing, "a worm and no man." Well do I know that my strength is in God, and that my only position of safety is that of total prostration at his feet.

CHAPTER XII.

1822—1823. ÆT. 34—36.

EXTRACTS FROM LETTERS AND JOURNAL; COMMENCEMENT OF WORK ON THE DISTINGUISHING PRINCIPLES OF FRIENDS; HOME PURSUITS; LITERARY JOURNAL; ANTI-SLAVERY MOVEMENTS; RELIGIOUS SERVICES IN ESSEX AND SUFFOLK; HANNAH MORE; RELIGIOUS VISIT TO YARMOUTH.

THERE is a beautiful passage in Baxter's Saint's Rest, in which the believer is represented as thus addressing himself on his entrance into glory. "Now thou art sufficiently convinced that the ways thou calledst hard, and the cup thou calledst bitter, were necessary; that thy Lord had sweeter ends, and meant thee better than thou wouldst believe; and that thy Redeemer was saving thee as well when he crossed thy desires as when he granted them, and as well when he broke thy heart as when he bound it up."* Such was the experience which Joseph John Gurney was now invited to realise. The hand of the "Refiner" was upon him; the discipline was painful, but he knew its purpose, and had been, in mercy, taught to receive it as a discipline of love.

* Page 32, ed. 1677.

TO HENRY BRADY.

Earlham, 7th mo., 15th, 1822.

Through the awful dispensation which has been allotted me, I may acknowledge that, however sorely tried, I have not been forsaken. Sometimes I am permitted to feel an almost abounding happiness; and generally a great calm over my mind and spirit. So that I have been constrained to proclaim from past experience the tender mercies of our God.

During the few months succeeding his loss he continued mostly at home, in the enjoyment of the society of his sisters Catherine and Rachel; his children becoming increasingly the objects of his tender solicitude.

In the mean time, besides attending to the necessary claims of business, and to the various public objects that had long shared his interest, he sedulously devoted his leisure to study; finding relief, as he intimates, not in the indulgence of sorrow, but in a diligent attention to the calls of duty. "My time is fully occupied," he writes in his Journal,* "and I have no opportunity to nurse my sorrow. Had I more opportunity, I know it would be wrong to do so. It is, and will be deep."

6th mo., 24th, 1822. The last three or four days have brought with them times of great lowness; yet I believe my faith has not failed, and the prayer which I have repeatedly offered in secret, that I might be preserved, through all, in that submission which precludes a *single murmur*, has been much blessed to me, and I trust answered.

* Under date 7th mo., 29th, 1822.

6th mo., 28th. This morning has been passed in very satisfactory communications with the servants. It is cause of gratitude to the Author of all our mercies that the household generally appear to be in so feeling and serious a frame of mind; so that, even in taking their beloved mistress from them, the Lord has, in measure at least, accomplished her main desire for them, and will, I trust, continue to bless the event to that great end. Since I last wrote I have passed through periods of deep sorrow; but thanks be to my beloved Redeemer, I am not forsaken. The *weaning* process is wonderfully painful, but, no doubt, it is needful, and I humbly trust it makes progress.

7th mo., 8th. Affecting accounts are received of the sudden, and I fear fatal illness of Charles Parker, who has been so lately with us evincing his spiritual exercise on our behalf, and his own fitness for the eternal world.* Alas! what a shadow, what a dream is our life! Yet why should we complain because a shock of corn fully ripe is gathered into the Master's garner.

7th mo., 15th. * * Dearest Louisa has just left us, after committing me with prayer and praise to our heavenly Father. She was led to speak of my learning further obedience by the things which I suffer. I desire to remember this hint for good, for I feel persuaded that, as it relates to myself, it is the main import of this awful dispensation.

9th mo., 4th. From first day, 8th mo., 4th, to the following seventh day, I was vigorously employed in clearing off the various claims of business, and left home for Hunstanton, on the 9th ult., with clear hands, and I trust not without a feeling of thankfulness towards the Author of all good. Our journey was pleasant, but our arrival at Hunstanton, a place full of the most affecting and tender associations, was very mournful. I strolled down by myself in the dark to the cliff, and poured out my heart in bitter weeping, in the remembrance of my lost

* An interesting notice of Charles Parker is to be found in "Piety Promoted," part 11, p. 280.

treasure. How many hours of sweet and pure enjoyment have we been permitted to taste together in that place! I continued at Hunstanton three weeks, and in the society of my dear mother, my dear sister Fry, and Rachel, experienced much true tranquillity and enjoyment. The Edwardses were also valuable companions. Dear Elizabeth's health strikingly improved during our stay, and her company and influence were at once reviving and instructive. Her deep humility was particularly striking amidst the love and applause of her fellow creatures, who seem on all occasions to gather round her. With the consent of our Norwich elders, I ventured to invite the inhabitants to a public meeting, which, though a time of personal humiliation, was followed by great relief and peace of mind. Two first days were passed at Lynn, where there is a very interesting little company of "convinced" individuals. Would that they may be led onwards in that narrow way which has been thus cast up for them! * * My dear home seems peaceful, notwithstanding its covering of mourning; nor do I find a great rush upon me, of things to be done and cared for. But diligence is very needful, and brings consolation with it.

Whilst at Hunstanton, he entered upon the composition of his work, on the Distinguishing Principles of Friends. In a letter to Jonathan Hutchinson, he describes it as "an attempt at something more easy and familiar than Barclay, and deeper than Henry Tuke."

"I hope," he writes in his Journal, "the task is rightly undertaken. O for that humble, self-denying, waiting state, in which our works are not our own, but the Lord's. Were it more attained to, how pure, how beautiful, would become the offerings of the righteous!"

9th mo., 9th. Second day morning. The solemnities of yesterday were far from being destitute of the divine blessing. Amidst all our trials the Lord is with us, and at times, he is pleased to proclaim a sabbath from the evil imaginations of the heart, and the temptations of the adversary.

Retiring for a few days to Cromer Hall, he found a large and interesting circle. Amongst others, the late William Wilberforce, and Zachary Macaulay were there, deliberating with his brother-in-law Thomas Fowell Buxton, on the position and prospects of the Anti-Slavery Question. It was the occasion on which the latter appears to have arrived at his "final decision," to accept the responsible post of advocate of the cause, as successor to Wilberforce.* In this important undertaking, and throughout the succeeding struggle, Joseph John Gurney gave him his warm and efficient encouragement and support.

Earlham, 9th mo., 28th. Wilberforce, his wife, daughter, and two sons, are our guests; and, after a visit of four days, are about to leave us this morning. My communications with him have been of an interesting and very animating nature. To describe him is difficult; for seldom, if ever, have I met with anything so beautiful as his mind. He lives, or appears to live, in perpetual sunshine; humility and love may be said to cover him, and the variety of his intellectual powers, and profusion of mental ornaments, render him, in a very peculiar degree, a delightful companion.

We have just been permitted to enjoy together, an opportunity of solemn waiting and fervent prayer, during which I was strengthened to minister to him, his wife, and his children, and to commit them to the everlasting Father of his people; also to pour out our united petitions on behalf of the poor slaves, and for their oppressors; and for the hastening of that day, in which the universal sabbath from those cruelties and

* See Life of Sir T. F. Buxton, p. 122.

contentions which now lay waste mankind, shall be proclaimed in the earth.

10th mo., 6th. Our Bible Society parties have been large but quiet, and a spirit of love and humility has, I hope, in a measure, reigned amongst us. Charles Simeon and John Cunningham, have been both interesting guests. The former is of a very marked character; full of elevated hopes, and Christian joy and love. I have enjoyed his society, and prized his influence; at the same time I find myself reverting with feelings of peace and satisfaction to the unexciting simplicity of my own religious profession.

First day evening, 10th mo., 13th. "Out of the depths have I cried unto thee, O Lord. Lord, hear my voice; let thine ears be attentive to the voice of my supplications. If thou, Lord, shouldest mark iniquities, O Lord, who shall stand? But there is forgiveness with thee, that thou mayest be feared." Such is the language of my soul this evening, after a week of much depression, and after a sabbath in which my gracious Master has been pleased to display a glimpse of his own countenance; so that I am, on the one hand, prostrated before him, and on the other, not destitute of some degree of ability to rejoice in the hope set before me in the gospel. Our two meetings have been to me, through divine favour, opportunities of much silent reverent waiting on God; and I have, both inwardly and vocally, prayed that I might be armed afresh of him, for the combat with my spiritual adversary.

Second day, 11th mo., 11th. * * Truly, I may adore the mercy of a long-suffering and gracious God, who has not left me to perish in the corruptions of my fallen nature, but wonderfully proclaims to me, from season to season, his great salvation. Seldom have I felt such deep lowness as I did yesterday; but I found it was wholesome for me thus to suffer. The morning meeting was spent in silent, awful prostration of soul before God. In the afternoon, with much fear, I preached on the invitation of the halt, poor, blind, and maimed, to the marriage supper, and on the wedding garment of the righteousness of Christ.

TO HENRY BRADY.

Norwich, 11th mo., 13th, 1822.

* * It is not Christian to be cast down without measure, by the death even of our dearest friends. I dare not allow it in myself, and I must venture to forbid it in thee. Why should we mourn as those that are without hope? And how is it that in the affairs of affection, we are so dependent upon the flesh? I know of nothing more to the credit of religion, than cheerfulness and thankfulness under affliction. Our consolations are unspeakable and abounding. As to thy *inward* trials of mind, I can indeed sympathize with thee, for I know what it is to be deeply cast down; and the corruption of the human heart is the very thing which has often brought me, as it has been bringing thee, into this state. But be of good courage, there is one, whose holy hand will, I believe, however secretly, sustain, uplift, protect, and deliver through all. *Cultivate a sound, deep, scriptural view of the redemption which is in Christ Jesus.* Accustom thyself not to dwell on thyself, but on him, as assuredly made unto thee of God, "wisdom, righteousness, sanctification, and redemption." Let his mercies and his merits be thy strength and thy stay, and pray for ability to "rejoice in the Lord." We mourn and pine because we dwell so much in and on ourselves; no sooner is our faith in Christ strengthened and illuminated, than we rejoice in him.

TO JONATHAN HUTCHINSON.

Cromer Hall, 11th mo., 17th, 1822.

* * * Thou wilt believe me that it is my desire to be preserved in cheerful submission. I endeavour after this state, and sometimes I am uplifted into natural cheerfulness without any effort of my own. O! that I may learn obedience from that which I suffer! that "the sword" which hath "entered into my bones" may cut and clear away everything that defileth. I well know that I had need of this discipline: pray for me, that it be not in vain. * * *

11th mo., 19th. I have found myself of late much melted in sorrow. My own demerits are often spread before me, and I ought far more than I do, to lift up the song of gratitude and praise, that, such as I am,—I am "not appointed unto wrath," but freely invited "to obtain salvation through Jesus Christ my Lord."

12th mo., 8th. "He putteth his mouth in the dust and keepeth silence, because he hath borne it (the yoke) upon him." This description is, I trust, in a degree applicable to my experience, during this low and sombre sabbath day! I have uttered a few words in ministry; otherwise, the day has been passed much in silence, and I hope in prostration of soul. I may acknowledge that now, at the approach of night, and in the prospect of a week of peculiarly active, and not very pleasing business, I find such a sabbath strengthening. And oftentimes have I known myself most strengthened in the result, when I have been most clothed, in my own apprehension, with weakness, coldness, and lamentation: a fresh lesson not to depend upon ourselves, but upon him that raiseth the death. Lord, grant that I may have my fruit unto holiness, and the end everlasting life.

The year 1823 was one of peculiar and varied exertion. Besides carefully revising for publication his Letter on the Authority of Christianity, and preparing for the press his work on the Distinguishing Principles of Friends, to which he devoted much time and diligent research; the book which had already occupied him so long, and which ultimately formed the basis of his Essays on Christianity, and the Biblical Notes, still engaged his attention. "I cannot add to my literary labours," he writes to a friend, "for I have already three works on hand." He found time, however, as will be seen, for considerable effort in the Anti-Slavery cause. Some idea may be formed of his home pursuits by the perusal of the following extracts from his literary journal* at this period.

1st mo., 9th, to 1st mo., 19th. Two weeks. Wrote an introductory chapter, (vasto labore et mentis et pennæ,) on universal religious privileges, and four folio pages on oaths. Finished Barclay on Saving Light, also on Oaths and War. Finished Tuke's Principles. Read Jesse Kersey's ditto. Read three or four of Cowper's didactic pieces; half the Life of Dr. Doddridge, and part of Samuel Scott's Diary.

1st mo., 19th, to 1st mo., 26th. A rather ineffectual week; wrote chapter ii, on Religious Peculiarities, only three folio pages; and three more (roughly) of chapter iii, on the Perceptibility of Spiritual Guidance; (I must get on at a greater pace if possible;) finished Doddridge's Life; some of Cecil's Remains.

2nd mo. 2nd, to 2nd mo., 8th. Corrected chapter iii; altered and rewrote part of chapter ii; wrote note and passage on Conscience in chapter i; studied for chapter iv, read original one; read Selden, Hammond, Lightfoot, Rees, Wall, and Robinson on Jewish Baptisms; read R. Barclay on Baptism and the Supper. Finished first Epistle of John, and read second Epistle; proceeded with Cecil's Remains. Epistolæ variæ and accounts.

4th mo., 13th, to 4th mo., 20th. Alterations in chapter ix; researches and reading continued, especially R. Barclay and the "Fathers" for chapters x and xi, and one page and a half written. I must be very diligent for these three weeks, or I shall be foundered. Plato continued: Gibbs on Baptism read. Isaiah, &c. Made speech on Slavery, wrote letters, &c.

11th mo., 9th, to 11th mo., 17th. Finished the Revelation, in Greek Testament; letters, &c.; corrected three sheets of Appendix; read over and reconsidered Letter to a Friend on

* Besides his ordinary journal, Joseph John Gurney was in the habit of keeping in a distinct form a regular account of his reading and literary labours. It extends from about the year 1811 to 1837, when it was interrupted by his journey to America.

Christianity; thought much on the subject, and read Soame Jenyns, J. Scott, Porteus, Doddridge, and Cecil on the Evidencies of Christianity.

To return to his ordinary Journal: —

1*st mo.*, 6*th*, 1823. * * * I find myself still sorrowful; I hope and believe not murmuring. The pains arising out of my bereaved situation are of a very abiding kind. The apostle knew how to abound, and how to suffer need. How needful is such a knowledge, especially for ministers of the gospel! It was my lot to abound yesterday; it is not much less so to suffer need to-day. The waters have passed through me; and, though I trust they have cleansed in their course, they have left me empty and poor. Yet I do not approve of too close a notice of the variations in one's state of mind. We ought rather to think little of ourselves, and steadily to dwell on Christ, who changes not.

2*nd mo.*, 8*th*. The history of the week just passed much resembles that of its forerunner. Some heavy cares connected with temporals, and public affairs very awful and threatening. The rumours of many wars prevalent, and great danger lest this country should become engaged in the conflict. Yet I am not destitute of some sustaining hope that it may please the God of all comfort to stay the desolating sword, and to calm the turbulence of his creatures. This was the substance of a prayer I felt engaged publicly to offer in our morning meeting. I also prayed for the king of this country, that he might be brought into the fear and faith of God, and be prepared by divine grace for the exchange of a mortal crown for one invisible and eternal; also, and more especially, for the universal church of Christ, that, amidst all the courses of providence, and the turmoils of the world, she might flourish, and be more and more filled with love.

* * * * * *

Sweet is the recollection this evening of the *mother** and the *daughter*. Ah, what a world of dreams is this, and shall

*Joseph John Gurney's mother-in-law, Martha Birkbeck, had died a few weeks previously, on the 11th of the 12th month, 1822.

it indeed be succeeded by one of infinite realities? How awful, yet how animating is such a thought.

2nd mo., 15th. I fear I am going but lamely on my way; and have sometimes apprehensions, lest my theological studies should separate me from Him, who is to be worshipped not in the letter but in the spirit.

O gracious Lord, who knowest all the infirmities of the heart of thy servant, and art acquainted with my deep sorrow, and with the dismay which is at times my allotment because of the power of my soul's enemy, may it please thee to arise for my help and deliverance. Keep me from the power of temptation, and shelter me amidst all the storms and anxieties of life. Draw me nearer to thyself, thou everlasting fountain of all good; and, as thou hast been pleased to take away from me my tenderly beloved partner in life, enable me to bow with ready cheerfulness under thy chastening rod; and so quicken and preserve me by thy grace, that I may finally inherit, with her, the joys of thy salvation, through our Lord and Saviour Jesus Christ.

3rd mo., 3rd. The principal features in the past week have been excessive labour in completing my chapter on Baptism and the Supper, and a very pleasant visit from C—— and Lady J. W——. The communication with them was, to me, both profitable and refreshing, and affords a lesson against too great a shutting up of ourselves. Yesterday I rode by myself to Tasburgh meeting, and was comforted in the company of fourteen friends, to whom I had little to administer but encouragement. I felt it very salutary to be taken out of myself. Truly we serve no hard master.

3rd mo., 16th. The last two weeks have floated on much in the usual manner. My book has brought me discouragements, and labours also. Two visits to the sick chamber of my old friend, Joseph Geldart, whose death seems now rapidly approaching. His humility, submission, quietness, and hope in Christ, plainly indicate the latter end of the righteous. He seems polished, purified, and brightened for the last solemn stage of his mortal pilgrimage. * * Other visits to the sick have also been satisfactory.

3rd mo., 28th. I remember being a good deal oppressed, about two weeks ago, under the apprehension, that, through unwatchfulness, and perhaps through study, my gift in the ministry was declining; but it has seldom been brought more thoroughly into exercise, than in the present week. On third day, at the Quarterly Meeting, I felt constrained under the gentle influences of divine love, to preach Christ crucified; and my way opened very satisfactorily as I went along. I thought that I afterwards lost a little ground, in taking too active a part in the discipline—a memorandum this for the Yearly Meeting; one, I trust, which will not be forgotten. The love and unity felt were reviving; and a little fresh hope appears to arise, from time to time, that we shall yet be maintained as a society on the face of the earth.

Anti-slavery operations were now commencing with vigour in various parts of the country. Early in the present year, William Wilberforce had published his Appeal on behalf of the Slaves. About the same time the Anti-slavery Society was formed. "Public feeling," says the editor of the Life of Sir Thomas Fowell Buxton, "was soon roused into activity, and petitions began to flow in; the lead was taken by the Society of Friends, and it was determined that the presentation of their appeal by the hands of Mr. Wilberfore should be the opening of the Parliamentary campaign."* Joseph John Gurney was not inattentive to the occasion. He had met Zachary Macaulay a few weeks before at Keswick, and had but just parted from his brother-in-law Thomas Fowell Buxton, who had been spending some days at Earlham on his way to London. Though pressed with engagements, he consented to explain the present position of the

* Life of Sir T. F. Buxton, p. 127.

question, before a public meeting of his fellow citizens in Norwich.

He afterwards writes:—

Seventh day; (26th of the 4th mo.) Yesterday morning we held our public meeting at Norwich, for petitioning Parliament for the gradual but complete abolition of slavery throughout the British Colonies. It was largely attended. It fell to my lot to lay the subject before the meeting, for which purpose I spoke for about an hour-and-a-half. The meeting was conducted with great spirit and unanimity. I thought it a cause for thankfulness, that the affecting and interesting subject should meet with so many open and zealous hearts, and personally, I am, I trust, thankful at having been favoured with the needful ability to meet the occasion.

In the fifth month, after attending the Yearly Meeting in London, he was engaged in holding religious meetings at several places in Middlesex, Essex, and Suffolk, and in visiting the families of Friends at Saffron Walden and Woodbridge. After an absence of about five weeks, he writes:—

6th mo., 20th. I can acknowledge that my prayer has been abundantly answered. The Lord has been with me, in my going out and in my coming in. He has preserved my best life from destruction or decay. He has poured forth of his Holy Spirit upon me, and again and again has he empowered me to declare his righteousness and his praise in the great congregation. He has also been graciously present with those whom I left behind, preserving them in health, both of body and soul, and the darling children have sweetly flourished under his parent wing. Peace marks my return to this delightful spot, and I feel entirely relieved of my burthen; but over that peace and relief, sorrow and the memory of past happy days still diffuse a tone of deep seriousness and perhaps, in some degree, of melancholy. But I will seek for ability to rejoice in the Lord, and to joy in the God of my salvation. What a year has rolled over my head! and now, though the affecting anniversary is past, the brightness of the sunshine, the beauty of the summer flowers, and the abundant verdure of this place, powerfully recall the period, when nature wore a similar aspect, and when inexpressible sorrow and conflict of soul raged in the midst of that lovely scene. O Lord, bow me in the dust before thee; that, in the utter humiliation of the pride of man, I may be preserved from all murmuring, and may receive ability to adore thy holy name, for all thy unspeakable goodness to me and mine. * * * *

On my arrival at Upton, after a fatiguing journey, on 7th day, (5th mo., 17th,) I was met with the mournful intelligence of Mary Hanbury's * death. Deep was the conflict into which this most touching event was the means of introducing me. I was brought into the very depths with the sufferers, nor did I obtain relief till I had seen them, and poured forth my heart with them in prayer and praise. The funeral at Winchmore Hill, on the following sixth day, was memorably calm; and sweet and heavenly was the influence spread over us. The chief mourners on this touching occasion have been throughout eminently clothed in the protecting armour of their Lord. * * * *

9th mo., 3rd. Last week ——— and ——— were with us. Their visit was interesting. Some discussions on our peculiarities into which we fell were not very pleasant, and brought me into secret conflict of mind. But all was removed, and the power of truth remarkably manifested to our humiliation and instruction, in our meeting on fifth day, which was attended by our whole party. What can be compared with thy wisdom and power, and with the influence of thy Holy Spirit, O Lord!

On first day my dear uncle and I went together to the funeral of a Friend at Tivetshall. It was to me a day of

* The only child of William Allen. Her death occurred but little more than a year after her marriage with Cornelius Hanbury. See Life of William Allen, vol. iii, p. 222, and 348—351.

much trial, and of little comfort; and though I prized a quiet ride with my uncle, I had reason to apprehend I should have been more in my place, in my own meeting. Such mistakes are instructive; they give us a useful warning, and call for closer watchfulness.

From London in the ninth month, he accompanied his sister Elizabeth Fry in a short journey to Bristol, where, as usual, they found much occupation. In allusion to a call on Hannah More, he writes:—

We were delighted with our interview with this extraordinary and excellent person. She is now 78 years old, but most vivacious and productive. Very like Wilberforce. She was greatly pleased at the opportunity of seeing my sister; and we parted after solemn prayer.

Soon after his return he met with an accident by a fall from his horse, which severely bruised his arm and elbow joint. Though much disabled, he did not wholly discontinue his exertions. The feeble tremulousness of the hand-writing in the original, gives an additional interest to the following extract.

9th mo., 29th. I have felt low, chiefly because of the apprehended low estate of the church. But we must wash and anoint, and endeavour to encourage a hopeful view. O that the Lord may arise, and have mercy upon Zion! Why should I doubt his doing so?

John and Sarah Grubb have paid me a highly acceptable visit. How affecting when compared with their former one, when they had so deep a sense of our sufferings to come! They were brought into much feeling of unity with the beloved departed spirit, and expressed an assurance both of her happiness, and of the specialty of the providence which directed the fatal shaft. How entirely do I still feel that the most intimate tie is no more! How impossible that such a loss should be supplied by any other description of human association. Solitude, as to the outward, is now my greatest happiness. It gives the wounded mind leisure, both to know and to bear itself.

TO JONATHAN HUTCHINSON.

Earlham, 10th mo., 14th, 1823.

With a fractured elbow, of which thou mayest probably have heard, I find much difficulty in writing, but I know well how greatly I am in thy debt, and must attempt to *scratch on paper* a fresh testimony of the love I continue to feel for thee. It gives me pain to hear of thy indisposition. Thou art precious to many of us, and we are unwilling to let thee go; but our Heavenly Father knows what is best for us and for his church. He may remove prop after prop; but, thanks be to him, the chief corner Stone can never be taken away. "*The Son abideth ever.*" Did I tell thee how busily I have been engaged during the last twelve months by composing a book on the peculiar views and practices of Friends? I have now sent it to my printer, but suppose it will hardly be published before the second month. I hope it may be of some use to our little Society, "stripped, robbed, and spoiled," as it is, in a spiritual sense. Would that we might once more arise and shine in the brightness of true light, the light of the Lord's countenance! Yet if this be denied, let us cultivate such a disposition as will ever prompt the language, "Not our will, but thine be done." It may be that we have already served our appointed purpose. But I encourage brighter and better hopes. * * *

11*th mo.*, 9*th.* Dined on fifth day with Sir J. Smith, to meet William Roscoe, and was gratified by his zealous and able defence of anti-slavery. I have been since reflecting on the state of the world; the abounding of vice; the slave trade; the cruel murders that have been lately committed;

the obstructions to good; the influence of popery and political despotism, increasing, I fear, rather than diminishing; and I have felt amazed and afflicted. But, through all, the *one thing needful* exists and spreads. The gates of hell shall not prevail against the church of God.

Second day; 17th. Another week floated away, and added to the amount of the reckoning, which I must sooner or later make of my stewardship. Awful thought! Yesterday was one of spiritual fasting, and of very deep humiliation. How earnestly have I desired, that in the use of my gift in the ministry, (which I feel to be very precious to me,) I may be preserved in purity and simplicity, and that the *life* may never be withdrawn from it. I trust I feel an increasing love for the cause, and for him whom I am endeavouring to serve.

12th mo., 1*st.* [In allusion to various religious engagements at Yarmouth;] I have seldom passed through a time of closer exercise, being led deeply to sympathize with the afflicted, and loudly to arouse the careless. The family visiting particularly, I found to be an exercising work of faith, and at times I hardly knew how to proceed in it. Yet the opening which appeared to be afforded me on each successive occasion, was wonderful to myself, and the impressions which I felt in meeting on first day morning, were confirmed and cleared as I went along from family to family. The public meetings were, I trust, favoured with life.

First day night, 12*th mo.,* 28*th.* May the privilege of holy communion with the Father and the Son, through adorable mercy, be my portion more and more, that all my life and works may be thereby sanctified and consecrated. To-day, the Cromer Hall party all at meeting with us. Both meetings very serious times to me. In the morning, I was engaged first in prayer, and afterwards, at some length, on the right preparation for heaven. The cause of righteousness is, I trust, increasingly precious to many of us. May it prosper! saith my soul.

CHAPTER XIII.

1824. ÆT. 36.

VISIT TO FRIENDS AT BURY; AMELIA OPIE; ANTI-SLAVERY SPEECH AT NORWICH; PUBLICATION OF HIS LETTER ON THE AUTHORITY OF CHRISTIANITY, AND OF HIS WORK ON THE DISTINGUISHING VIEWS AND PRACTICES OF FRIENDS.

THE opening of the year 1824, found Joseph John Gurney still busily occupied.

Seventh day, 1*st mo.*, 10*th*, 1824. The week hitherto has been a fagging one; literature, banking, letters, slavery committee. I am going to-day to Ampton, with a view of holding one or two public meetings at Bury; and one for the upper classes is appointed for to-morrow evening.

1*st mo.*, 18*th*. Arrived at Ampton [Lord Calthorpe's] to dinner on 7th day, the 10th; found the Wilberforces, Lady Olivia Sparrow, &c. My engagements at Bury occupied first, second, and sixth days, and consisted of two meetings with Friends, two public meetings, and about seventeen religious visits to the families of Friends. The retrospect of these services is satisfactory.

TO JONATHAN HUTCHINSON.

Earlham, 1st mo., 19th, 1824.

* * The low state of our little church is sometimes cause of secret mourning; but when we are favoured to arrive on the heavenly shores, shall we not find an innumerable host of *true Quakers?* Will there be any worshippers there in the letter, and not in the life? Any prayers and praises uttered out of the immediate influence of the Holy Spirit? Any

ceremonial observances? Any oaths? Any compliments? Any war? A broad negation meets every one of these questions. And surely we may hence derive a confirming evidence that we are not altogether in the wrong. May we patiently persevere to the end, placing our whole confidence in Him, who I believe will not suffer the pure light of truth to be quenched, even within the borders of his church militant. * *

1st mo., 22nd. I never before more entirely appreciated the excellence of our religious principles. They are invaluable. May we cleave closely to them, at the same time that we embrace, in the arms of true love, all who are serving the same Master, though in different ways. It is an inexpressible privilege to be brought into what appears to my apprehension, with great clearness, to be the purest, truest, and most spiritual administration of the Christian system.

The warm and steady friendship which subsisted between Amelia Opie and the various members of the family at Earlham, demands some notice in the present memoir. It was about this time, that after passing through deep mental conflict, she believed it her duty to become more closely united in religious profession with Friends; though her admission into actual membership with them did not take place until the following year, [1825,] a little previously to her father's decease. So remarkable a change could not fail to be watched with great interest by Joseph John Gurney. Known in earlier life as the accomplished daughter of Dr. Alderson, of Norwich, she became in 1798, at the age of twenty-nine, the wife of John Opie, the eminent painter; and soon afterwards entered upon a career of authorship, which, joined to her brilliant powers of conversation, quickly secured for her a distinguished position in a widely extended literary and fashionable circle. Upon her husband's decease in 1807, she returned to Norwich, where she continued to reside during the remainder of her life; though her frequent visits to London enabled her to maintain her former intercourse with the literary and fashionable world, among whom her tales and her poetry were alike popular.

"Admired for her amiability, her talents, and her accomplishments," says Joseph John Gurney, in a short notice of her contained in his Autobiography, "she was received in London at the houses of many of the nobility, and wherever she went she was a welcome guest. But she gradually discovered that all her vanities, her position in the world, and her novel writing, in which her reputation was high, must be laid down at the foot of the cross of Christ. Not satisfied with the forms of the Church of Fngland, or of any class of the Dissenters, she took refuge in the quietness of our silent meetings, which she attended with great assiduity. In the meantime it was evident that Christ himself was becoming her peaceful and permanent home; and by degrees she became thoroughly convinced of the principles of Friends. Her friendship with Priscilla and myself appears to have been one principal means allotted in the order of providence for the working of this change."

Among the letters addressed by Joseph John Gurney to Amelia Opie, two have been preserved among her papers, from which the following extracts can scarcely fail to interest the reader.* They are both dated, it will be observed, in the year 1814.

* The Editor is indebted for these letters to the kindness of Thomas Brightwell, Amelia Opie's executor.

The first opens with an allusion to his brother John's illness.

Norwich, 6th mo., 14th, 1814.

I remember with true pleasure thy affectionate conduct to us all, during the last few months of affliction. Thy sympathy has been like that of a sister, and has been prized by us, I trust, as it ought to be. Thou mayest assure thyself, therefore, that, however thou mayest be engaged in the gay whirlpool of London, thou art not forgotten by thy retired friends at Earlham.

Thy last note is an instructive inmate of my pocket-book, inasmuch as it bespeaks a *tender conscience.* It appears to me that thy mind is particularly alive to the duties of Christian charity, and I would express the desire that the same fear, (shall I call it "godly fear?") may attend thee in all thy communications with *the world.* I will refer thee to two texts. "Pure religion and undefiled before God and the Father is this, to visit the widow and fatherless in their affliction, *and to keep oneself unspotted from the world.*" "Be not conformed to this world, but be ye transformed by the renewing of your mind, that ye may prove what is that good, and acceptable, and perfect will of God." Thou wilt perhaps say that thy friend knows nothing of "the world," misinterprets the meaning of the apostle, and is frightened by the bugbear of a name. There may be some truth in this observation, and I must allow that the world is not idolatrous now as it was then; that we are all alike citizens of "the world;" and that there is no department of it which is not tinctured with evil. But I refer particularly to the fashionable world, of which I am apt to entertain two notions: the first, that there is much in it of *real evil;* the second, that there is much also in it, which, though not evil in itself, yet has a decided tendency to produce forgetfulness of God, and thus to generate evil indirectly. On the other hand, there is little in it, perhaps, which is *positively* good. * * It is my earnest desire for thee and for myself, that we may be redeemed from a *worldly spirit,* and that in our communications with the world, whether fashionable, commercial, or common-place, we may be enabled simply to follow *an unerring guide within us*, which will assuredly inform us, *if we will but wait for direction*, what to touch and what to shrink from; what to follow, and what to eschew. * *

Earlham, 7th mo., 22nd, 1814.

I am sure I had some meaning in my mind, my dear friend, when I requested thee "not to be angry with me" for my last letter. I might indeed use a wrong word, for I really believe thy temper very seldom suffers thee to be angry; but did I not run some risk of being thought impertinent, by addressing something in the shape of advice to one so much older and more experienced than myself? Of one thing I beg thee to assure thyself, that, though more than a month has elapsed since I received thy letter, I have not forgotten thee. Indeed I have often thought of thee; and often secretly wished thee well on thy way to heaven. It is a great favour to feel, and to feel acutely, about our religious state; it is a great favour to be gifted with a devotional spirit; and I heartily rejoice to find how sensitive thy mind is and how lively are its impressions on this subject, of all others the most important. It affords a clear proof that the blessing of God's presence has attended thee; and I doubt not that thou art sensible not only of the consolations of his presence, but of his secret direction to the particulars of thy duty. My chief desire for thee is, that thou mayst be made willing simply and obediently to follow this direction, and to give up everything which the light of truth may, by degrees, point out to thee as inconsistent with the holy will of God. True happiness here or hereafter can consist in nothing, but in conformity with that will. The world has undoubtedly many pleasures to bestow; perhaps no pleasure so great as that of being universally *liked, admired, and flattered;* but it is not in the world, that we are to find that peace "which passeth all understanding." It is striking to observe the essential difference which exists between the pleasures of the world, and the religious happiness of the soul. The temporary nature of the former seems to be proved by their all being conveyed to us through our natural senses; but "eye hath not seen, neither hath ear heard, neither have entered into the heart of man the things which God hath prepared for them that love him." How clearly one sees that the one belongs to our mortal, the other to our immortal part! Thou wilt observe, my dear friend, that I have underscored the words "liked, admired, and flattered." It is because I know that thou art "liked, admired, and flattered;" and unless thou art of a very different composition from myself, I am satisfied it must afford no small temptation to thee, and require on thy part the utmost stretch of thy watchfulness. * * * Wilt thou allow me to quote a few texts? "The path of the just is as the shining light, which shineth more and more unto the perfect day." "Thy word is a lamp unto my feet and a light unto my path. I have sworn and I will perform it, that I will keep thy righteous judgments." "O send forth thy light and thy truth; let them lead me! let them bring me unto thy holy hill, and to thy tabernacles." The "word" to which David refers in the second text cannot mean the *written word*, because the written word, with the exception of the Pentateuch and the first historical books, was not then written. Dost thou not think that the "word of God" in Scripture means generally that by which the truth of God is communicated to the soul; whether by speech, writing, or the secret influence of the Spirit? And dost thou not think that the "word," which David here speaks of, is the very same as is alluded to by John, when he says, "But the anointing which ye have received of him, abideth in you: and ye need not that any man teach you: but as the same anointing teacheth you of all things, and is truth, and is no lie, and even as it hath taught you, ye shall abide in him." May we not trace the same doctrine and principle in the 14th chapter of John? "He that hath my commandments and keepeth them, he it is that loveth me, and he that loveth me shall be loved of my Father, and I will love him and will manifest myself to him." "But the Comforter, which is the Holy Ghost, whom the Father will send in my name, he shall teach you all things, and bring all things to your remembrance whatsoever I have said unto you." "Thus saith the Lord thy Redeemer, the Holy One of Israel; I am the Lord thy God which teacheth thee to profit, which leadeth thee in the way that thou shouldest go. O that thou hadst hearkened unto my commandments! then had thy peace been as a river, and thy righteousness as the waves of the sea." The subject is so interesting that I have multiplied my texts already perhaps too much, and could remultiply them, with a few references to my concordance; but what I have now cited will suffice to show, that there is indeed a spiritual communication between God and the souls of his creatures, which constitutes at once their happiness and their safety. May we be enabled, in our respective situations, to hold fast this blessing, and, by a strict adherence to the dictates of divine truth thus manifested to the mind, may we, my dear friend, "work out our salvation with fear and trembling."

Perhaps thou art now saying to thyself, this is true Quakerism. *Quid mihi refert?* Indeed I had no intention to plead for Quakerism as such, but only for that which must, after all, constitute the practical part of Christianity, (connected as it is with all the other branches of the system,) in whatsoever shape Christianity is to be found.

I see I am involved in an essay which may carry me into my next sheet. Shall I go on, or shall I not? I know thou wilt allow me a few lines more.

Well then, Christianity appears to me to consist of the work which is wrought *for* us, and the work which is wrought *in* us, justification and sanctification. By the one our sins are forgiven, by the other, they are purged away; by the former we are reconciled to God, "who imputeth not our trespasses unto us," by the latter we are made fit for the inheritance prepared for us. I feel some delicacy in making my statement; because I do not know how far the habits and principles of the denomination of Christians,* amongst whom my friend has been educated, may have impressed her with different views. Thou must, therefore, take what I say, as a statement of my own belief; as a proof of intimacy with one for whom, under every possible difference of opinion, I feel the most sincere friendship. Now the two branches of

* The Unitarians.

Christian truth, to which I have referred, are undoubtedly one in design and origin; inseparably and intimately connected; flowing together from the boundless mercy of God, in Christ Jesus our Lord. Yet I have believed, and do still believe that obedience to the will of God, as declared by his Holy Spirit in our souls, is the main thing for us to attend to; because it is not only the means whereby we become sanctified and capable of heaven; but it will bring us to that near and nearer union with our Maker, in which our spiritual understanding becomes enlightened about Christian doctrine in general. By co-operation with the work which is wrought in us, we are effectually made acquainted with the work which has been wrought for us. None are so truly aware of their dependence upon the merits of Christ, as those who obey his precepts. "He that doeth my will shall know of my doctrine." "The secret of the Lord is with them that fear him, and he will show unto them his covenant."

Thou wilt not imagine that I am for superseding the use of means, which are mercifully bestowed upon us by God, and are talents for which we must give account; and I suppose we shall unite in considering that of the means given us, none are more important than the study of the Scriptures. Still it can never *suffice* to cultivate the intellect on this subject, which seems to me much the object of thy friend Bishop Horsley. "No man knoweth the things of a man, save the spirit of man which is in him. Even so the things of God knoweth no man but the Spirit of God."

I need say no more about Horsley; perhaps I am prejudiced about him. Whatever he was, he certainly does not wear the garb of much Christian simplicity and humility. He was not much of a little child. As to Paley, he is pellucidly clear, and of a sound and practical understanding. Still I do not feel when I read him as much as I should wish to feel. Is he sufficiently spiritual? But I am not very greedy of sermons. I think I like Friends' Journals better. I have only one thing to add, which is, that my letter is a great deal better, (little as thou mayest esteem it,) than myself. Again farewell.

In a few stanzas addressed to her in the year

1817, after alluding to some of the excellent points of her character—

"The sympathies that all thy bosom fill,
The charity that speaks and thinks no ill,
The temper, genial as the western breeze,
The haste to help, the watchfulness to please."—

Joseph John Gurney continues:—

"But most I love to mark devotion's flame
Rise from thy bosom in thy Maker's name:
O how I bless the ray of love divine
That first, within thee, taught that flame to shine,
From mists of error drew thy steps away,
And bade thee freely own a Saviour's sway!"

Concluding with the following earnest appeal:—

"And canst thou join the unsubstantial dream,
Where pleasure's idle votaries vainly gleam?
And must thou with the painted crowd, be hurled
Down the gay eddies of a thankless world?
Shall fashion's lure, shall flattery's heartless smile,
Thy higher, better, safer hope beguile?
Ah think again! that Saviour bleeding see;
That thou might'st live to him, he died for thee:
He died to save thee from a world of woe,
Tricked in the flippant pageantry of show.
Though in sweet chime its gilded fetters ring,
Thou know'st its sorrows, *thou* hast felt its sting.
Ah! think again! and from the busy strife,
The gay delusion and the pride of life,
Let Israel's God thy pliant footsteps lead
By the still waters in the verdant mead!
Thine be the spirit willing to obey,
The faithful watching and the narrow way;
Thine be the Christian's daily cross to bear,
His labour and his burden thine to share!
Light is the burden, easy is the yoke,
Rest for thy soul, a meek Redeemer spoke,
Rest for thy soul, and peace without alloy,
And overflowing balm, and everlasting joy."

"Great was the conflict," continues Joseph John Gurney, in his notice of his long valued friend, "when she found nerself constrained to make an open profession of Quakerism. I remember her telling me of the agony of her mind in the view of changing her dress, and of addressing her numerous friends and acquaintances by their plain names, and with the humbling simplicity of 'thee' and 'thou.' But her great Master was with her in this time of need, and with remarkable decision and fortitude, she made the change at once, and openly declared herself a Friend. Seldom has a more striking improvement been wrought in any one who has passed under my notice. Truly may it be said, that her valuable qualities have been sanctified; whilst her play of character has not been lost, but has been rendered more interesting than before. Every one who knows her is aware of her *truthiness*, and appreciates her kindness; and 'Quaker' as she is, and a determined one, she is still sought after by some of her old friends in high station."

"May the Shepherd of Israel," he adds, "be with her to guide, instruct, and comfort her during the remainder of her pilgrimage; and may she be his to all eternity."*

* Amelia Opie died on the 2nd of the 12th month, 1853, at the advanced age of 84. I have retained the concluding paragraph in the above extract in accordance with her own desire, expressed in an interesting correspondence which I had with her in connexion with the present Memoir. The following brief extract from a note then received from her, written in her 82nd year, is strikingly descriptive of the state of her mind towards the close of her long life.

"How I love to repeat those lines—

'Just as I am, without one plea,
But that thy blood was shed for me,
And that thou bid'st me come to thee,
O Lamb of God, I come!'

I am deep in Chalmers's Life, and humbly desire to be enabled to profit by it.'

The Journal proceeds:—

2nd mo., 22nd. Amelia Opie made her appearance to-day in a Friend's dress; her mind being now fully made up to be in all respects a Friend. I thought she had been marvellously helped through her conflicts, and had been a striking example of faithfulness. A song of praise was raised in my heart on her account. May she be preserved to the end!

3d mo., 1st. * * * I have no value for the peculiarities of Friends' *quasi* peculiarities, but solely because I think they are the natural and necessary consequences of what I consider to be the highest and purest standard of Christian truth and worship; and, in holding out the highest and purest standard, as, in my best judgment, I deem it to be, I entertain the humble hope that I may be made of some little use to the flock of Christ, however diversified. Yet the very fact of being thus obliged to dwell for a time on our distinguishing features, ought to be guarded by its antagonist *muscle*—I mean a godly watchfulness to dwell deeply in those fundamental truths of Christianity, in which the whole of that flock is one, and under one Shepherd.

3d mo., 8th. To see Friends prospering in the best sense of the term; to behold a real "growth in the truth" amongst them, together with some little encouragement from convincement, would, indeed, be an inexpressible joy to my soul; but even in these things I must learn to be content with little—very little,—and cast myself on the Lord alone; that in him my soul may rest and be satisfied.

To turn once more to the subject of slavery. Since the anti-slavery meeting at Norwich in the preceding spring, the cause had assumed a different aspect. The debate which had followed the motion then made by Thomas Fowell Buxton, had drawn from the House of Commons certain important resolutions, tending to the amelioration of the condition of the slaves, and the Government had issued a circular letter, founded upon them, to the various colonial authorities.* The steps thus taken at home had exasperated the planters, and, in many of the colonies, "for some weeks after the arrival of the dispatches, not the slightest restraint seems to have been put upon the violence of their rage, which drove them to the wildest designs."† News of the excitement at once chilled the zeal of Government, and it required all the ardour and steady determination of the older abolitionists to maintain their stand. "Even at Norwich," writes Thomas Fowell Buxton to Zachary Macaulay, "our friends were somewhat intimidated." Clarkson, however, had been there and had done his work well. "His address to about forty persons at the Town Hall," says Joseph John Gurney, "was satisfactory and singularly interesting. I was much pleased with the simplicity, constancy, gentleness, and firmness of the man." The crisis was important. The vacillating disposition of Government made it obviously desirable that the hands of the anti-slavery leaders in parliament should, as far as practicable, be strengthened by a demonstration of feeling in the country. Anxious to serve the cause, so far as his influence extended, Joseph John Gurney zealously co-operated with other warm friends in Norwich, in obtaining the appointment of a public meeting in that city, for the purpose of petitioning parliament to support and carry into effect, the late resolutions of the House of Commons. His speech was forcible and effective. It was subsequently published; and, as an example of

* See Life of Sir T. F. Buxton, p. 134. † Idem, p. 137.

his mode of address on such occasions, a somewhat lengthened extract may be here given. After alluding to the resolutions of the House of Commons, and to Lord Bathurst's official despatch to the Colonies founded upon them, he proceeds:—

Were the abolition of slavery a perfectly easy matter, were there no opposition to encounter and no difficulties to surmount, it would be wholly unnecessary for the people to repeat their petitions. We might sit still in the comfortable persuasion that the government would effect the object without unnecessary delay. But what is the real state of the question? How has Lord Bathurst's communication been received? In several of the islands it has been met by a determined, and even furious contradiction. By the legislature of Jamaica, a series of resolutions has been drawn up in opposition to the minister's recommendations, which, were it not almost too ridiculous to imagine, might even be construed as expressing an intention of rebellion against the mother country. * * Among the senators of the colonial legislature, one gentleman in Barbadoes, is pleased to meet the injunctions of our colonial secretary respecting the flogging of women, not only with violent opposition, but with vulgar jokes on the gallantry of Englishmen. Such raillery on a subject of so delicate and affecting a nature, does, I confess, appear to me to be utterly abominable. In the island of Trinidad, a large public meeting of the planters has been held, to pass a series of resolutions, in which they declare that the flogging of women, as well as of men, is indispensably necessary to the good order of the colonies; that it is quite a mistake to suppose that the holding of Sunday markets is any profanation of the sabbath; and that nothing more is needed, with respect to the evidence of slaves, since that evidence is already received, *when it is corroborated by two free men.* The vengeance of West Indians has even been wreaked on the ministers of religion, and the *gentlemen* of Barbadoes have united their forces in demolishing the meeting-house of a methodist missionary, and in forcing him to flee from the island for his life, on account of his supposed connection with "*the villainous African institution.*" And when a proclamation was issued by the governor, offering a reward on the conviction of the offenders, it was received by these gentlemen rioters with nothing but insult and mockery.—Such is the nature of the opposition which renders it so desirable for us to strengthen the hands of Government by our petitions to parliament.

In reference to "the vehement declarations of some of the colonial legislatures, that the benevolent proceedings of Government could not fail to be productive of the most formidable insurrections among the slaves; that the planters would be the martyrs to a heedless philanthropy; and that all the islands would unquestionably overflow with blood;" he remarks:—

Is it kindness? is it benevolence? is it the hope of future relief from hardship, which induces a man to rise up in anger against his neighbour? Certainly not, for these things have no other tendency than to pacify and to please. It is the continuance of oppression, it is the despair of amelioration in the condition of the oppressed, which produces a disposition to rise in arms against the oppressor. * * These observations may serve to exemplify and confirm a very plain principle of which our friend Clarkson reminded us a few nights since, that we ought ever to distinguish between the *occasion* and the *cause* of events. Whatsoever may have been the occasion of the insurrections which have at various times taken place in the West Indies, the *cause* of them is unquestionably to be found in slavery, and in slavery alone. Nor shall we ever get rid of a liability to these frightful disasters, until we are delivered from that unrighteous system, out of which they arise.

Adverting to "the heavy condemnation," by one of the leading periodicals, of the assertion of "that great and good man, William Wilberforce," that the proposition that the condition of the West Indian slaves is fully equal to that of the free peasantry of this country, "is monstrous in itself, and implies a total insensibility to the native feeling and moral dignity of man,"

"Let us," continues Joseph John Gurney, "briefly run through the comparison between the two parties. The slaves, it is said, are clothed, fed, and housed; and we grant that a certain provision of clothing, such as that warm climate requires, is directed by the Colonial law to be given to them,—that they have a small allowance of salt fish, and have provision grounds, which they are permitted to cultivate principally on the sabbath day. In these two points I conceive that the comparison is still to the advantage of the British peasant. The same may certainly be said with reference to habitation, as the huts of the negroes are greatly inferior to English cottages. And with regard to labour, our peasantry would, I presume, be very unwilling to change their condition with that of those unfortunate bondsmen, who not only work like themselves for nine or ten hours during the day, but who, for several months in the year, are compelled to continue their drudgery during half of every night, or the whole of every other night. But let it be conceded for a moment, that in point of clothing, food, housing, and labour, the condition of the West Indian slave and that of the free British peasant are equal. There are still a few other particulars of no very inferior moment, in which a strange difference will be found between the two parties in the comparison. The British peasant settles when he pleases in married life, as easily as any other person, and thenceforward no man may interfere with his domestic comforts. The slave who takes a woman for his companion, is for the most part not married at all. * * But be he married in form or not, his connubial connexion is totally unprotected by law; and the caprice of his master, or the sale by auction of the property of which he forms a part, may at any time tear his wife from his bosom, and separate his helpless children from their parents. The negro works under the stimulus of the lash, and the laws of our colonies bestow upon his master or overseer a full authority for inflicting upon him, his wife, or his daughter, thirty-nine lashes for any fault or misbehaviour. Now I do not know what one of our free peasants would say to such assault and battery, but I rather apprehend that he would be found to rise up in his own defence, and that in no very inefficacious way. Be that as it may, the law is always open to him, just as open as to our worthy chairman himself, or to the king upon his throne. But how is it with the miserable slave? If his master even exceed the prescribed number of his lashes—if he multiply the tens into hundreds—if he absolutely murder him in cold blood, and if there be present ten thousand witnesses; yet, if all those witnesses be slaves like himself, the laws of the colonies afford no effective redress or satisfaction, and the offender may enjoy an *absolute impunity.* * * In short the British peasant is his own master, and a free man. The West Indian slave is a mere chattel. He is reduced to the condition of the beast of burden. He may, it is true, be very kindly treated. He may also be bought, sold, divorced from his wife, separated from his children, worked hard, flogged, tortured, branded with red hot iron, and under particular circumstances, even murdered, according to the arbitrary determination of his fellow men. I may appeal to the whole of this meeting whether it be not indeed true, that the proposition to which I have been alluding is "monstrous, and that it implies a total insensibility to the native feelings and moral dignity of man.

Utterly is it at variance with the dictates of Christianity, that one man should be regarded as the mere chattel of another; utterly at variance with those dictates, that we should compel our fellow creatures to labour for us, and give them no wages for their labour; that we should inflict upon them the cruel punishment of the whip at our own discretion; that we should degrade, expose, and torture, even the female sex; that we should subject whole families to writs of *venditioni exponas*, by which the nearest ties of affection may be forcibly torn asunder; and finally, that we should allow of a system, under which, persons who like ourselves possess immortal souls, are regarded and treated like the beasts that perish. Assuredly, all these particulars are in absolute contradiction to that golden rule—"Do unto others as ye would have others do unto you." * * * While, therefore, I would encourage every disposition to moderation and charity, while I can sincerely declare that no persons connected with the present question appear to me to be so much the objects for deep commiseration as the oppressors themselves, yet I cannot but remember that in grounding our proceedings on the noble principles of the British Constitution, and on the celestial sanctions of Christianity itself, we are standing on a rock which cannot be shaken. I must, therefore, implore our benevolent and energetic Chairman, I must implore our worthy Member for the County, (now present,) I must implore you all, whatever situation you may occupy, never to relax your efforts in this holy cause, but to go forward with a step at once measured and determined, at once gentle and resolute, until that happy day shall arrive when every individual within the whole circuit of the British dominions, shall be able to lift up his head with thankfulness and joy, and say, *Behold I am free.*"

His faith in the ultimate success of the cause was strong, and the formidable opposition that was now aroused against it did not dishearten him. The difficulties from without were at this time increased by a difference of opinion in the anti-slavery councils, as to the course to be pursued in consequence of the altered disposition of Government. Without venturing to advise at a distance upon questions of detail, Joseph John Gurney was one who felt bound to support his brother-in-law in making a decided stand.

A few days before the debate upon the question, in which the latter had determined to attack the vacillating policy of Government, he thus writes to him.*

Norwich, 3rd mo., 10th, 1824.

MY DEAR BROTHER,

I feel much for thee and for our cause in the prospect of the approaching discussion in parliament, and having been enabled to remember both the one and the other in my prayers, I feel inclined to remind thee (however needlessly) of the apostle's injunction, "Quit you like men, be strong." I do not mean to advise against that course of moderation, or rather spirit of moderation, to recommend which I have already been busy; but to administer my feeble encouragement, in the belief that the cause is identified with that which is just, holy, and true; that it has been in the line of thy Christian duty that thou hast undertaken it, and that therefore there is assuredly one, who will "send thee help from his sanctuary, and strengthen thee out of Zion." I am well assured that on this momentous occasion thou art looking for grace to help in time of need, and as this is the case with thee, he will, I believe, be found unto thee "strength and wisdom, tongue and utterance." * * *

* * * I look upon colonial slavery as a monster who must have a very long succession of hard knocks before he will expire. Why should we expect to get his extinction into full train, in less than ten years? * * Public opinion is now, I think, much advancing in our favour. A knowledge of the subject is extending, and with it a great deal of feeling; and all this, in the long run, will tell.

Nor do I think the extravagance of the West Indians, especially where it issues in such abominable injustice as at Demarara, at all unfavourable to our views.

With regard to thyself, as I am fond of thy popularity, I am prone to dislike the contrary; but I have a strong belief that in due time thy history will afford a plain exemplification of the certainty of the divine promise, "Them that honour me, I will honour." Till then, be content to suffer

* Part of this letter has been already printed in the Life of Sir T. F. Buxton, p. 145.

thy portion of persecution, and let no frowns of adversaries, no want of faith, no private feelings of thy own incompetency, either deprive thee of thy spirits or spoil thy speech!

In the spring of this year he published his Letter to a Friend on the Authority of Christianity, already referred to, and soon afterwards his Observations on the Distinguishing Views and Practices of the Society of Friends. The history of the latter work is thus reviewed in the Autobiography.

In the latter part of the [to me] sorrowful summer of 1822, I spent some time quietly at Hunstanton, on the sea coast, with my bereft and beloved mother-in-law. There I commenced the first sketch of my work on the Religious Peculiarities (since called the Distinguishing Views and Practices) of the Society of Friends.

I soon became warmly interested in this undertaking, and pursued the object with the diligence which it required. Here, indeed, I found some refuge from sorrow, and I can say, from my own experience, that the steady and determined occupation of mind in the pursuit of any desirable object, is one of the best alleviations of grief that this world affords. When the work was completed, I took it up to the revising body appointed for the Society, the Morning Meeting.* The principle on which I have acted in reference to this subject has been to publish general views of doctrine, without this check on my own responsibility; but whenever I have written on behalf of the body, then to give Friends the opportunity of revisal; a course which is obviously dictated by common justice. I believe the distinction now drawn is

*The Morning Meeting is a meeting of the ministers and elders among Friends in and about London, which sits monthly; to which manuscripts written by Friends "relating to the Christian principles and practices" of the Society, are recommended to be submitted previously to publication: see Rules of Discipline, p. 170.

fully recognized amongst us; and it is a ground, on either hand, which ought, in my opinion, to be steadily maintained. A committee was appointed by the meeting to revise the work. This committee gave much time to the object, and remarkably interesting and satisfactory to me were the hours which were spent over it. The work finally received the cordial confirmation of the meeting, and, on my return home for the purpose of publishing it, memorable was the flow of peace with which I was mercifully favoured. This seal of peace was the more valuable, as the work, when published, gave offence to some very dear to me, on the ground of its opposing the outward rites of baptism and the supper; or rather of its showing that Friends have good scriptural reasons for disusing them. These were tender points with some of our circle, and though I had handled the subject with much care, I had more than a little to suffer respecting it. Among Friends the work met with an extensive circulation, and the seventh edition, with some important corrections and addenda, was published in 1834. After the experience of many years, I am not aware that I regret anything in the work; much less do I feel at liberty to shrink from those Christian testimonies to the purity and spirituality of the gospel of Christ, which it is intended to develope and defend.

The first chapter of this work contains a brief exposition of the grounds of religious union between the true followers of Christ everywhere. Joseph John Gurney's statement of his views of the universality of divine grace, of the efficacy of the atoning sacrifice of Christ to those who are destitute of the outward knowledge of it, and of the free extension to all men of the love and mercy of their one Father and Creator in heaven, is striking and appropriate; and when he dwells on the peculiar privileges which are common to all true believers, his heart warms with the theme, and he does not repress his longings that "the love which cements together the varied members of the mystical body of Christ may more and more abound; that the barriers which ignorance or prejudice has reared amongst them may be broken through and demolished; that Christians may be enabled increasingly to *strive together* for the hope of the gospel; and that, whilst they individually draw nearer to the Fountain of all good, they may be enabled yet more perfectly to enjoy 'the communion of the Holy Ghost;' to 'keep the unity of the Spirit in the bond of peace.'"*

From these general views he proceeds to the consideration of the Peculiarities of Friends. "The term *peculiarities*," he says, in an explanatory note which ought not to be overlooked, "has been adopted for the sake of convenience and perspicuity, and I conceive it to be accurately descriptive of those opinions and customs which distinguish from other parts of the church any one community of Christians. It is far from my intention, by the use of such a term, to convey the idea that such distinctions are of little practical consequence."† The term as it stood in the title page of the work was afterwards exchanged for another more appropriate, but it is right that the reader should have before him the author's own explanation of it as originally used. The third chapter, on the Perceptible Influence and Guidance of the Spirit of Truth, deserves the attentive perusal of every serious reader. The doctrine involved in it must ever be of the utmost practical importance; as upon its complete acceptance depends, in no small measure, our appreciation

* Page 48, seventh ed. † Page 69.

and enjoyment of "the fulness of the blessing of the gospel of Christ." Joseph John Gurney's belief that the operations of the Holy Spirit upon the soul are "immediate, direct, and perceptible," that "all are furnished with an inward guide or monitor who makes his voice known, and who, if faithfully obeyed and closely followed, will infallibly conduct us into true virtue and happiness,"* a belief which he here explicitly declares and largely insists upon, was to him increasingly precious. And who that has traced his progress in his Journal can doubt but that he now wrote of what he had himself known and experienced, "tasted and handled?" To that large class of professing Christians who are deterred from accepting this truth by the dread of falling into the snares of enthusiasm, his observations on the marks by which the voice of the Holy Spirit are to be discerned from the voice of the stranger may be especially commended.†

In the 4th chapter the reasons which have led the Society of Friends to the disuse of all typical rites in the public worship of God are stated with clearness. In connexion with his own experience, as recorded in his Journal, this chapter is peculiarly interesting, as marking the progress of conviction in his own mind. And they who are willing to admit, (and what serious reader of the New Testament will shrink from the admission?) that Christianity is *an essentially spiritual religion*, can hardly fail to be impressed with the force of the author's conclusions. One remark appears to be especially applicable in the present day.

* Page 76. † See pp. 90—96

"I would suggest," he says, "that the ceremonies which we have been considering, so far from being, like the moral law of God, *universally* salutary, are evidently fraught with no little danger, as occasions by which the deceitful disposition in the human heart is naturally excited, and brought into action. Here our appeal may be made, not only to theory, but to facts; for it is indisputable that the outward rites of baptism and the supper, as observed among the professors of Christianity, have been the means of leading multitudes into gross superstition. How many thousands of persons are there, as every spiritually minded Christian will allow, who place upon these outward rites a reliance which is warranted neither by reason nor by Scripture; and which, so far from bringing them nearer to God, so far from reminding them of Christ, operates in the most palpable manner as a diversion from a true and living faith in their Creator and Redeemer! How often has the ignorant sinner, even in the hour of death, depended on the 'sacrament' of the Lord's supper as upon a saving ordinance! And how many a learned theologian, both ancient and modern, has been found to insist on the dangerous tenet, that the rite of baptism is *regeneration!*" *

The succeeding chapters, "on the nature and character of the Christian Ministry," "on the selection, preparation, and appointment of the ministers of the gospel," on their "pecuniary remuneration," "on the ministry of women," and on "silent worship," will all repay an attentive perusal, as well as those in which the principles of Friends on the important subjects of war and oaths, and upon plainness and simplicity in dress, and the disuse of complimentary language, are stated with much force, clearness, and feeling. In the seventh edition, a chapter was added explanatory of the Christian discipline and internal government

* Page 169.

of the Society. They who peruse the work in a humble, serious spirit, can hardly fail to profit by it. And if the younger members of his own society do not find every difficulty that may suggest itself to their minds fully cleared, they should not forget that in this state of being, and until the eye is opened to see the whole truth in its completeness, the portion which may already be discovered must necessarily appear imperfect, and, in consequence, present difficulties greater or less, according to the extent of such imperfection. Let them carefully weigh not only the difficulties which may appear to them attendant upon the author's conclusions, but also those which necessarily attach to the opposite ones. And above all let them be very faithful to that which they know to be the truth, and never suffer any doubts as to that which they do not yet fully understand, to draw them away from those convictions, which, in moments of serious reflection, when their hearts have been humbled and made tender, have been plainly manifested to them to be *of the Lord.*

CHAPTER XIV.

1824. ÆT. 36—37.

EXTRACTS FROM JOURNAL AND LETTERS; JOURNEY TO THE NORTH OF ENGLAND; LETTERS TO THOMAS FOWELL BUXTON AND LORD SUFFIELD; RETURN HOME; VISIT TO SUFFOLK.

Earlham, 4th mo., 8th, 1824. How probable that this may turn out to be the last volume of my Journal! How little do we know what a day, a month, a year may bring forth! How many are cut off in the midst of their plans of usefulness and service whilst those plans are still immature, or only half executed! I have, certainly, interesting views of usefulness before me, especially in my literary career; and should I be enabled to accomplish them before the thread of life is cut, I shall be thankful. But the Lord only knows what is best for me; best for the church; best for his own cause. May I ever be found believing and submitting. While, however, the day and the strength of life are continued, let me endeavour to labour diligently, remembering the advice of Solomon; "Let thine eyes look right on, and let thine eyelids look straight before thee. Turn not to the right hand nor to the left, and let all thy ways be established."

The Essays on Christianity were now closely engaging his attention. After noticing the kindness of his partners in the Bank, through which he was enabled not unfrequently to devote himself exclusively to this object, he writes:—

4th mo., 19th. I have been closely engaged in writing my essay On Man: not without some painful exercise of mind in reference to parts of the subject. The doctrine of eternal punishment, a doctrine far too explicitly stated in Scripture to admit, in my opinion, of any refutation, has especially dwelt with me; and at times my own hopes have been very considerably clouded. But I have found consolation in endeavouring after an entire submission to the divine will as it relates to myself; and a childlike willingness to receive the truth as it is, without murmuring. * * I can acknowledge that *Christ alone* is the way through whom I can obtain salvation; and am permitted in my inmost spirit to believe, that he *is* my Saviour, and that therefore, notwithstanding every past sin, I shall be forgiven and *live*. May I abide more and more in this only effective and sustaining faith, and may the Lord be pleased to cleanse my inward thoughts and secret motives, and to present me blameless before the throne of his glory. * * I have ventured during the past week to read a little in my beloved departed wife's Journal. It is written in a heavenly spirit, and though it has brought mournful things to my recollection with fresh force, it has administered consolation and instruction.

TO JONATHAN HUTCHINSON.

Norwich, 5th mo., 1st, 1824.

[After alluding to the state of his health.] It is a mercy that the inevitable change is so gradual, and a far greater one to know something of the renewal of the inward, during the decay of the outward man. What could the apostle mean by the "inward man," but that never dying part which holds communion with God, and is formed after the image of his own eternity? How unspeakable the importance of having that never dying part washed white in the blood of the everlasting covenant, and clothed in the perfect righteousness of the Son of God! That it is so with thee, that it ever will be so, I can and do believe; and I heartily desire that as thy hoary head descends towards the grave, thou mayest know every cloud more and more to give way to sunshine, and every note of mourning to the song of thankfulness and praise. I well know that while mortality lasts, the enemy who has the power of it, lasts also, and will continue to buffet and afflict at seasons. Let us humbly bear it; and endeavour always to remember that he is possessed neither of omniscience nor of omnipotence, attributes which do most assuredly belong to the Saviour whom we love and serve, and who is and ever will be, (I humbly trust,) on our side. I am busy preparing for second editions of my works: and have other literary labours in hand. * * Farewell! Excuse the lameness of the effusions of a *banker* on a *market day*.

5th mo., 16*th*. I have passed an interesting time since I last wrote. A pleasant journey by the Day coach, in company with the Sidneys and Francis Cunningham, during which we talked much and read much, brought me to Upton on second day evening, the 4th, where I found all well and happy. Third day, the 5th. Peaceful meeting at Plaistow, delightful again to be sitting beside dearest Elizabeth. I was pleased by a warm and affectionate greeting from dear John Barclay, my partner (alas) in young widowhood. Fourth day. Went to the meeting of the Bible Society at Freemason's Hall. The meeting was very large, admirably conducted, and fraught with high interest. The report, which unfolded many a blessed prospect, was well read by the able new secretary, Andrew Brandram. The speakers were Lords Harrowby, Bexley, Roden, Barham, Teignmouth, Charles Grant, Sir R. H. Inglis, Sir George Rose, Morrison, myself, Wardlaw, John Cunningham, &c. The Earl of Roden detailed, with uncommon feeling, simplicity, and apparent integrity of intention, his own conversion, occasioned, in the first instance, by the attendance of a meeting of the Bible Society. I made a speech of some length, in which I revived the consideration of the main, original principles of the Bible Society; that all Scripture is given by inspiration; that divine truth is to be trusted by itself; and that sectarian distinctions sink into almost nothing, when Christians are engaged in promulgating their common gospel.

Second day, the 11th. To London with Samuel. Meeting of the British and Foreign School Society—Duke of Sussex in the chair. A warming, useful occasion. Buxton spoke capitally, and I followed him on religious instruction, &c. Third day. Meeting at Plaistow. The voice of warning sounded as an alarm. May it have entered the hearts of some! Afterwards, to London to the African Institution Meeting. This, also, was highly interesting, and, on the whole, satisfactory; but many gloomy things were that day reported. The death of Macarthy* particularly, and the dreadful enormous prevalence of the horrid trade in men. I spoke, advancing the proposition, that the true remedy for the slave trade was to be found in the emancipation of the slaves in our own colonies. Buxton drew a capital comparison between the King of France and the King of Madagascar. Fourth day. Returned by Day coach to Norwich. Reading and very fair company rendered the journey agreeable, and I was rather glad of the opportunity of withdrawing my frail mind from the influence of public excitement. Dearest Louisa gave me a good hint when I was with her, chiefly in reference to my works. "Do thy duty, and care not whether people praise or blame—leave it."

Second day morning, [*5th mo.,* *24th.*] It seems to me the leading defect in my religious life, that the course in which I am treading derives its deep interest, (and deeply interesting it assuredly is,) too much from present associations, and too little from future prospects. It is very seldom that I enjoy a tangible, unquestionable sense of the soul's immortal bliss. And yet, at times I have known it, and I trust, through adorable grace and mercy, I shall know it more and more.

Sixth day morning, [*5th mo.,* *29th.*] I can scarcely describe the pleasure which I have felt for some days past, in observing that a work of spiritual religion is really (through adorable and unmerited mercy) going forward among our young people. I have had to notice it to my inexpressible comfort, in several individuals. May the Lord preserve them! May no enemy

* The Governor of Sierra Leone. See Life of William Allen, vol. ii, p. 383.

be permitted to mar the work! May the wilderness still become (as I humbly believe it will) the fruitful field, the garden of roses!

On third day evening I went out for a ride, and the gentle intimations of divine love in the heart, brought me into considerable service. I felt it right to shape my course to ———. There I had an encouraging conversation with ———, and a somewhat powerful opportunity with the poor, struggling, and yet unwilling, mother of the family. May the Shepherd bring her into the fold! Afterwards, I went to see a poor woman in the last stage of a consumption. I found her in a suffering state, but I believe open to the word of the Lord. I ministered the gospel to her; and solemn prayer on her account followed. There was both power and peace to be felt on the occasion, and I subsequently found that she died six hours afterwards in peace.

In allusion to a letter from a valued relative, strongly disapproving of his work on the Distinguishing Principles of Friends, he writes:—

6th mo., 7th. ———'s letter on the subject of my book has been answered deliberately, and with a degree of serenity in which I have felt comfort; and I have been favoured to feel also, after considerable exercise of mind, an increased settlement in the blessed truth, as Friends have been led to hold it. This I can say without judging others; for I do fully believe that grace will be with all them who love the Lord Jesus Christ in sincerity. On the whole, seriousness of mind seems extending itself a little amongst us, which I esteem an unspeakable favour.

TO JONATHAN HUTCHINSON.

Norwich, 6th mo., 30th, 1824.

It seems to be my lot to give satisfaction and dissatisfaction, to pass "through good report and evil report:" and being rather sensitive, I sometimes a little shrink from the touch of man. These observations are suggested by some kind, but very disapproving remarks sent by a valued relative, who views things in a different light from myself, on the subject of my work on Friends' principles: but I should say that from Friends uniformly who have mentioned the subject, and from several others, I have received much encouragement. May I look less and less to man, and more and more to God!

To his sister Elizabeth Fry, who was then at Brighton, in a feeble state of health, he writes:—

Earlham, 7th mo., 2nd, 1824.

My beloved Sister,

* * It has been a matter of painful feeling to me, even selfishly, to have thee brought so low; and now I can equally rejoice in the happy prospect of thy gradual recovery; for I often find myself much alone, without one in my own *home* circle with whom I can fully communicate. * * I had been occupied in perusing some sheets of almost unmixed disapprobation of my book from ———, when thy letter arrived, stating "John Glaisyer's satisfaction in every sentence." I was quite thankful for such a verdict, from one whose judgment I so highly respect; for it is impossible not to be sensible to pain from the decided turn against my authorship, which it has given to a certain small proportion of our own connexions. The ceremony of the supper is certainly as the "apple of the eye," to many in our circle, to a degree which it is difficult to me to comprehend. Should we be favoured to land safely on yon blissful shore, we shall be all Quakers there, requiring no commemorative ordinances; no uninspired ministry; no judicial oaths; no defensive warfare! It appears to me that ours is not what some would make it out to be, a narrow system of human construction, but the absence of system, the natural result of genuine and unmixed Christianity. This is what Quakerism ought to be; and what it is, when the life of truth has full sway with us. However, the occasion which I have lately found to insist so much on our peculiarities, has made me very sensible how needful it is to dwell in that love, which can overflow all obstructions and

distinctions of feeling between party and party, and sect and sect. And yet with the deepest desire to be preserved in this root of harmony, I am much bound in spirit to the promotion of our own cause; and have often, of late, felt constrained to uphold it very boldly in the ministry of the gospel. Is it not, after all, essentially connected with that which is best in the world? * * *

The duodecimo edition of my book, is begun to be printed; and I suppose will appear in about two months. I have a fourth edition also in hand, of the octavo size. The universal approbation of Friends has certainly been very satisfactory; and there are the scattered few amongst others also, whose minds it has remarkably met. Last evening we had a party of Friends, which was pleasant, and ended with a sweet solemnity. Indeed, we have in these parts, cause for thankfulnesss in observing no ambiguous symptoms of a "growth in the truth." Some of our young men especially, have now given in their names; and as a little evidence of it, have become plain in their dress and language. The meetings too, have been sweet and solemn, and well attended. What a mercy this is! Some tangible evidence that we are not forsaken.

7th mo., 2nd. Night. If the Lord appoint me the continuance of that solitary path which I am now treading, often in great loneliness of feeling, may I be more than willing to tread it, and with regard to the darling children, may I be enabled to assist a little in training them up for eternity. * *

I am low at this dark and silent hour, and have no one to whom it is possible for me fully to unfold my heart, except my beloved Lord and Master, whom I trust I have not by any wilful errors greatly offended. I am sometimes favoured with a sense of his love, so that a little hope arises for myself, for Friends, for the church at large. But cannot I say "I am a worm and no man."

In the prospect of religious service in the North of England to which he now believed himself called, he writes,

7th mo., 26th. The week passed in as close and determined occupation as I could well manage, the result of which was the complete clearing off of all business engagements, and the satisfactory finishing (except the notes) of Section 2, Essay 10. To crown the week, I found it necessary to go to Acle on seventh day evening to attend their Bible meeting, in a barn, an effort which I did not regret, as it was a very favoured time. Lord Calthorpe, who had been paying me a visit at Earlham, was our excellent chairman. I value the steadiness and almost nearness of his friendship. Enoch Jacobson, (the Friend from Norway,) again pleasantly with me one day. In the adjournment of the Monthly Meeting on 5th day, I laid open to men and women Friends, my view of holding meetings with Friends in Yorkshire, Durham, Lancashire, Nottinghamshire, and Lincolnshire — an arduous prospect — one which, though of old date, has become more defined within the last few days, and has spread not a little. Yesterday I was furnished with a full certificate, signed by all present, and evidently signed heartily. By this sweet unity of my brethren and sisters, I trust I may be strengthened in the prosecution of my undertaking. * * * The afternoon meeting (on the following first day) was very touching. I spoke on the declaration of Paul, that our citizenship is in heaven; and the flowings of the tenderest Christian love, under which I was enabled, in parting, to set forth the virtue, the unspeakable virtue, of the name of Jesus, brought myself and many others, I believe, to tears.

TO SAMUEL AND ELIZABETH GURNEY.

Norwich, 7th mo., 22nd, 1824.

MY DEAREST BROTHER AND SISTER,

I have quite longed for some communication with you, and sometimes pined over our inevitable separation. I want to enjoy more of a fellowship with you outwardly, in the gospel of our Lord and Saviour. Inwardly I trust we do enjoy it, and increasingly prize it. Mayest thou, my beloved brother, be preserved in a condition of close watchfulness, WITH PRAYER, that the trammels of the world may not hinder the growth of the precious immortal seed, or prevent thy being wholly dedicated to the love, fear, and service of God. The world will have its cares, but we need not imbibe its spirit; and let us henceforth endeavour yet more sedulously to keep our hands clean, perfecting holiness in the fear of the Lord.

The following details of his journey are from his Journal. After describing his progress as far as Wansford, in Northamptonshire, he continues:—

I left Wansford on third day morning, 7th mo., 27th, at half-past five, on the outside of the Edinburgh mail; and an agreeable journey, in the company of a pious, well-informed, and travelled stranger, Dr. Gaultier, with whom I read the Greek Testament and Magee, brought me to Robin Hood's Well, about six miles from Doncaster, in the afternoon; whence I came in a chaise to Ackworth. Many friends had arrived before me, and others were fast collecting. The meeting for worship on fourth day morning was large, and much favoured with what I apprehend to be an immediate divine influence. I had breakfasted very pleasantly at Luke Howard's agreeable villa, and walked thither again in the evening, when, with the family and several other friends, we heard read some of Hannah Kilham's letters,* and had, in a very precious religious opportunity, to remember with close sympathy our distant friends who are toiling for the cause of Christ under a burning sun. O that a true missionary spirit, in accordance with our own principles, may more break forth amongst us!

On fifth day the general committee digested their report [of the examination,] and the whole discussion on it was attended with feelings of satisfaction and I hope thankfulness. Certainly after an absence of four years, I am greatly struck with the real progress and improvement of this most interesting institution. There is in the whole system more of spirit

* Hannah Kilham was at this time engaged in religious labours on the coast of Africa.

and effect; and among the dear children, more of civility, more of piety, more of mind. On reflection, I felt best satisfied to go through the scriptural examination of the whole school. Accordingly sixth day was devoted to the girls, and seventh day to the boys. Both days brought their blessing with them. The girls performed very well on the whole; the upper classes exceedingly well. After their examination, and tea with my dear friend Luke Howard, I returned with him to read with the girls at seven o'clock. The opportunity which followed was indeed an hour of weeping to the dear children. How precious are the tears of softness and contrition!

To examine in succession the five classes of boys on the following day, I found somewhat laborious, though highly interesting and every way encouraging. After tea we settled down to a religious opportunity with them at seven o'clock. I attempted to read to them the eighth of Romans, but explanation became ministry, and I was under the necessity of laying down the book, after reading a very few verses. The little fellows were soon melted; the greater part of them I believe; and there was a precious solemnity over us. I afterwards visited many of the children in bed, and found them very sweet and tender. * * * *

On second day morning, (8th mo., 2nd,) an agreeable ride over a fine, and in parts almost a mountainous country, brought me to Manchester. This was (though I forgot it at the time,) my birthday; and I have now lived somewhat more than thirty-six years. How clearly does this consideration bring home the inadequate fulfilment of my stewardship! In the afternoon proceeded to Stockport, where a very kind reception awaited me at the house of Ollive Sims. George Jones called upon me, and we made arrangements for his republication of my letter on Christianity; and I have since adopted similar measures at Manchester and Liverpool. Elizabeth Robson has also taken it out to America, to be reprinted there; so that Friends appear to have taken up this performance, as well as the work on our principles, warmly and decisively.

After noticing meetings at Stockport and Manchester, he proceeds: —

Before I left [Manchester] I earnestly recommended the formation of an association for promoting moral and Christian order in factories, which I trust will lead to some practical fruit. The object is of the first importance in my view, considering that the great mass of the population is engaged in these factories. A wet ride on the outside of the Liverpool mail, after a warm leave taking with Friends, brought me in the afternoon to Prescot, whence I took a chaise for Knowsley. Lord and Lady Derby gave me a cordial reception. It was their public day; and we had a magnificent dinner in their almost royal new dining room. Our party consisted of Lord and Lady Derby, Lord Stanley, his daughters Louisa and Eleanor, and several others. I endeavoured to give the conversation in the evening something of a religious turn, and read a little to them.

Sixth day was pleasant and interesting. Many hours were spent in Lady Derby's sitting room, in scriptural investigation. The divinity of Christ was our subject; and the conversation and intercourse were highly interesting. I also rode with Lord Derby about the park, and pleaded in vain against cock-fighting, racing, &c. The next morning I felt under a weight of exercise, which seemed as if it could have no vent; but at last opportunity offered for the reading of a psalm, with silence, ministry, and prayer, in Lady Derby's room with herself and her husband. It was an affecting time, and I afterwards parted from them under a sense of reciprocal love. Sarah Benson's carriage came for me, and conveyed me to her son Robert Benson's house of mourning at Linacre, four miles from Liverpool, on the mouth of the Mersey. His dear and excellent wife died after her confinement, a few weeks since, and has left him with four children. I have not often seen a more real mourner. Sarah Benson is a nobly comprehensive person, of deep piety and sound judgment.

First day [at Liverpool] was one of much close exercise, and of some real suffering for the truth. The Friends at the morning meeting numerous; the ministry close and almost severe. I felt myself much a mourner and much "in bonds." These, however, were broken asunder in a large and favoured public meeting in the evening, in which the gospel had free course, and was, I humbly trust, glorified amongst us.

On second day morning we were agreeably surprised by the appearance of the gallant "Canada" coming into the Mersey, her mark being known to Robert Benson, and we had the pleasure of descrying Anna Braithwaite in her, through the telescope. I did not however see her face to face till my return to Linacre at night, when I was much gratified by observing her to be in health, and at ease. Her story respecting America is, in a high degree, interesting and affecting. She seems to have indeed gone forth in the needful hour, to detect the secret places of infidelity, and to proclaim the truth with boldness. I should conceive, from her statements, that divine truth is gradually regaining its ascendency among our transatlantic brethren. On third day morning, the 12th, I breakfasted with the family of the Waterhouses. One of the sons, [Benjamin,] an interesting young man of twenty-two, is now my travelling companion. After breakfast to the prison; very defective; but the women under the kind care of a committee. With them we held a solemn meeting. Then a visit to the beautiful docks. What a wonderful, busy, ingenious, adventurous creature is man! How unlikely that such an one should be created for the mere span of seventy years, and for that only! We dined at James Cropper's, and after a little needful rest, he and I called upon his neighbour and my worthy friend William Roscoe. I asked for silence, and in ministry encouraged him in the continuance of his works of benevolence, and preached to him the gospel of Christ, very shortly, but, I believe, in the *life*. We left him tender and grateful. He is not, I believe, far from the kingdom of God; but oh! the obstructions thrown in the path of men by an unsound or incomplete faith! * * * *

Fifth day; parting opportunity after breakfast with ——; close exercise felt and expressed on his account, that without further delay he might close in with what I believe to be the divine will for him, and become a consistent Friend. How happy should I be to hear of this result! There is much in him greatly to esteem and value. A high integrity of character, and a love for the truth as it is in Jesus.

The Friends met me very generally at their week-day meeting that morning. It was our parting assemblage; and very close and clear was the exercise of mind into which I found myself introduced. * * The love felt after the meeting concluded was almost inexpressible, and it appeared to be mutual. I felt particularly bound to some of the young men. After dining with —— and a religious opportunity in their family, my dear young friend Benjamin Waterhouse and myself, ascended the outside of a crowded stage coach, which conveyed us, with rather a frightful rapidity, to Preston, thirty-two miles. Tired and exhausted, I found a comfortable abode at the house of my kind friends, Ralph and Mary Alderson.

From Preston his course was directed, by way of Lancaster and Settle, to Darlington. Writing to his brother-in-law Thomas Fowell Buxton, after an affectionate remonstrance on the subject of shooting for diversion, he says:—

Settle, 8th mo., 18th, 1824.

* * I do feel an earnest desire that all thy ways may be ordered by the noon-day principles of Christian truth; that thou mayest remember how considerable a degree of questionableness attaches to every path in life, in which *self is not denied;* and that every thing may drop off from thy system of living and action which cannot be done to the glory of God, and in the name of our Lord Jesus. Great confidence in thy Christianity I have long felt, and still feel; and yet I think thy public life affords reasons why a deep, determined, steady, abiding watchfulness and continued religious exercise of mind,

are peculiarly needful. "The whole world (says the apostle) lieth in wickedness," and they whose interests in connexion with it are the strongest, (and I consider thy parliamentary life, however right, a most powerful worldly interest,) have the more need ever to watch and pray, "lest they enter into temptation," lest their standard should become lowered, lest they should slide down-hill. Thy personal religious growth is more connected with the welfare of man and the glory of God, than that of many. With thee not a few deeply interesting objects, (as far as the measure of an individual goes,) appear ready to stand or fall; and I am intimately persuaded that nothing will serve thy purpose, or the purposes which in some degree centre in thee, but *divine grace.* It ought to be the root and spring, and protection of all thy proceedings. It will make its way, where to all other principles the door is shut. It comes from Him, who can and will gradually execute his own gracious designs; and, as for thyself, thou hast in my apprehension, nothing of so much importance to do, as to lie low under the mighty hand of God, that he may sanctify all thy talents, enlarge all thy capacities, direct all thy movements, and preserve the instrument in its true brightness and sharpness, free from the rust of the world, which would soon render it comparatively inefficacious. Pray, therefore, that thou mayest dwell deeply in the root of life, even in Christ Jesus, "the wisdom and the power of God."

At Darlington, besides holding two public meetings, he visited the families of Friends. In allusion to these services, he writes in his Journal:—

The burthen seemed very considerable; but I found it greater than I expected, for my private opportunities were upwards of seventy in number. The week was, of course, a very laborious one; for besides these private visits, (almost all of which were accomplished before the conclusion of the following first day, four only being left till the next morning,) there were the meetings with the Darlington Friends on the following first day morning, and with the public on third day, and again on the following first day evening; and on fifth day, a meeting, a funeral, and several private opportunities at Stockton. The family visiting was, (as it always is,) a peculiarly close labour. Earnestly, however, did I crave divine assistance to divide the word of truth aright; which prayer was the more needed, because I find myself almost constantly led on these occasions, as well as in meetings, to speak to particular states; to enter into feeling for almost every individual, individually. On the whole, I like solitary family visiting best. The visits were generally satisfactory, quite confirming the favourable impressions received in the preceding meetings. Tears almost everywhere, the fruit, in my estimation, of real sensibility, not of sentimentality. In some instances, the work was painfully close and searching, I fully believe rightly so, but I was reproved *in foro conscientiæ*, for mentioning, though in intimacy, a case or two of this sort. A holy discreetness in keeping counsel is, indeed, essential to the Christian minister. * * The concluding meeting with Friends at Darlington, on first day morning, the 29th, was very solemn and affecting. I trust some were *reached* in the heart, to use a quaint but expressive word. I left this interesting and truly flourishing place, (O may it through watchfulness and humility long continue so!) for Durham and Sunderland, on second day, the 30th of the 8th month.

From Darlington, by way of Sunderland and Shields, he proceeded to Newcastle, and thence, by way of Redcar, to Whitby. At Sunderland he writes:—

I held a satisfactory meeting with the young people, among whom (as I have since done at Shields, Newcastle, and Whitby,) I endeavoured to institute an association for reading Friends' books in company, each sex separately, and of course under proper superintendence. I believe a real blessing would attend such little efforts for good.

* * [At Newcastle] on first day, [the 4th of the 9th mo.,] the morning meeting was, I believe, larger than usual. It

was one of close exercise with me. * * I dined afterwards with my dear friend George Richardson, where I met a small party of Friends. He is the individual under whose ministry dearest Priscilla was brought home to Friends, and is a person whose light is shining brightly all around. Would that such more abounded amongst us. Several family visits were paid in the course of second day, through no inconsiderable fatigue. The most interesting was one to David Sutton and his wife, the old man 88, and his wife a complete invalid. There was true life to be felt in their company. After taking tea at our aged Friend Robert Foster's, I held a meeting in the evening with about eighty young people. It lasted two hours and a half, for the life rose into something like dominion, and it was a time of great solemnity. I hope my plan for reading Friends' books will go on among them.

In the afternoon of third day, Margaret and Mary Bragg accompanied me, very pleasantly, to Durham, where a public meeting was appointed. It was not large, and a time of some real lowness and difficulty. It seemed clearly laid upon me to uphold the doctrine of the universal light of Christ in the heart, and to explain our several peculiar religious testimonies. I hope and believe there were individuals present who could receive, perhaps rejoice in the doctrine.

Two days afterwards, the 8th of the 9th month :—

* After a short stormy night, the more so to me from the fracture of a large pane of glass by my bedside through the violence of the wind, I rose a little after four o'clock, and my two young companions having joined me from the inn, we went forward [from Redcar] over a wretched road, a long ride of five hours, to Whitby. The meeting of the Friends there was appointed at half-past ten, and after a hasty meal, we found ourselves seated in it before eleven o'clock. Never scarcely did I feel more entirely oppressed with bodily and mental infirmity, so that entering into religious exercise seemed impossible. But with my gracious Saviour and Leader all things are possible, and I shall not soon forget how I was unexpectedly and

almost suddenly brought into close sympathy with a suffering, afflicted, mournful company of brethren and sisters, for many such, as I afterwards found, there were present, chiefly from outward causes. I ministered to them the sweet oil of consolation, and was also much engaged in endeavouring to arouse, alarm, and bring to Christ the children of the world, who had a name to live but were dead. * * In the evening I met the young people, about thirty; on which occasion, though I greatly felt my own weakness, I believe the necessary help was afforded.

From York, Joseph John Gurney wrote

TO LORD SUFFIELD.

(On the decease of his wife.)*

York, 9th mo., 30th, 1824.

I cannot express, my dear friend, how deeply I have felt interested in the events which have been passing in thy family. I well know the sore distress which must have been thy portion during the time of afflicting suspense, and during the bitter change from hope to hopelessness; and how the whole is summed up by the mournful blank of such a termination of anxiety. But I feel confident that mercy has been richly mingled with the cup of woe. I doubt not but thou hast found that there is, in such scenes, much which tends to satisfy the mind that, in striving after the attainment of vital religion through faith in a Redeemer, we have not been following any cunningly devised fable, but substantial and ever enduring truth. * * *

I cannot help writing freely to thee, my dear and honoured friend. With regard to thyself I cannot but believe that thou hast been strengthened to bow in reverent, holy resignation to the will of thy heavenly Father, and that he has been pleased to administer that precious support by which alone such trials can be rightly endured. Ah! my dear friend, may this severe affliction abundantly yield the peaceable fruits

* See Memoir of Lord Suffield, by Richard Mackenzie Bacon, pp. 202—203.

of righteousness. May it be the means of more entirely weaning thee from a too attractive world, of fixing thy whole heart on God, and of exciting thee to a holy dedication of thyself and of all thy talents to *his* service, who has bought thee with a price, even with the precious price of his own blood. In the path of religion and duty, I can venture to say thy consolations in Christ will abound, and a precious union of spirit will still be felt with her who has (I humbly trust) winged her flight before thee to the realms of light and bliss. * * *

I am almost daily engaged in these parts, chiefly on a visit to the Society of Friends, and expect to be detained a few weeks longer from home. I hope Buxton has been with thee.

I am, my dear friend,
Ever faithfully thine,
J. J. GURNEY.

The remainder of Joseph John Gurney's journey was occupied by engagements similar to those already described at various places in Yorkshire, and the adjacent counties of Lincoln, Nottingham, and Derby.

Earlham, 11th mo., 5th. At most of the larger towns I passed two or three days, and held public meetings very generally, and youth's meetings in many places. Deep and various, I may truly say, were the exercises which I passed through; yet ought I gratefully to acknowledge, that in every place the power of truth seemed to prevail. If the question be asked, "lackedst thou anything?" I can, indeed, humbly answer, "nothing, Lord;" for my merciful Saviour has not failed me, that I am aware of, in a single instance. Sometimes, indeed, the strength given seemed only just equivalent to the need. At other times it was dispensed abundantly and powerfully. My gift has often been searching, dissecting, severe; yet, I trust, always in true love.

On second day morning I returned to this dear place, and

found Rachel and the darling children at home. I have to record with thankfulness the health, sweetness, good behaviour, and general improvement of these little ones. May they ever be the children and followers of the Saviour. His for life, his for eternity. They were overjoyed to meet me; we had been separated fifteen weeks. Dearest Catherine came home to dinner; and Francis and Richenda, Louisa, and her little ones are with us, very delightfully. And yet, in this change, (shadowed as it is by old causes of deep sorrow,) I have, to tell the truth, passed through much lowness. The solitude of my path, as it relates to Friends, was almost overpowering to my spirit on my return, but I am cheerful and happy now. I was truly thankful to find the meeting of yesterday large, and something very precious to be felt with that beloved flock, as if there had been a little growth in grace, an increased settlement in the truth. O that it may be so!

TO A FRIEND.

Earlham, first day night, 11th mo., 7th, 1824.

It is sweet and consoling to me, amidst many discouragements, and some deep trial of mind, on my return home to an allotment which is, in some very important respects, solitary, to think of thee; and to dwell on the happy prospect of thy becoming more entirely united with Friends. Thou knowest my opinion of "plainness of speech and apparel." It is my deliberate conviction that it is a good testimony, founded on true gospel principles, and that, however familiar and universal the contrary may have become, Friends are truly bound not to sacrifice one jot or tittle of that testimony. I am pleading for no form, but for that which I thoroughly believe to be a fruit of the Spirit of Christ; and I am certainly anxious that nothing should prevent thy acceding to it; not only because I am persuaded it is a branch of our duty, but because I well know that in thy case, as in that of many others, it is likely to be a little door to a wide field—a little link on which a great chain will hang. What would have become of my dear sister Fry's labours, had she resisted the early call of duty, and reasoned away the required sacrifice?

Let me earnestly invite thee to make this a subject of prayer, and to refrain from any farther reasoning or speculation respecting it. Follow the Shepherd's voice with childlike simplicity. Ours must be a life of faith; and we must sometimes suffer our gracious Lord and Master to lead us for a season as the "blind, in ways which we knew not, and in paths which we have not known." He is powerfully alluring thee into "the wilderness." Follow him closely. Cleave to thy holy guide, who hath loved thee and given himself for thee. He will give thee thy rich and pleasant vineyards from thence, and the valley of Achor—of deep humiliation—for a door both of hope and of usefulness, which no man shall ever shut.

11th mo., 12th. Yesterday at our Monthly Meeting I delivered in my certificate, and had to acknowledge the kindness and mercy of Israel's Shepherd who was with me in the way, guiding me and helping me; also the peace I felt in the humble belief that I had not been out of my right place. I added a few words on the evident gathering of the people in many places to Christ: and on the great importance that Friends should bear all their testimonies consistently in the sight of the world. I felt much true peace afterwards. In the evening I began to re-read Butler, with pleasure.

This morning, I have been conversing with dearest Rachel, who thinks me a little disjointed from home associations, and has her jealousies respecting my course. Her cautions have often been useful and salutary to me. May I be preserved in close watchfulness against all the wiles of the enemy!

O my dearest Lord and Saviour, who art my only refuge and way to the Father, in this often dark and cloudy world, permit me at this time to cast myself at thy feet, and to crave thy gracious aid and protection. Make thy way straight before me. Defend me, I humbly beseech thee, from the wiles of the enemy of souls, who is ever ready to play upon the deep deceitfulness of the human heart. Let him not mislead me, I reverently pray thee; but be thou my prophet, my priest, and my teacher, my guide and my comforter in all my ways, words, and works. I humbly thank thee for the knowledge of thy truth, and for the hopes of eternity: and grant, I beseech thee, that I may be strengthened of thy grace for the performance of my daily duty; and that I may more abound in pure, unfeigned, uninterrupted love towards all who love and serve thee. Let me ever maintain my footing on the only sure foundation. Let me be kept in the valley of real humiliation. Let me ever adhere to the sobriety and simplicity of thy most holy truth: and since thou hast seen meet to intrust thy unworthy servant with a gift in the ministry, let it be preserved, I pray thee, deep, clear, sound, wholesome, to my own peace, to the good of others, and to thy glory!

Second day morning, 11*th mo.*, 15*th.* * * * Yesterday was a very peaceful and even consoling Sabbath day. Both the meetings large, and both meat and drink to the soul. Ah! may it please our gracious Master to gather our flock in this place more entirely to himself, and to draw others into the enjoyment of this peculiarly sweet and salutary rest. Surely the work of convincement must in the end go forward. For what, after all, can be compared to the preciousness of that principle, which truly leads into the silence of all flesh before the Lord Jehovah?

First day night. Conflict of mind, the secret buffeting of the enemy, a strange mixture of unaccountable bitters in my cup, continued to be my portion, till last night, in a very considerable degree; but, all, it may be, was no more than a needful preparation for the blessed hope and elevation, the sweet peace and flowing comfort of the day which is now brought to its conclusion. "Bless the Lord, O my soul, and all that is within me, bless his holy name!"

12*th mo.*, 17*th.* Yesterday I heard of the instantaneous and easy death, (after a few days' indisposition,) of my beloved and truly honoured friend, Samuel Alexander, aged 75. I have often said of late, that I scarcely knew any one who so much corresponded with my idea of Christian perfection as this dear friend. I had a peculiar reverence for him, the more so because of his deep humility, for self was of no reputation with him. In such a case as his, I am inclined to think that sudden dissolution may be esteemed a real blessing. But O the necessity of being ready at a moment!

12th mo., 30th. My religious principles are likely to be put (I mean in my own mind) to rather a severe test, by the reviews which are now rapidly coming out of my work. How can I expect that the world, or the church at large, will do otherwise than frown, at present, on the peculiar tenets of our little sect? Yet I may, I think, with humility and gratitude confess, that, after much conflict from fears and doubts which are very apt to assail me, I am permitted time after time, to find rest in the persuasion, that the truth, as we have been taught to hold it, (without any disparagement of others in their own place,) is, "the truth as it is in Jesus." And never am I so sensible of this satisfaction, as when my soul, in the hours of public worship, is gathered into deep quietness and solemnity before God.

CHAPTER XV.

1825. ÆT. 37—38.

EXTRACTS FROM JOURNAL; LETTER FROM WILLIAM WILBERFORCE ON HIS RETIREMENT FROM PARLIAMENT; VISIT TO LINCOLNSHIRE; ALFRED CORDER; YEARLY MEETING; COUNTY MEETING ON SLAVERY; PUBLICATION OF HIS ESSAYS ON CHRISTIANITY.

THE year 1825 was spent by Joseph John Gurney mostly at home. The Journal of this period derives its interest more from the value of the experience which it unfolds, and the reflections which are here and there scattered through it, than from the newness or variety of the incidents recorded. Not a few will read with an additional interest the numerous and emphatic allusions made by Joseph John Gurney to the peculiar principles of his own religious society, whilst they recollect that he was now deeply engaged in the completion of his Essays on Christianity.

1*st mo.*, 30*th.* The past week has been exceedingly full. Earl B——— here two days. I hope the right standard has been in some degree maintained.

A considerable weight of discouragement has been my companion with regard to our religious society. I am sometimes laden with mournful apprehensions that it is decaying and withering away; and that this "good thing," as I apprehend it to be, should after a season be no more seen on the earth. Perhaps there is nothing which requires so deep a submission of soul to the divine will, as a point of this description. Yet how obviously incumbent upon us it is to bow very low before the Lord our God, and in every thing to breathe the language "Thy will be done." Sometimes brighter hopes arise, and the strong persuasion that the thing *is* good, and calculated in an eminent degree to promote the glory of God, gives rise to the belief that it will yet take root, and again in due time spread among men.

2nd mo., 6th. I have been much engaged in "overseership" with some individuals. One case has interested me rather anxiously. It is that of a young woman, who I believe would do well in adopting the language and simple dress of the Friend. Such examples are wanted amongst us, yet we have need of long patience. The power of an endless life is the great thing to aim at; which I believe is much promoted by obedience in the day of small things; and I humbly trust more of this power will, in the end, be manifested within our peaceful borders. "I will raise up the tabernacle of David that is fallen, and close up the breaches thereof, and I will raise up his ruins, and I will build it as in days of old."* I cannot doubt that this prophecy is being accomplished, and will be accomplished in the Christian church; and it appears to me to involve the ultimate growth and establishment of those spiritual and unsophisticated principles which our Society professes. But the Lord only knows his own wise and gracious designs.

Early in this year William Wilberforce retired from parliament. On this occasion he addressed to Joseph John Gurney the following "brief but expressive note."†

Near Uxbridge, Feb. 8th, 1825.

MY DEAR FRIEND,

If I do not deceive myself, you will be rather glad than sorry to hear that I have determined to retire from the House of Commons. My physician's advice

* Amos ix, 11.

† From the Familiar Sketch of William Wilberforce. Minor Works, vol. ii, p. 243.

was such as, all circumstances taken into account, led me to believe it to be my duty so to do; and an event so interesting to me, I do not like you to hear from rumour or the newspapers. I scarcely need assure you that I trust I shall not be less occupied, though I may be less *noisy* than heretofore. Were it not for the weakness of my eyes, I should be strongly tempted to pour forth the train of thoughts which is rising in my bosom; but I must check myself and say farewell, my dear friend. I hope you and yours are in good health, and that you are blessed with that peace which I know you prefer to all earthly enjoyments.

May you be favoured with a long course of usefulness and comfort in this life, if it be the will of God, and may you at length be an abundant partaker of those pleasures which will be infinite in degree, and eternal in continuance.

I am ever

Your sincere and affectionate friend,

W. WILBERFORCE.

2nd mo., 14*th.* I have been a good deal struck and affected with the extraordinary want of spiritual apprehension which appears to me to be evinced by the reviews of my work on Friends, in religious publications. How is it that the religious world refuses its sanction so entirely to *practical* principles, especially as it relates to the ministry and the guidance of the Holy Spirit, which I may say, we *know* to be true? Lord, send forth *thy* light and *thy* truth! What is man without them?

2nd mo., 27*th.* The present day has been one of very close exercise of mind. The former part of it occupied by a journey with two Friends to North Walsham. There we attended the meeting for worship, and the preparative meeting, in which the queries were answered; the whole of which was satisfactory. We returned to Norwich to tea, and at seven o'clock were seated in the Goat Lane meeting house, in pursuance of the appointment of a public meeting, to which the gentry were, in my name, specially invited. Notwithstanding the weather, many were there; and after much deep exercise of mind, all has again ended well. The truths of Christianity were plainly declared to a very mixed, a very attentive, and a very reflecting congregation. "Without faith it is impossible to please God." I felt much relieved, and very full of love towards all, when the meeting was over. How ought my spirit to overflow with humble gratitude to that most Gracious Being, who has never yet failed me in the needful hour!

I wish solemnly to record my full and clear apprehension (much sealed on my spirit this week,) that, when unassisted by the Spirit of truth, I am, as to every religious work, dry and unprofitable. God alone is sufficient for these things. *The unction is everything.* May I not then heartily subscribe to the inspired exclamation, "Not unto us, not unto us, O Lord, but unto thy name be the glory!"

4th mo., 8th. My time and mind have been much occupied since first day. Some successful operation on the book: discussions relative to business, involving no little feeling and thought. Emma O'Brien's visit, with Augustus and Angelina and Julia Noel. They came on fourth day morning, and proceeded with me to Aylsham, where we held a good meeting of the Bible Society. Our meeting [for worship] yesterday was attended by our guests, and was very touching and solemn. O that the mental eye of more of the Lord's children might, through grace, be opened to behold more clearly the excellence of such a mode of worship, and of the principles of Friends in general! They increasingly appear to me to be very, very precious.

Sixth day morning. I have just parted from my interesting guests, after a solemn reviving time of religious intercourse and prayer. O the sweetness of the heavenly oil! How well worth waiting for; how well worth being a fool for! And truly it is not to be obtained in man's will, or at man's time. It is poured forth when the Master pleases; and happy those ministers of gospel truth, who are, in any degree, favoured to know when to speak, and when to be silent!

4th mo., 18th. The past week has been very busy; and in it I have satisfactorily finished my whole Essay on "Redemption." The Monthly Meeting on fifth day was deeply interesting. I laid before Friends my prospect [of religious service] in Lincolnshire; and the applications for membership afterwards brought great solemnity over the meeting. It is reviving to *gather*, instead of scattering. * * I am clearing off to-day. To-morrow I expect to be on the wing for Lincolnshire. May the Shepherd of the flock graciously condescend to be my helper and guide.

5th mo., 4th. My course was Wisbech, Gedney, Spalding, Boston, Leak, Wainfleet, Holbeach, Gedney again, Long Sutton, Wisbech again, Downham; and throughout I was much assisted by my dear and sympathizing companion, Alfred Corder. How delightful it is to me to see a young man so prepared and anointed for the Lord! * At all the above-mentioned places I held public meetings, some of which were very arduous times. In others there was an easier flow, and a quicker entrance for the word of life; in all considerable, in some profound solemnity. The Friends are a scattered few, but my meetings with them were generally much favoured; and, on the whole, a hope has been felt, that the precious principles we profess, and which in some of the public meetings I felt a full liberty to unfold, will yet be maintained in these districts. I was much pleased with green rural Gedney; and dear Jonathan Hutchinson, though infirm, was, as usual, a highly interesting and truly paternal companion.

* Joseph John Gurney had soon afterwards to record the early removal of this promising young man. With his usual affectionate warmth and simplicity, he thus briefly notices the circumstance in the Autobiography. "The autumn of 1825, is marked in my remembrance by the death of Alfred Corder, a young Friend who had resided at Ipswich, and who travelled with me in Lincolnshire, &c. He was the son of a farmer, and an ironmonger by trade, but nature and grace had, as it were, conspired in polishing him, and his mind was one of peculiar sensitiveness and refinement. Seldom have I known any one who more excited the lively affection of his friends, and for my own part I loved him as a brother. Little adapted to the rigours of this rough world, he bore his living testimony in our religious meetings; and soon afterwards, to the inexpressible grief of his friends, sickened and died."

5th mo., 13th. After a somewhat disturbed night, I find myself languid and spiritually poor. But how good it is for us to be brought and kept low! We are not capable here of continued spiritual elevation.

I have been sauntering in the meadows this fine morning with my tenderly beloved children: they are truly very sweet and precious. O may the Shepherd of Israel keep these tender lambs in his own bosom.

TO HENRY BRADY.

Earlham, 6th mo., 9th, 1825.

* * I have been often led of late to reflect on the very strong encouragement held out to us in Scripture to pray for the Holy Spirit. I wish to be more diligent myself, and to encourage those I love to greater diligence in this duty. The Holy Spirit can yet do wonders for us, in consoling amidst sorrow, in cleansing from sin, in anointing for service. May the gift of grace be thine, my dear friend, in all these respects.

I never, I think, felt more thoroughly persuaded of the importance of your labours in the religious instruction of the children at Ackworth. The late Yearly Meeting evidently showed forth the fruits of the Society's increased care in this respect. Such a hopeful rising generation I think I never before witnessed; and many Friends who had attended twenty or thirty Yearly Meetings or more, have borne a similar testimony. The arising of the power of divine life from meeting to meeting was most cheering and animating. My dear sister Elizabeth Fry and myself held a youth's meeting; an evening being appointed by the Yearly Meeting for the purpose. It was a noble assemblage: I suppose nearly two thousand were present, and some hundreds, it was said, could find no entrance. I trust it was a time of instruction and gathering to them, as it was of the deepest exercise to us. * *

I have been holding several meetings since the Yearly Meeting, chiefly in Suffolk. There are many symptoms, I trust, abroad that the truth is making progress, and this ought to cheer our hearts. And though I suppose we are never likely to be a great multitude, yet I feel much hope that we shall in due season be a strong and lively, if not a numerous body.

I returned home to the funeral of my beloved aunt Gurney, at Keswick. She has long been declining, and of late rapidly so, and made a very peaceful close. She was a true Dorcas, and *lowly in spirit.*

TO ANNA GURNEY.

London, 6th mo., 4th, 1825.

MY DEAREST ANNA,

On arriving at Plashet yesterday evening, I received the deeply affecting tidings of my beloved aunt's decease. And yet what can I say when I reflect on the peacefulness of her exit, and on her calm and exemplary reliance on the unconquerable Captain of Salvation. I must, and I do rejoice in such a close of such a life; a life much chequered with sorrows and cares, though on the whole one of much happiness, and certainly one of no common humility, patience, and virtue.

TO HIS BROTHER AND SISTER BUXTON.

Earlham, 6th mo., 13th, 1825.

I have enjoyed returning to this delicious place, more, peaceful and sweet I am ready to think than ever, and hope soon to resume my usual *stroke* of work. * * I am not I trust, disposed to dwell on sorrow, or in any respect to turn sweet sunshine into gloom. Let us rather dwell on the hopes of the gospel, and on the joys of eternity. Let us take a little hope and courage in the name of our Lord; and press forward with alacrity towards that better country where there is no sorrow, nor sickness, nor sin, nor *slavery.*

6th mo., 24th. George Withy and Mary Alexander were with us on first day. In the evening, at George Withy's request, we held a public meeting. It was full and very *capital.* O that the truth may spread; the original, unsophisticated, unsectarianized truth as it is in Jesus. Yesterday our flock met, with little exception; George Withy being with us; he was very singular, very close, and very powerful; and I think made no small impression. A large party of young men from Norwich breakfasted here a few mornings since. There is much hope to be felt respecting them; and some of the more faithful ones are evidently advanced in their career.

Having returned home after attending the General Meeting at Ackworth, he writes:—

Second day morning, [*8th mo.*, *8th.*] How much humbled ought we to be under the sense of the Lord's unmerited mercies, always remembering that all that we possess of either natural or spiritual talent, we have received; and what is more have to account for, before the judgment seat of Christ.

O most merciful Father, the creator and governor of all things, suffer one of the most unworthy of thy children, who is often secretly buffeted and tempted by his soul's enemy, to draw near to thee for help, strength, and deliverance. Let thy holy baptism again and again pass through me and over me, until all is subdued and purified. Continue, if it please thee, to anoint me abundantly with the oil of thy kingdom, that I may preach thy word instantly; that I may avail myself of all right opportunities for the promotion of thy precious cause of truth and righteousness. Be mercifully pleased so to regulate my temporal circumstances, that I may be set more at liberty to serve thee; yea, to dedicate myself unto thee as a Priest and a Levite. Enable me to complete my present work, I humbly and reverently beseech thee; and bless it largely to the increase of thy true church, and to the glory of thine own great name. O my God and Saviour, suffer not my faith to fail. Be all in all unto me, the fulness of strength, joy, and peace. Cover all my transgressions. Let me rejoice daily in wearing the spotless robe of the righteousness of Jesus. Bless my darling children from their early youth upwards. Let them always be thy children. Let them be deniers of self, cross-bearers; willing, persevering, diligent, fruitful followers of thy Son Jesus Christ, to whom with thee and the Holy Spirit, one God, all-wise, all-merciful, eternal, be addressed for ever from my prostrate soul, the melody of honour, glory, power, and praise! Amen!

8th mo., 18*th*. On fourth day we finally arranged those matters of business which have been for some time past so weighty, sometimes so oppressive to me. This settlement has afforded me that peculiarly sweet feeling of peace which I know to be indicative of the Master's signet. Often have these word run through my mind — "*In his quidem hæc mihi ambitio est, mi Jesu, vacare tibi.*"

FROM JONATHAN HUTCHINSON.

Selby, 8th mo., 22nd, 1825.

I was last evening much comforted and encouraged by hearing my son read in his family, the first six chapters in the 2nd of Corinthians. What love and sympathy at this distance of time we sometimes feel for eminent Scripture characters! I think mine runs the strongest toward Paul and David, always reserving an unmeasured and indescribable portion for the once suffering, now glorified Redeemer; to whom, with the Father, be all honour, thanksgiving, and praise, in time, and in eternity!

A short visit in the early part of the ninth month to his friend William Forster, on his return from America, scarcely interrupted his varied pressing home occupations.

"It is no time for idleness," he writes to Jonathan Hutchinson,* "I am deeply engaged in many things, as usual. Just now I am publishing my Essays, which is a considerable effort. Next week we are to have a County Meeting on Slavery. We have had a great, and I hope, good Bible Meeting already.

* Under date 10th mo., 12th.

But what, after all, is so truly exercising as the duty of the *Christian Minister?* Indeed, I find it to be so.

Second day afternoon, 10th mo., 10th. Yesterday was one of inexpressibly deep exercise to me. In the morning I was long engaged on the great prophecy in Isaiah ii, and was unexpectedly led to dwell on the views of Friends respecting the true nature of worship, types, &c. The same strain in prayer—that the great Anti-type might be over all types, and his power over all forms. It certainly was very confirming to myself to be thus powerfully led on this subject. Sweet time between meetings, at the hospital with two poor men.

10th mo., 17th. Yesterday was spent away from Norwich. After some uneasiness about our own flock, and some notion that I might hold a public meeting in the evening, I felt quieted in the belief that I might leave Norwich, and all its concerns, to the Master; and I wish to record it, that on this and other occasions, I have felt quite as much peace in abstaining from services, suggested by my own zeal and natural ardour in pursuit of the great object, as I have felt at other times in a faithful performance of that which he really requires. Let me take the lesson deeply home!

My dear uncle and myself passed the morning in attending Wymondham meeting, and in fulfilling our commission respecting a visit to the tithe-payers. The day was satisfactory.

10th mo., 24th. Since I last wrote, I have been, as it were, flooded by a rapid current of interest, chiefly in the Slavery concern, which, with the party at Earlham connected with it, occupied fourth, fifth, and part of sixth day. The party staying here consisted of Lord and Lady William Bentinck, Lord Gosford, Lord Calthorpe, the Lushingtons, Buxtons, Hoares, Hankinsons, &c. It was particularly satisfactory, pleasant, and useful, without undue excitation; and, through preserving favour, I did not feel dislocated from my usual condition. The readings on fifth and sixth day mornings were attended by all the party, and were very solemn and reviving. The holy oil was poured forth for our instruction and refreshment—a favour for which I cannot be sufficiently thankful; and O, that under such mercies, self may be kept prostrate in the dust!

The Anti-slavery County Meeting on fifth day, was all that could be desired, and far better than we had reason to expect. It was a flowing and interesting occasion, rendered more especially so by Buxton's entire success. I hope the impression produced will be found abiding, and productive of important results. We dined afterwards—upwards of fifty; a delightful party; quiet, orderly, happy, entertaining. On the whole, I have great reason to value the friendship of these persons, whom I believe I have never gone out of my way to meet.

It was at the close of this year that he published the elaborate work, in which, under the title of Essays on Christianity, he has embodied, in a condensed form, the result of the meditation and research of many years. With singular perspicuity of arrangement he here unfolds the evidences and fundamental doctrines of the Christian religion; dwelling with peculiar force upon the great truths of redemption, more especially upon the glorious offices and divine character and perfections of the Redeemer, and the being, power, and work of the Holy Spirit. The tenth essay, in which the scriptural argument in proof of the Deity of Christ is carefully and powerfully stated, contains the substance of the more extended unpublished work upon the subject, which, as has been already noticed, he had commenced so early as the year 1815. The whole is enforced as well by a continued reference to the practical object and tendency of all Christian truth, as by a particular essay devoted to the important subjects of "faith" and "obedience," in which the reasonableness and necessity of their combined and harmonious exercise are strikingly exhibited.

Deeply sensible of the mysterious, and, to use his own expression in his Journal,* "unembraceable" character of many of the subjects treated of, it was his desire to keep strictly within the limits of that which has been revealed respecting them.

"I wish to remark," he writes in his Autobiography, "that throughout this work, as far as relates to doctrine, I profess nothing more than to present a clear arrangement of Scripture evidence. To attempt to be 'wise above that which is written,' must surely be esteemed one of the greatest of follies.† May I ever be preserved from it; and, in dependence on the enlightening and guiding influence of the Holy Spirit, may I be enabled both to understand and apply Scripture with 'simplicity and godly sincerity,' which may be said to be, under Christ, the keepers of the true key to its hidden treasures."

The whole work breathes the spirit of one whose heart is warmed and animated by the love of Christ. Taught as he had been in the school of experience, and strengthened, in no small measure, to consecrate his faculties to the service of his Divine Master, he was enabled in this volume, and often with singular success, to employ his extensive acquaintance with the original languages of Scripture, as well as with Jewish and Rabbinical learning, and the remains of early Christian antiquity, in throwing a clear and steady light upon the momentous topics of which he treats. Indeed it may be said, without disparagement to the many other valuable treatises

* Under date 3rd mo., 15th, 1825.

† A similar remark occurs in the Preface to the Essays.

extant upon these subjects, that it would be difficult to find a volume in which so much sound and important information is digested in so small a compass, and in so useful and practical a form, as in that now under consideration. Notwithstanding the sound scholarship, apparent in almost every page, the style is clear, and adapted to the merely English reader; whilst the diligent student of the Hebrew and Greek Scriptures, can hardly fail to derive instruction from the many incidental explanations, scattered throughout the work, of obscure or difficult passages.

Amidst his numerous other avocations, and his frequent interruptions from company, much steady perseverance was necessary to the completion of such a work.

"To wind up the mind to the effort of writing," he remarks in his Journal in allusion to it,* "is one of the difficulties of my course of life. But," he adds, "as my object is the promotion of truth and righteousness, I believe I may rightly pray, that the Lord would send me 'help from his sanctuary, and strengthen me out of Zion;' and if I should succeed in this important and interesting undertaking, may I be preserved from seeking the least praise for myself, but give the glory where alone it is due!"

It was in the same spirit that it was brought to a conclusion.

"To finish it," he writes, under date 12th mo., 5th, "after the long labour and thought bestowed upon it, was strange to my feelings, with an intermixture of awfulness. I trust I was enabled to pray that the divine blessing might rest upon the undertaking."

* Under date 6th mo., 27th, 1825.

The work, upon its publication, was very favourably received, and has since passed through numerous editions.* In a few warm but expressive lines, the Bishop of Norwich assured Joseph John Gurney of "the high opinion which he entertained" respecting it; and from his brother-in-law Thomas Fowell Buxton he learned the satisfaction which it had given to the Duke of Gloucester. "I read it," said the Duke, "over, and over, and over again." His old tutor John Rogers wrote with a warmth that may be excused towards a favourite pupil:—

In the composition of these essays, you have discovered an intimate acquaintance with the subject on which you treat; you have shown that your mind is impressed with a full sense of its importance, and that it has occupied your most serious thoughts; you have displayed a great knowledge of the original languages, in which the old and the new covenants were written, as well as of the Jewish and Christian antiquities; you have conducted your work in a regular and perspicuous method; and, (what gives it the greatest value,) you have evinced, in general, that excellent temper, and that Christian spirit, which ought always to characterize writings of this nature.

FROM ROBERT SOUTHEY.

Keswick, 4th January, 1826.

I have gone through your volume, with wonder as well as satisfaction, and I hope not without profiting by it. It would have been a surprising book from one who had been bred to the profession of divinity, and pursued the study with ardour during a long life. The evidence is full and complete, the

*It has been re-published in America, and has been translated into German and Spanish. It has also been lately published in a cheap form by the Religious Tract Society, from stereotype plates presented by my friend John Henry Gurney.—*Editor.*

deductions everywhere logical, the spirit truly Christian; and I cannot doubt, but that it will be the means of bringing home many who have gone astray, and of preserving others from error.

My heart went with you everywhere. There are two points only on which I hesitate in opinion. * * * * Do not think me presumptuous. From the changes through which my mind has passed I have learnt the useful lesson of distrusting myself; and for some twelve years I have been conscious of no other change than an increasing sense of weakness, and the necessity of a saving faith.

FROM HANNAH MORE.

Barley Wood, June 15th, 1826.

It is a necessity to which I am too frequently driven, when I have been favoured with a presentation copy of a work from an author, whose mediocrity I either knew or suspected, to return my thanks almost immediately, that I might not be compelled to the painful alternative of rudeness or flattery. You, my dear sir, are an author whose work, to borrow the language of one of the collects of our church, one may "read, mark, learn, and inwardly digest" before one acknowledges the obligation conferred. There is much judgment in the arrangement, great perspicuity in the style, as well as depth and truth in the argument. I pray that it may please our gracious Heavenly Father, without whom nothing is strong, nothing is holy, to make this book an instrument of much good.

FROM CHARLES SIMEON.

K. C. Cambridge, January 25th, 1826.

MY BELOVED FRIEND AND BROTHER,

I have proceeded half through your book *regularly* according to your direction,* and have read it with great delight and edification. Your statements throughout

* See the Preface to the Essays.

are judicious and satisfactory, and the richness of your appeals to Scripture renders your book invaluable. * * * * I love your recapitulations exceedingly. The vast advantage of them to your readers is obvious; but they are not less useful to your own mind, in that they induce a habit of order, of terseness, of perspicuity. It is almost impossible for a man who recapitulates, either to run riot, or to talk nonsense. Bishop Pearson's perorations have always delighted me, and yours also will delight and edify many.

I have just perused your most elaborate defence of the divinity of our blessed Lord. I think that the whole church will bless you for it; and in your dying hour it will be no grief to you to have taken so much pains in elucidating and confirming a point that is of such unspeakable importance to all who feel their need of a divine Saviour. Go on, my beloved brother, and may God long preserve you to be a blessing to the church and the world.

"What an extraordinary production it is," wrote his early friend Edward Edwards, "for a young layman—for a banker—above all, for a *Friend*." Not a few of his acquaintance who did not belong to the same religious body with himself, were in fact ready to join in this last exclamation. Accustomed, it may be, to view Quakerism through a somewhat prejudiced medium, to take the opinions of the early Friends from the reports of their opponents, or from a view of their writings, too much confined to those published in the heat of controversy, they were perhaps hardly aware that the early Friends steadfastly maintained the great doctrines of the proper manhood and Deity of Christ, and the reality and efficacy of his propitiatory sacrifice; and that the burden of their exhortations was, that others might be brought in faith and obedience, through the work of his Spirit in their hearts, effectually to know him in all his gracious offices.* It had been scarcely, perhaps, enough considered that some of their most important and distinguishing principles — those on the subjects of worship and ministry — were simply results, necessary ones, as they believed, of a complete, heartfelt apprehension of the mediatorial, priestly, and regal characters of the Son of God.† Nor had it been sufficiently recollected, that whilst nothing short of regard for his divine authority could have supported them, almost single-handed amongst the professors of Christianity, in the maintenance of their testimonies, grounded upon his plain precepts, against all oaths and war; so it was their reverence for him and for his truth, their deep sense of the all-importance of his one peculiar and distinctive baptism "of the Holy Ghost and of fire," and of the necessity of eating and drinking, by faith, of his body broken, and his blood shed upon the cross for them, that had led them, in rejecting the commonly received outward rites of Christian communion, to press after the reality rather than the representation, the substance rather than the shadow. The more the true character of the gospel-dispensation, as drawn by the inspired

* See Selections from the Epistles of George Fox, by Samuel Tuke, pp. 12, 63, 150, 214, 224, 260. Indeed the whole of this little volume is replete with instruction. See also the valuable body of evidence on the Christian principles of the early Friends, especially on the important subjects of the Three that bear record in heaven, of the Divinity and Offices of Jesus Christ, and of the Holy Scriptures, contained in the "Exposition of the Faith of the Religious Society of Friends on the fundamental doctrines of the Christian Religion," by Thomas Evans, Philadelphia, 1828.

† See in particular the little Tract issued by the Yearly Meeting of 1840, entitled, Testimony to the Authority of Christ in his Church.

penmen of the New Testament, and the extent to which it is apprehended by the early Friends, are considered and understood, the less will it excite surprise, either that the writer of the Observations on the Distinguishing Views of the Society of Friends should maintain the truths so clearly set forth in his Essays on Christianity, or that the writer of the Essays should feel bound to the principles which he has advocated in his earlier work. In his view, the two works were consistent with each other, both equally represented his own deep-felt convictions, and both required to be perused in order to the full comprehension at once of the extent and the limits of his religious belief.

After what has been said, it will not be necessary to do more, than to insert extracts from a very few of the letters which he received, upon its publication, from the members of his own religious society.

FROM WILLIAM FORSTER.

Bradpole, [2d of 3d month,] 1826.

"Thou must allow me, in true brotherly love, to offer thee my warmest congratulations, that thou hast been enabled to bring out thy Essays. I entertain a most lively and cheering hope of the usefulness of thy work; that in this cloudy and dark day, it will tend to the establishment of the wavering, to the fortifying of the feeble-minded, and put to silence the cavils of many a proud and self-sufficient gainsayer. To the anxious inquirer after the truth as it is in Jesus, I firmly believe it will be rendered peculiarly helpful and valuable. In short, I cannot but look upon it as one of those labours of love that will be made to abound 'by many thanksgivings unto God.' It would be strange if I did not feel more than a common and passing interest in the work; for, I think, I never found myself upon any occasion so much anticipated; it gives utterance to my own views and feelings in such lucid and convincing language, and withal it solves some of my difficulties so thoroughly and satisfactorily."

FROM JONATHAN HUTCHINSON.

Gedney, 5th mo., 1st, 1826.

I have lately finished a very deliberate reading of thy Essays, and, on the whole, with a satisfaction which enables me honestly to say, that I am glad to have seen such a book before I die. I rejoice that a friend so dear to me, should, consistently with his own avowed principle of human incapacity for any work that can be denominated good both in motive and act, have been *enabled* to write it. I hope this effort of labour and of love, for such I consider it, will prove of advantage to many, as I think it has been of edification to myself, by exciting me afresh, even under life's declining energies, to "thank God and take courage," and, under some renewal of faith and hope, reverently, I trust, to "put on strength in the name of the Lord."

It was with peculiar satisfaction that he received the following from the well-known author of the English Grammar, then far advanced in years.

Holdgate, near York, 2nd mo., 1st, 1826.

MY DEAR AND MUCH ESTEEMED FRIEND,

I am obliged and gratified by thy kind remembrance of me, in the distribution of thy volume.

Being able to read but little myself, I have had the book read to me, and very much to my satisfaction. Proofs thou hast given abundantly of the positions contained in the volume being conformable to the Holy Scriptures. The work is happily calculated, both in its matter and manner, to comfort those who unite in the author's views and sentiments, to disperse the doubts of those who hesitate, and to produce conviction in the minds of gainsayers. Thou hast indeed by this pious labour, very materially served the cause of truth and righteousness ; and I trust thou wilt be blessed for it by Him whose blessing makes truly rich, and will accompany thee to the latest hour of life.

Farewell, dear Joseph, in the best sense of the word!

I remain thy very affectionate friend,

LINDLEY MURRAY.

Two weeks after receiving the above letter, he writes in his Journal :—

On seventh day I received the affecting tidings of the decease of my beloved and honoured friend Lindley Murray. A fortnight before his death he wrote me a letter expressive of his unity with my Essays. How valuable that letter now!

CHAPTER XVI.

1825—1827. ÆT. 38—39.

PANIC IN THE MONETARY AND COMMERCIAL WORLD; ENGAGEMENT IN MARRIAGE WITH MARY FOWLER; JOURNEYS IN THE WEST OF ENGLAND, AND IN THE MIDLAND COUNTIES; EXTRACTS FROM JOURNAL AND LETTERS; PROSPECT OF A VISIT TO IRELAND WITH HIS SISTER ELIZABETH FRY.

THE panic in the monetary and commercial world, and the sudden run upon the banks in London and the country, have rendered memorable the winter of 1825–26. As a banker, Joseph John Gurney did not escape his share of anxiety. A few months previously he had written in his Journal:—*

Business has been productive of trial to me, and has led me to reflect on the equity of God, who measures out his salutary chastisements, even in this world, to the rich as well as to the poor. I can certainly testify that some of the greatest pains and most burdensome cares which I have had to endure, have arisen out of being what is usually called a "monied man."

These cares now pressed upon him with unaccustomed force. It was a time that put men's characters and principles to the proof. Houses of old and established reputation were giving way; the weaker ones had been already forced to yield. Credit seemed for a time annihilated. Men hardly knew whom to

* Under date 7th mo. 10th, 1825.

trust. Each post brought the news of fresh disasters, and none could tell whose turn might come next. Had Joseph John Gurney been the mere man of business, his constitutional timidity would have ill fitted him to meet such a crisis. But in his case, the man of business was also the servant of Christ. And they who witnessed the quiet courage with which he faced the storm, his wholemindedness to the occasion, the clear and sound judgment, and steady firmness with which he met each new emergency, and through all, the deep repose of his own spirit, could not but acknowledge the reality and excellence of the fruits arising out of such a combination of character; whilst all may be instructed in recollecting that had the Christian minister ceased to be the man of business, the opportunity for thus illustrating by example, the practical results of the religion of Jesus would have been lost.

His Journal at this period strikingly illustrates these various points of his character.

11*th mo.*, 23*rd*, 1825. Since I last wrote, I have had true cause, amidst much trial of faith, to set my seal to the declaration, that the "Lord is good, and that his righteousness endureth for ever." What a week it has been! The post of 3rd day, the 15th, brought me an unexpected letter from my brother Samuel, which rendered it necessary for me to go the next day to London. There I passed 5th, 6th, and 7th days; an interesting but deeply trying time; the city in general being in a state of great distress for want of money, and affairs at their acmé of anxiety. However I was favoured with much calmness, and even cheerfulness, feeling the Lord to be near to us; and was enabled, to a point which could scarcely have been looked for, to assist in arranging everything comfortably, and to quit London and my dear brothers and sisters with an easy mind, by mail, on seventh day night. Seldom have I more signally experienced the special providence of our heavenly Father. I arrived in Norwich on first day morning, in time for meeting. It was well attended, and was a favoured occasion. I was engaged in thanksgiving and prayer, and in ministry on the declaration, "Happy is the man who hath the God of Jacob for his help, whose hope is in the Lord his God." The afternoon meeting was also highly favoured.

Second day. Norwich Anti-slavery Meeting. Driven up into a corner as I was, and absolutely deprived of the opportunity of previous study or much reflection, I found it necessary to wind myself up to a great effort. In this I was favoured to succeed; and the meeting passed off excellently.

12th mo., 5th. After our successful anti-slavery meeting, on this day fortnight, I was variously and closely engaged for three or four days. On the sixth day morning, I corrected the last sheet of my Essays on Christianity. That afternoon I went to Yarmouth, where I attended a large and hopeful Bible Society Meeting in the evening, and made a long speech, I trust with some effect. The next day in the evening, by the mail, fifty miles to Ipswich. The following first day there was one of close exercise. It was hard work to raise the living spring from the hidden well. The public meeting in the evening was very large and relieving. I was much engaged in prayer, and in preaching on the universality of the grace of God, and on the beauty of holiness. Elizabeth Dudley followed me in the same strain, and concluded the meeting with solemn supplication.

Second day was very affecting to me. With James and Emma Corder I travelled to Coggeshall, where I passed several hours with that family, and much of the time with dear Alfred. I found him much wasted and tried with a sad cough, but beautifully calm, quiet, and resigned. I have not often seen Christian principle more brightly exemplified. After a quiet, affecting leave-taking, and much spiritual exercise in the family circle, I left him in the evening for Colchester; whence, after a few hours' sleep, the mail brought me to Norwich on third day morning. A close trial of faith and patience daily going forward from continued London anxieties. It has been a stormy time indeed! and I fear my dear brother has had much to endure. Two of our partners went up on fourth day. This has enabled me to stay quietly in my own berth, which was the more needful, as I had appointed a public meeting for yesterday evening. It was very large, and I believe passed off well.

1st mo., *11th*, 1826. The very day after I last wrote in this Journal, arrived a letter from Samuel, requiring my immediate presence in London, on account of the gloomy state of money affairs. His letter coincided with my own plans; for I had previously taken my place for that day, in the Ipswich mail.

The day to which I allude was fifth day, 12th mo., 8th. It was the day of our monthly meeting, at which Friends signed my certificate for my intended journey to the south and west. Large and solemn were the meetings both for worship and discipline, and eminently with us appeared to be that Lord of life and glory, who ever has been, and, I doubt not, ever will be, "for a crown of glory, and for a diadem of beauty, to the residue of his people." My address to the assembly was that of a friend parting from them for a time, and deeply concerned for their spiritual welfare and progress. I called upon them to walk more worthy of their high vocation, as Christians, as Quakers; being led to insist on the genuine excellence, both of the foundation, and of the superstructure, of what I believe most firmly to be a temple in which God delights to dwell.

He thus continues his history in a letter:—

TO JONATHAN HUTCHINSON.

Norwich, 1st mo., 21st, 1826.

* * * When I arrived in London the next morning by the mail, I found myself entirely arrested by the very painful and anxious state of the monied world. The path of duty was clear, viz., to continue in London for two or three weeks. An awful stormy time it was. I never saw the like before, and truly I can say that the only sure refuge was the "strong tower"—the name of the Lord. Many were deeply distressed,

and I never witnessed any thing so like the judgments of God on a people who had made for themselves idols of gold and idols of silver. It has occasioned me more than a little suffering, from the feeling of my own numerous and important ties to the earth; ties which it would be wholly out of my power to sever. However I endeavoured quietly to repose in that providence by which I seem to myself to have been brought into my present situation in life; and which will, I trust, open the way for my nevertheless performing my religious duties. Ah! how closely do I feel, through all, bound in spirit to Zion—the city of the saints' solemnities! How do I delight in her privileges, in her quiet palaces, in her streams of living water! And how infinitely desirable does it appear to me, to be devoted in heart and soul to the very best, the very dearest of all masters!

When things had become a little quiet I ventured into the west for rather more than a week, and held meetings with Friends and others at Melksham, Bath, and Bristol. At the last place I spent a memorable Sabbath day, in which, I trust, the "truth as it is in Jesus" was in some degree exalted, and finally in dominion.

A few weeks later he writes in his Journal:—

2nd mo., 20th. The week has, in part, been one of deep trial; almost overwhelming solicitudes about business, &c., and the state of the country in general, alarming to every thoughtful mind. Memorable are the lessons which these events are calculated to impress on our own Society; and earnest are my desires that we may, in our various allotments, be favoured with ability to preserve clean hands, and to uphold with integrity the cause of our Redeemer. I do not know that I feel condemned in the retrospect and examination of my temporal calling; nor am I aware, that I have ever seen an opening for quitting my post. Yet my soul is exercised in fervent desires that nothing may stand in the way between me and my Maker; and that I may be more entirely brought into the innocence of the Christian life, through the mighty power of that Saviour, in whom is my confidence, and whose blood cleanseth from all sin.

Another circumstance was at this time deeply interesting his feelings. It is thus adverted to in the Autobiography:—

When the commercial troubles had subsided, I went down into the west of England; and, whilst at Melksham, passed a few days at Elm Grove, a lovely place in the country, with Rachel Fowler, a cousin of my late wife's, and widow of Robert Fowler, whose grave and expressive speeches used to fall with so much weight upon my ear and soul during my earlier attendances of the Yearly Meeting. She was left with three sons and two daughters. Mary, the youngest, immediately attracted my attention. She was fourteen years younger than myself, but appeared in every other respect precisely adapted to my taste and need; and truly may it be said that wisdom was "grey hairs" to her, for never did I meet with, in any young person, so accurate a discernment, or so sound a judgment. I had previously paid the family a visit; and, having now enjoyed a more complete opportunity of intercourse, my mind became quite clear, and I mentioned my views first to her mother, and afterwards, with her mother's full sanction, to herself. It was evident that there was a close correspondence between us in sentiment, taste, and feeling; and, although nothing was then decided, I was well satisfied with my visit; except only that her rapidly increasing delicacy of health made me anxious. After a little time, her mind quietly settled in the affirmative of the question; a decision for which she believed she had the sanction of that gracious Lord whom she desired to serve. But her health soon appeared more and more to fail, and although we were not greatly alarmed, continued to excite our anxiety and close watchfulness for nearly a year and a half. Thus was I introduced to a new description of trial, a new exercise of faith and patience; but hope lived through all, and, whilst involved in inevitable suspense on a most interesting point, I endeavoured as steadily as I could, to pursue the path of duty, and to do the day's work in the day.

To return to the Journal:—

First day night, 1st mo., 29th. I may record with thankfulness a peaceful Sabbath, after a more than usually busy and *careful* week. It is a great mercy that there is provided one day in the week, for the stopping of the big wheel which involves so many rapid interests.

Third day morning. The sweetness of the Sabbath has been mercifully prolonged, amidst much business, and much infirmity. The Lord knows, that notwithstanding all my infirmities, *I love him and his cause, as with all my heart,* and graciously is he pleased to speak peace to my often wounded spirit.

2nd mo., 3rd. This morning I have been re-perusing my chapter "on the disuse of typical rites,"* and am favoured to feel much satisfaction in it; so that I can praise the Lord, in the humble belief, that he has been graciously pleased to lead me into his truth, not only as it relates to the common Christian ground, but as it regards the peculiar views and testimonies of our scattered, and to a great degree despised, society—despised not as individuals, but as a profession.

2nd mo., 7th. Amelia Opie here. We have passed a solemn time in the family reading; all the servants, the children, and ourselves present. I felt it right to exhort to economy, moderation, seriousness of mind, to the fear of the Lord and the love of Jesus; and was afterwards engaged in prayer for the servants, the children, &c. There seemed to be an open door in the hearts of those present. I feel in some degree inwardly gathered to the centre of light and life, which is, I believe, a condition peculiarly needful, in the present day, to be sought after and carefully maintained.

After an absence from home of several months, during which he was principally occupied by re-

* See Observations on the Distinguishing Views of Friends, chap. 4.

ligious labours in the West of England, he writes:—

Earlham, 6th mo., 19th. A strange and unusual break in my history! Much, indeed, has passed since I last wrote. I left home on my mission, on seventh day, 3rd mo., 11th, and passed the next day at Plaistow; thence proceeded by mail to Bristol to their Quarterly Meeting. Most closely, and, I may add, arduously, was I engaged in visiting the three Quarterly Meetings of Bristol and Somerset, Devon, and Cornwall, and all the meetings within their compass, one very small one excepted; holding public meetings in most places, and paying many family visits.

During this journey, I was, at times, inexpressibly baptized into deep suffering and affliction of spirit; but mostly found that this experience prepared the way for subsequent elevation in the power of the gift, and sometimes for joy in the Lord. My general concern towards Friends was, to awaken them to a more lively sense of the great principles of truth, and to wean them from a dependence on a mere religion of system and education. In Bristol, I had warmly to plead amongst them for "the faith once delivered to the saints." Nothing could exceed the kindness with which I was received in that city and elsewhere. It might have been spoiling to me, had it not been for the lowering efficacy of the deep and frequent conflict of my own spirit.

Towards the public my general duty was clearly to proclaim the essential truths of our common Christianity, and where more preparation was evinced, especially in Cornwall, to unfold the most spiritual views of religion.

TO MARY FOWLER.

Norwich, 7th mo., 13th, 1826.

* * I often think that I am happier in meeting than any where else. It is indeed a high privilege to be emancipated for the time from the discomposures, cares, and sorrows of this rapidly passing and constantly varying scene, and to be permitted to sit down as in the secret place of God's holy tabernacle. * *

TO THOMAS FOWELL BUXTON.

Norwich, 7th mo., 15th, 1826.

* * I feel myself to be so intimately bound up with thee in mind and circumstances, that everything which touches thee, touches me also, and probably often more to the quick than it does thee. It has therefore been a real pain to me to know of thy being under some discouragements. Yet I trust that thou wilt derive benefit from them, in weaning thee still more entirely from all things temporal, in elevating thy thoughts more towards heavenly things, and in strengthening thy already strong resolution, to glory only in Christ crucified, and to be indeed one of his faithful soldiers; a soldier invincibly simple-hearted, and persevering in the great contest which is now going on between light and darkness, good and evil.

7th mo., 24th. Last third day, Amelia Opie and I went to Acle, where we met Lord Calthorpe at E. Sidney's, and held a successful anniversary of the Bible Society. On my return at night, I found Wilberforce and his family at Earlham. They staid till seventh day morning. Lord Calthorpe here part of the time. It has been a memorable visit, and a sweet renewal and confirmation of our now old friendship. Numbers came to meet Wilberforce from day to day, and very delightful have been his conversation and influence. The spirit of prayer was much poured out upon me during this time, especially in a solemn religious opportunity just before their departure.

The eighth month of this year was devoted to various religious services in Worcestershire, Shropshire, and the Midland Counties. Writing to his cousin Priscilla Hannah Gurney, whom he had lately visited, he thus briefly alludes to some of these engagements :—

Wellingboro,' 8th mo., 29th, 1826.

My beloved Cousin,

I need scarcely tell thee that since we parted, it has been my lot to pass through much and various exercise of mind. At Worcester I met a cordial reception from the N—— family, at their pleasant residence; and my visit to the meeting there was interesting and enlivening to myself. The time which I passed with the young people one morning before breakfast was peculiarly touching. I held a satisfactory meeting in the prison, besides a large public one; and then two with Friends, who form a body of tolerable size. Thomas and Lydia Newman accompanied me on third day morning, (now a fortnight ago,) to Coalbrookdale, where I continued until the following seventh day. I held public meetings at the Dale, and at Madeley, in Mary Fletcher's barn. The latter was a touching occasion, and I was much interested in afterwards visiting the house and the room where both the Fletchers paid the last debt of nature. * * At Birmingham I held two public meetings, one with upwards of two thousand people in the Independent meeting house. Through mercy it was much crowned with peace. On fourth day we were favoured with a comfortable farewell meeting with Friends. Fifth day evening at Coventry. Sixth day at Warwick, besides a very arduous and suffering meeting with the butterfly visitors of Leamington Spa. We reached Northampton on seventh day night, where I found plenty of work. I am just returned from a very exercising meeting with Friends of this place and neighbourhood, and purpose a public meeting in the evening. To-morrow the same at Huntingdon. Fifth day I mean to devote to my old friend Lady Olivia Sparrow, at Brampton; and on sixth day, hope to hold a public meeting at Cambridge, which place I have for some time felt bound to, and then to Lynn, on my way home.

TO MARY FOWLER.

Brampton, 8th month, 31st., 1826.

* * We are now at Lady Olivia Sparrow's. The scene on our arrival last night was very striking. The approach to

the hall is through a large conservatory, and as we entered the latter, we saw the hall crowded with people all kneeling, and Malan (from Geneva,) a saint-like looking person engaged in fervent prayer. We stood contemplating the scene for some time; it was something like enchantment from the mixture of splendour and apparently deep piety: not to mention the mingling in one common offering of earnest prayer, of many individuals of high rank with the servants, cottagers, &c., &c. We have been warmly received and most kindly treated. There are many religious persons of the party; Lord and Lady Mandeville, Lady William Bentinck, &c., &c. and I have been much engaged in ministry among them this morning after the morning reading.

His visit to Cambridge is thus noticed in the Autobiography.

It was the third time of my there convening a public meeting, and my dear friend Simeon being aware of my intention, a large number of the young gownsmen attended; but nothing could I preach on the occasion but those views of the spirituality of worship, ministry, &c., which distinguish our own Society. Power appeared to go forth with the word, and certainly it was clothed in love. Nevertheless, my open avowal of these views gave considerable offence; and I have but little reputation to lose at Cambridge, as a preacher!

Whilst I heartily deprecate sectarianism, principle is principle, and truth is truth, and they cannot be concealed. To be misconstrued by the good, is a trial to which I am no stranger. Such things belong to the peculiar infirmity of our present condition; but they must be patiently borne. All will be set right in that better world, where error and prejudice will for ever give place to unmixed truth and absolute unanimity.

The somewhat brief intervals of leisure which he enjoyed at home at this period were not unimproved. In the autumn of this year he wrote a few observations addressed to his friend Lady P——, on the state of the "religious world," in which he briefly but pointedly adverts to three subjects of much practical importance; the proneness to place too much dependence on *ceremonies*, on *ministers*, and on *words*; adding a short but expressive observation on Christian practice in connexion with "that most desolating of the scourges of the world —the practice of war." * But his principal literary engagement was one of much more weight and importance; the composition of the Biblical Notes and Dissertations, intended chiefly to illustrate and confirm the doctrine of the Deity of Christ. "I had long been collecting materials for this work," he writes, "and pleasant, though by no means very easy, was the labour of digesting them, adding to them, reducing them to order, clothing the bones with muscles, and thus preparing them for the public. But great care was necessary, and I moved on slowly."

TO MARY FOWLER.

Norwich, 11th mo., 4th, 1826.

* * * I have begun my studies once more in good earnest, and hope I shall become quite interested in them. Real study is peculiarly wholesome for the mind. Indeed I know of scarcely anything that gives me the same satisfaction, so long as I can believe that it is in any degree in promotion of that one great and glorious cause to which my soul is bound. I have collected, in my own line, a very useful and comprehensive library, and I think thou would'st have been

* These observations were subsequently published under the title of The Contribution of a Member of the Society of Friends to a Lady's Album, and passed through two editions.

amused to see me this morning amidst a sea of books and papers, looking, I doubt not, very grave and abstract.

I am expecting some public calls in the service of the Bible and Anti-slavery Societies, but have otherwise a prospect of much quietness, which is very preferable. However, the root of quietness lies deeply seated in our own hearts. It is a conscience void of offence in the sight of God and man. Would that this might become more and more our blessed and soul-satisfying portion.

TO THE SAME.

Norwich, 11th mo., 11th, 1826.

* * I do most cordially agree with thy sentiments on the subject of literature and study. There is scarcely anything which makes me more sick at heart, or which more convinces me in what a wrong state is this fallen world of ours, than to see men of many and various talents making idols of intellectual pursuits, instead of steadily aiming *through them* at the promotion of the glory of God, and of the welfare of mankind. It is, on the other hand, very pleasant to reflect how much a single eye to the glory of God will enable a man to effect, even in the cultivation of mind and intellect, and how much the work of divine grace refines and illuminates the natural faculties. How delightful is the combination, in some persons whom I know and love, of intellectual vigour and childlike submission to the grace and government of our Lord Jesus Christ. How abundantly true it is that "in *Him* are hid *all* the treasures of wisdom and knowledge."

To return to the Journal:—

9th mo., *10th.* I have heartily desired to have my drowsy powers quickened for the service of God. This is often needful, especially in the pursuit of my studies. I have a line of study before me, but am fearful these pursuits may never again be very productive. Yet I trust I may be preserved from allowing the garden given me to cultivate, to run to waste. Be pleased, O Lord, to forgive my innumerable transgressions and to blot them out of thy book; and bestow upon me, I pray thee, a comforting assurance that my name is recorded in thy book of life. Be with me in all my pursuits, and in the performance of all my duties, that perpetual protection from the snares of the enemy, both in prosperity and adversity, may be my peaceful lot. Suffer me to cast on thee the burden of all my temporal cares, and of all my spiritual solicitudes. Graciously bless the little flock over which thou hast been pleased to call me to be an overseer in the Gospel, and grant that our scattered, and in some respects degraded, Society, may still be enabled to show forth the purity of thy law, and the spirituality of thy worship. And be thou, O Lord, with thy universal church, to confirm, increase, and multiply, that thy servants may rejoice, and thy own holy name be exalted above all.

TO MARY FOWLER.

Norwich, 9th mo., 10th, 1826.

* * It has been very instructive to me to be brought during the last fortnight so much into the society of pious people not of our profession. I trust it has still further enlarged my heart towards all who love the Lord Jesus. At the same time it has had, in no common degree, a confirming effect as it relates to my own principles. I have felt the beneficial influence of my Quakerism, and have had repeatedly to believe that we should not have been so preciously baptized together into the unity of the Spirit, had not the arrangements been upon *Quaker principles.* Our silence has been peculiarly solemn.

TO HIS UNCLE AND AUNT JOSEPH GURNEY.

Norwich, 9th mo., 16th, 1826.

* * I am ready to marvel at now finding myself the only one of our family in Norfolk of my generation, who is maintaining the peculiar religious principles handed down to us by our forefathers. Such a state of things, is, indeed, humbling, and has led me, as I doubt not it has you, to close

searching of heart. The result, as far as I know it, is a degree of peaceful confidence that, notwithstanding all discouragements—and just now they appear to me to be more than a few—our little Society is not, and will not be forsaken; and that a people will still be preserved, who shall bear a consistent testimony to the truth as we view it; that is, (as I still believe,) to the truth in its unmixed simplicity and spirituality. Never did I more highly value our simple mode of worship; and when a little tempest-tossed, I am, perhaps, too apt to conceive that to be at meeting is not only the happiest, but the only happy thing in life. With respect to the outward ordinances, I apprehend, that in the entire disuse of them, we are bearing a noble testimony to the spirituality of the gospel dispensation. Oh! that our lives and conversation may, more and more, correspond with such a testimony!

I may just add, that I increasingly feel how much an abiding in the root of our own principles, is the means of enlarging the heart towards ALL who truly love the Lord Jesus Christ!

After the week of the Bible Society and other religious meetings at Norwich, in the course of which they had enjoyed a flow of "peaceful and not soon to be forgotten Christian love and harmony," he writes:—

9th mo., 22nd. I sit down in deep solitude of soul, and in the privacy of my own study, the throng being gone to hear our dear friend Simeon preach; and my cousin Anna G—— and Legh Richmond being together in the drawing-room. My spirits are very low, and I have been both weeping and praying. After the extraordinary flow of the present week, the circumstances of this evening have strongly reminded me of my solitude, that I have lost the beloved wife and sister, who once sweetly united in my peculiar course; and the recollection of them has been blended, in a somewhat melancholy manner, with that of dear Alfred Corder, with whom, for a short but bright season, I enjoyed more intimacy, as a Friend, than I have ever done perhaps with any other person. May I not hope that these beloved ones, and many others with them, are, through the infinite mercies of God in Christ Jesus, for ever centred in bliss? And must I not humbly endeavour to press forwards after the mark for the same prize?

My soul has been deeply revolving how far my peculiar principles can stand the double test to which they are now subjected; that of the solitude, poverty, nakedness, and apparent decline to which we poor and misunderstood Quakers are exposed; and on the other hand, that of the flowing association, the high tone of religious feeling, and the evangelical prosperity of the many pious persons, not Friends, by whom I am surrounded, and with whom I have been lately permitted very sweetly to unite in essentials, and in the social, though not public, worship of Almighty God. Can I under such circumstances, and especially under that probable deepening and heightening of the picture, to which I may look forward, live and die a Quaker? The question is to me one of awful and solemn interest; and I think I am favoured at this time, in the humiliation and silence of self, with a degree of quiet decisiveness to answer it in the affirmative. Little as our peculiar profession is thought of, and even despised as it is by many, I yet have had renewed cause during the past week, to believe that the power of our principles is felt, that they really have a strong practical influence. Thus a hope lives with me, that in the tender mercies of our God, we shall not be forsaken or destroyed; and that testimony-bearers will yet be raised up, who shall, after this sort, testify of the perfection and spirituality of the gospel dispensation.

Quakerism is, I trust, nothing to me as a name, and nothing, I would hope, as the inscription of a sect. I abhor sectarianism. I crave to possess the impartiality and comprehensiveness of the wisdom and of the love of God, so far as they are bestowed upon man. All I desire is, that there may be preserved among the living members of the universal church, those who shall uphold a complete standard of spirituality in worship, and of true innocency in conduct, which have long appeared to me genuine and most essential marks of real Christianity.

FROM LEGH RICHMOND.

Turvey, Olney, Bucks, October 4th, 1826.

MY DEAR FRIEND AND BROTHER,

Once more returned to the bosom of my family and my parish, refreshed by the recollections of your Christian hospitalities, and strengthened in my spiritual course, as I trust, by the public and private intercourse of Norwich and Earlham, can I help telling you how greatly you and yours are thus endeared to my heart? It was indeed a season of holy festivity, and I desire to bless God for it. Such times are like the oases of the wilderness, to invigorate the wearied traveller, and fill him with peace and joy through believing. My Norfolk excursion has left indelible marks of gratitude and satisfaction on my mind: may they be cherished for time and eternity by the goodness of Him "in whom we live and move and have our being!" Greatly as I have felt obliged to you for personal kindness towards myself, I have felt, if possible, still more indebted to you for your Christian affection shown to my very dear and beloved son. He is so near to my heart's tenderest feelings, that whatever concerns his welfare both in soul and body excites the most earnest breathings of my soul towards God. I hope you will not forget him. I know you will not in prayer;—but sometimes write to him. Your friendly conduct has won his heart and may be of essential service to him. I have had severe trials in the successive loss of his two elder brothers. The one, after ten years' absence in India, died on his passage home; but I have every reason to believe that he died in the Lord. The other died at home, exhibiting beautiful tokens of the divine love towards him; his death was blessed to not a few. Deeply grateful to God for these special mercies, I nevertheless feel much; above all I often anxiously enquire whether these affecting bereavements have produced their right effects upon my own soul, upon my ministry, upon my domestic habits.

Your Essays please me more and more; I delight in finding such unity of sentiment with other Christians. The Christian Observer reviews them this month with much approbation, and so it ought.

TO HENRY BRADY.

Norwich, 11th mo., 1st, 1826.

* * I paid a very satisfactory and comforting visit last week to the school at Croydon. It seems now to be animated with an Ackworth spirit; and I was particularly well satisfied with thy cousin E. F. B——, the present superintendent, who seems superior in point of both intellect and piety. We had all the children collected, both boys and girls, and I had them under instruction for two hours and upwards. A sweet solemnity crowned all. * * * Art thou favoured to perceive in any of the dear children at Ackworth, marks of the work of grace in the heart; something, I mean, beyond outward propriety of behaviour? How affecting have been the deaths of various hopeful young persons in our society, and how animating would be the belief that others are coming forward to supply their place!

TO JONATHAN HUTCHINSON.

11th mo., 1st, 1826.

* * I am just returned home from a short western journey. My principal object was to pass a few quiet days with my beloved friend at Melksham, and I had the happiness to find her radically improved in health. I persuade myself she is a person whom thou wilt value and love. Hopeful, however, as I am respecting her health, I do not look to the *speedy* accomplishment of our wishes. It may be that while she is gradually regaining her strength, I may be again sent forth to labour in the vineyard.

The prospect of a lengthened visit to Ireland, in company with his sister Elizabeth Fry, was now opening before him.

First day evening, 11*th mo.*, 26*th.* After a week of considerable exertion, I have been graciously permitted to enjoy an edifying peaceful Sabbath. The reward of sweet and deep inward quiet, has been most undeservedly bestowed; apparently in consequence of my having been made willing, at both the meetings and in families, to labour in the vineyard. The exercises of the morning meeting were painfully searching; I humbly trust, not in vain; those of the afternoon were more easy and comforting to myself, and the Scripture was opened to me to my own admiration. The prospect of service among Friends and, others, in Ireland, has gradually gained an ascendency over my mind; and, I am strongly inclined to believe, I shall have to lay it before my friends at our next Monthly Meeting. The undertaking is, indeed, one that calls for close, unreserved dedication. The Lord alone is sufficient for these things. May he be my perpetual help and protector. How inexpressibly precious is his anointing. May I ever be preserved from crude attempts to exercise my ministry without it. Indeed, I never was more fully sensible of the necessity of being moved in all things appertaining to God's kingdom, by the gentle impulses of divine wisdom and love, or otherwise of not being moved at all.

Fourth day morning. I can breathe a sincere prayer, that every thought and imagination within me may be brought into captivity to the obedience of Christ; that his mind may be my mind; that I may be thoroughly conformed to the whole will of God respecting me; and that his blessed, pure truth, may never be wounded through my want of faithfulness or courage.

12*th mo.*, 3*rd.* The week agreeably concluded by the arrival of my dear sister Fry. Our Irish prospect seems a good deal opening upon us; and it is a great satisfaction to me to find her views, as to the time of throwing it before Friends, correspond with my own. Indeed, it seems pretty clear now, that I must mention it at our next Monthly Meeting. May all be done to the glory of God!

12*th mo.*, 11*th.* My uncle was telling me, the other day, on the authority of the late John Bateman, that our great grandfather, Joseph Gurney, a meek and humble man, scarcely ever failed to be engaged both in prayer and preaching, at every meeting he attended; but always in the *life*.

The frequent repetition of services of this description, to which I find myself called, often tries my faith, and brings me into close and deep exercise of soul: but I must follow my holy Leader. O that I may never be found presenting unsavoury offerings on the Lord's altar! How remarkable it is, that from generation to generation, there are those raised up amongst us who have thus to bear a public testimony to redeeming love and power. May it continue to be the case, through the unmerited goodness of Israel's Shepherd, and in due season may the number of anointed priests and Levites be multiplied on the face of the earth! I fully believe that this description applies to many out of our pale, and yet, perhaps, not in the same way and degree.

His friends having given their sanction and encouragement to his proposed visit to Ireland, he writes, after a week spent in religious labours, in Suffolk, and subsequent short visits to London and Melksham, the intervals being closely occupied by literary and other engagements at home:—

First day night, 1*st mo.*, 28*th*, 1827. I am likely to leave home with clear hands; and may, with humble gratitude, confess that a remarkable feeling of repose has been my portion, as I have quietly yielded to the stream which is conveying me onwards to an arduous and extensive field of gospel labour.

CHAPTER XVII.

1827. ÆT. 39.

DEPARTURE FOR IRELAND; LABOURS IN DUBLIN; VISIT TO THE MARQUIS WELLESLEY, THE LORD LIEUTENANT; PRISONS; DR. MURRAY; ARCHBISHOP MAGEE; ARCHBISHOP OF TUAM; TRIM; COOTEHILL; ARMAGH; LISBURN; JOHN CONRAN; LURGAN; BELFAST; LONDONDERRY.

JOSEPH John Gurney left Earlham on his way to Ireland, on the 2nd of the second month., 1827. "We were in that island," he writes in his Autobiography, "for about three months, in all its counties except four, paying a general visit to Friends, holding many public meetings, inspecting prisons, communicating with persons in authority as occasion required, and mingling with members of various denominations in the pursuit of works of benevolence, Roman Catholics, at times, as well as Protestants. When not engaged in ministerial labours, it was very much my office to help my beloved sister in her comprehensive designs for the benefit of her fellow men."

TO MARY FOWLER.

London, 2nd mo., 3rd, 1827.

I was favoured yesterday to leave home with a degree both of clearness and peace — clearness, because all my memoranda and *agenda* were swept away to my satisfaction; peace, in the belief mercifully afforded that my going was in the ordering of divine wisdom and love; and in the secret persuasion that my beloved sister and children on the one hand, and myself on the other, would be preserved to a happy meeting again. However, this is not to be stamped higher than an agreeable presentiment. * * * I increasingly feel the necessity of dwelling deep in the root of true wisdom; that I may not be deceived by any superficial, unauthorized sensations, but may be enabled quietly and faithfully to follow the true Shepherd. I hope thou wilt be enabled to pray for my preservation particularly in this respect; for I imagine that my naturally sanguine temperament exposes me to the danger of error more than many others. Probably thou hast found this out, and therefore dost not regret (nor do I) that much of the necessary ballast of secret suffering falls to my lot.

His Journal of this visit, is contained in a series of letters to his sisters Catherine and Rachel, from which the following extracts are taken.

Holyhead, 2nd mo., 9th, 1827.

My dear Sisters,

We are just arrived at this place, in good health and spirits, after an interesting journey. E—— and I much enjoyed our peaceful journey to Worcester. It was a peculiar pleasure to me, to pass so many hours with her, in undisturbed *tête à tête*. We drove through the vale of Rodburg, and were quite inspirited by the scenery. A large party of Friends met us at Worcester, at my particular request; persons about whom I had been interested at my last visit. It was a pleasant rendezvous, and ended in a religious opportunity. A young man present poured forth an acceptable prayer for our preservation; and it was cheering to me, to observe an evident piety prevailing in the circle. Yesterday, after an early breakfast, we left Worcester, and reached Coalbrookdale in a few hours. There we dined at Barnard Dickenson's, and met another interesting and interested circle of Friends. Our evening journey was somewhat long, and we did not reach the beautiful Llangollen, till ten o'clock last night.

Our journey of to-day has been delightful, notwithstanding the coldness of the weather. I have occupied the box much of the way, and we have all feasted on the delightful scenery. The vale of Llangollen was the first lovely object which greeted us. Afterwards we passed through some magnificent, wild, mountain districts; particularly by the lake Ogwen; scenery which appeared to me, about equal to that of the Trosachs in Scotland; and though we missed the summer verdure and foliage, these were in some measure supplied by the full cataracts and large icicles. We dined at an inn, within a mile of Bangor; and after dinner, examined and passed over that wonderful work of human ingenuity, the Menai bridge.

We have been travelling all day by the finest road in England. It has been really curious to trace this smooth and perfect work of art, winding along through the roughest and wildest scenes of nature. There is something very animating in the beauty and magnificence of these scenes; and it has given quite a flow both to health and spirits. Our dear sister is writing her journal home, and drawing the Menai bridge for her children. We hope to sail at eight o'clock to-morrow morning. We are favoured with a feeling of tranquillity and comfort, though sensible of the weight and importance of our undertaking. The sympathy and prayers of our friends have been truly welcome.

Dublin, 2nd mo., 15th, 1827.

Since I wrote on second day morning, we have passed three very full and very interesting days, having gradually found our footing on this island, and our way amongst Friends and others. On second day, we were much occupied in paying a variety of visits; first to the Deaf and Dumb Institution, about two miles from our residence, and to Joseph Humfreys and his wife — superior Friends, under whose superintendence it is placed. It was a pleasant sight and especially instructive to observe J. Humfreys' manner with the children, to whom he had managed to communicate much religious instruction. Some of them seemed under the power of religion. Then to the bed-ridden widow of the late John Hilton, of Bristol; then to an afflicted family, known to dear Priscilla, of the name of Stott. In all these visits, and many similar ones, we have had religious opportunities; and it is particularly comforting to find ourselves, both in public and in private, brought into such remarkable unity of mental exercise. Before dinner I called at the Secretary of State's office, to deliver a letter from Peel, and was very kindly received by the Under-secretary of State, William Gregory, who promises every assistance. We dined at Robert Fayle's. This was the family with whom dear Priscilla lodged. Her memory is precious among Friends in Ireland.

Third day was devoted to the Monthly Meeting, the largest and longest I have ever attended; for I think that even in the meetings for business (both being included) there were not less than 400 Friends; and the men's meeting did not conclude (with an interval, of course, for dinner) until half-past nine at night. The weight and variety of business excited my sympathy towards the bearers of the burthen. It was a memorable day—the divine unction continuing to flow on, very remarkably, for many hours. * * *

Yesterday, after making arrangements for the printing of my Scripture Instruction documents, in the form of a tract, we again set off on a series of visits. Seven or eight interesting private opportunities with Friends, individually, or in families, occupied the morning. We paid a visit to the Dublin "Retreat," where are about fifteen patients, kindly managed on the improved system, and under the care of judicious Friends. We afterwards dined with the Doyle family, and in the evening attended a youths' meeting, held at seven o'clock, by our appointment. It was a very solemn but exercising time; about 500 persons present. Some were there who had no connexion with the Society.

2nd mo., 19th, 1827.

We breakfasted on fifth day, at Major Sirr's, at the Castle. The rest of the morning was passed in receiving and paying visits. Before dinner we went together to the Secretary of State's office, and met a very cordial reception from William

Gregory, the Under-Secretary. We dined with an elderly and pious Friend, Sarah Phelps, and had to entertain and instruct a party of fifty in the evening. It passed off well, though I was poorly, the commencement of rather a trying attack of cold and fever. Notwithstanding my poorliness, we were under the necessity of attending a public meeting appointed for sixth day morning. This proved a memorable occasion, and did me no harm. I was enabled to unfold the doctrines appertaining to the person and character of Christ, with a good deal of clearness and power, being made strong out of much bodily and mental weakness. Dear E—— passed part of the morning with the "Sisters of Charity," at their nunnery. They seem to have been delighted with her visit. On seventh day morning she took an early drive through the "Liberty," where the lowest part of the population dwell. At eleven o'clock, we held a meeting with the heads of families, &c., among Friends. It was one of deep and close exercise of mind; numerously attended, and I hope for good. Various calls from gentlemen and ladies at our lodgings afterwards; amongst the rest the pious Lady L—— and her daughter. At three o'clock we went by appointment to call on the Marquis Wellesley, the Lord Lieutenant, at the Vice-regal Lodge, Phœnix Park. The park is beautiful, about a mile from Dublin, with a noble view of the Wicklow mountains. The Viceroy is a clever, easy, polite, sensible, elderly man; small and grey-headed. He entered fully into our views; promised us every assistance in his power; and agreed with our sentiments on capital punishment, prisons, &c. Perhaps there may be a little of the courtier about him, but I believe him to be sincere. His wife, (a Roman Catholic American lady,) was confined up stairs with illness. We afterwards dined at Samuel and Jane Gatchell's, where in the evening we met a large party; among the rest John Leslie Forster's wife, a pious and exemplary woman. We returned home very tired. I was not well in the night, but rose refreshed in the morning. The meeting on first day was crowded by Friends and others. It was a good time, in which the truth was, I trust, exalted. Afterwards we made some calls on the afflicted; dined with the Bewley family, interesting and pious Friends. Drank tea at James Martin Pike's, one of the Dublin Philanthropists, a clever Friend, with a lovely family. Held a large public meeting at seven o'clock, in which the doctrines of the Atonement and of the Holy Spirit were largely set forth. It was a very solemn meeting. * * *

At John White's, near Edenderry, King's County, 2nd mo., 25th, 1827.

Since I last wrote, we have passed six days of strong and rapid interest, and having been all of us but poorly in the course of it, we consider it no small favour, that we have been permitted to quit Dublin in peace, and to enter unhurt on the country part of our engagement. It would have been unsafe to have continued longer in that city; for our dear sister's strength would probably have failed under the impetuous attentions of the thronging multitude. But to continue the thread of our history.—On second day, after breakfasting at a Friend's house with a large party, we commenced our visits to the prisons, and examined four principal ones that morning. Two of them very bad, particularly the Dublin Newgate; an awful scene of multitudinous wickedness and misery! Vast crowds of criminals, without occupation, without instruction, without any provided clothing, and therefore half-naked, herded together in great dens; for such was the character of some of their day rooms. Thence to the City Marshalsea prison, for small debtors, which was, if possible, still worse. Then another large debtors' prison, very bad also; and, lastly, the Smithfield Penitentiary, where there are a great many women and boys, in pretty good order. We dined that evening at the Secretary Gregory's, in the Phœnix Park. He is one of our kind Friends. We met a select and interesting party; amongst others, two ladies of rank of the Clancarty family, of which Lady Anne Gregory, the Secretary's wife, is a member, and their brother the Archbishop of Tuam; a person full of kindness, intelligence, and piety. The great subject of conversation at these Dublin parties, now seems to be the religious stir among the Roman Catholics, which is already technically called the "Reformation." The Protestants are delighted with it; consider that it is spreading, and will spread; and mix up their feelings on the subject with a certain degree of party zeal, against which we have done our best to hold up a yet purer standard. There is prevalent in Dublin great zeal, and great love for the truth; but there is wanted more of the garment of universal charity, and more of the ornament of a meek and quiet spirit. Yet there is a blessed work going on, which is far more conspicuous in the upper classes of society there, than in any part of England with which I am acquainted.

I forgot to tell you, that while we were visiting one of the prisons, the judges, then on the bench of a neighbouring Court, heard of us, and sent a message to invite us into their presence. We thought it right to go, and were ushered through a little door, on to the Judge's bench, in the front of a crowded and inquisitive assembly. We conversed some time with Judges Johnstone and Jebb, both eminent men, and found them true men on the subject of Capital Punishment. On third day we attended Meeting: (they hold two week day meetings in Dublin, on third and sixth days:) it was large, flocked to by many not Friends, and a very solemn, I hope profitable, occasion. Our dear sister's ministry was, as usual, very touching. I think it has produced a very considerable impression, her way having been remarkably made to the hearts of the people. After meeting we resumed our course of prison visiting, and that morning inspected two more debtors' prisons; and Kilmainham, the county jail. This jail is well conducted and superintended, and forms a striking contrast to the Dublin Newgate. We met several gentlemen of importance there, among whom were the Sheriff of the County, Sir Thomas Needham, and John David Latouche, the banker, a man of eminent liberality and respectability. E—— and I (she with a sad cold on her chest) went at six o'clock to dine at Baron Pennefather's, one of the judges, where we were handsomely entertained by some very superior people. The Baron is a highly cultivated, enlightened man, and his wife a solid Christian character. We met there two interesting clergymen: Cleaver, the son of the late Archbishop of Dublin; and James Dunn, a person of high reputation, who continues to preach in the Church of England, but from motives of conscience, has given up two valuable livings. We returned home very tired, and dear E—— was quite poorly for the next day or two, but nursing was impossible. Out of weakness we were made strong for services various and arduous.

On fourth day tō breakfast at a lady's named Hoare, where about forty serious persons were assembled to meet us. It was a good time I hope. Thence to the Richmond Bridewell, a great prison, where we were met by several gentlemen, including the Inspectors General of the prisons of Ireland, and I suppose nearly one hundred ladies, many of them of consideration and station. The object of the meeting was to organize a Ladies' Association for visiting prisons; our dear sister was, of course, in the chair, and I sat by as her secretary; the Inspectors General on either side. She managed the whole affair with great ability. The association was formed, and large Visiting Committees appointed for the four principal prisons. We had afterwards to examine the prison itself. We returned home, dear E—— much fagged, but obliged to prepare for a visit to Lady Wellesley, at the Phœnix Park. * * On our way back we spent a short, but very interesting time with Dr. Murray, the Roman Catholic Archbishop of Dublin. He is a pleasing man, of humble and Christian deportment, and did not appear to object to any of our views. There was something very sweet in the manners, and apparently in the mind of this Archbishop; but with it, we apprehend, a strong and determined attachment to his own church. In point of simplicity of life and appearance, he is an example for Christian prelates. We dined that evening at the house of John Henry North, a person of evident genius, and of great urbanity and elegance. Dr. Singer, of the College, a learned man, was there, and a pious clergyman in great repute, of the name of Magee. After dinner, many religious persons flocked into the room. Immediately after tea, —— stood up, holding a little Bible in his hand, and began to read, then to preach, and then without a moment's pause, called on "our dear friend and sister" to pray. Forthwith the company dropped on their knees. I was obliged to ask them to sit down in silence, and after a time dear E—— prayed very sweetly. I had also to address them. This description will give you some idea of the state of society in Dublin. I should imagine that these Bible readings are extensively supplanting cards and other such amusements. We rather fear that there is with it all, a pretty full infusion of high Calvinism.

Fifth day was equally remarkable. We breakfasted at home, and afterwards received an interesting visit from the famous Magee, Archbishop of Dublin. We conversed together nearly an hour, particularly respecting his book on the Atonement, Friends' Principles, &c. He appeared to be high church in his views, an acute and very clever man. He promised to read my Essays, as did Dr. Murray; Lord Wellesley also intends reading them. They are but little known in this land; but where known, appear to be liked. Many besides the Friends seem to be acquainted with the "peculiarities."

When the Archbishop had left us, we went to the House of Industry; a vast receptacle of aged, infirm, lunatic, and idiot paupers, under the government of Colonel Morris, who gave us a most cordial reception. It is a wonderful institution, supported by Government, and finely managed. The same may be said of the Richmond Lunatic Asylum, which we next visited with Dr. Jackson, the physician. In both these institutions the patients are kindly treated, and to a great extent employed and instructed. Then to the Richmond General Penitentiary, a sort of home Botany Bay. Here, however, the Governor, who considers himself amenable only to the Lord Lieutenant, refused to allow us to speak to the prisoners, or to see those who were in solitary confinement and under punishment. As we had engaged to quit Dublin on the morrow, it was difficult to know how to act; but on our return to our lodgings, we found our kind friend the

Archbishop of Tuam; and he and I went to the Secretary's office, where I was furnished with the Lord Lieutenant's commands to the Governor, to show us every thing we wished. I much enjoyed my walk with the Archbishop. There is something very noble and pleasing about him. His Christian course is a decided one. In the evening we were at home and received numerous guests.

On sixth day we rose with an almost overwhelming prospect of service: the morning meeting with Friends; the difficult task of re-examining the penitentiary; a report to make of the result to Government; and then a journey of nearly forty miles to be accomplished. However, way opened for the whole, and very satisfactorily. When we reached the meeting-house, we found it thronged to excess, and had considerable difficulty in reaching the gallery. Hundreds went away disappointed of a place. About 1500 were supposed to be present. With full minds, and tired bodies, we found it no easy task to cope with such a meeting; but it proved a memorable one. There was, I think, a true effusion of the Spirit on the occasion; and our dear sister was wonderfully enabled to surmount her bodily weakness and mental fears. I hardly ever heard such preaching as hers was that day; and the whole was concluded by the hearty ascription of all glory where alone it is due. Her text was, "Holiness becometh thine house, O Lord, for ever."

Soon after meeting, I had a happy *rencontre* with the Governor of the Penitentiary in the street. We took him to the prison in our carriage, delivered the Government order, and made a thorough visitation of the institution. Happily, there was no great evil lurking, and we parted with our defeated friend in harmony; and I had real pleasure in going to Secretary Gregory, and making a favourable report.

In the end we got through all our labours: dined; packed our carriage; left Dublin at five o'clock, truly grateful to our friends, of the Pim family, for their uncommon kindness and attention; and, after travelling until eleven o'clock at night, we arrived at Christians-town, county Kildare; at the hospitable house of our dear friend, James Forbes. * *

At Jonathan Richardson's, Lisburn, 3rd mo., 4th, 1827.

* * I last wrote from John White's, near Edenderry. We left his house about ten o'clock on second day morning (the 26th ult.) for Trim, the county town of Meath; passing through a country very incompletely cultivated, with wretched earthen huts on the sides of the road, the inhabitants of which appeared to be but little elevated above the condition of the heathen world. They seem to understand little that one says to them, and nothing can well exceed the filth in the midst of which they live. Knowledge, with a sense of need, both temporally and spiritually, is that first step to improvement, which does not seem yet taken, in many parts of this unhappy land. I believe, however, that education is making rapid strides; and the more it prevails, the more uneasy the people become, both with their physical and their spiritual degradation. I find there are almost daily tidings of the progress of "the Reformation" in many places. Trim is a wretched capital. The Duke of Wellington's towering monument being in true Hibernian contrast with the filth and misery which surround it. The prison was once the pride of the county, but is now considered one of the worst in Ireland. We found it, as we do all the county jails, full of prisoners, chiefly for rioting and the work of the shillelah. It is kept in good order, and is carefully superintended. We endeavoured to lay the foundation of a ladies' committee. Thence over an improving country, and past several gentlemen's seats, through the town of Kells, to our friend Lord Bective's, at Headfort. It is a fine extensive nobleman's place, conducted with great care and economy. We arrived in time for dinner, and were most kindly received by the Earl and Countess. There is something truly amiable about them both. We passed, however, rather a sleepy evening, for we were tired; and Lord B—— was obliged to leave us at night, on his way to attend Parliament, on the Roman Catholic question, of which he is a warm supporter. He and his wife promoted our religious intercourse with their household, and the next morning we had the family together, including a number of Roman Catholics; a general anxiety

prevailing to see the stranger guests. Dear E—— read Matt. xxv, and we had a remarkably interesting meeting afterwards, a little like that at Lord Derby's, in days of old. Much love towards us was manifested by all the party, especially the servants, who seemed full of zeal in helping us. We spent an hour or two with Lady B—— at Kells, their neighbouring town, in inspecting her public charities, and a wretched little prison, happily not often used; and we then drove off to a desolate place called Ballyborough, on our way to the next meeting of Friends. The people seemed anxious for tracts, of which we distributed a large quantity; and there being no horses to be had in the place fit to use, we were happy enough to meet with two pairs on their return home, which we kept for two days' service. It is a desolate country and the roads very bad; and very tired we were when we arrived at Cootehill, a little town in the county of Cavan, where we were most hospitably entertained by J. C—— and his two sisters. The change from the vast chateau to their humble abode, was far from unpleasant; there was so much cleanliness and comfort in the accommodation provided.

There are only a few scattered families of Friends in this place, (Lisburn,) which is one of some importance, being a principal linen mart for the north of Ireland. The domestic manufacture of linen is the staple of this part of the country, and every poor man is his own flax grower, weaver, and merchant. As we advance towards the north, the peasantry assume a more respectable appearance. The children may like to know that we met on our road, a day or two since, a vast body of peasants, neatly dressed, attending the corpse of a young woman to its burial, and the attendants round about the coffin were chaunting the funeral cry, very improperly called "the Irish howl." It was a touching sound. This is a fine harvest for the priest, who levies a handsome subscription on the people present at the burial. We held a meeting at Cootehill on fourth day morning. It was largely attended by a mixed company of Friends, Protestant church-people, and Roman Catholics. It was a time in which the truth was, I trust, exalted, and many, especially of the Roman Catholics, have since been applying to our host for tracts. He tells me his whole stock has been exhausted, by the sudden demand our meeting occasioned. The inquisitive state of the public mind, where education has at all prevailed, is deeply interesting. From Cootehill, our four horses, which we had met with the day before, brought us through some fine nobleman's domains, and afterwards through a dull country to Monaghan; where we spent an hour in visiting a new and very tolerable county jail, full of prisoners; and in sowing the seeds of a ladies' committee. We dined at the inn, and reached the hotel at Armagh in the evening. The travelling in these parts is uncommonly tedious, the Irish stages swelling to an unreasonable length; and no mile stones. It is difficult to get on without four horses. Fifth day morning at Armagh, was highly interesting. It is a fine inland town. We first visited the county jail, and found a peculiarly open door for intercourse with the prisoners; the first time this has happened to us in Ireland. Popery has, in general, appeared to block up the way in the minds of the prisoners. From the prison we proceeded to the lunatic asylum for five counties, admirably managed, none under restraint, and a considerable number of both men and women employed. We then went to Lady Lifford's, at the deanery. She knew dear Priscilla, and is a close ally of Lady Gosford's. Here we met several ladies, and laid the foundation of a visiting association. Lady Lifford is a charming, elderly lady; an humble, solid, practical Christian, abounding in good works. On separating one from another, we were favoured with a true solemnity. Thence to Richill, where a large meeting of Friends and others were assembled at two o'clock; I believe to a good purpose, as the gospel was fully preached and gladly received. That night we reached Rhoane Hill, near Grange, where we were kindly entertained by an interesting family of Friends, and on sixth day morning we held a large meeting at Grange. It was to me a time of deep exercise of mind. These were the parts in which Friends were once so led away by infidelity, and their present state reminded me of the condition of the Jews after they came from Babylon; returned indeed from captivity, but yet without the Urim and Thummim, and after a time without prophets. Through all, there seemed a strong hope of revival, and two young people have lately begun to minister there. After a tedious journey, we reached this place (Lisburn) on sixth day evening, and find ourselves quite at home, under the care of our young friend, Jonathan Richardson, in his father's comfortable house; the parents in England. There is an excellent Friends' school here, the Hibernian Ackworth, and most of yesterday was employed in the examination of the children, and in setting on foot the Ackworth plans of scriptural instruction. I found the wheel move rather heavily, but believe success is likely to crown the effort. The meeting of ministers and elders was held in the evening. I am sitting up now to finish this letter after a laborious day. A large meeting with Friends this morning, and with the public this evening, besides a continued stream of family engagements. One of our companions in the work has been John Conran, a veteran preacher of 88 years, who stood his ground valiantly in the time of the secession, and was for some years afterward the only minister, or elder, in the north of Ireland. He has already been joined by six more, and many others seem likely to follow in the train. Nothing can well exceed the loveliness of this dear old man's spirit. His preaching highly animating, his fine white locks flowing over his shoulders. Our meetings have been much favoured to-day, and I think we all retire to rest with the feelings of thankfulness and peace.

Grace Hill, County Antrim, 3rd mo., 14th, 1827.

My Journal is sadly in arrear. I last wrote on first day the 4th from Lisburn. The public meeting that evening was remarkably interesting; many Roman Catholics there; and my doctrine, as I supposed, very anti-papistical; but the report made by one of their community was, that I preached the same things as their own priest!

The following day was devoted to the business of the Quarterly Meeting, which was large; twice the size of ours. It was a day of unction. Our dear sister and her sister

E. F—— visited the men's meeting; and John Conran, that veteran warrior in the army of the Lamb, preached in the course of the morning one of the best sermons I ever heard, on the Sonship and Divinity of our Saviour. A young man in a low line of life, knelt down and supplicated very powerfully. There is a remarkable breaking forth of the ministry in these parts, chiefly in the poorer class of the Society.

On third day a concluding meeting for worship, with a very large and interesting body of Friends; it was an extraordinary time, and one that could not fail to leave very encouraging impressions. Then to the County Infirmary, a valuable institution, a Ladies' Committee established; then to the Provincial School, to drink tea with the children, amongst whom I finally established my plan of scriptural instruction; then another large public meeting. The state of the public mind in this country requires a nice and delicate touch, and the greatest care is requisite to keep clear of all sectarian and party feeling.

On fourth day we left Lisburn on our way to several country meetings. The weather wild. After attending a large meeting at Ballinderry, we went through a driving snow to Lurgan, county of Down, the original settlement of Friends in this land. A large old meeting-house, and a small scattered flock. There was no invitation, and the weather was very severe, yet the inhabitants of the place flocked to meeting, evidently athirst, in no common degree, after living waters; and a very solemn assembly we had. Dear E—— was much strengthened for the occasion. A long drive through wind and snow, brought us late at night to the hospitable mansion of Thomas Christy Wakefield, of Moyallen. This was once a flourishing colony of Friends in a beautiful country; a village of pretty villas; but, alas! the bright scene has vanished under the deadly touch of infidelity. Many of the principal Friends seceded many years ago, and have remarkably come to nothing. There is a little faithful band preserved from the wreck, some of whom are particularly pleasing. Notwithstanding the snow, we had a meeting with Friends in the morning, and with the public in the evening. The next day, more snow having fallen, we could not proceed on our journey, the roads being impassable. I called on the Friends, and in the afternoon and evening we were met by a large party of young people. We were anxious to go off the next morning, and four horses took us, with considerable difficulty, to Hillsborough, where there is a small settlement of Friends. We held a meeting there, to which many came through a pouring rain.

On seventh day night we returned to our old lodgings at Lisburn, and proceeded on first day morning to meeting, at Belfast; a beautiful drive of seven miles, through a fruitful valley, under fine mountains. Belfast is the Liverpool of Ireland. A few years ago there were only two or three Friends; now there are thirty families. A remarkable seriousness seemed to prevail among the young people, and here we heard another young man minister very acceptably. Our public meeting that evening was held in a large school room, on an upper floor. There was an almost frightful *effusio populi.* When we arrived punctually at the time appointed, we found the people going away by hundreds, disappointed for want of room. We were put to difficulty to get into the room. The crowd was very overpowering to our dear sister, and I was afraid she would have fainted. However we got to our places at last. Protection and strength were graciously afforded. I was enabled to declare the gospel with rather unusual power, and all was soon profoundly quiet; and, in the end, the vast assembly dispersed in quietness and safety. I am sure you would have felt for us, could you have watched our movements that night.

The next day we had abundance of work as usual. First, a a visit to the House of Correction, with a crowd of ladies and gentlemen flocking after our dear sister; amongst the rest, the clergy, English Church, Presbyterian, and Roman Catholic. Dr. Croly, the Roman Catholic Bishop, was with us, a very liberal man. All these denominations unite in the religious instruction of the prisoners. I sent the bishop both my works. They say his liberality enables him to proselyte more successfully. Then to Carrickfergus, a long and beautiful drive under the mountains by the coast. There is a large county jail there for Antrim; and very thoroughly we inspected it. While I visited the male side, E—— succeeded in forming a ladies' committee. We returned to a late dinner at our friend William Bell's; a crowd of Friends, chiefly young, came in the evening; and it was no light matter to meet the occasion after the fatigue of the day. However, all passed off well. But alas! on our return to our lodgings to supper, behold another party to meet us, some of the principal Presbyterians. The Presbyterians form the largest portion of the population in this part of Ireland, and are at Belfast divided into two parties, Orthodox and Arian. By dear E——'s desire, another public meeting was appointed for yesterday morning, at eleven, to which the upper classes were principally invited. It was a beautiful congregation of upwards of 1000 orderly, attentive, well-dressed people; and a highly favoured occasion. The place which our dear sister has among them all, is truly remarkable; amongst other effects, it seems in a singular degree to stop the objections entertained to women's preaching. A clergyman who had expressed these objections before the meeting, said after it, "No one who loves the truth would dare to prevent them." A variety of public institutions were next to be visited. E—— went to the Penitentiary, and I to the Schools; both of us to the Poor-house, a place of refuge for the aged and infirm, and for orphan children; very well managed. In the evening dear E—— had a congregation of ladies at the meeting-house, to arrange committees for visiting the Poor-house, the Penitentiary and the Prison. I went to Carrickfergus again, having been brought under a concern of mind to hold a public meeting there. The rain poured in torrents; but there was a pretty good congregation in the Methodist meeting-house. * * * *

Omagh, county Tyrone, 3rd mo., 19th, 1827.

MY DEAREST SISTERS,

I wrote to you from Grace hill, the Moravian settlement, on fourth day evening. That morning we passed an interesting hour in surveying the settlement; the first I had ever seen. The single sisters, about fifty in number, occupy one large house, and seemed very cheerful and happy; but they do not appear to live greatly for the benefit of mankind; not attending much to the education of the poor, and leaving the sick to their ministers. We left our various books, and proceeded to a little meeting at Low Grange, consisting of an aged widow, and her son and daughter, with a few others. However, many persons came in, including two clergymen, and we had a very comfortable meeting.

We took a repast of eggs and bacon at a public house in a small town hard by — Portglenone. Here we distributed tracts. The *empressement* of the people to obtain these treasures, is really interesting. They seemed delighted with my letter on Christianity, chiefly because of its neutrality. We find it does not at all answer for us to issue any controversial tracts, or to mix ourselves in the questions now so warmly agitated between the churches of Rome and England. It seems our business to bring home to the one Foundation.

We arrived in the evening at a Friend's house in the country, where we held a meeting, with a very small flock: including a young Roman Catholic lady, who seems convinced of the principles of Friends. Her brother trod the same course before her, and underwent great persecution, and has since died in early life. We travelled that day on the banks of Lough Neagh. Some of the scenery was fine, especially in the demesne of Earl O'Neill, whose castle overlooked the lake, till it was consumed by fire. It is now a pile of ruins. * *

On seventh day, we proceeded, chiefly by the sea coast and the banks of Lough Foyle, to Londonderry; where we arrived early in the afternoon, having appointed a rendezvous at the jail at three o'clock.

The situation of this little city is highly beautiful, on the banks of the river Foyle, and with a good harbour; the town is encircled with a wall, on the top of which is a fine walk; and the cathedral, finer than Irish cathedrals in general, towers over the whole scene.

On our arrival at the jail, we found our letters had not reached their destination, so that no one was there to meet us. But it was curious to observe how soon the scene was changed. Forth came, on the notice of the moment, the mayor, the government inspector, the clergy, (Presbyterian and Church of England,) the bishop and his lady, and many others. The openness of everybody towards us was interesting. After our business had been effected, we three dined at the bishop's, at half-past six, and met rather a grand party; chiefly of the Northland (or Knox) family, of which he is one. He is a generous, and liberal-minded man; freely spending the large income which his see produces. He is the head and supporter of all the charitable institutions. It was amusing to see him and his lady, with other authorities, arranging the seats of the great court house, for our meeting in the morning. We may truly say that times are changed. How different from the persecutions Friends once endured!

Yesterday was one of deep and varied exercise of mind. We felt it very much in prospect. At half-past ten, the hour appointed, the court house was rapidly filled with the gentry of the town and neighbourhood. It was a solemn and satisfactory meeting; many seemed deeply impressed, particularly a lady of rank, who was completely broken down. She said, after our afternoon meeting, that she must have come to it, had it even cost her her life. The afternoon meeting was held at the Presbyterian meeting house, at half-past three. About 2000 persons there; the bishop himself and his family sitting immediately in front of us. It was no light occasion. I never found one more arduous. But all ended well, though through deep humiliation. After it was over dear E—— met the ladies, and completely succeeded in forming her committee. The bishop took me in his car, to see the Infirmary and other institutions. We turned our backs on Londonderry, with peaceful minds, at half-past six this morning; still accompanied by our four active and agreeable guides, Thomas and Charles Wakefield, John Christy, and William Bell. We have visited two large jails to day, two Infirmaries, and one

Lunatic Asylum at Lifford, the county town of Donegal. Here at Omagh, the county town of Tyrone, there are 104 prisoners for trial; ten for murder! They are cases of violent political feeling and revenge. The assizes begin to-morrow, and we are stopped for want of horses. It was entertaining to see the members of the bar, in numbers, running down the street, on our arrival being known, to meet us at the prison. We have formed our committee, and our dear sister has been with the judges, who happily agree with us on the subject of Capital Punishment. We mean, if possible, to reach Sligo to-morrow.

CHAPTER XVIII.

1827. ÆT. 39.

ROUTE TO SLIGO; STATE OF THE COUNTRY; HIBERNIAN BLUNDER; GALWAY; ILLNESS OF ELIZABETH FRY; CLONMEL; CARLOW; DR. DOYLE; BALLITORE; YEARLY MEETING IN DUBLIN; FINAL VISIT TO LORD WELLESLEY; WICKLOW; ENNISCORTHY; WEXFORD; WATERFORD; RETURN TO ENGLAND.

Mountmellick, Queen's County,
3rd mo., 25th, 1827.

I WROTE last from Omagh, in Tyrone, where we stopped in the midst of the confusion of the assizes. This was last second day. I went to bed very tired, and rose at half-past four in the morning, not greatly refreshed by the damp little bed which had fallen to my lot. We were obliged to rise thus early, as we had a long day's journey in prospect. A very difficult stage of about twenty English miles, over a road dangerous for night travelling, brought us to Tempo, a little village, where we obtained some breakfast in the mud-floored room of a public house. The Roman Catholic population of the place were very eager for our tracts, of which we distributed many. Indeed, I may say that the dissemination of them, and particularly of the Letter on Christianity, has been one of our very interesting objects during the past week. We meet on the roads vast numbers of intelligent looking people, to whom the gift of a tract is most acceptable. They commence reading them forthwith, with much zeal. Sometimes, however, they are afraid to receive them. I happened to give a poor man a copy of the Letter, just as a priest was riding towards him. The man immediately delivered up his treasure to the priest, who, with an expression of peculiar bitterness, tore it in halves, and threw it into a ditch:—a sly little boy, however, ran off with the fragments. The thirst for information which prevails in the parts of Ireland where we have lately been, is most remarkable. I believe that the system of the papal priesthood begins to be shaken to its centre; and we have seen enough to convince us, that provided *truth*, and not *infidelity*, is the alternative, the sooner it falls the better; for it is an iron yoke.

From Tempo to Enniskillen, a populous town, prettily situated on the banks of Lough Erne. Here we visited the infirmary, and a very indifferent jail, in which were six persons under a charge of desperate murder. This is no uncommon crime in Ireland. Deeply settled revenge is in general the cause; and it is often attended with awful barbarity. I do not exaggerate when I say that we have seen dozens of murderers during the last week. In Roscommon jail were ten more, for the murder of a member of our Society, a mere nominal Friend, who had a quantity of arms in his house, which were in part, the object of pursuit. He defended himself vigorously, but it was all in vain. He was shot by the assailants; and more desperate characters than they appeared to be, I never beheld. At Sligo there was a prisoner who had roasted a poor woman alive! Nothing can exceed the ferocity into which the unbridled passions of this unhappy people lead them, when party spirit has the sway over them. After forming our Committee of Ladies, we left Enniskillen in the afternoon, on our way to Sligo, in some hopes of reaching that place before night. Our drive during daylight was delightful; the scenery like that in the Highlands, under fine mountains, and by the side of a beautifully wooded lake; Lord Enniskillen's castle, at Florence court, being a principal object in the scene. The peasantry very numerous, well dressed, decent, and intelligent. We enjoyed supplying them with tracts. The linen manufacture extends as far as Sligo, and has a great effect in promoting the decency and welfare of the population, it being entirely a domestic manufacture.

Our efforts to reach Sligo proved fruitless. We were benighted just as we arrived at an inn, called the Red Lion, which the persons we met on the road described as a "very grand" place; but it proved so wretched, that we determined to push forwards to Manor Hamilton, ten miles farther, notwithstanding the risk which attends travelling by night on these roads; both from the deep ditches on each side, and from the prevalence of violent robbery. We found it difficult to get along, and when at last we reached the town, O the extreme filth and poverty of the accommodation which awaited us! I never before lodged in so sad a place; and felt really anxious for dear E———, and her sister, who had risen at four in the morning. But we ought to be more than content to suffer a little—and it is but a little—for the sake of a good cause.

I set off, with two of the guides, early for Sligo, on fourth day morning, to prepare the way. Our visit there was uncommonly interesting. We came total strangers to the place, but all sorts of people had open arms to receive us. I soon found a few pious persons, they called on others, and early in the afternoon we visited the prison, in company with a crowd of ladies and gentlemen, including the High Sheriff. The assizes were going on in the town, and not a bed, room, or hovel, was to be had at any inn. We took private lodgings, but this was unnecessary, so many were desirous of making us their guests. In the evening we went to the rector's, where we were met by a large inquisitive party. We did what we could to interest and instruct, and formed a Ladies' Committee very satisfactorily.

The next morning was very interesting. We breakfasted at the house of some pious people named Whitacre, who had provided me with a lodging. After breakfast, several of the late converts from Popery came to see us. Sligo has already added forty-two names to the "reformation," and fourteen more were to come forward to-day as recanters of error. The people who met us that morning excited our sincere regard and interest. They were intelligent men of the lower middle class, and had been all brought to a knowledge of the truth, chiefly through the reading of the Scriptures. Their account of the faith that was in them, and of their scriptural reasons for renouncing Popery, was wonderfully clear. They were evidently enlightened by a power more than human, and appeared spiritually minded, hungering and thirsting after righteousness. There was an obvious approach in some of their minds, towards the principles of Friends. It is, indeed, a wonderful work, which now appears to be rapidly going forward in the minds of this afflicted, but interesting people.

As the morning advanced, we held, in the Linen Hall, a large public meeting; which we understood to have been the only one that had been held there for thirty years and upwards. It was genteelly attended, which I attributed chiefly to E——'s public character, and was a time of remarkable openness, the word appearing "to run" and find entrance. It was difficult to make our escape from Sligo, the people were all so loving. However, after an early dinner we drove off, and arrived in the evening at the pretty town of Boyle, county of Roscommon, (still in Connaught,) where we found a comfortable inn. On sixth day we travelled through much of that desolate looking county, and reached Roscommon to dinner. There we visited the Infirmary, Jail, and Lunatic Asylum; the last a horrid place indeed, which we have represented to Lord and Lady Lorton, the most influential people in the county, the latter of whom was repeatedly with us in Dublin. Some of the scenes we have of late witnessed in the public institutions have been most distressing; vice and misery in abundance. Nobody can tell what this country is, without visiting it; but long must be our visit, were it required of us to obtain a full knowledge of the Irish character. We held our evening meeting at a little village called Ballymurry, where there are a few Friends; and lodged at the clean comfortable house of a widow, Margaret Robinson, with an interesting family of young people. Yesterday morning we went more than twenty miles, to a ten o'clock meeting at Moate, in Westmeath, from which place we came hither last evening. Westmeath is one of the most disturbed of the counties; murders very frequent. Fifteen poor men are expected to be executed at the jail at Mullingar! You may depend on our not running any unnecessary risks. I fully believe we have nothing to fear.

We find a large Quarterly Meeting assembled here, about four hundred Friends, and the day has, I hope, been a good one. Dearest Priscilla is remembered with peculiar love and delight. We have been spending the evening at the house of her intimate friend, Ann Shannon, where we have seen a party of one hundred, chiefly young people. I hope they were ministered to with some effect. Friends are not satisfied here with a large circle round a room; the whole square surface is filled like a Lancasterian school-room. * *

Galway, 4th mo., 1st, 1827.

After a deeply exercising, and, in various respects, serious day, I sit down to continue my journal; though I despair of giving to any persons, who do not see Ireland for themselves, a full notion of what it is, and what the people are.

Last third day morning the large Quarterly Meeting at Mountmellick, for the province of Leinster, concluded with a meeting for worship; in which there was an uncommon outpouring of that influence which prepares both for the utterance and the reception of the gospel. Friends parted from us in much love. Afterwards I had three considerable schools to visit, in all of which I succeeded in establishing my system of scriptural instruction. The Provincial Friends' school at Mountmellick, has been reduced to a very low ebb; and, I rather hope, our visit to it will have a considerable effect in its revival. In the evening we held a public meeting, which was largely attended.

On fourth day morning, a day of continued and impetuous rain, we went to breakfast at the country seat of James Pim, of Monkstown, the brother of our host at Dublin; where we met about twenty-four of that family. We passed an interesting hour with them. Then to the county jail for Queen's County, at Maryboro'; carefully superintended by a pious clergyman, named Harper; for all the jails in Ireland are under the care of local inspectors: a very good arrangement. The state of immorality in these parts is tremendous. There were eleven cases of murder for trial at the assizes, which were then about to commence. Whilst E—— was forming her Ladies' Committee, I was engaged with these wretched felons, who appeared considerably affected, especially one of the poor murderers.

It is a sad circumstance, that the priesthood are now entirely set against the schools for "all," especially in the diocese of the famous Dr. Doyle, where we find all the children of the Roman Catholics removed, and many a noble Institution miserably ruined in consequence. It may truly be said, that the blind teachers of this blind people, prefer darkness to light. The effect produced by the reading of Scripture, has alarmed them thoroughly, and the consequence is, at present, very lamentable; but there are cheering symptoms of the gradual breaking of this truly iron yoke.

We held good meetings at Mountrath and Abbeylieux, in Queen's County, and took up our quarters for the night at Abbeylieux house, Viscount de Vesci's. Here, in consequence of an Hibernian blunder (and in this land accuracy is a scarce article,) we found ourselves in the humbling character of uninvited guests. We had been led to understand that we were warmly invited, whereas nothing of the kind had taken place; and this was not intentional deception, but only that total want of exact representation of the truth, to which the traveller in Ireland is frequently exposed. The result in the present instance was curious; a party of seven Friends drove up to a nobleman's house, on a dark night, knocked at his door, and quietly informed him that they were come to lodge.

Lord and Lady de Vesci are truly kind, hospitable people, resident on their own beautiful estate, and the benefactors of the population around them. They received us kindly, and took five of us in. The next morning we held a public meeting, which passed off well, and left them in peace, on our way to Rathdowny, where we dined with a newly settled young couple of Friends; and proceeded onwards to Knock, to attend a little country meeting. It was a darksome evening, but the meeting was well attended by Friends and others, and was a very solemn one. We lodged at Ballymalish, the house of Joseph Thacker, a county magistrate. He is connected with Friends, has an interesting family, and received us with great hospitality; his family accompanying us in their carriage to Roscrea meeting the next morning. He gives a curious account of the Popish population by which he is surrounded. Their late "jubilee" has been attended by very injurious moral effects; the ceremonies practised on the occasion being thought to have the effect of procuring free forgiveness for the sins of seven years past, and free license for the sins of the seven years now to come. This, at least, appears to be the notion of the extremely ignorant amongst them.

The meeting at Roscrea, a large town in Tipperary full of curious remains of antiquity, was a large one; and the truth seemed to make its way. In most of these meetings, besides the small company of Friends we have their neighbours also, which we find relieving to our minds. Indeed, a greater degree of selectness seems impossible, for there is a vast eagerness on the part of the people to come to our meetings. In the evening we held a large public meeting at Birr, in King's County; a fine town; where the Roman Catholics are in a state of much agitation, in consequence of quarrels between their priests. Many of them came to the meeting. I was much led to insist on the right and duty, common to all, of reading the Scriptures, and on the guidance of the Spirit. I believe they were generally satisfied. This town belongs to the Earl of Ross, who resides near it. He, and his wife and children, were at the meeting, and seemed much pleased.

On seventh day we travelled seventy English miles, through the county of Galway, to this truly foreign place; and in the course of this long day's journey, held a good public meeting at Ballynasloe, a large town. There are several serious clergymen in that part of the county, who gave us a warm reception; amongst the rest Archdeacon Trench, one of the Archbishop of Tuam's brothers, who was lately in danger of his life at one of the discussion meetings. The "Reformation" is going on at Ballynasloe. The Roman Catholics flocked to our meeting, which was an open and favoured opportunity. We could not but believe, that a work of true religion is going on there. The drive to Galway is through an uninteresting country.

The population appears pretty well attired; but, in some parts, the hovels are wretched in the extreme. On visiting one of them, we found a poor Roman Catholic widow, a true Christian, living upon almost nothing, and full of a peaceful, thankful spirit. She had contrived to impart an uncommon degree of neatness and cleanliness to her miserable hut, though her pig has free egress and ingress. We arrived here late at night. Galway is an old Spanish town, containing 40,000 inhabitants in the depths of popery, 150 priests, three nunneries: filth and ignorance abounding, notwithstanding a fine harbour and considerable trade. We have passed a truly strange day. Early in the morning the mayor came to us, to say that if we chose to hold meetings here, he should feel it his duty to mount a guard of soldiers over our congregation; at the same time, professing a readiness to assist us. He seemed completely alarmed at the prospect, and it required a little steadiness and faith to go forward in the path of duty. We, of course, declined a guard, and endeavoured to quiet his fears. We have since held our meetings: the first at eleven o'clock in a large room at the inn; about 200 people with us. The power of truth was remarkably to be felt; and we found ourselves enabled to preach the fundamental doctrines of Christianity, and the peaceableness of true religion. They were chiefly Roman Catholics, and were going in and out during most of the meeting. I believe we were as strange to them as possible. Another meeting was appointed for four o'clock in the Corn Exchange, a large room. This was to us all an inexpressibly exercising meeting; a time of real conflict of mind. There was a vast crowd, chiefly of Roman Catholics, in spite of their bishop, and some tumult on the stairs and at the doors; the congregation itself of the more respectable order. In the present irritable and touchy state of public feeling, with the poor frightened mayor in the room, we had, indeed, need of the "mind of Christ." We were marvellously helped through. I preached on faith in the Father, in the Son, and in the Holy Ghost. Dear E—— unfolded the practical part with admirable force and clearness, and E. F—— concluded with prayer. At the close of the meeting the poor Irish *stamped* approbation.

We were greatly relieved, and the Roman Catholics of the upper class appeared fully satisfied, as well as the Protestants; who are here a small minority, about one-fortieth part of the population. The Roman Catholics were heard to say, that if we had meetings every night, they would be sure to come, and that all the priests in the kingdom should not prevent them. I have since been walking by the harbour, and through the crowded streets. It is like one of the populous towns in France, quite foreign in its appearance. We have jails, schools, and nunneries to visit to-morrow.

On third day we are going, (if not prevented) to Sir Edward and Lady O'Brien's, on our way to Limerick. We are all well, though the weight of our engagements is great indeed.

TO MARY FOWLER.

Cork, 4th mo., 8th, 1827.

* * * On third day we proceeded to Ennis, in the county of Clare, where we were met by a crowd of ladies and gentlemen; inspected the county prison, poor-house, and infirmary, and parted after a short, solemn meeting with them. We dined and slept at Dromland, the seat of Sir E. O'Brien. The openings for religious service amongst them and their friends were numerous; especially in a little town called Newmarket, where Lady O'Brien employs a great number of the poor in fine needlework, which sells well in London. Our visit being noised abroad, we had a flock to meet us there, chiefly I suppose, from a desire to see my dear sister; and, amongst the rest, the Roman Catholic dean was quite caught in the net. I read the Scriptures to the assembled crowd, and we had, I trust, a very precious and solemn meeting. We went thence to Limerick, where we were most kindly entertained by our dear friends Joseph Massey Harvey and his wife. We passed three nights under their roof. Whilst in that city we could a little understand what the apostle Paul meant by "being pressed out of measure," for the multitudes that came after my dear sister put us to some inconvenience at the prisons; and the meeting house was so completely filled, that on one occasion it was said

500 went away. However, I trust and believe, the Master was with us: the hearts of the people seemed wonderfully opened towards us. * * *

At this period of their journey the health of his sister, Elizabeth Fry, began to give way under the effects of over-exertion and fatigue, and they were glad to avail themselves of the repose and unremitting attentions afforded them under the hospitable roof of John Strangman, of Waterford.

Joseph John Gurney subsequently writes to his sisters:

Carlow, 4th mo., 26th, 1827.

We passed a very anxious week at Waterford, our invalid requiring the closest watching and attention. The attacks of fever were certainly violent, and we could not tell what might come of it, as a dangerous fever was very prevalent in the place. It was some trial of faith and patience to be detained day after day; but I endeavoured to make some use of spare moments, in calling upon Friends, &c. Last fifth day after meeting I went to examine the Mendicity Institution. There is one of these in most of the principal towns—a receptacle where the extremely indigent, who would otherwise have no resource but begging, are fed and employed, and their children instructed; very useful institutions, but not now adequate to meet the wants of a half-starved population. It is affecting to think of the sufferings of the poor, in the towns particularly. The landed proprietors have driven them off their estates, in large numbers, taking advantage of the expiration of the leases on which they once held their miserable huts; and they have no refuge but in the towns, where many of them are reduced to an extremity of want. They meet their afflictions with a very strong principle of resignation. It is one of the effects of the Roman Catholic religion here, which above everything else preaches "submission."

I believe the bloody and riotous part of the population are

far from being the most distressed. It is no wonder, with all this want and misery, that the low fever should so abound. In Waterford there were, while we were there, from twenty to thirty applicants, day after day, for admission to the Fever Hospital. This hospital I did not visit, but it is admirably attended to, and there are two or three noble minded men, (Friends,) who have long been accustomed to risk their lives in close personal attention to its poor inmates. Happily, there are very few large towns in Ireland without a similar provision.

On sixth day morning last, though dear E—— had passed a poor night, and was very weak, we all felt it right to move for Clonmel, where the Quarterly Meeting was to commence on the following day. The way opened for us beyond expectation; and at one o'clock we were in the carriage. The drive of about thirty miles, English, lies through the "golden valley," a rich and beautiful green district, watered by the Suir. The contrast between the extreme fertility of the land, and the wretchedness of the inhabitants, which we never observed more striking than in the town of Carrick on Suir, is melancholy and almost unaccountable; partly to be attributed to the whiskey shops, which abound on every side. Alas! what a work the Prince of darkness has wrought in this land! In the evening we arrived at Melbrook, the picturesque residence of the widow Mary Strangman, and her agreeable daughters. Dear E—— bore the journey very tolerably, and slept fairly. Whilst she remained quiet in her room, on seventh day, I passed some hours, after the select meeting, in a laborious visitation of the prisons, and the house of industry.

The county of Tipperary has been in a very disturbed state, and the outrages committed, almost nightly, have been of a horrid character, not much connected with political causes. They are rather, I fear, symptoms of a deep moral degeneracy. In illustration of this, I may mention that about 150 ruffians were discharged by proclamation, at the late assizes at Clonmel, because the prosecutors were prevented by the law of terror from coming forward against them. These prosecutors are liable to a fine in consequence, which is paid by the offending parties, and so the matter is, in many cases, compromised. But this state of things is only in two or three of the counties. Dearest E—— was able to attend the morning meeting on first day, (the Quarterly Meeting,) and was wonderfully helped to minister. It was a time of close and rather painful exercise of mind. In the evening she went down to Anner Mills, where we took up our abode for two days; a delightful place, inhabited by a veteran in the good cause, Sarah Grubb, a widow upwards of 80, and strong in her intellectual, as well as lively in her spiritual faculties. She lives with her daughter, Elizabeth Clibborn, who has twelve fine children. It is truly an abode of peace, a Christian family. Here we were most comfortably accommodated. E——'s sister and I joined her there after attending a large public meeting in the evening, in which it was particularly laid upon me to unfold the spiritual nature of the gospel, and the universality of the grace of God. It was a time of deep solemnity. We dined that day with Margaret Grubb, an aged, but lively minister, daughter of the late Richard Shackleton, and were enabled, I trust, to minister to her consolation. There is nothing more enlivening than a green old age. We have seen much of this lately, and ought to be confirmed in our course by it.

On third day, the concluding meeting for worship was held, a very large one, and I have not often sat in a meeting in which there was a more evident effusion of the Spirit of the Great Baptizer. It was a great comfort thus to end well at Clonmel, and to leave the place with minds so much relieved. After parting visits of an interesting nature, to our dear Friends at Melbrook and Anner Mills, we journeyed on for about forty miles through the county of Kilkenny, a fine, arable, cultivated district, to the Royal Oak, a country inn, where we slept; our beloved invalid evidently improving.

Dublin, 5th mo., 2nd, 1827.

I wrote from Carlow last fifth day morning. That day turned out to be one of rather peculiar interest. Whilst dear E——

and her sister visited some of the Friends, I undertook the more laborious task of inspecting the jail, &c. The public mind was a little afloat about us, and numbers of the gentry of the county met me. In the course of our round the Roman Catholic priest made his appearance, and began to lodge his complaints with me (as if I was umpire) against the crowd of Protestants present, and chiefly the Protestant clergy, for interfering with his spiritual cure in the jail. The two parties have been a good deal aggravated against each other in these parts, and it seemed peculiarly important that we should pacify and reconcile, if possible. I therefore begged the priest and the Protestant clergy to come to our lodgings to discuss their knotty qnestions, (chiefly relating to the use of the Scriptures in the jail,) with my sister and myself quietly. We happily brought them to terms, and I went afterwards to the Roman Catholic Bishop Doyle to get the arrangement confirmed. He is considered by far the most able and powerful supporter of the Popish system in this land, and is painted very black by the Protestants, very undeservedly so I believe. He gave me a polite reception, and is not more acute than gentlemanlike and pleasing. He gave his full sanction to the arrangement; but you will a little judge of the state of things here, when you are told that the only terms on which we could get the Scriptures read to these miserable criminals were, that only the Douay version should be used, that the priest should select the chapters, and that either he or some Roman Catholic prisoner should be the reader. It is unquestionable that Popery presents an effective bar to free and fair religious instruction. There is a perpetual fight going on between the tyranny of their system, and the desire for knowledge which is every where arising. I was glad to add Dr. Doyle to the number of extraordinary men seen and known by us in Ireland. Whilst I was with him, dear E—— paid a visit to the nunnery, where she was warmly received. We proceeded in the afternoon a long stage to Ballitore, not expecting a meeting there till the next morning, and being very weary with the day's work; but on our arrival, we found both Friends and other people assembling to meet us, and many already seated in the meeting-house. I was frightened for our weary invalid; but there was no alternative, and she was wonderfully carried over the difficulty, being enabled to minister to what we afterwards found to be the state of those present, with much effect. The minister of the parish was there, as is the case in most of our meetings. He seemed a serious character, and expressed much satisfaction.

Ballitore is classic ground among Friends in Ireland, having been from generation to generation, the residence of the Shackletons, by one of whom Edmund Burke was educated. Burke's schoolfellow and intimate friend, Richard Shackleton, a venerable elder, is still remembered in Ireland with reverence and affection. Infidelity made sad ravages in this little meeting at the time of the secession. The school is still maintained by a learned Friend, named James White. I had an opportunity of establishing my plan of scriptural instruction, and have been truly glad to find so general a willingness on the part of Friends to co-operate in the prosecution of this object.

On our way from Ballitore to Dublin, on sixth day, we visited the jail at Naas, the county town of Kildare, reaching the house of our hospitable friend Jonathan Pim, in the evening.

On seventh day morning Richard Pope came to breakfast with us. He is the talk of Ireland just now, and a highly interesting person. He has broken off his connexion with the Church of England, which clears him of all ecclesiastical authority, and he moves about in the work of the gospel where and as he pleases. His late public disputation with "Father" Maguire, in Dublin, which lasted several days, has excited intense interest. The Papists claim a "splendid victory," and I believe the Jesuit troubled poor Pope more than was expected, but there is little doubt that the cause of truth will be promoted by the discussion. They say that Pope's arguments were solid and convincing, and his eloquence at times surprising. I felt a real love for him, he is modest and deep. I fear, however, that his bodily powers are rapidly giving way. He has worked too hard.

I hardly know how to enter on the particulars of our Yearly Meeting. It has been so far a remarkable occasion; much life and solemnity in most of the sittings; and the meetings for worship highly favoured by the presence of Him, who can alone teach his disciples how to worship aright. The Friends are collected in great numbers, and we have the company of many from England. The labour is considerable, many pressing after us, and a variety of visits to the houses of Friends filling up all the intervals between the meetings. Yesterday we had a very agreeable interview at the castle, with the Lord Chief Justice Burke, a very superior man, who enters warmly into our views, and promises all the aid he can give, both now and in future. We have been certainly much gratified with the acquaintance we have formed with the Irish judges, many of whom are very useful characters.

To-day we again paid a visit to Lord Wellesley, at the Vice-regal Lodge. He is particularly intelligent, and evidently very desirous to promote the good of the country. Like the king, in England, he has the power of life and death, and his hatred of capital punishment made it easy for us to intercede for one poor man, whom we are anxious to save from the gallows. Ever since our dear sister spoke to this poor creature, (at Ennis, in the county of Clare,) he has shown marked evidence of contrition and reformation. I have no doubt that the man's life will be saved. The Lord Lieutenant listened with the greatest attention to our suggestions on various points, and it is agreed between us that we are to provide him with a written report, addressed to himself, on every subject which we may deem worthy of notice in connexion with the state of Ireland. This he intends communicating to the government at home. We feel the responsibility much, and I heartily wish I may be enabled to draw up such a report as will be useful to this afflicted people.*

* See *infra*, p. 373, a notice of the Report subsequently prepared by Joseph John Gurney.

Milford Haven, 5th mo., 11th, 1827.

My dearest Sisters,

I shall begin this concluding sheet of my journal, by telling you that fair wind and fine weather were our agreeable companions in crossing the sea to-day, and we arrived safely at our desired haven after a good voyage of ten hours.

The Yearly Meeting in Dublin concluded in great solemnity on sixth day evening, and we afterwards met a very large Irish party at our lodgings. There was a remarkable influence over us of divine love, and this was eminently the case the next morning when we parted from our kind friends at William street, as well as in the concluding meeting for ministers and elders.

We got clear of the great city after a final call at the Secretary of State's office, that afternoon; and a drive of thirty English miles, through a very pleasant, rich, and fertile country, brought us at night to Joseph Pim's, at Wicklow, a little town on the sea coast, something like Cromer. There we passed a very interesting "Sabbath;" a meeting with Friends in the morning, a public one in the evening; besides a visitation of the county jail, and a successful effort in forming a Ladies' Committee. There are some very pleasing and serious people in that neighbourhood. The public meeting, held in the court house, was excessively crowded, and brought us into deep exercise of mind. Such meetings in Ireland, under its present circumstances, are occasions of peculiar responsibility. A curious circumstance in connexion with this meeting deserves to be recorded. The rector's usual service was appointed, at the same hour. His whole congregation was with us, with the single exception of his clerk, who forthwith preferred a humble petition that he also might go and hear the Quakers. The rector consented, and he and his clerk came to the meeting together. The Protestants are in general very good tempered towards each other, of which this is a specimen.

On second day we took a fine journey through one of the most romantic districts in Ireland—the vales of Avoca and

Arklow. The weather was fine, and the scenery very admirable —much on a level with some of the finest parts of the Highlands. It was refreshing to us to revel a little on the beauties of nature, and our numerous guides were delighted by our pleasure. The land in the fertile valleys of Wicklow lets in parts for five pounds or six pounds per Irish acre. The barren mountains which they intersect are chiefly of fine granite. We arrived in the evening at the little village-city of Ferns, a bishop's see of many thousands per annum, with an old ruined castle. In the neighbourhood is a quiet meeting of Friends: few in number, but of the right sort. We had much satisfaction in paying them a visit. On third day morning we held a meeting at Enniscorthy with Friends of that district, a scattered flock, which is the more affecting, as the last generation made so noble a stand in those parts at the time of the rebellion. Their deliverances were truly wonderful. The meeting was spontaneously attended by numbers of strangers. The hearts of many are open to receive the truth in the love of it. We were kindly entertained there by Ann Thompson, a young woman who devotes her time to the education of the poor, and accompanied Hannah Kilham to Africa. It is proposed to her that she should go again to Africa. We rather advised her to continue in Ireland. No mission more important I believe. The county of Wexford is a very interesting part of Ireland; the people are of English origin, and in some parts talk the old Anglo-Saxon. They are much more decent than the Irish poor in general, though deeply distressed at present by the failure of the potatoe crop.

We arrived at Wexford, a large town on the sea coast, early in the evening, and truly it was an evening of overpowering exertion. Crowds were waiting for us at the jail, at the entry of the town. It was in vain to attempt to pass by it, though a public meeting was appointed for seven o'clock: we visited it, and my sister formed her committee. When we went to the appointed place of meeting in the evening — a large assembly room on an upper floor — we found it fearfully crowded, and almost insufferably close. Dear E—— seemed much overcome, and what with this, and what with the ticklish state of the people, the noise of a hooting boy-mob under the windows, and the idea that the floor might possibly or probably give way, it was a time of some real conflict of mind to us. However, we were enabled to get pretty well through it, and the truths of the gospel were plainly uttered, and, I trust, joyfully received; and no accident occurred beyond the occasional breaking of a form. You can hardly imagine how really appalling some of our public meetings have been in this land; and yet, I believe, we have been engaged in no service which has told so much. This place is one of the strongholds of Popery, and it was in vain that we proposed to the Romish priesthood, our conciliatory plans for the reading of the Scriptures in the jail. They set their faces against it, under every modification. How long will such a bondage be maintained?

The next day (fourth day) we held meetings, summoned for Friends, but public in effect, at Forest and Ross, and passed through a country interesting for its recollections. Vinegar hill, so infamous for the horrid cruelties practised there by the rebels, and Scalabogue, where they burnt the barn, full of their Protestant victims. This part of the country is now peculiarly peaceable, and free from crime. We dined at Hoareton house with a county magistrate, once a Friend; and at Ross were most kindly entertained by Samuel Elly. The meeting there formed the peaceable and solemn conclusion of our public services in Ireland.

On fifth day to Waterford, where we found a variety of things and people to attend to, and, in the evening, with many kind attendants, we went down to Dunmore, the harbour, where we were glad to take refuge in the Vixen steam packet, which has now so happily restored us to our own land. On the retrospect of our whole deeply interesting journey, we feel quiet, peaceful, and unexcited; and, I trust, can most sincerely adopt the language of David, "What shall we render unto the Lord for all his benefits towards us?"

CHAPTER XIX.

1827—1829. ÆT. 39—42.

ARRIVAL IN LONDON; ALARMING ILLNESS OF HIS BROTHER-IN-LAW, THOMAS FOWELL BUXTON; MARRIAGE WITH MARY FOWLER; HIS SISTER RACHEL GURNEY'S ILLNESS AND DEATH; PUBLICATION OF REPORT ON IRELAND; VARIOUS JOURNEYS; EXTRACTS FROM LETTERS AND JOURNAL.

JOSEPH JOHN GURNEY'S return from Ireland was somewhat clouded by the gradually increasing illness of his sister Rachel, who, with his children, had been staying at Brighton during his absence, for the benefit of her health. On his arrival in London he found his brother-in-law Thomas Fowell Buxton deeply absorbed in preparing for the impending debate upon the question of the continuance of the slave trade in the Mauritius. His brother's state of health awakened some anxiety, though he little anticipated the alarming attack of illness which soon afterwards threatened suddenly to put a period to his important labours.*

TO THOMAS FOWELL BUXTON.

Upton, fourth day, 5th mo., 23rd, 1827.

* * * Pray, my dear Buxton, take entire rest and recreation; and do not overwork the Mauritius case. A few broad

* See Life of Sir T. F. Buxton, pp. 189—194.

proofs will tell better in the House than any vast quantity of detail. I believe the best of helpers will not fail to be with thee; and, after all, nothing will do but putting our trust in Him.

Be sure to get into a truly Christian spirit towards the supposed offender, which will tell more than much scolding.

Earlham, 6th mo., 6th, 1827. Four interesting and important months have passed away, and I find myself once more in this profoundly quiet and peaceful spot, having returned hither by the Day coach last second day evening. * *

On fourth day, the 23rd ultimo, I went down to Brighton, where I was greatly comforted and refreshed in being once more with my beloved sisters and children. I found dearest Rachel, however, a good deal fallen in my absence. The dear children gave me a most affectionate reception. * * *

On second day, we received, by a special messenger, the account of Fowell's extreme illness. He was lying insensible at Upton. We waited the next post, which brought somewhat better tidings, and with Richenda and Edward, I reached Upton on third day afternoon, the 29th. There we had the happiness to find our beloved brother gradually recovering; and since then he has been making a rapid daily improvement. The relief has been inexpressible. I am remarkably favoured on my return with quiet waters outwardly, and with a precious degree of inward peace. Praised be the name of the Lord!

The following are from his letters to Mary Fowler at this period.

Norwich, 6th mo., 6th, 1827.

* * * Having passed a very salutary and reviving Sabbath at Upton, Plashet, and Plaistow, I was the more prepared to enjoy a quiet journey hither; in the course of which I read, with much pleasure, nearly a whole volume of Bishop Watson's Apologies. * * *

In the tender mercy of my heavenly Father I am favoured, on my return to this place, with more than a common portion of the reward of peace. The whole place is clothed in abounding verdure, and I promise myself that thou wilt find it a peaceful and pleasant home. For my own part, I feel very thankful that such a resting place is provided for us, and I see no reason to believe that it may not be our permanent residence; to be exchanged only for one infinitely brighter, purer, and sweeter. I find my solitude not only very pleasant, but very convenient, as it affords me the opportunity of continuing with some portion of vigour and stillness my Report to the Irish Government. I shall not be thoroughly relieved about Ireland till this is finished and despatched. * *

Earlham, 6th mo., 15th, 1827.

* * To-day, I am staying at home to write my Report. I find it hard work, and am too much disposed to an indolent feeling about it. I am sure, however, it cannot be right for me to be idle, since it was but yesterday that I was preaching on "Whatsoever thy hand findeth to do, do it with thy might." * *

In allusion to a visit to the school at Croydon, he writes:—

6th mo., 25th, 1827.

* * My visit was interesting. Though tired with my journey, I got well through the examination of the whole school on seventh day. With the boys I was pleased, with the girls delighted. I never saw children in better training; and their knowledge of the Scriptures, corresponding, as it does, with their conduct, is very gratifying. In the evening we had a table spread on the lawn, covered not with meats, but with a variety of books for rewards. About seventy children received prizes. The next day I had the boys and girls assembled for an hour before meeting. They all had their Bibles, and turned to a variety of passages by way of commentary on the part which principally engaged us — Rev. xxi.

Earlham, first day evening, 7th mo., 1st, 1827.

* * * How apt are we to fail both in faith and in thankfulness! In myself I can truly acknowledge this failure, and it is my prayer that in both of us, peace, love, gratitude, and joy in the Holy Ghost, may more and more abound. Our meetings to-day have been solemn and edifying. I have been but little engaged in ministry since my return until this morning, when the stream flowed, I believe, from the depths. The feelings, thoughts, and words, came to me as if they rose spontaneously out of a fountain over which I had no command, and with which I had no right to intermeddle. * * *

I am getting on pretty well with my Report, and have received a very polite communication on the subject from the Lord Lieutenant. I hope it will not turn out a very dry document. It is well I have it to do in this interval, I might otherwise, possibly, be fretful and impatient.

I have been meditating, during my solitary walk this morning, on the infinite advantage of having an all-wise and almighty Friend; and, I think, I have been in some slight degree enabled to commend myself and my beloved ones, our pleasures, pains, cares, wishes, and hopes, to him. * *

On the 18th of the 7th month he was married to Mary Fowler. "Bright, hopeful, and happy," to use his own words in the Autobiography, "was our wedding day. We dined on the lawn, a large united company, and rejoiced together, I trust in the Lord. Mary and I left the party at Elm Grove in the afternoon for North Devon." He afterwards writes: —

Linton, North Devon, 7th mo., 24th. We are now on the point of quitting the delightful scenery of this place, on our way to Ilfracombe, dearest Mary being my only companion. In waiting from time to time on the Lord, chiefly in silence, we have, I think, notwithstanding our great unworthiness, (and my own is great indeed,) been favoured with a sweet, enlivening sense of the divine presence and favour. It is, I believe, our great and separate desire to be devoted to the service of truth in this evil world. And O that we may be preserved from all the snares of the enemy!

Earlham, 8th mo., 5th. On sixth day evening, after a pleasant journey, viâ Oxford and Cambridge, I brought my dear wife home. Our arrival was very comfortable, and the darling children gave us a truly cordial reception. We have since settled most agreeably, our only cloud being our dearest Rachel's state, who is very ill, and suffering much. It is a deep interest to us all, but adds to our sense of the value and comfort of my beloved Mary's arrival. The preciousness of the gift bestowed upon me is inexpressible.

8th mo., 10th. The death of Canning, of which we heard yesterday, is an awful stroke. It is a singular circumstance, that he should have ended his career in the same house, and I believe the same room as Fox, under political circumstances so very similar. Each of them attained the summit of his ambition and fell. I cannot help entertaining a strong hope, that his repeated warnings may have been the means of bringing him to his God before he died.

TO JONATHAN HUTCHINSON.

Norwich, 8th mo., 25th, 1827.

My dear sister Rachel is greatly sunk, and it has been for the last two weeks our affecting task to watch her entrance on the valley of the shadow of death. In the frame of her spirit she is as one who has *begun to die.* Remarkably redeemed does she appear to be from all dependence on human help. She finds the reality of those things in which she has so long believed, and speaks sweetly of the inexpressible privilege of feeling and knowing that her "Redeemer liveth."

8th mo., 27th. On our return with Richenda, from Lowestoft, on third day, we found our dearest Rachel a little further sunk, and we have been chiefly occupied during the week in attending to her. She seems wonderfully helped to meet the approach of death. On ——'s throwing out a hint respecting the "sacrament," she disclaimed any wish or intention to partake in that ceremony, acknowledged that in past days she had received benefit from the services of the Church of England, but that she was now feeding exclusively on the substance, and did, indeed, eat the flesh and drink the blood of the Son of Man. I am truly thankful for her being brought to this experience. Indeed her abstraction from all dependence on human help is wonderful.

His sister's illness continued to engross much of his attention for several weeks. The following are a few selections from his own more detailed account of her last days.*

One morning on going into her bed-room after our reading, I found her enjoying a sensible visitation of divine love, and she sweetly uttered the words of the Psalmist, "I have none in heaven but thee, nor on all the earth that I desire beside thee." Another time when my sister Fry went to her in the night, and expressed her belief that peace was prevalent: "yes," she said, "I feel the Ruler and Head of his people to be very near to me." "Yesterday," she added, "was one of great suffering; such an one as I never passed before, but, through all, I leaned on the Beloved."

A few days later, upon her medical attendant's coming into the room, she said, "I *must* tell you that there is but one principle which can support us, the love of God in Christ Jesus;" and speaking of her own feelings she added, "Divine love and power are with me every moment."

The day before her death she had a most affecting and striking interview with the dear children and their attendant, whom she summoned to her bedside. The children brought her nosegays, and my dear wife and their attendant H—— S—— stood beside them. Nothing could exceed dearest

*In making these selections, a few slight additions and verbal alterations have been made, in order to connect the sentences, but not so as to alter the sense.

Rachel's tender and affectionate manner towards them, and their intense interest in what they saw and heard was strongly marked. She spoke to them of the fear of the Lord, of her own happiness, of her love to them, of the danger of all sin, and that evil thoughts were sin, &c. The whole picture and group cannot easily be forgotten.

Her death took place on second day morning, the 24th of the 9th month, whilst we were all assembled round her bed; dear Louisa being engaged in very solemn prayer for the accomplishment of the blessed work. After the close had taken place, dear Elizabeth uttered a song of thanksgiving in the midst of our great sorrow.

"A sister," adds Joseph John Gurney, "so persevering in kindness, so entirely interested in one's concerns, and so affectionately and devotedly attached, few brothers have ever enjoyed. She was to me much of a watcher and guardian, and never withheld a hint that could be useful. Her advices are deeply engraven on my heart and recollection; and I can, with respect to her, feel the full force of the expression, 'she being dead, yet speaketh.' May I be enabled, through the love and power of the Lord Jesus, to rejoice with her purified and glorified spirit."

Joseph John Gurney now completed his Report on the state of Ireland, which he addressed, in the joint names of himself and his sister Elizabeth Fry, to the Marquis Wellesley, and, with his permission, subsequently published. In this report, he takes a comprehensive survey, in three distinct sections, of the Prison, the Lunatic Asylums, Houses of Industry, Mendicity Associations, and Infirmaries; and lastly, of the general condition of the people. The observations on this last subject, in particular, will still repay the perusal of the reader whose heart is alive to the welfare of Ireland. The questions of pauperism and its remedies, of the uncertainty of tenure, of the system of middlemen, of absenteeism, emigration, crime, intemperance, and scriptural education, are, amongst others, successively passed under review; and, much as has been attempted and accomplished for the improvement of Ireland since its first publication, nearly thirty years ago, the intelligent reader cannot fail to notice how many of the observations are applicable, with nearly equal force, at the present day. The Report has passed through three editions, the last of which was printed in 1847, in a size uniform with the octavo edition of Joseph John Gurney's works.*

*In the course of the late Session of Parliament, at the close of the year 1852, the late Attorney-General for Ireland, (Joseph Napier,) on moving for leave to bring in "a series of measures, having for their object, the adjustment of the relation between Landlords and Tenants in Ireland," alluded to this Report in terms of high, but not undeserved commendation. After referring to the labours of the Parliamentary Committees of 1819 and 1823, who "had appeared to arrive at the conviction that the people of Ireland were a nuisance, and that the main question was how to get rid of them," and stating that the Committee of 1827 had "achieved only the proposition of some equally temporary nostrum," he continued:—

"He had perused a Report from another source on the same subject, to which he would direct the attention of the House. It was a Report emanating from some members of the Society of Friends. In the year 1827 the excellent Mrs. Fry and her brother, who had conceived a deep interest on the subject, visited Ireland; they examined every county, and made the most minute inquiries into every element of her condition, and the result was that they prepared a kind of Report on the subject for the Marquis of Wellesley; and a better State Paper on Ireland never was produced. They stated that what they found in Ireland was want of employment, a defective administration of justice, and a want of education prevalent throughout the country; and they added, as a remarkable feature, that scarcely anything was made the

TO HIS SISTER-IN-LAW, ELIZABETH GURNEY.

Earlham, 10th mo., 20th, 1827.

The longer I live the more I become persuaded that the Lord's children, unworthy as they are, are the objects not only of his spiritual grace, but of his especial providence; that they are of more value in his sight "than many sparrows," who yet fall not to the ground without him, and that "the very hairs of their head are numbered." If this belief is well founded, if it is proved both by Scripture and experience, what a repose we may feel in it, in the various turns and changes of our mortal pilgrimage! Truly "all things shall work together for good to them that love God." * *

Dear Catherine is, on the whole, wonderfully well, pursuing her objects, especially the teaching of our children, with vigour.

most of, and that everywhere the country presented the spectacle of a fair and fruitful land with utterly inadequate cultivation. They expressed their conviction that if sufficient cultivation was applied to the soil by the adequate employment of the people, any failure of the potato crop, under existing circumstances so terrible a calamity, would be amply and most beneficially met by a regular supply of the more suitable and far more nutritive description of food, *wheaten bread*. They considered, they said, that employment would be a far better remedy for the distressed people of Ireland than emigration, although, to a limited extent, this latter remedy also might be useful; and they insisted as a grand remedy, upon the effectual alteration of the system under which high nominal rents, low wages, and insecurity of tenure afflicted the country; and they also recommended (for this was before the Emancipation Act of 1829) the establishment of equality of civil rights; adding that the less distinctions of religion were insisted on in civil polity, the greater would be the probability of the establishment of a state of things leading to permanent tranquillity. Had the suggestions made by these able and benevolent persons been acted upon at the time, he would venture to say—not scrutinizing the designs of the Almighty in the dispensations which had befallen the country, nor causes over which men had no control—he would venture to say, humanly speaking, we should have been spared calamities which Ireland had, of late years, endured." *Hansard's Debates*, House of Commons, 3rd Series, Vol. 123, column 312.

Mary and I read a good deal together; the prophets in the morning, and Barclay's Apology in the afternoon. Our Bible Society week was passed through with a considerable degree of facility, and I hope not without edification. Our dear sister Fry may be informed that I have received a polite letter from Colonel Shaw, with Lord Wellesley's full permission for the reprinting of our Irish Report. This I have begun doing.

TO HENRY BRADY.

Norwich, 10th mo., 6th, 1827.

It is very satisfactory that thy first engagement in the ministry was accompanied by such a flow of peace. I well remember the happy day I passed after a like occurrence. Yet it is more than probable that thou wilt have thy deep tribulations of spirit in connexion with the work. In such case thou wilt, I trust, be able to recur to the love and joy of "thine espousals," as an evidence that the work is the Lord's, and that all will yet be well.

TO A RELATIVE.

10th mo., 14th, 1827.

* * Blest as thou and thy dear partner in life are; led along by so many tender mercies, how peculiarly are you bound by the ties of gratitude and allegiance, to devote yourselves and your all to him who hath loved you; or, to use the expressive phraseology of our own Society, to give yourselves up to "the service of truth." That this may be the case with both of you is my earnest desire; and if either of you are sensible of a call to the more open services of the gospel, it will be well to exercise the active as well as the retiring virtues, and not to wait until the ripe fruit begins to wither and decay. That I would have the fruit ripe, I trust, I need not assure you. But the time is short, and the responsibility infinite.

First day night, [*10th mo.*, 21*st.*] Our meetings have been peculiarly solemn. In the afternoon, I found it my place to exalt the doctrine always professed by Friends, of a divine seed, or principle, placed through the mercy of God in Christ Jesus, in the hearts of all men. O! may I more and more vitally understand this myself; that I may more and more effectually present it, both by example and precept, to the attention of others.

The close of the year was devoted by Joseph John Gurney to various religious engagements, principally in Buckinghamshire and the counties of Gloucester and Wilts. "Some of the meetings," he writes in his Journal, "especially those at Cambridge and Aylesbury, were evidently times of great solemnity and of the putting forth of what we may believe to be the divine power; and in all of them, I may humbly acknowledge that sufficient strength was afforded to meet the duties of the day." A single incident deserves to be recorded. At one of the meetings where he was present, a marriage was solemnized, and notwithstanding the apparent unsuitableness of the occasion, he felt "constrained," as he expresses it, to preach upon the subject of death. A few weeks had scarcely elapsed before three of the assembled party, including the bridegroom himself, were called to meet their God.

1*st mo.*, 25*th*, 1828. How silent, how imperceptible, yet how awful is the approach of death and eternity! The Lord grant that I may be ready when my change cometh; that all my pollutions may then have been cleansed away, and all my doubts and fears scattered before the Sun of Righteousness.

2*nd mo.*, 25*th*. Never that I remember has the rapid flight of time been so awfully impressed on me as of late; "the sand is running out of the glass irresistibly;" and every grain that falls is bringing me nearer to death and eternity. Is it possible that there should be any true repose but in Christ?

First day night, [*3rd mo.,* 16*th.*] Deep discouragement was the clothing of my soul during the greater part of our two nearly silent meetings, chiefly in the apprehension that several amongst us are taking retrograde steps. Alas ! for the power of the world, the flesh, and the enemy ! An increasing neglect of meetings is apparent in some of our members and attenders ; and how can we expect it to be otherwise with those who refuse to take up their cross and follow Jesus ? Some painful fears have also found their way to my heart, lest a lurking infidelity should have insinuated itself into the bosoms of some of our juniors. In the midst of these sources of anxiety and depression, I was a little gladdened by a visit to old Sarah Aldrich, whom I found in a lively, loving frame of mind ; full of joy and thankfulness in the midst of her infirmities. She said, that the Lord, in bringing her into trial, had brought her into his "banqueting house," and that her consolations in Christ were inexpressible.

FROM JONATHAN HUTCHINSON.

Gedney, 3rd mo., 22nd, 1828.

* * We must not spend all our time and our strength in merely exclaiming "O wretched man that I am!" but rather consider what a favour it is, that amidst all our trials and changes, even our passions may be restrained and regulated by a superior principle, and directed into their proper channels by the pointing of an unerring hand. And does not this view of our situation raise us from the dust, and inspire the devout and grateful ejaculation, "thanks be to God?"

3rd mo., 23*rd.*. I am permitted to feel some substantial relief this evening, after a well attended afternoon meeting, in which I was brought into deep exercise, and had not only to supplicate for the visited ones, the wanderers, and the poor prisoners appointed to die, but also to preach Christ to the people as the Rock, the very rock. The ministry has, I trust, arisen from a right source, but it has of late been to me unusually difficult of utterance ! O ! that I may be more deeply humbled; more willing to be as a fool; as one of no repute, if it can but serve the cause of truth and righteousness!

In the fourth month he was again engaged in the service of the gospel in Lincolnshire and Yorkshire, and some parts of the counties of Nottingham and Northampton. From Halifax he wrote

TO HIS BROTHER SAMUEL GURNEY.

4th mo., 9th, 1828.

MY BELOVED BROTHER,

In the midst of some deep exercise of mind, which must be expected to attend me as I pass along in this work, my heart very much turns toward thee, from whom I have in every way derived so much assistance and encouragement. I find myself bowed before the Lord in a sense of great weakness and of utter inability to serve him and promote his cause, except through the gracious renewal of his love and power. We left Ackworth early this morning, and arrived here in time for meeting with the increasing body of Friends in this place. I am resting this afternoon in the prospect of a public meeting this evening, appointed to be held at seven, in a large Methodist meeting house. To-morrow the like services appear to await me at Huddersfield; and on fifth day I propose being with Friends of Wooldale in the morning, and with Friends of Sheffield in the evening. On seventh day to take coach for Leicester. On the whole, the journey has produced a feeling of some renewed encouragement as to the prospects of our own Society.

I feel it profitable to be extricated for a season from the thoughts of this world, and am the more easy in it, as I left the business after thoroughly attending to my own department of it. That thou mayest be favoured to arise from time to time above the trammels of business, and to hold daily communion with God in spirit, is my earnest desire and prayer.

4th mo., 27th. I have felt a peculiar desire to-day, that the ministry in me may be preserved within its true limits, bright and deep. It is a powerful principle on which our ministry turns, if faithfully kept to. O that it may be more and more appreciated and understood!

5th mo., 2nd. Notwithstanding this desire, I have some reason to believe, that in the exercise of the gift, I have not always the unity of those whom I greatly love and approve: and this sometimes happens, when, to my own apprehension, the unction has been rather peculiarly bestowed upon me, and when the seal of peace has been more than usually impressed. On such occasions I do not wish to say, "I am right." I rather look upon such circumstances as evidences of the deep imperfection which hangs about us in this comparatively clouded condition; and desire that every discouragement of the kind may tend to my further humiliation in the presence of Him, who is perfect in wisdom, and who, through good report and evil report, unity and disunity, has an undoubted right to be obeyed and served to the very best of the ability which he is pleased to bestow. In the mean time, love and forbearance, and the spirit which can prefer another's judgment to our own, are great matters.

Third day morning, [*5th mo., 6th.*] Yesterday the anti-slavery meeting was well got through; large and interesting. The exertion, however, was considerable. O! that the friends of religion may be more and more awakened and bound to the cause, and that it may, in due season, please infinite wisdom and grace to loosen the bands of the oppressed! The detail of the subject is horrid indeed!

First day afternoon, [*5th mo., 11th.*] The scythe of the fell destroyer of mankind seems put forth, stroke after stroke. O that I were divested of the fear of death! O that I had faith and love enough to rejoice in the withering away of that which is mortal! Rapidly advancing towards the completion of my fortieth year, with the prospect before me of but a short additional journey, and with the retrospect of innumerable sins and infirmities on my part, and of many great mercies on the part of my God, I think I can preach to myself a sermon on the following text of Scripture: "Thou shalt remember all the way which the Lord thy God hath led thee, these forty years in the wilderness, to humble thee and to prove thee, to know what was in thy heart, whether thou wouldest keep his commandments or no:" Deut. viii, 2.

7th mo., *14th.* We left home in the expectation of a three weeks' excursion, and returned on seventh day evening after an absence of eight weeks. So little are we in our own power!

On my journey to London, I was exposed for a short time to extreme danger from an accident, being thrown from the coach-box; but was mercifully delivered without material injury. Dearest Mary, however, suffered from her journey; and during the whole of our sojourn in London was very unwell; so much so as to excite great uneasiness and even alarm in her mother and myself. It was a comfort to me to be able, nevertheless, to attend our Yearly Meeting; my dear wife being laid up in the interim at our lodgings, hard by, in Bishopsgate street; so that I could undulate between private and public duties without difficulty. The Yearly Meeting was memorable; deeply interesting to me, from the nature of the subjects brought before it, especially that of the disturbances in America.* We were addressed in an epistle by the seceding Yearly Meeting at Philadelphia; but without any dissenting voice, it was resolved neither to read nor to receive the communication. The unity and harmony of the body were never, in my recollection, more comfortably experienced.

Towards the close of the Yearly Meeting, a meeting of the young people was appointed at my request. It was a large and beautiful assembly, and I hope it was not in vain, that gospel principles were unfolded, under the influence, I trust, of the love and power of Christ.

Amongst the many dear friends who were at the Yearly Meeting, it was peculiarly pleasant to me to be again in close intercourse with my beloved friends, William Forster and Jonathan Hutchinson. I also enjoyed some precious intimate hours with my uncle Joseph. After the Yearly Meeting

* This alludes to the separation from Friends in America, of Elias Hicks and his followers. See *infra*, chap. xxvii.

we took up our abode for a time at Upton, where my dear wife gradually improved. I was occupied in the mean time by the meeting for sufferings, preparing Friends' petition on slavery, attending Gracechurch street Monthly Meeting, &c. As soon as my dear wife was fit to move, we went to Hastings and passed three weeks there, and at Brighton, Worthing, and Bognor. On our return we made short visits to Bury Hill, Tottenham, Upton, and Saffron Walden; all of which were satisfactory, and were favoured at length to arrive in safety with our beloved mother, at this peaceful and pleasant home.

7th mo., 29th. During the past week, visits to the Bethel,* visit from Friends, and the meeting of the Bible Association at Melton, were satisfactory points; also our reading meeting here last evening. To live, in any measure for the good of others, gives a feeling of satisfaction not to be derived from any other mode of life. But surely a vast deal of self indulgence is worked up into my whole system. And as to philanthropy, how tainted sometimes are its secret springs!

9th mo., 17th. The time which has passed since I last wrote, has been fraught with lively interests. My dear sister Fry's satisfactory and comforting visit, from fourth to seventh day last, was perhaps the principal. I never saw her, that I remember, in a more favoured condition, and she was the means of raising me considerably in the scale of spiritual feeling, wherein I am so very apt to find a low place. Greatly gifted she assuredly is, both by nature and grace, and is enabled to exercise a gentle and unseen, yet powerful, influence over all about her. She was present at our large and highly favoured Monthly Meeting, last fifth day, and was memorably engaged amongst us as a daughter of consolation.

9th mo., 22nd. Solemn and sober silence was the almost uninterrupted characteristic of our meeting on fifth day. I felt the value of it as a release to myself, and as profitable to all. On sixth day a pleasant and successful expedition with Kinghorn and Brightwell, to the Aylsham Bible Meeting. I

* An establishment for the insane, at Norwich.

found the Wilberforces here on my return, and very much feasted on his society the next morning, before his departure.

In the tenth month he again left home in the service of the Gospel. Upon his return he writes :—

11*th mo.*, 9*th.* * * During my late journey I visited all the meetings of Bedfordshire and Hertfordshire, Cambridgeshire and Huntingdonshire, a large proportion of the families, particularly at Hitchen and Hertford, and held nineteen public meetings. It has been a time of deep occasional depression; but, I clearly experienced the value of the guiding hand. The public meetings were generally favoured times, especially so at Bedford and Cambridge.

During the autumn the institution at Ackworth was visited with typhus fever, which, besides carrying off several of the children, proved at length fatal to Henry Brady, in whose gradually maturing character Joseph John Gurney had long taken a lively interest, and whose loss to Ackworth seemed to him at the time almost irreparable. This event, together with the continued delicacy of his beloved wife, the decease of his valued cousin Priscilla Hannah Gurney, and more than all, the deep sorrow into which his sister Elizabeth Fry was now plunged, all contributed to throw a shade of mourning over the conclusion of the year. Cast down and brought very low, it was, to use his own expressive words, "at the foot of the cross," that, "in prayer and supplication" he was permitted to find refuge and consolation.

12*th mo.*, 1*st.* The gloom which rather remarkably hangs over the world of temporals, has been accompanied with a measure of painful anxiety. I wish I may be enabled to imitate the example of Wesley, who tells us, that although he grieved, he never *fretted*, which he speaks of as the result of many fervent prayers. I think there is good reason to suppose a period of some strift and considerable loss to be at hand. Well, let it be so, if it be the divine will and purpose, and let me be quietly resigned. Why should I perplex myself by anticipations? Why should I not rather fix my whole soul on God, and grasp, more firmly than ever, those unsearchable riches, which are in Christ my Lord?

12*th mo.*, 13*th.* The accounts received on fifth day determined me to go to Upton the next morning. On first day the meeting at Plaistow was instructive and affecting. The necessity and benefit of complete humiliation, and the saving power of the Redeemer were livingly before us; and temporals in some measure were bidden to recede from our view. In the evening, previously to my departure by the Ipswich mail, my dear sister Fry and I went to Newgate to pay a farewell visit to a convict who was appointed to suffer the awful penalty of death the next morning. The interview was affecting, but in a short and solemn time of religious retirement a remarkable degree of hope and encouragement on his account was felt by us both.

TO A FRIEND.

Earlham, 12th mo., 22nd, 1828.

I am grieved to hear the tidings of thy dear wife's renewed, and I fear severe illness, though I hardly like to use the word *severe*, in reference to any of the dispensations of a most merciful God towards his unworthy but believing children. O that we may all be enabled, amidst the various painful vicissitudes, to which in this world we are exposed, to place a yet firmer trust in Him who is head *over all things* to his church, and who undoubtedly orders *all things* well for those who love and serve him! It has certainly been a period of deep affliction to our religious society since thou and I met. What can we do but quietly resign *all* into the hands of our heavenly Father, and encourage the hope, that from the depth of these humiliations, his children may yet arise to serve and praise him in the beauty and strength of true Christian principle?

At the opening of the following year, Joseph John Gurney writes: —

1*st mo.*, 2*nd*, 1829. I rose early and have been endeavouring to pour forth my heart in prayer to the Almighty, and to commend all my cares, and, above all, my own soul, to his merciful providence. In temporals, I have many weights and somewhat extensive solicitudes. I pray to be preserved from fretting on these subjects, doing my daily duty with faithfulness, and leaving all results in quietness to Him who hath the disposing of all our matters. * *

The condition of that part of the church of Christ, which is within the borders of "Quakerism," is a cause, from time to time, of much humiliation and depression. Life is at a low ebb amongst us, I greatly fear; and the removal from the scene of warfare of so many promising young persons, seems, to our finite eye, almost to preclude the hope of revival. And yet in such a notion, I am sure there is a radical want of faith. At the commencement of this new year, which begins in clouds, I feel a renewed persuasion, that it is my place and duty, to maintain an unbroken testimony, whether Friends survive or perish, to the spirituality, simplicity, freedom, peaceableness, and perfection of the gospel dispensation.

TO THE BISHOP OF NORWICH.

(Then under severe domestic affliction.*)

Norwich, 1st mo., 3rd, 1829.

MY BELOVED AND HONOURED FRIEND,

Though I have for some days hesitated respecting the propriety of intruding upon thy sorrows, I cannot feel satisfied without just saying that, under thy present circumstances,

* See the Life of Bp. Bathurst, by his daughter, p. 345.

thou and thy family have my sympathy and my prayers. For many years have I now enjoyed the privilege of thy friendship, and I can truly say that I have never more felt the value and pleasure of it than during our late intercourse. I have contemplated thee as one gradually descending with a peaceful step to the grave, mercifully endowed with unimpaired faculties, and still enabled to communicate comfort and happiness to thy family and friends. That events should have occurred, one after another, to disturb thy repose, and to occasion thee heartfelt sorrow, can be no matter of indifference to one who has so long experienced thy kindness. Nevertheless I entertain a firm conviction that these painful dispensations are graciously intended for the promotion of thy eternal welfare, through a yet closer communion with God, and *a yet more intimate dependence on that Redeemer, whose blood alone cleanses from all sin.* * * *

1st mo., 5th. In the afternoon of yesterday, a satisfactory time of solemnity, beside the dying bed of poor old Roger Norman, who, I trust, is about to enter into the rest prepared for the righteous. In our silent waiting this morning, (my dearest wife and I being alone,) I could not do otherwise than express "my desire that we might, during this week, dwell near to God, and be found at the foot of the cross of Christ; that we might be faithful in our stewardship; that while diligent in the performance of daily duty, we might have our conversation in heaven ; that even the little circumstances of life might be sanctified to us ; that the life which we now live in the flesh, we might live by faith in the Son of God, who loved us, and gave himself for us."

1st mo., 12th. Much prosperity, and much care and responsibility, seem to be my allotment in things temporal, and I often feel anxious that neither the advantages, nor the perplexities of riches, may divert me from the one thing needful. I would have deeply impressed on my soul, our blessed Saviour's precept, "Make to yourselves friends of the mammon of unrighteousness, that when ye fail, they may receive you into everlasting habitations." Comp. 1 Tim., vi. 17—19.

2nd mo., 14th. The trying position of the affairs of some of my near friends, is one of the crosses of the day. Some exercises of patience must be expected; yet a secret hope lives with me, that, with patience and watchfulness, I shall know my way to open for such services in the gospel, as may be in store for me. In the mean time, it is my wish to be like the poor penitent, who lay at the feet of Jesus, washing them with her tears, and wiping them with the hairs of her head.

3rd mo., 18th. Some precious communion with God graciously permitted this morning, and often of late. Inward conflict drives even wandering minds to a throne of grace.

Having been again occupied from home in various religious engagements, he writes, after an absence of rather more than ten weeks:—

Earlham, 6th mo., 20th. I visited all the meetings in Berks and Oxon, several of those in Bucks, including a general visit to families, and holding nearly twenty public meetings.

The visits to Reading and Oxford, were both particularly interesting to me. At the former place, two meetings, with a large company of young people, were relieving and cheering. The public meeting at Oxford was very large, and very fairly attended by the students. A great many Friends met us there, and it was a memorable occasion. Through the zealous intervention of A—— H——, I was introduced to many of the pious collegians, whom I met at his rooms, the day after the meeting, at breakfast and dinner. More ingenuous youths than the young students among them, I have scarcely ever met with, and their piety seemed very genuine. Several of them accompanied us in the evening to Farringdon, where the public meeting, though deep and difficult exercise to me, proved to be a very uniting time; and the young men seemed afterwards to overflow with love. * * *

The Yearly Meeting was very absorbing during its whole continuance, and certainly was an occasion of powerfully renewed favour. It was well attended, and the unanimity which prevailed among Friends, especially in issuing the document respecting America, and declaration of our faith in our blessed Redeemer, was peculiarly precious.*

On the whole retrospect of this interesting time, I feel that I have, under a deep sense of my own unworthiness, abundant cause for thankfulness to the Author of all good, who has most mercifully led me about and instructed me, and supported me in times of more than common mental trial; covering me with favour as with a shield, and anointing me from time to time for the work and service to which, I believe, he was pleased to send me forth; and now, on my return home, I am favoured to feel a degree of tranquillity and of renewed encouragement to trust in his holy name.

6th mo., 13th. On waking this morning, I was favoured with a precious tranquillizing sense of the Lord's preserving care and undeserved love. How delightful it is to feel the extension of the wing of divine goodness!

After writing the above, I went to the bank, and came home with a tried and perturbed spirit, the world not having pleased me. Alas! how great is my weakness! Our dear friends William and Martha Smith came to dinner. On sitting together after tea, we were eminently favoured with a sense of divine love; and M—— S—— was particularly enabled to minister to us, according to our necessities. The trial of mind which I have lately passed through, was aptly described by her, and strong encouragement given to persevere in the work of the Lord, *fearing nothing but disobedience to his will.*

6th mo., 22nd. * * I am afresh persuaded that I shall never gain strength by committing myself to the guidance of other people's scruples. I heartily desire to follow the "anointing," and verily believe that our society, (never more dear to me than at present,) can be preserved and improved,

* A copy of this document is inserted *infra,* in the Appendix to the second volume.

only by our individually following on to know and serve the Lord in the way which he condescends to point out to us. In the mean time may we be preserved from judging one another; may love reign and abound; and may the ungodly part in us all be judged, condemned, and die, through the Lord's own power, that nothing may obstruct our final and perfect union with him.

7th mo., 10*th.* Friends of our Monthly Meeting have set me at liberty to hold a few meetings in the course of our intended Ackworth journey, as "Truth may open the way." I have, of late, heard objections raised to this quaint expression, in which the word, "truth" appears to stand for Christ, or rather the Spirit of Christ; as it operates on the understanding and will. For one, I cleave to it as sound and scriptural, (John xiv, &c.,) well understood by Friends, and rendering unnecessary the too familiar or frequent expression of the name of Jesus Christ.

After his journey to Ackworth, and the attendance of a few meetings in connexion with it, which occupied little more than two weeks, he continued mostly at home until towards the close of the year. During his intervals of leisure at this period, he was still closely engaged in the completion of the Biblical Notes.

8th mo., 30*th.* Yesterday my mind was brought into a considerable degree of conflict, but in the evening peace seemed remarkably restored, and was permitted to flow in my soul more than I have known it for some time past. This day has also been a favoured one; in the morning particularly we were permitted to know the breaking of bread as at the Master's table. On the whole, a little rest to the sole of the foot is just now experienced.

9th mo., 11*th.* Our party has come, and is gone; our meetings have been held and are over. Our Earlham lodgers were Fowell, Edwards, Steinkopff, Fitzgerald, Tyrell, Long,

Weyland, Lord and Lady Radstock, &c.; and we have been mercifully favoured with the quieting and delightful influence of an infinitely more glorious and powerful Visitor and Guest; and on fourth day morning especially were enabled to obtain living access to the throne of grace. The public meetings have been also excellent. That of the Bible Society a noble one indeed.

TO JONATHAN HUTCHINSON.

Earlham, 10th mo., 4th, 1829.

The sanguine hopes of youth are now pretty fairly passed away with me, (for I am 41,) and I no longer entertain glowing expectations of great things within our borders; but still in my best moments, I am the most settled in the belief, that a remnant will be preserved amongst us, by whom the principles professed by us will still be manifested in some degree of brightness and purity. For ourselves, as individuals, I am increasingly convinced that the only resting-place is in the fulness and perfection, which are in Christ. Come what may of height or depth, of life or death, we may still flee to him as to an all-sufficient Saviour, and find safety. That this is thy constant refuge I am assured, and cannot doubt; and that it is one which will never fail thee, either for time or eternity, is my comforting conviction.

Towards the close of the year he was engaged in a visit to all the meetings and families of Friends in the Quarterly Meetings of Essex, besides holding many religious meetings with others not in profession with Friends; an arduous engagement which "afforded close hourly occupation," for the greater part of six weeks. He returned home commemorating the mercy through which his "wants in every way had been graciously provided for." "May we," he adds, "be filled with gratitude, trust, and love."

"I have been often led to think lately," he writes to Jonathan Hutchinson,* "of the Christian grace of *hope.* We are to be 'rejoicing in *hope*,' as well as 'patient in tribulation;' and I am apt to think that many of our dear sorrowing Friends are more exemplary in the latter, than in the former duty. But I find it easier to preach this doctrine, than to apply it to myself, as a dark cloud is often permitted to rest on my path, at which time, patient submission seems to be nearly all that I can attain to."

* Under date 12th mo., 25th.

CHAPTER XX.

ILLUSTRATIONS OF CHARACTER.

INTEREST IN NORWICH POOR; BREAKFAST TO OPERATIVES AT EARLHAM; VISITS TO PRISON; JOHN STRATFORD; THE BETHEL; RECONCILING LETTER; VISITS OF SCHOOL CHILDREN TO EARLHAM; ADVICE TO A YOUNG FRIEND ON HIS MARRIAGE; GIVING AND RECEIVING; DAY UPON A STAGE COACH; HOUSEHOLD DISCIPLINE; ECONOMY OF TIME; YOUTHFUL RECOLLECTIONS OF EARLHAM.

NUMEROUS as are the details of the "inner life," furnished by such a Journal as Joseph John Gurney's, it is yet not always easy to collect from them the materials necessary for the full illustration of his character. In that mirror in which he appears as reflected to himself, we do not perceive with sufficient distinctness how he appeared in the sight of others. The disclosure of the inward warfare is necessarily very much unconnected with the exhibition of those practical results that were conspicuous to all around. It is the object of the present chapter to endeavour to furnish a few hints that may asssist the reader in supplying this deficiency.

None can have attentively perused the foregoing pages without perceiving that one leading feature of Joseph John Gurney's character was an unwearied active benevolence. Like his sister, Elizabeth Fry, he seemed continually to live under a deep sense of his responsibility toward others.* A cheerful and bountiful giver, it was not merely by large pecuniary assistance that he proved his interest in objects connected with the welfare of his fellow men: to these objects he was exemplary in devoting no common share of time and personal attention. His steady devotion to the Anti-slavery and Bible Societies is already before the reader. In addition to these great and often absorbing interests, his exertions for the distressed labouring population of Norwich were unremitting. Year after year, during the winter, or on any occasion when their distress was aggravated by want of employment, he was at his post, stirring up his fellow citizens to the necessary measures for the alleviation of their wants. The District Visiting Society, (which he was himself mainly instrumental in originating,)† the Soup Society and the Coal Society found in him a steady and effective supporter. Often would he say that the painful consciousness of the poverty and suffering of many thousands around him, almost prevented his enjoyment of the abundant blessings with which

* "I may say, I am morning, noon, and night under a deep impression of my responsibility towards others." From an address of Elizabeth Fry to a Bible committee, preserved by one of her nieces. A great example was before them, Rom. i, 14.

† He led the way towards the raising of the necessary funds by a donation of £500. The formation of the Society is thus noticed in his Journal under date 11th mo., 26th, 1830. "In Norwich I have been deeply interested in the endeavour to form a District Society, for visiting and relieving the poor; and, I may confess, it has been a subject of daily prayer. After several preparatory meetings of gentlemen, in a private way, we launched our vessel yesterday, under the kind and masterly pilotage of Charles Wodehouse, for which I have felt truly thankful."

he was himself so richly favoured. On one occasion, he expended a considerable sum in providing the capital for an attempt to supply the poor weavers and mechanics with employment during a scarcity of work. But though, like many similar attempts, it failed to answer the expectation of the promoter, and was abandoned, it served at least to furnish another proof of the sincerity and earnestness with which he laboured for their welfare.

The depression in trade occasioned by the "panic" of 1825 will be long remembered. Norwich did not escape its influence. As a banker, Joseph John Gurney was more than usually absorbed in his own more immediate cares, but his heart at once turned towards his suffering fellow-citizens. "The dreadful distress," he writes to a friend,* "which prevails in the great mass of our once labouring, now, alas! idle population, has been such as to call forth my strenuous efforts on their behalf. In this, success has been mercifully vouchsafed, and many thousands of families have been already fed. We have raised £3300 in five days."

One more illustration deserves notice. In the winter of 1829–30, the manufactures of Norwich were again greatly depressed. The weavers became unsettled, holding riotous meetings and using threatening language against their employers. The state of things was alarming. Joseph John Gurney felt it his duty to use his influence in checking the spirit of discontent that was rapidly spreading. He attended one of the very large and tumultuous meetings of the operatives, and endeavoured to persuade them to desist from their disorderly proceedings,

* Under date 1st mo., 21st, 1826.

and quietly to resume their work. With a view of still further winning them by kindness, he invited a deputation from those assembled, to breakfast at Earlham the following morning. Between forty and fifty of them came, with Dover, a notorious Chartist leader, at their head. After the usual family reading of the Scriptures, they sat down to a plentiful repast, which had been provided for them in the large dining room, of which they partook heartily, and their host afterwards addressed them in a kind, conciliatory manner upon the subject of wages, and their duty to their employers. The men conducted themselves in an orderly manner, and appeared grateful for the attention shown them. The scene was one not soon to be forgotten.

His visits to the prisoners at the jail have been already alluded to. These visits, whilst doubtless greatly contributing to the benefit of many a poor degraded criminal, frequently introduced him into considerable personal labour and great mental suffering. This was particularly the case in regard to prisoners left for execution. In their behalf he would spare neither trouble nor expense, if he thought the circumstances such as to warrant an application for a reprieve. Several instances of this kind have been already noticed. To another case arising out of his prison labours, we owe the well-known Tract containing the touching account of John Stratford. The story is thus simply recorded in the Autobiography.

"It was at the summer assizes at Norwich, in the year 1829, that John Stratford, one of our most ingenious mechanics, was condemned to death for poisoning. He had been guilty of gross immorality; and, in attempting to destroy the husband of the object of his shameful passion, he occasioned the death of another individual, and endangered the lives of several more. His complicated wickedness was the practical result of infidelity; and afforded me, when I visited him in prison, an awful example of the effect of those dreadful publications, which are employed by the enemies of religion to sap the principles of the working classes. He was a man of strong understanding and warm feelings. In his low estate the Lord opened his eyes to behold his aggravated sinfulness. I was with him in private shortly before his execution, noted down his confessions, and listened to his earnest petitions for mercy. His doubts respecting the truth of religion fled swiftly away at the awful approach of death. As far as I could judge, he was a deep and thorough penitent, who turned to Christ with much fervour of spirit; and I entertain a humble belief, that in his extremity he found mercy of the Lord. He died, calling on the name of Jesus. As soon as possible after his execution, I published a tract, containing an account of the case, and put out an advertisement, offering it gratis to any of my fellow citizens who chose to apply for it. About 10,000 copies were, on these terms rapidly taken; and it has since been largely circulated by Tract Societies, and through other means.* I trust the Lord of whom it testifies, may have blessed it to some.

The afflicted inmates of the Bethel and the Norfolk and Norwich Hospital were also objects of his Christian solicitude, and, for several years, he was

* Besides the 10,000 copies which were thus disposed of, more than 10,000 were afterwards sold at 1d. each. Norwich did not then possess a steam press; and the comparatively slow operations of the ordinary printing press were insufficient to satisfy the eagerness of the applicants. So great was the rush when a fresh handful was brought out of the printing office, that it was not safe to deliver them in the shop or at the door; but it was found necessary to carry them some paces into the market-place, where they were eagerly seized, all wet and unfolded as they came from the press.

in the habit of regularly visiting them at short stated periods. The time between the two meetings for worship on the first day of the week was frequently devoted to this object. Not very long after his return from America, as he was travelling in an omnibus between Yarmouth and Lowestoft, a well-dressed female, with an anxious countenance, who had sat gazing at him for some time, suddenly exclaimed, "You are Mr. Gurney—I am sure you are. Ah! it was a bad day for us when you went away, Sir; we felt as if we had lost our best friend. How well do I remember your blessed Scripture readings and your solemn prayers!" He recognized her as a former inmate of the Bethel, and, taking advantage of a pause, observed, "Then I hope, my good friend, my visits to thyself and thy poor fellow sufferers were not all in vain." "O no, indeed, Sir," she replied, "we used to watch for your coming; all you said had such a soothing effect upon our minds; and we missed you sadly when you went away. I shall never forget the last chapter you read to us, Sir. Here it is:" and she pointed to the 103rd Psalm. "We used to read it over and over again; and, for my own part, I learned it all by heart." He then took the Bible and read some verses: the poor creature, says an eye-witness, seemed to cling to him, as if she thought he had indeed the power to heal the malady, which, (though she was no longer an inmate of the Bethel,) was evidently not yet removed.

The following letter affords an apt illustration of another feature of his character. It relates to a member of another denomination of Christians, an individual whom he greatly esteemed.

TO ———

Earlham, 8th mo., 31st, 1832.

DEAR FRIEND,

From information which I have received from a friend of mine, not connected with your congregation, I have reason to believe that the illness of our valued friend —— is partly to be traced to great vexation of mind arising from some difference in his church; and I very much fear that, unless this vexation can be removed, his recovery will be greatly endangered. I understand, on further inquiry, that certain resolutions proposed by thyself are matters of great grief and agitation to him; indeed I am pretty certain that this is the fact, to an extent probably quite unknown to thyself. I have no doubt that thy resolutions were brought forward with a good intent; and, of course, I can be no judge of the affairs of your church. But, as a member (I trust) of the Church of Christ, I do feel a very high value indeed for the life of our honoured friend; and I am deeply convinced that the carrying of a point in your own body, ought not to be put in competition with the interest which the church at large has in the labour and influence of this our exemplary fellow-citizen. I venture, therefore, to entreat thee, if possible, to set his mind entirely at rest on the subject. As a common friend I thought I might make this appeal, but I can assure thee that it is from my own sense of duty, and of true regard to both parties that I do it; for no one has suggested such a thing to me.

I am thy sincere friend,

J. J. GURNEY.

After what has already appeared in the preceding chapters, it will not be needful, in this place, to dwell long upon his warm and affectionate interest in children and young persons. And yet a trait so prominent and characteristic claims some further notice. "It has long been one of my greatest pleasures," he writes in his Autobiography, (and they who knew him most intimately will best appreciate the truth of his words,) "to communicate at my ease with children, especially in schools, to amuse them, and play upon their minds as on an instrument of music; to bring forth their powers, and to lead them as through a flowery path into the habitations of Zion." Perhaps few occasions presented a more complete illustration of this part of his character, than the happy summer evenings which the children of many of the different schools in Norwich used to enjoy at Earlham by his invitation. Year by year he delighted to share in their holiday pleasure; and beautiful was the sight of the youthful parties seated upon the lawn in front of the house, in companies of from 100 to 200, whilst he would assist in handing the tea, cake, and fruit provided for them; or, with joy beaming upon his countenance, would listen to their happy voices reciting the hymn or psalm which he had given them to learn; or when, in the pause which followed, he would himself affectionately address them, reminding them of their duty to their teachers, their parents, and above all to that Heavenly Shepherd who had given his life for the sheep.

The playful seriousness of his character is strikingly exhibited in the following letter to a nephew, who had gained one of the highest positions in the university examination.

Earlham, 6th mo., 7th, 1827.

MY DEAR NEPHEW,

I received thy laconic epistle, the "*veni, vidi, vici*" of our family Cæsar, with true pleasure. As right I have—

"I swell the triumph, and partake the gale."

At the same time, to be sincere and serious, I may just tell thee in addition, that the intelligence conveyed to my mind a little touch of anxiety; first, lest thou shouldst overwork thyself, and spoil a good constitution both of body and mind, by a vast surplusage (not usable in after life) of logic and algebra: and secondly, or rather principally, lest the glitter of this gilded chaplet should, by any means, divert a dear, innocent lad from "the simplicity which is in Christ."

For the first point; endeavour to bear in mind the "*modus in rebus*," the "*certi denique fines.*" Unloose the bowstring; take a few weeks of perfect pastime. Come and grace the green solitudes of Earlham, or swim over the sea to France. Be any thing, for the next month, but a mathematician and a scholar. Forget that thou art "*celeberrimus*," one of the "οἱ πάνυ"—be a child.

As to the second point, it is a serious one, and I must now look grave. Truly it would be an ill exchange, if academic honours, and the love of thy own doings, and the flattery of this fair world, were to deprive thee of that old-fashioned apostolic ground of joy:—"This is my rejoicing, that with simplicity and godly sincerity, not with fleshly wisdom, but by the grace of God, I have had my conversation in the world." So said a man of learning and genius, under the powerful influence of pure Christianity. So mayest thou say, my learned nephew, under the same influence, in every stage of thy career, and especially at the near approach of that hour when thy honours must sleep in the dust, and thy soul awake in eternity! As I can rise no higher in my wishes for thee, I had better conclude, and with warm congratulations to a fond father and mother,

I remain, thy affectionate uncle,

J. J. GURNEY.

TO A YOUNG FRIEND ON HIS MARRIAGE.

Norwich, 11th mo., 13th, 1827.

MY DEAR ——,

I have ordered Barclay & Co. to pay Denison & Co. £100 on thy account. I quite disapprove of thy borrowing money, either of me or any body else, either now or henceforward. Let me as an old and, I trust, dear friend, advise thee never to do it; but, whatsoever sacrifice it may involve, to cut thy coat to thy cloth, and to pay for everything at once. I am satisfied that if thou and thy dear friend are willing, with all simplicity and humility, to meet your real situation, you may make two ends meet without difficulty, and save a little into the bargain, which I consider indispensable. Make it a Christian duty to be a rigid and perfect economist, and let thy partner do the same, and you will, I believe, find this the road to ease and comfort, if not to wealth.

Having bestowed this advice upon thee, I need scarcely add that the £100 is a gift and not a loan. * * *

"Wilt thou execute a little commission for me at Arch's? said Joseph John Gurney, addressing another of his young friends, whom he had kindly taken one day to dine at his lodgings, during the interval between the sittings of the Yearly Meeting. His young friend, of course, readily assented. Joseph John Gurney wrote a few lines on a slip of paper, which he handed to his young friend, enclosed to his booksellers, but without giving to his young companion any intimation of its contents. The note was duly delivered, and the circumstance was forgotten until, after the lapse of a few weeks, the young friend, no less to his surprise than to his delight, received a large parcel sent to him, as he was informed, at Joseph John Gurney's request, consisting of upwards of thirty volumes, comprising the Lexicons of Simonis and Schleusner, and the Scholia of the Rosenmüllers (the father and son) on the Old and New Testaments: a great prize indeed to a youthful student. Many were the instances in which he thus encouraged, amongst his young friends, a taste for reading, more especially in connexion with those pursuits in which he himself delighted.

His gifts were made additionally acceptable, by the "simplicity" and "cheerfulness" with which they were bestowed. He gave as one who remembered that he was but a steward, having nothing that he had not received.

"Rest assured," he writes on one occasion to a Friend whom he had assisted, "that I have no feeling of the kind alluded to in thy letter. I believe that the assistance I gave thee was, on my part, a matter of duty, and, on thine, a providential help. How precious is that love which overflows the boundary line of giving and receiving, and levels us all in one feeling of our unworthiness of God's unspeakable gift."

His watchfulness to seize and to take advantage of openings for usefulness, was another striking point in his character. He might be deceived again and again by false appearances, (and perhaps his charitable view of others, contrasted as it was with his severe judgment upon himself, might be considered by some to amount almost to an infirmity,) yet still he went on, sowing his seed "by all waters," humbly confiding the result to Him, who could alone cause it to be "found after many days." But it is worthy of remark that this Christian liberality was rarely, if ever, allowed to interfere with his great habitual caution and discrimination in matters of business. "Constantly," says his son, "was he found helping, as an individual, parties to whom he refused accommodation as a banker."

His intercourse with the poor failed not to afford him many illustrations of the practical power of the Gospel, when received in living faith; — a theme on which he loved to dwell. One day, at Earlham, a poor man in the servants' hall attracted his attention. He was old and blind. Joseph John Gurney addressed him with the voice of sympathy, but he seemed to be more alive to his blessings than his privations. "It is true," he said, "I have not much of this world's goods, and my sight has almost failed me; but I have food and clothing, and every thing I need during my earthly pilgrimage, and then I am *heir to a kingdom—think of* THAT." Joseph John Gurney was greatly affected by the cheerful and contented spirit of the good old man, and much impressed by his childlike confidence; and turning away, he observed to one of his sisters, with tears in his eyes, "Who would not exchange the wealth and honours of this world for the simple faith of this poor old man, that it is his Father's good pleasure to give him the kingdom?"

When engaged in travelling with others, it appeared to be Joseph John Gurney's habitual aim to make such opportunities occasions of interesting and profitable communication. A day passed with him upon a stage coach is thus described by one of his fellow passengers:—

It was on a lovely day, in spring, that I had the pleasure of travelling from Norwich to London with Mr. Gurney. We met unexpectedly at the coach office; and, with our respective companions, had taken outside places. Mr. Gurney's companion was a lady whom he was escorting back to London after a visit to Earlham; and, besides the friend who was accompanying me to the "May meetings," two excellent dissenting ministers, known to us all, had taken their places by our side. We were a party of six, just filling up the space behind, and happily leaving no room for intruders. It was not very long after Mr. Gurney's return from Ireland, and the subject of Ireland being introduced, he gave us a very animating account of his visit to that country in company with Mrs. Fry. Although some questions were asked as he proceeded, we were listeners rather than talkers; and when he had finished, there was, very naturally, a pause. After a short interval of silence, Mr. Gurney, addressing us, said, "I always make it a rule to read a portion of Scripture every morning;" and, having proposed to read a chapter aloud, inquired whether any one had a Testament. There was no lack, as it happened, of Greek Testaments, but, singularly enough, no one had an English one. He accordingly took out his pocket Greek Testament, and, translating as he went on, read us a chapter in very literal English, adding a few remarks, explanatory and practical, and pausing at its close, as was his wont, for inward devotion and prayer. I very much regret that I made no memoranda of the conversation of the day; for though the general impression of it is left deeply engraven on my mind, the incidents and remarks that contributed, in so large a degree, to make it what it was, have faded from the memory. A little before noon we arrived at Bury, and were quite prepared, by a ride of two-and-forty miles, for breakfast. Mr. Gurney seemed to enjoy his wash and his breakfast as much as any of us, and when he took his seat again on the coach, called for the bag of books I had in charge, and handing a book to each of us said, "I have been giving out all the morning, I must now be taking in." We had left one of our party at Bury, and had taken up in his stead a young man, who proved to be a student at the University of Glasgow; and having lent him the Edinburgh Review, which I had been reading, and called his attention to certain paragraphs, he and I fell into conversation. Mr. Gurney, seeing this, said to me quietly aside, "I see thou art interested in that young man; if thou wouldst like to give him a copy of my Essays, thou mayst call at Arch's and get one." This was but one instance among a thousand, of his being "instant in season and out of season," ever looking out for opportunities of usefulness. The commission was not forgotten; the young man received the book, and if he still lives, remembers, I doubt not, as we all do, "the day upon the stage coach." Towards evening there was a shifting of places, and the seats vacated by one and another were filled by drovers. Mr. Gurney adapted himself equally to his less refined companions, and, after a time addressing them said, "We commenced the day by reading a chapter of the Bible, perhaps you will not object to our closing it in the same manner." There was a hearty consent, and he read a chapter from one of Paul's Epistles, making a few explanatory remarks as he went on. He had not long concluded, and relapsed into silence, when we arrived at the inn, where, finding his brother's carriage in attendance, he took his leave, bidding us all farewell.

But it was at Earlham that he was emphatically at home. To this beloved retreat, he again and again returned with new delight. Here he was to be seen at his ease, and it was here that the peculiar brightness of his character was displayed. Love was the ruling principle that reigned in his household; a love not degenerating into a weak indulgence, but strong in its combination with Christian discipline. Upon his servants, upon his children, upon all that came within the range of his influence, he inculcated by precept, and more than all, by his own example, the inestimable value of order, method, and true economy of time. It was a grief to him when moments were squandered away to no purpose. Even when walking for health or recreation, he would often employ himself in storing his memory with some new hymn or passage of Scripture. And he was especially careful, that the time spent with his family, or with a more extended social circle, should be improved by intelligent conversation, or useful reading. In later years he practised the art of sketching from nature, in which he attained considerable facility and skill, and which he often pursued, as an agreeable recreation, whilst listening to reading or conversation.

Amidst the widely extended claims upon his interest and sympathies, the villagers of the little hamlet of Earlham were not forgotten. Besides the liberal attention to their varied wants afforded them from the hall, they were accustomed for nearly thirty years to assemble with the family on the evening of the first day of each week; when a portion of Scripture, a religious tract, or a selection of Christian Biography was read; the opportunity concluding in deep religious silence, broken, at times, under the constraining influence of divine love, with affectionate Christian counsel and fervent prayer. They were occasions long to be remembered by those present.

His beloved daughter, in a little sketch which will find a more appropriate place at the conclusion of this memoir, has beautifully illustrated his character as a father. It may not, however, be improper here to introduce the following letter written to his son, soon after his first settlement at school, which may serve as a specimen of the style in which he was accustomed to communicate with his children :—

Earlham, 2nd mo., 28th, 1830.

MY DEAREST J. H——,

Since thou hast been at school nearly two months, I begin to be impatient to receive a nice, long, intimate letter from thee, and I hope thou wilt send me such a one without delay. I think thou ought to write a few lines to some one of us every week, or at least every fortnight. We all love thee dearly, and none so much so, perhaps, as papa and mamma. My own heart has been much with thee, and I cannot tell thee with how much earnestness I desire thy welfare. Not merely temporal prosperity and good bodily health, though I trust thou mayst be mercifully favoured with a good share of even these blessings, but I mean chiefly, the welfare of that part in thee which will endure for ever and ever. O, my precious child! how greatly does thy father desire that thy soul may be happy through all eternity! Remember, my dear boy, that thou art born for eternity, and that the great object of the present uncertain state of being, is to prepare for a state which will never have an end. In order to be perfectly good and happy in the world to come, we must repent of all our sins, humble ourselves before God, come to Christ as our only Saviour and Redeemer, and in all things endeavour to obey and follow his blessed Spirit, which visits and enlightens our dark hearts. This Spirit will lead thee to live in the fear of God, and to serve him with a perfect heart and a willing mind.

I shall now repeat some of the advice which I have often given thee.

First. Never begin or end the day without prayer. Wait on the Lord more often than the day, and call upon his holy name, for without his help we can do nothing truly well. Secondly. Read a small portion of Scripture every day, by thyself, in thy own private chamber, besides attending the family reading. The Scriptures are the best of books. Learn to love them dearly, to prize them highly, and to use them diligently. Thirdly. Keep carefully to the plain language, and never be ashamed of being a consistent Friend. Rest assured that to be half a Christian and half not, and half a Friend and half not, will never answer any good purpose. Fourthly. Be a whole man to everything. At Latin, be a whole man to Latin. At geometry or history, be a whole man to geometry or history. At play, be a whole man to play. At washing and dressing, be a whole man to washing and dressing. Above all, at Meeting, be a whole man to worship. Fifthly. Never speak or think highly of thyself. Thou art a poor unworthy creature; a mere worm of earth. Thou hast not a single talent or faculty which thou hast not received from God. Dwell in humility before him. Sixthly. Avoid all vain and evil thoughts. Remember dearest aunt Rachel's saying, "Evil thoughts are sin." Seventhly. Mind thy manners as well as thy morals. Do not be clumsy and awkward. Be always ready to serve and please all around thee. Be swift to give up thy own will to the will of others in little things: this is the way to be a true gentleman. Finally, "whatsoever thy hand findeth to do, do it with thy might, for there is no work, nor device, nor knowledge, nor wisdom, in the grave whither thou art going."

So farewell, my dearest boy. We are all well and happy.

I am thy loving father,

J. J. GURNEY.

The following graphic reminiscences of youthful days spent at Earlham, may form an appropriate conclusion to the present chapter.

"Activity of benevolence, *practical* kindness, seemed to me to be the ruling spirit of Earlham. I did not hear much of great schemes, but I saw much of real acts of charity; and these recollections, on that account, are both pleasant and profitable. The whole household seemed imbued with the same happy feeling. As I sat pondering on how little I had ever done, and making in my inmost heart, first excuses, and then resolutions, I caught sight of some lady's maid, or upper servant of the family cheerfully crossing the scarcely tracked path, amidst the drifting snow, on some errand of mercy to a poor neighbour. I have forgotten many and many a sermon and lecture on the duty of benevolence: that one little act of self-denial has remained in my memory for a long course of years. * * * *

"One night—I remember it well—I received a severe lesson on the sin of evil-speaking. Severe I thought it then, and my heart rose in childish indignation against him who gave it; but I had not lived long enough in the world to know how much mischief a child's inconsiderate talk may do, and how frequently it happens, that great talkers run off the straight line of truth. I was talking very fast about some female relative, who did not stand particularly high in my estimation; and was proceeding to give particulars of her delinquencies, failings of temper, &c., to the amusement, I suppose, of one or two of my hearers. In a few moments my eye caught an expression, in that of one of my auditors, of such calm and steady disapprobation, that I stopped suddenly short. There was no mistaking the meaning conveyed by that dark, speaking eye; it brought the colour to my temples, and confusion and shame to my heart. I was silent for a few moments, when Joseph John Gurney asked very gravely,

"'Dost thou not know of any *good* thing to tell us of—— ?' I did not answer, and the question was more seriously repeated. 'Think, is there nothing good thou canst tell us of her?' 'Oh, yes I know of some good things certainly, but——' 'Would it not have been better then to relate those good things, than to have told us that which must lower her in our estimation? Since there is good to relate, would it not be kinder to be silent on the *evil?*' 'Charity rejoiceth not in iniquity,' thou knowest.' * * *

"It was our custom every morning,—that of Miss Gurney and any little visitor she might have with her,—to go before breakfast into the room adjoining her father's dressing room, and recite certain portions of Scripture, either of our own choice or his selection. There was a particular appropriateness in the 13th chapter of 1st Corinthians, which, on the following morning, I was desired to read, and afterwards to commit to memory. There was no comment made on what I read. It was unnecessary; the reproof was felt even to the shedding of tears; but the kind voice and silent caress soon spoke love and peace, and I was comforted. 'A word spoken in season how good it is!' * * *

"Children are so observant of inconsistency in those who reprove, that had I ever found my mentor guilty of the sin of uncharitableness, I should not have failed to put it down in the note-book of my heart; but I can truly say that the force of that beautiful precept was never weakened by a contradictory example. I never heard a censorious word pass those calm lips, nor knew a cloud of unworthy suspicion to darken his bright trusting hope of the best of every one. Most eminently was that grace his, which 'hopeth all things.' Every one who has visited Earlham, must have been impressed with the superior tone of conversation there; with the absence of scandal and small talk; and when persons, rather than things, were a little too prominent in the discourse of the juniors, how ingeniously and yet how kindly has the subject been put aside, and some other matter of innocent interest introduced in its stead.

"Such was the home of Joseph John Gurney as it appeared to a child. Clouds there were, doubtless; from human frailty and infirmity it was not entirely exempt; but few Christian households display a happier scene of concord, consistency, and holiness, than that which we have just visited." *

* From Reminiscences of a Good Man's Life, by H. R. Geldart, whose father, the late Simon Martin, was one of Joseph John Gurney's partners in the Norwich Bank. It was originally printed in the Monthly Christian Spectator for the third month. 1852, and has since been published in a separate form.

CHAPTER XXI.

1830. ÆT. 42—43.

VISIT TO FRIENDS IN SUFFOLK; LETTER TO SIR JAMES MACKINTOSH ON CAPITAL PUNISHMENT FOR FORGERY; YEARLY MEETING; CHALMERS AND WILBERFORCE; JOURNEY IN SCOTLAND AND CUMBERLAND; DETENTION AT EDINBURGH; CHALMERIANA; SOUTHEY; CARLISLE; PENRITH; KENDAL; MANCHESTER; RETURN HOME; DEATH OF HIS UNCLE JOSEPH GURNEY.

JOSEPH JOHN GURNEY commenced the year 1830, with two weeks of close religious labour in the county of Suffolk. "I traversed the snows in my gig," he writes to Jonathan Hutchinson,* "in order to visit the scattered meetings. I do not know that I ever "roughed it" so much before, nor do I remember many occasions in which a little sacrifice in the cause of truth was more rewarded."

TO HIS SISTER ELIZABETH FRY.

Norwich, 1st mo., 19th, 1830.

My heart and mind have been much and closely with thee for some time past, and I trust I have been enabled to remember thee, when access has been permitted to the throne of grace. Thou mayest rest assured of my constant unity and faithful sympathy with thee, in every tribulation, and under every wave of conflict. * * I often think of —— with great interest. I plead not for forms; but a thorough, unqualified submission to the internal power of the cross of Christ in the heart, is that

* Under date 3rd mo. 17th, 1830.

which I fully believe will alone satisfy and give true rest. * * We had a very uncomfortable alarm last evening at Earlham, in consequence of some beams, near the flue in the hall, igniting. What a mercy that it did not happen in the night! As it was, we were apparently in imminent danger of an overwhelming conflagration; but happily, the fire was surmounted before it burst forth. We have felt humbled under a sense of gratitude for this merciful deliverance.

2nd mo., 1st. The continuance of this very wintry weather is affecting, as it relates to the poor. Indeed, the chastising hand seems rather remarkably put forth on this nation; and who can wonder, when we consider the vast multitude of those who are living in sin, and in open rebellion against the Most High? Neither ought our faith to be shaken, if those who are not partakers of the pollutions, are "partakers in the plagues." The time is coming, when all apparent inequalities will be made even; when He shall "return, and discern between the righteous and the wicked, between him that serveth God and him that serveth him not."

2nd mo., 19th. Much enjoyment of the quietness and loveliness of this dear place, and of the domestic happiness which it is still permitted to contain. Should it be right for me to quit business altogether, it would follow, I think, that Earlham must be given up. If the Lord condescends to require the sacrifice, I trust a willingness to offer it will be wrought in me. I think I desire no more than clearly to see his will.

Reference has been more than once made to Joseph John Gurney's strong feeling upon the subject of capital punishment. For any crime short of murder, he was, in fact, altogether opposed to it.*

* "I cannot say," he writes in his Journal, under date 8th mo., 17th, 1829, "that my spirit greatly revolts against life for *life;* though capital punishment for any thing short of this, appears to me to be execrable." In later life he became opposed to capital punishment even for murder.

This view of the question had been for some years gradually gaining ground. Among the many salutary practical reforms for which this country is indebted to the late Sir Robert Peel, not the least was the complete revision and consolidation of the criminal law; by which many barbarous enactments were swept from the statute book, and a milder and more efficacious system of punishment was introduced. This distinguished statesman, who was at this time Home Secretary, was now turning his attention to the amendment of the laws relating to forgery. On this subject, however, he was not prepared to go so far as the advocates of the abolition of capital punishment desired. His bill retained the punishment of death in several cases of forgery. The opportunity was felt to be an important one, and the advocates of a more lenient system lost no time in availing themselves of it. Joseph John Gurney exerted himself in Norwich, in procuring a petition to Parliament for the entire abolition of the punishment of death in these cases; and, availing himself of his practical experience as a banker, he subsequently addressed the following letter to Sir James Mackintosh, with the view of strengthening his hands in his noble advocacy of the cause of humanity.

Norwich, 4th mo., 20th, 1830.

ESTEEMED FRIEND,

Although I have not the pleasure of more than a very slight personal acquaintance with thee, the useful and honourable public part thou hast taken in the cause of the abolition of capital punishments, will, I trust, afford a sufficient apology for my addressing thee on the subject.

It has been a matter of deep regret to me to observe, that

the alterations and amendments proposed by the Home Secretary, in regard to the penal acts respecting forgery, are almost exclusively in matter of form, and not of practice. It seems that the pristine ferocity of the law is to continue without alleviation, as it relates to all instruments representing money, such as bills of exchange, drafts, and notes, — all instruments, in short, with which a banker has any concern.

I have long been engaged extensively in the business of a banker, and have always considered it a heavy grievance that the law, as it now stands, leaves me wholly unprotected from the attacks of the forger. I cannot in conscience take any steps towards destroying the life of a fellow creature, whose crime against me affects my property only; being deeply convinced that, should I do so, I should thereby sacrifice as plain a principle of equity as was ever proposed to the attention of mankind. Besides I am in possession, like other men, of the feelings of common humanity; and to aid and abet in procuring the destruction of any man living, would be to me extremely distressing and horrible. And yet I consider forgery a shameful and heinous crime. I well know the cruel losses and inconveniences to which it subjects the money-changing world; and if the law would but help me to put such an offender on the tread-wheel for a couple of years, I should feel the highest satisfaction in availing myself of its provisions. * * Mine is no insulated or uncommon case: multitudes in the commercial world are placed, by the severity of the law, in the same uncomfortable and unprotected situation.

Being thoroughly persuaded that all penal enactments with which the public cannot heartily co-operate, are bad in principle, and injurious in operation, I have only to express, in conclusion, my earnest wish, that thy great powers may continue to be steadily directed against a system at once so unjust and so ineffective.

I am, with much respect,

Thy sincere friend,

J. J. Gurney.

It is satisfactory to know that, although the efforts made at this time did not then result in any modification of the proposed measure on this point, the abolition of capital punishment, in these cases, has been since conceded by the legislature, and that no person has suffered death for forgery, in this country, since that period.*

To return to the Journal :—

5th mo., 3rd. How entirely do I feel that all my hope of a happy futurity depends on my casting myself, or, rather, on my being cast by a divine hand, on the mercies, merits, and righteousness of Jesus Christ; that I may be seen in him; judged in him; justified in him; glorified in him. Be thou for ever abased, O my soul! polluted and degraded as thou art in thyself, in the contemplation of his glorious attributes, his perfect sufficiency for thy eternal salvation.

5th mo., 14th. Our beloved friends William and Anna Forster left us this morning for London. Their company and ministry amongst us have been very acceptable. Yesterday especially, at our Monthly Meeting, the former was largely and nobly engaged in preaching. It was a time of much sweetness and comfortable ingathering, for which we cannot be too thankful. The same precious feeling continued here in the evening. Some banking exigencies have been more trying to my sensitiveness, this week, than they ought

* The punishment of death is now abolished in all cases of forgery, except where the act amounts to High Treason, as in the case of counterfeiting the Royal sign manual, or the Great or Privy Seal. This desirable change did not, however, take place until the commencement of the present reign, in 1837. Even in the last reign, several new forgeries were made capital felonies. The gradual progress of humane legislation, on this subject, may be seen by reference to the statutes 11 Geo. iv, & 1 Will. iv, c. 66, (Sir Robert Peel's Act, to which Joseph John Gurney's letter refers,) 2 & 3 Will. iv, c. 123, and c. 125; 5 & 6 Will. iv, c. 45; 1 Vict., c. 14; and 4 & 5 Vict., c. 66: and as to counterfeiting the coin, see statute 2 Will. iv, c. 34.

to have been. Unworthy as I know myself to be, I venture to crave divine protection even in these affairs; and I think I feel a degree of confidence in the dealings of that gentle and paternal hand, which has hitherto led me along. O that I may be blessed with quietness, diligence, faith, and fortitude; that I may be arrayed, earth-worm as I am, in the whole armour of my God!

Second day morning. I have many things to attend to; but am favoured with a precious degree of calmness. How delightful, and I hope edifying, has been my intercourse with my beloved Mary during the past spring! Such happiness I feel to be quite a store; a privilege to have enjoyed it, let the future produce what it may.

6th mo., 13th. I continued alone at home till sixth day, 5th mo., 19th, when I went by mail to London, exchanging the delightful summer solitude of Earlham, for a busy and exercising scene, into which I made my plunge on seventh day. The Yearly Meeting was a time of remarkable interest. On the men's part well attended, sometimes much *gathered;* at other times too much of what was superficial, and of ourselves. We seem to want a greater depth, and O that it may be graciously bestowed upon us! Yet we had cause for thankfulness on account of the general harmony and abounding sense of brotherly love. Of the sittings I should distinguish, as the most remarkable, that in which the claims of the heathen were considered, which resulted in the recognition of the concern as worthy of the deliberate consideration of the meeting next year; and the last sitting but one, in which a Friend spoke most powerfully on the doctrine of the atonement.

It was about this period, whilst on a visit at Hampstead, at the house of his brother-in-law, Samuel Hoare, that Joseph John Gurney was first introduced to the late Dr. Chalmers, who was then in London. In the interesting memoranda of their intercourse, which has since been printed, Joseph John Gurney writes:—

"We walked together for an hour before dinner in the garden; and soon found that we were led, by a feeling of congeniality, into familiar intercourse. He had just been presented by a friend with a copy of my Essays, which led to much interesting conversation on the Evidences of Christianity, on which we had both written — their cumulative and harmonious character, and the enlargements which had been made in this branch of theological knowledge of late years. It was a noble encouragement to a good cause to find that these evidences were better understood, and more fully appreciated, eighteen hundred years after the introduction of our religion, than at any period of Church history, since the days when men were brought into actual contact with miracles.

"We talked over the subject of a moral law, universally written by the Moral Governor of the universe on the hearts of mankind. He allowed the existence of this principle, and its universality, although we were both aware that the light, though pure, is often faint. The darkness of fallen human nature comprehendeth it not. I remarked the distinction which exists between this law and the natural faculty of conscience; the law being the light, the conscience the eye; the law the guide, the conscience the presiding judge. He admitted this distinction; but when, after the example of Butler, I misnamed this law the moral sense, he corrected me, and said, 'No, the moral sense is identical with the conscience: the law you speak of is that which the moral sense perceives.' I argued, that the law thus written on the hearts of all men, although faint, and perpetually misread by an obscured and perverted conscience, is in itself perfectly pure and holy, an efflux of the divine character. When therefore I reflected on the utter corruption of human nature, and on the apostolic doctrine, 'In me, that is, in my flesh, there dwelleth no good thing,' I could not but conclude that this universal law is a work of the Spirit.

"Chalmers. 'I have no objection to admit that it is a work of the Spirit.'

"This was a conclusion, worthy of the breadth and liberality of Dr. C's mind, and of the simplicity which he displays in admitting truth, from whatever quarter it may come. It reminded me of the broad assertion twice made to me, in private conversation, by William Wilberforce, that, according to his full belief, an effective offer of salvation was made to every man born into the world. I will just add, that since Christ is expressly declared to have died for all men, and since the law of God—a principle, when obeyed, in its nature, *saving*—is, as we believe, universally communicated to men, it is only reasonable to believe that our fallen race has obtained this blessing through the redemption which is by Christ Jesus our Lord.

"At dinner, we had an interesting party—Dr. Bird Sumner, Bishop of Chester;* Dr. Lushington; Buxton; and a family party, including our sister Elizabeth Fry. The conversation during dinner turned to the subject of capital punishments. Lushington, in the warmest terms, expressed his abhorrence of the system; and declared his opinion, that the poor criminal was thus hurried out of life, and into eternity, by means of the perpetration of another crime, far greater, for the most part, than any which the sufferer himself had committed. He even indicated a feeling, that the worse the criminal, the more improper such a punishment.

"On this Buxton rallied him, and re-stated his argument with great pleasantry; 'The doctor assures us that if your Lordship were condemned to the gallows, or that you, Dr. Chalmers, were about to suffer the *ultimum supplicium*, he would be the last man to interfere with the execution of the law, or prevent the translation of the virtuous to a happier state. But to terminate the probationary existence of the most degraded of our race, of the worst of robbers or the most outrageous of murderers, was opposed at once to all the feelings of humanity, and to all the principles of religion.' After all, there is a great deal of truth in Dr. Lushington's statement, and substantially we were all agreed.

"After dinner a brisk discussion arose respecting the

* Now Archbishop of Canterbury.

comparative religious condition of the long parliament, and of our representatives, in the present day of latitudinarianism and laxity. Lushington contended that the advantage lay on the side of our modern senate; and that the looseness of the present was a less crying evil than the hypocrisy of past times. The bishop and Chalmers took the other side; and not only demonstrated the religious superiority of the Puritans, but strongly insisted on the great principle, that it is godliness which exalteth a nation, and which can alone impart true strength and stability to human governments. Chalmers stated the points of the argument with great strength and clearness, and the bishop confirmed what he said.

"In the evening Joanna Baillie joined our party; and, after the bishop and others were gone, we formed a social circle, of which Chalmers was the centre. The evidences of Christianity became again the topic of conversation. The harmony of Scripture, and the accordance and correspondence of one part with another were, I think, adverted to. This evidence of accordance is one to which Dr. C.'s mind is obviously much alive. He knows how to trace, in the adaptation between one branch of truth and another, and especially between God's religion and man's experience, the master-hand of perfect wisdom and goodness.

"CHALMERS. 'The historical evidences of Christianity are abundantly sufficient to satisfy the scrutinizing researches of the learned; and are within the reach of all well-educated persons. But the internal evidence of the truth lies within the grasp of *every* sincere inquirer. Every man who reads his Bible, and compares what it says of mankind with the records of his own experience; every man who marks the adaptation of its mighty system of doctrine to his own spiritual need as a sinner in the sight of God; is furnished with practical proof of the divine origin of our religion. I love this evidence. It is what I call the *portable evidence of Christianity.*'

"On the following morning Dr. Chalmers read the Scriptures to the family circle, and selected the latter half of John xiv. The verse which peculiarly attracted his attention was the twenty-first; 'He that hath my commandments, and keepeth them, he it is that loveth me; and he that loveth me shall be loved of my Father; and I will love him, and will manifest myself to him.' The observations which he made on this verse, and on the whole bearing of what he had read, were excellent; and completely accordant with the views which Friends have so long been accustomed to take of the true method of obtaining religious knowledge. 'While we are bound,' he observed in substance, 'to make a diligent use of the Scriptures, that appointed depositary of all religious information, we are ever to remember, that *obedience to the law of Christ* is the means of bringing us into a capacity of rightly understanding and appreciating their contents; as our Lord has himself declared, that those who do his Father's will shall know of his doctrine, and of its divine authority. Every act of childlike obedience to the dictates of the Spirit of God prepares the way for an increase of light; and where Christ manifests '*himself*,' there will be a true and saving apprehension of religion.' In setting forth these views, Dr. Chalmers was, I believe, speaking from his own experience; for it seems to have been by the gradual following up of his convictions of duty, and through the operation of a remarkable *moral* energy, that, under the grace of God, he found his way out of the dark regions of barren speculation, into the green pastures of the fold of Christ.

"When comparatively ignorant and worldly he was called upon by his learned friend, Dr. Brewster, to write the article on Christianity for the Edinburgh Encyclopedia. He obeyed the summons, though himself scarcely a believer; and his researches in order to this end, especially the study of Scripture itself, were the means first of convincing his understanding of the truth of religion, and next of impressing his heart with a sense of its unspeakable importance and excellence. In the whole of this process he was doubtless marvellously assisted by that childlike *simplicity* of mind which he recommended to us so beautifully; and which is so marked a feature in his own character. 'The meek will he guide in judgment, the meek will he teach his way.'

"Before he concluded his familiar yet impressive discourse, he powerfully contrasted two methods of religious education. The former — no stranger in Scotland — that of imparting to the minds of children a complete system of doctrinal orthodoxy; and, without moral culture, leaving that system to produce its own fruits as it might. The latter, that of training children in such a course of virtuous obedience to the divine law, as would prepare them for the reception of greater and greater light respecting the doctrines of religion. He pointed out the vast superiority of the latter system. He would neglect neither moral nor religious culture; but he would make the former the pathway to the latter. * * *

"When our conversation was concluded, my brother, Samuel Hoare, took me with him on the box of his chariot, and drove Dr. Chalmers and his pleasing wife to Wilberforce's, at Highwood Hall, beyond Hendon. Dr. Chalmers and his lady were engaged to stay some days there; and we were glad of the opportunity of enjoying the company of the *senator emeritus*, together with that of Dr. C., for a few hours. Our morning passed delightfully. Chalmers was, indeed, comparatively silent, as he often is when many persons are collected, and the stream of conversation flowed between ourselves and the ever lively Wilberforce. I have seldom observed a more amusing and pleasing contrast between two great men, than between Wilberforce and Chalmers. Chalmers is stout and erect, with a broad countenance; Wilberforce minute, and singularly twisted; Chalmers, both in body and mind, moves with a deliberate step; Wilberforce, infirm as he is in his advanced years, flies about with astonishing activity: and while, with nimble finger, he seizes on every thing that adorns or diversifies his path, his mind flits from object to object with unceasing versatility. Chalmers can say a pleasant thing now and then, and laugh when he has said it, and he has a strong touch of humour in his countenance; but in general he is grave — his thoughts grow to a great size before they are uttered: Wilberforce sparkles with life and wit, and the characteristic of his mind is 'rapid productiveness.' A man might be in Chalmers' company for an hour, especially in a party, without knowing who or what he was — though in the end he would be sure to be detected by some unexpected display of powerful originality; Wilberforce, except when fairly asleep, is never latent: Chalmers knows how to veil himself in a decent cloud; Wilberforce is always in sunshine. Seldom, I believe, has any mind been more strung to a perpetual tune of love and praise. Yet these persons, distinguished as they are from the world at large, and from each other, present some admirable points of resemblance. Both of them are broad thinkers and liberal feelers: both of them are arrayed in humility, meekness, and charity: both appear to hold self in little reputation: above all, both love the Lord Jesus Christ, and reverently acknowledge him to be their only Saviour.

"Wilberforce was the son of a wealthy merchant at Hull, and was scarcely more than of age when he was elected member of Parliament for that town. But he was not long to occupy this station, for a higher one awaited him. Immediately after the Hull election, he attended the county election at York; where, to the vast assembly collected in the castle yard, he made a speech on the popular question of the day — Fox's India bill. His eloquence, especially in the earlier stages of his course, was, as I understand, of a most animated and diversified character; and his voice sonorous and mellifluous. The speech produced an almost magical effect on the assembled multitude; and under a strong, and apparently unanimous impulse, they cried out, 'We will have the little man for our member.' In short, though without pretensions from family or fortune to the honour of representing that vast county, he was elected its member by acclamation.

"Wilberforce was now one of the most popular of men. His fine talents, his amiability, his wit, his gaiety, adapted him for the highest worldly circles in the county. Happily, however, that heavenly Father, whom his pious parents had taught him to love in early life, was preparing for him 'better things' than the blandishments of the world, even 'things which accompany salvation.' Not long after his election he was travelling through France, in order to visit a sick relation at Nice, in company with his friend, Isaac Milner, afterwards Dean of

Carlisle, a person somewhat older and more serious than himself. In the course of their journey they happened to converse about a clergyman in Yorkshire, who, having been impressed with evangelical views, was remarkably devoted to his parochial duties.

"WILBERFORCE. 'That man carries things a great deal too far, *in my opinion.*'

"MILNER. 'Do you think so? I conceive that if you tried him by the standard presented to us in the New Testament, you would change that opinion.'

"WILBERFORCE. 'Indeed, Milner—well, I have no objection to try the experiment. I will read the New Testament with you, if you like, with pleasure.'

"Important, indeed, were the results of this casual and unexpected conversation. The two friends read the whole of the New Testament together as they journeyed on towards Nice: and this single perusal of the records of inspiration was so blessed to Wilberforce, that he became a new man. His opinions and feelings underwent a rapid revolution. He found himself to be a sinner, and rejoiced in the discovery of his Saviour. He renounced the world, and devoted himself to the fear and service of Almighty God. When he arrived at Nice, he found, in the chamber of his sick relative, a copy of Dr. Doddridge's Rise and Progress of Religion in the Soul. This useful manual of religious experience he read with extreme eagerness, and it appears to have been the means of confirming and completing his change.

"The news now swiftly flew into Yorkshire that their popular young member was gone mad. Wilberforce followed the report, *in propriâ personâ;* threw himself, with noble boldness, amongst his friends and supporters; plainly told them of his change of sentiment; and with good reason adopted (as it may be presumed) the words of a yet more eminent convert, 'I am *not* mad, most noble Festus—I speak the words of truth and soberness.' From that time his influence in the county was constantly extending itself; and when, many years afterwards, a contested election took place between Colonel Lascelles and Lord Milton, he polled almost double the number of the votes of either of the other candidates; and a voluntary subscription flowed in of about £40,000, to defray his expenses. A great part of this subscription was returned. Wilberforce afterwards voluntarily retired from the representation of the county, being unable, from want of health, to cope with the weight of business which it threw on his shoulders.

"It is impossible to reflect on this story without much pleasure. What a mercy to Wilberforce was the petty and apparently fortuitous circumstance, which led him to an attentive perusal of the New Testament! And how divine the book which, through the blessing of its almighty Author, could bear with so irresistible a moral and spiritual force on the intellect, the genius, and the dispositions of Wilberforce! In like manner, what a mercy to Dr. Chalmers was the unexpected, and at that time unlikely, application made to him by Dr. Brewster! It was in the order of Providence that two chance circumstances, as the world would call them, should be the means of translating two mighty minds from the region of spiritual darkness, into the kingdom of light; converting the sceptical philosopher into the profound theologian, and the witty songster into the abolisher of the slave trade, the faithful and ardent Christian labourer in the cause of justice and humanity.*

"The author of that extraordinary book, the Natural History of Enthusiasm, proposes a beautiful analysis of the order and harmony of providence. He says, that events may be divided into two classes—those which arise in the ordinary course of experience; and which, being regulated by certain known laws, natural or moral, may, to a certain and often a great extent, be calculated beforehand; and thus bring into exercise the quality of prudence, or the useful faculty of long-sightedness. Indeed, a careful observation and right estimate of such causes and effects, may be said to constitute the best

* The foregoing incidents are related by Joseph John Gurney from information received in conversation with Wilberforce himself. For Wilberforce's own reflections on the circumstances of his life here referred to, see the first vol. of his Life, Appendix pp. 379—384.

kind of worldly *wisdom*. Another and more limited class of events may be described as incidental or fortuitous. These intersect the common course—the straight onward line of our experience—from a multitude of different points. They bear laterally upon us, and arise out of an endless and ever varied train of causes; connected, very probably, with the life and conduct of others—originating, it may be, in some idle word, or some thoughtless action, of some unknown person, whose mortal existence has been closed for centuries. And yet these apparently stray circumstances often intersect our path, just at such a time and in such a manner, as enable them to serve the most important purposes for our temporal and spiritual good. How perfect must be the skill and wisdom of that omniscient Being, who wields this infinitely intricate machinery; often inclines its forces in answer to *prayer*, and never fails to apply them to the highest advantage of his believing and obedient children!"

TO JONATHAN HUTCHINSON.

(On the decease of one of his daughters within a year after her marriage.)

London, 6th mo., 3rd, 1830.

MY DEARLY BELOVED FRIEND,

Thou well knowest that the affecting intelligence from Leiston must come closely home to me and my wife; for we feel so nearly united with thee and thine, that whatsoever you suffer becomes our suffering by reflection. I can truly say, that we have grieved and mourned with you over the loss of your beloved Lydia. I am aware that she was peculiarly precious—that she was one of those who imparted a charm to life in the circle in which she moved. And of such as these it often pleases a wise Providence to deprive us, that we may be the better prepared to say, "Whom have I in heaven but thee? and there is none upon earth that I desire beside thee." Thus the Lord claims an undivided sovereignty over our affections, as well as over our actions.

Amidst your deep sorrowing, you will not, we feel fully assured, be disposed to murmur. We trust that the Christian's faith, by which he sees things invisible to mortal eye, will gild the dark cloud, and lead you ever to rejoice for her emancipated spirit with "a joy unspeakable and full of glory." Such is the nature of the Christian's joy, that the tongue of human wisdom cannot utter it; and there is a fullness of glory in it, even here, which the eye unanointed cannot perceive. Nevertheless we know it is progressive, admitting of almost infinite enlargement and elevation. We will not therefore mourn for those who have happily exchanged its fainter irradiations for its meridian fulness. What a solidity, as well as brightness, my beloved friend, characterizes the Christian's life! It is like the paving of that holy city of apostolic vision, transparent glass, and yet pure, weighty gold.

In reference to your dear departed one, I have been led to dwell with much satisfaction, on the security which attaches to the absence of self-righteousness; and to a quiet, steadfast dependence on the mercy of God, through the appointed Mediator. Comparatively blameless as she was in the eye of man, I feel a persuasion that her hope rested, not on the rewarding of her virtue, but on the pardoning of her sins. She was not (I fully believe) a stranger, either in heart or understanding, to the efficacy of that blood, by which all sin is obliterated for the humble believer.

A large Committee had been appointed at the late Yearly Meeting for the purpose of making a general visit to the various meetings of Friends in Great Britain and Ireland. As a member of this committee, Joseph John Gurney, in company with several other Friends, attended the meetings in Scotland and Cumberland, and was also engaged in other services as a minister of the gospel. He was absent from home nearly four months.

"On seventh day, the 24th of the 7th month," he writes in his Journal, "I left home for Upton, in order to attend the interment of our beloved friend and cousin, Lucy Sheppard. I found the Upton party in deep sorrow; and truly rejoiced in being present to sympathize with them, and help them a little, during the scenes of that touching and sorrowful day. I joined my wife at Stamford, on second day evening, and proceeded with her to Ackworth, where the general meeting passed off much to our satisfaction.

On seventh day, a delightful journey by Fountain's Abbey and Richmond, brought us to Darlington; where, in the absence of all our nearer connexions, we were most hospitably received by our dear cousins E. and R. Pease, and remained until fourth day morning. Public meetings there, and at Staindrop, and Stockton. The public meeting at Staindrop much favoured, as was also one at Sunderland on fourth day evening. The meeting with Sunderland Friends on fifth day morning, was much to my satisfaction and relief; and there was a public one at Newcastle that evening, in a Dissenting Meeting House. Pleasant visit to our dear cousin Margaret Bragg. The meeting of Friends on sixth day morning largely attended by young people, and very hopeful.

TO SAMUEL GURNEY.

Darlington, 8th mo., 1st, 1830.

I believe that as Christians, and as Friends, we must adhere closely to our religious principles, and learn to bring everything more and more to that test; looking quietly forwards to the day when "the stone cut without hands" will become "a great mountain" and fill the whole earth. * *

The commotions in France are somewhat awful, but I trust they will end in a bloodless revolution. The worst feature in the case appears to me to be the *infidelity* with which the support of freedom is connected. Would that mankind knew more of that "perfect law of liberty" which is proclaimed to us in the Gospel of our Redeemer!

After attending the General Meeting for Friends

in Scotland, held at Aberdeen, he returned to Glasgow; and after various religious services there, and in the neighbourhood, proceeded to Edinburgh. Here he was detained nearly five weeks from the consequences of a severe bruise on the leg, received in the course of the journey. He did not, however, allow this interval of comparative repose to pass away unimproved. Under the hospitable roof of his valued friend Alexander Cruickshank, he had opportunities of religious intercourse with the individuals composing the small body of Friends resident at Edinburgh, and three meetings with the young people. He was also enabled to be present, one first day, at a public meeting, held at his request, which was attended by many in the upper circles. Besides these engagements, his sojourn at Edinburgh was agreeably relieved by much highly interesting social intercourse. Dr. Chalmers, amongst others, was a frequent visitor, "coming," writes Joseph John Gurney, "from a considerable distance about every other day to sit with me. We enjoyed much intimate and lively conversation, which I was accustomed to record from day to day, after he had left me, as I lay upon my sofa." A brief selection from these memoranda will give the reader some idea of the general character of their intercourse; and few will object to listen whilst they converse together.*

The conversation one day turning upon the

*The Chalmeriana have been published since this chapter was compiled; but I have not thought this a sufficient reason for omitting the extracts.

wonderful order and harmony of Divine Providence,

"I observed," says Joseph John Gurney, "that the great object of Bishop Butler's Analogy was to parry objections; and we agreed that in this respect that noble work had served a most important purpose in promoting the cause of truth. Chalmers expressed his admiration of Butler's unsophisticated mind and absence of affectation. But Butler possessed a mind of singular depth and originality, and such minds are beyond the limits of affectation.

"CHALMERS. 'I strongly recommend your reading Leibnitz, 'Essais sur la Theodicée.' He combines the mind of a philosopher, and a profound knowledge of metaphysics, with an unqualified regard for Christianity and its whole system of essential doctrine. I was telling Mrs. Gurney, at the Museum, of the hypothesis by which he accounts for the origin of evil. Take any complete part of creation—an animal for example. How perfect is the machine, how beautiful its proportions, how absolute the harmony of its constituent parts, how admirably it works! But look at some *fragment* of the creature; a piece of a nail, a broken bit of bone or a claw. How unsightly it is, how unmeaning! how little worthy, as far as appears, of the master hand of infinite skill and wisdom! Now all the evil which we perceive around us, afflicting as it is to our feelings, and trying to our faith, may be nothing more than a small unsightly fragment; and yet, in its connexion with the moral universe of God, it may form a part of a perfectly harmonious and glorious whole.'

"I mentioned a work, popular among the Unitarians, which resolves all the attributes of God into pure benevolence; denominates sin 'moral evil;' ascribes it to the direct appointment of God; and presumes to infer that it not only promotes the general good, but, taken in connexion with its corrective consequences, in the end enhances the happiness of the sinner.

"CHALMERS. 'It is a dangerous error to reduce the divine attributes to the single quality of goodness. Our best metaphysicians, (especially Brown) teach us that the ethical virtues are in their nature unalterably independent. Justice is an ethical virtue; distinct in its origin, character, and end, and must not be confounded with any other. These principles apply to the moral attributes of God.'

"Yes, I said, they are blended but not confused.

"CHALMERS. 'There is union in them but not unity. The harmony, yet distinctness, of the divine moral attributes, is most instructively inscribed on the atonement of Christ.'

"Truly, I replied, that is a point where justice and benevolence meet; where God has displayed at once his abhorrence of sin, and his mercy to the sinner.

"CHALMERS. 'Brown had very low and inadequate views of the character of God. The same may be said of Paley—witness his founding his system of morals on expediency. This was indeed a degradation in a Christian moral philosopher; and the more so, as even a Cicero could declaim against '*utilitas*' as the basis of morals.'

"I mentioned an anecdote which I had heard of Paley in his last illness, that is said to have had the authority of Wm. Hey, the late noted surgeon of Leeds; and which, if true, is remarkably consoling. When not far from his end, Paley, in conversing with some of his family or friends, took a calm review of his several works. He expressed the deep regret and dissatisfaction which, at that awful time, he felt in the recollection of his 'Moral Philosophy.' He was happy to believe that his 'Natural Theology' and 'Evidences of Christianity' were sound and useful works; but the book on which his mind then dwelt with the greatest pleasure was his 'Horæ Paulinæ.'

"CHALMERS. 'I am not surprised at this. It is an admirable statement of evidence, and displays a more masterly hand than any of his other works.'

* * * * * *

Dr. Chalmers' conversations with us have been much more frequently about *things* than *persons;* and indeed he has too much intelligence aud power of mind to descend to a species of conversation commonly called gossip, which is the frequent refuge of many whose understandings are meagrely stored with information.

"It is evident that he is deeply impressed with the opinion, that an overwhelming tide is but too likely, ere long, to sweep down many of our civil, literary, and religious institutions. The spirit which prevails abroad, he apprehends to be in somewhat active operation at home, and he ascribes its existence and increase to the wide dissemination of *superficial* knowledge.

"The new revolution in France, and the commotions which have since taken place in other parts of Europe, have all occurred since our lot has been cast in Scotland. They have, of course, been the subject of daily thought, meditation, and converse. Although there is much in these changes, especially as regards France, with which every liberal mind must sympathize, it is easy to perceive that the spirit of insubordination is increasingly prevalent in the world. I fear it runs through many both of our private and public relations; parent and child, master and servant, magistrate and citizen, king and subject. It is probable also that even the Christian church is affected by this change of feeling; and that in every denomination there is less of wholesome restraint, and a greater impatience of discipline, than was the case fifty or a hundred years ago. If this be one of the consequences of 'the march of intellect,' it is assuredly a fearful one; and I know of no remedy but the diffusion of the gospel. The Scriptures will never cease to teach us to fulfil all our relative duties aright, 'and to be subject one to another in love.' I believe the spirit of rebellion against man to be intimately associated with that of rebellion against God. That which can alone counteract both is GENUINE CHRISTIANITY.

"We were favoured one day with a call from a man of very superior parts, John Brown, the pious and able minister here of one of the largest seceding congregations. When we asked him, 'What dost thou think will be the end of all these national commotions?' he answered emphatically, 'the kingdoms of this world shall become the kingdoms of the Lord and of his Christ.' To this scriptural declaration we can all set the seal of a willing belief; but, in the meantime, tribulations and trials of faith may perhaps be ordained for the further purification of the followers of the Lamb; preparatory, it may be, to their final victory.

"CHALMERS. 'I think the Scriptures afford us good reason to believe, that the ultimate diffusion of pure Christianity in the world, must be preceded by commotion and confusion, and distress of nations. Look at the new French revolution. There is much that one approves at present, both in its tendency and in its results. But you see it has been effected by the growth of merely human intelligence; by the working of the unregenerate mind, without a particle of Christian principle. It is just the striving of the natural wisdom and pride of man, after that which we are apt to conceive to be the consummation of our happiness, a condition of independence. I am not one of those who underrate the value of civil and political liberty; but I am well assured that it is only the principles of Christianity, which can impart true security, prosperity, and happiness, either to individuals or to nations. I am prepared to expect, that on the efforts which are now making in the world to regenerate our species, *without religion, God will impress the stamp of a solemn and expressive mockery.*'

"We parted from our dear friend Dr. Chalmers, his wife, and daughters," writes Joseph John Gurney at the conclusion of the memoranda from which the above extracts are taken, "as well as from some other persons who have been endeared to us in Edinburgh, after a solemn and refreshing time of silence, ministry and prayer, on the 25th of the 9th month, 1830."

From Edinburgh, Joseph John Gurney's course was directed to Cumberland. Though not yet equal to his usual amount of continued exertion, he attended the Quarterly Meeting at Cockermouth, on the 30th, in company with the rest of the Yearly Meeting's Committee for that county; and after a meeting with the Friends there on the following morning, he, with his wife, proceeded, by way of Keswick, to Whitehaven.

"At Keswick," he writes in his Journal, "we spent an agreeable and interesting evening with Robert Southey and family. He read us some of his unpublished poetry, and we had much conversation, ending with some religious communication. Southey's religious feelings are sincere and warm, but his prejudices more than a few. On the whole he is a man whom one cannot help liking, and I have no doubt, that he engages the love of those who know him well.

"On seventh day, 10th mo., 2nd, we drove through a country of delightful scenery, the weather being fine, first round Derwentwater and into Borrowdale, and afterwards over the mountains to Scale Hill, and thence by Crummock and Lowes-water to Whitehaven; which place we reached in the evening, weary, yet delighted with our journey, and were hospitably received by our dear friends, John and Mary Spencer.

"We continued at Whitehaven until fifth day morning, during which time the families were visited, much to my comfort; for there are many hopeful Friends there, especially young married persons. O that the enemy of souls may not be permitted to mar the work! There was a good public meeting on first day evening, and a very solemn young people's meeting at John Spencer's. We parted from all our dear Friends in true love."

After various religious engagements at Pardshaw and Cockermouth, and the neighbouring district, they went forward to Wigton.

"Our visit to the school,"* says Joseph John Gurney, "was interesting and satisfactory. We were much pleased with the young master of the boys; and the examination of the children on both sides of the house was encouraging. That of the boys was delightful, and the tenderness of their minds was very remarkable. There appeared to be prevailing in this institution a really religious influence. May it more and

*An Institution similar in its object to the Friends' school at Ackworth, but on a much smaller scale.

more abound among them! On the whole, I think this school has served, and is still serving, an admirable purpose. We had a large and solemn public meeting in the evening. I was very poorly in the night, so as to be ready to conclude that it would be impossible for us to attend Beckfoot meeting, as fixed, the next morning; twelve miles off, and a desolate place on the sea coast. However in the morning our difficulties disappeared; and, after an early breakfast, we were on the road for Beckfoot. On our arrival, we found the meeting-house filled with a considerable number of country Friends, and the whole of Joseph Saul's school, more than one hundred boys, ushers, &c. I had to plead earnestly for Christianity, and for evangelical doctrine, combating with an infidel spirit. I hope it might not be in vain, as power was to be felt in the meeting. That night we reached Carlisle, and took up our abode, very comfortably to ourselves, with Thomas and Elizabeth Stordy. The week-day meeting there the next morning was largely attended, and a searching time. Afterwards we went to Scotby; dined with our dear Friends, Lydia Sutton and Tabitha Irwin, and held a meeting there in the afternoon; which to me was painfully exercising, but ended in peace.

Sixth day was spent in a long excursion to Solport and Kirklington meetings. It proved one of our most interesting days. Both these meetings were once large, but are now mere relics, especially Solport, on the borders of Scotland. There is, however, a valuable little body of Friends; and we had particular pleasure in visiting John and Peggy Story, at Moss-side; Friends in a very humble line of life, true originals, and alive to that which is good. On our way to Kirklington we drank tea at four o'clock with some other friends, not much above them in worldly dignity, Richard Graham and his worthy wife, little shopkeepers by the road-side; and, after an exercising meeting, walked across the country to old William Dodson's, where we met, in their neat little kitchen, an agreeable company of simple hearted Friends. After a solemn little meeting, we parted from them in much love, and returned to Carlisle, where seventh day was passed in writing, rest, and family visits. * * * *

On fifth day morning we left Carlisle and proceeded to Gillfoot meeting, about sixteen miles, over a fine country; the weather being inclement. We met a poor little scattered flock, the rain pouring, and the large old meeting house being now the picture of desolation. We dined at Joseph Priestman's; and in the afternoon proceeded, under the guidance of his son, to Penrith; where we took up our abode in the peaceful dwelling of our dear aged friends Elizabeth Ritson and Hannah Walker, who, with their niece Hannah Hayton, received us most hospitably. We much enjoyed the company of this interesting and truly peculiar trio; especially that of E. Ritson, who, in her ninety-third year, is all alive, intellectually and spiritually, and a cheerful, well informed companion. Meetings at Penrith, with Friends in the morning, and the public in the evening, brought close exercise of mind. I also visited most of their little flock (a comfortable body of Friends) in their own houses. Thomas Wilkinson met us at E. Ritson's in the morning, and although almost entirely blind and very infirm, he is very cheerful; doing credit to the cause of truth, which is so near to his heart. On seventh day, after a visit to the Beacon, and also to the workhouse, two stages, through a wild mountainous country, brought us to Kendal; where we met a cordial reception from our dear cousins, W. D. and Sarah Crewdson. At their house we lodged seven nights; and six days were passed amongst Friends of that place, in very close exercise and labour. There was a true baptism on the young; especially, perhaps, on many of the young men. The meetings with Friends were, I trust, good ones; particularly one on fifth day morning, in which the wondrous machinery of Christian motives was set in order before me, and through me, before others. In three successive evening meetings with the young, I had to consider the questions, "Why am I a Christian," and "Why am I a Quaker?"—the external evidences of Christianity; the internal evidences; (including a statement of essential doctrine;) and the principles of Friends. They were times of arduous exercise of mind to me, but I trust were of some use in the way of teaching. A large public meeting on first day evening also passed off well. My subject was "As in Adam all die, so in Christ shall all be made alive." We greatly prized the society of our friends and numerous relatives.

On seventh day, 10th mo., 30th, Sarah W. Crewdson accompanied us to Manchester. We were somewhat cheered on our way, by a visit to the Female Penitentiary in Lancaster Castle, where we had a heart-melting, though short meeting, with about fifty poor criminals. We arrived safely at night at the peaceful dwelling of our dear friends the Dockrays, at Ardwick.

The next day, first day the 31st, was to me an arduous one. Upwards of 500 at the morning meeting; a large mixed flock, with very few shepherds. The loss of Isaac Stephenson greatly to be felt and deplored. We dined and spent the afternoon with our dear friends, I. and E. Crewdson; and in the evening there was a vast public meeting, about 2000 people, respectable and quiet. I felt very calm on taking my seat; and voice as well as inward power were graciously given to me, to plead for "baptism, the *true and living* baptism, into the name of the Father, and of the Son, and of the Holy Ghost." There was afterwards much solemnity to be felt in prayer.

They returned to Earlham by way of Melksham, and London, arriving at home on the 16th of the 11th month.

FROM JONATHAN HUTCHINSON.

12th mo., 6th, 1830.

I was pleased with thy sketch of the grand scenery of some of our northern counties; and thy connecting it with a line from a beautiful and devout passage of my favourite Cowper, made it not the less acceptable. There, too, it seems, thou hast found a poet's corner, surrounded by mountain, lake, and river. In many respects, I think such a situation must be very favourable to literary pursuits, if, by thus abstracting the mind from practical subjects, it does not too much favour dreaming.

It might be well that thou wast there, and that thou hadst an opportunity of endeavouring to rouse a certain celebrated author from some of his reveries; into which, whilst I acknowledge his talents, I think he has proved himself liable to fall, perhaps both in prose and in verse. To some such cause may probably be attributed his classing Friends, as I think he has done, in his Book of the Church, among the "crazier" sects. If neither to slumber nor to absence of mind, to what must we ascribe this strange expression? I can find only one other solution—that the discipline of our Society, which, by way of distinction, we may call its morality, and for which he gives us high credit, was intelligible to his understanding, whilst the more spiritual parts of our profession, or its divinity, may have been as little comprehended by him as was the worship of the early Christians by those who called it heresy; or the reasoning of the apostle before Agrippa, when Festus thought him mad.

The close of the year was marked by the decease of his uncle Joseph Gurney; which took place, very suddenly, on the morning of the 25th of the 12th month. Joseph John Gurney afterwards writes:—

12th mo., 27th. I saw my dear uncle last on fifth day. He was silent at our meeting; which was, however, a solemn one: Lucy Aggs was well engaged in ministry on the sufferings of our Redeemer. My uncle expressed to me afterwards his satisfaction in her testimony. He was uncommonly glowing and tender. I met him at the Magdalen Committee, and walked with him thence to the bank. How little did I imagine that I should next see him stretched on the floor, a corpse!

Mild, cheerful, universally benevolent, strong in sense, in principle, and in manly fortitude; he was, above all, the tender, broken, and humble Christian. His humility was the most conspicuous feature of his character; and his lovely temper threw a gleam of sunshine over every person and thing around him. To associate with him has long been one of my greatest delights and privileges; and there was no one to whom I was so much accustomed to look for protection, advice, and help. I have sometimes been ready to conclude that I could not do without him; but I desire to bow submissively under the stroke; and the cutting of a string, at once so strong and so tender, will, I hope, be the means of compelling a yet nearer approach to the Fountain of all Good.

My dear uncle's ministry has increased in brightness as he advanced in age and experience. It was to me a source of lively pleasure, as well as edification. On the whole, nothing is so cheering, among many cheering things in the retrospect, as the clear views which he has of later times evinced, of the fundamental doctrines of Christianity; and especially of the exceeding great preciousness of that blood "which cleanseth from all sin." This was the subject of a short but memorable address which he delivered to our young men at the close of our last Preparative Meeting. May it have sunk deeply into many hearts!

CHAPTER XXII.

1830—1831. ÆT. 43.

PUBLICATION OF THE BIBLICAL NOTES AND DISSERTATIONS; LETTERS RESPECTING THEM; WORK UPON THE SABBATH; RELIGIOUS ENGAGEMENTS AT BRISTOL; "TEACHING" MEETINGS; LETTER TO HIS SON, DESCRIBING AN EVENING AT CAMBRIDGE AND A MORNING AT OXFORD.

1*st mo.*, 1*st*, 1831. The commencement of the new year is marked indeed. I hope I do not enter upon it heedlessly. Forgiveness for the past, and help for the future, are what I have to crave at the hands of a most merciful God and Father. When rejoicing predominates, let us not forget to tremble. When trembling more especially is our lot, let us still endeavour to rejoice!

First day night. 1*st mo.*, 30*th*. This afternoon —— has been our agreeable guest at Earlham; having been brought to Norwich by the death of a sister-in-law. We called for her at the Roman Catholic chapel, out of which a large crowd was issuing; and from her account it appears they are making many converts. What a strange tendency there is in man to believe too much or too little; or, in other words, to Popery or Infidelity! Yet these extremes are often found to meet. I do believe there is much amongst this people of an honest seriousness and pursuit of eternal things; but they appear to lose sight of the distinction between things *contrary* to reason, and things *beyond* reason. The doctrine of the Atonement is beyond reason. May I be preserved from ever doubting it!

Transubstantiation is contrary to reason. Therefore, as reason is a divine gift, I consider that I have divine authority for rejecting it.

The composition of the Biblical Notes and Dissertations, chiefly intended to confirm and illustrate the Doctrine of the Deity of Christ, had been occupying Joseph John Gurney's leisure for several years. This work was at length published in the year 1830. Though designed principally for learned readers, the first edition sold rapidly; and a second, with a few corrections and additions, was published in 1833. In the twenty-one chapters or dissertations of which the volume is composed, the author has carefully collected and arranged a large amount of evidence, historical and critical, on some of the most interesting and important topics of biblical research. The canonical authority of the Epistle to the Hebrews; the eternal pre-existence of "the Word;" the illustrations which this doctrine receives from the Chaldee Targums, and from the theological literature of the later Jews; the glorious character and attributes of Christ, as the Creator of the world, as the "image of the invisible God," as the "angel of the covenant," as our "great God and Saviour," and as he is "over all, God blessed for ever," together with the various testimonies of Scripture relating to these momentous questions, are severally treated with great depth and clearness; nor are the dissertations on the important and difficult prophecies in Isaiah vii, viii, ix; on the prophecy of Jeremiah xxiii, 5, 6; and on the correct reading of the original text of the memorable declaration of the apostle Paul, 1 Tim. iii, 16, less interesting and instructive.* The whole is concluded by a chapter in which the practical importance of faith in the Deity of Christ is powerfully stated and enforced. The spirit which pervades the work is admirably expressed in the motto from Athanasius, selected for the title-page. In the preface it is translated as follows:—

"I know that he (the Lord Jesus Christ) is truly God, from heaven, impassible. I know that he was of the seed of David, according to the flesh, man, and passible. I do not inquire *how* the same person is both passible and impassible; *how* he is both God and man; lest whilst I busy myself about the HOW, and am investigating the MODE, I should miss of THAT GOOD THING which is set before us."

* The more recent researches of the learned do not appear to support the conclusion at which Joseph John Gurney arrives in his elaborate defence, (pp. 372—410,) of the common reading, Θεὸς ἐφανερώθη, in 1 Tim. iii, 16, against the criticisms of Griesbach. It seems now clearly ascertained that the original reading of the codices A and C, is ΟC, not ΘC; and several other of the authorities on which Joseph John Gurney relied, in support of the received text, are now discovered to be favourable to the other reading. The evidence will be found briefly but clearly summed up in a valuable communication with which Dr. Tregelles has kindly favoured me, printed in the Appendix to the present volume. (See Appendix A.)† Those who desire a more complete discussion may consult the recent work of Dr. Davidson on Biblical Criticism, vol. ii, pp. 382—403. Without venturing to differ from such authorities, they whose opportunities do not admit of such investigations, may take comfort in remembering that the doctrine of the Deity of Christ is so firmly grounded upon other evidence, altogether conclusive in its character, that, to use Joseph John Gurney's language, "it is wholly unnecessary to insist on any passage of Scripture," in support of it, "of which the reading is justly liable to dispute." (Biblical Notes, p. 373.) Dr. Tregelles adds his strong testimony to the general excellence of Joseph John Gurney's work. "Thoroughly," he observes, "as the field of criticism has since changed, the value of that book remains."

† English edition.

"My own attainments in Biblical criticism," observes Joseph John Gurney, "are by no means great. Yet I know enough of that pursuit to be thoroughly convinced that, when conducted on just principles, it will never support those novel explanations of Holy Writ which have been seized upon with eagerness by modern writers of a speculative turn. If I am not greatly mistaken, it condemns all the floating fancies of the sceptic, and ranges itself on the side of that sound and simple interpretation of Scripture, which has been familiar, in all ages of the Church, to the humble followers of a crucified Redeemer."

It is not needful to dwell upon the commendation of a work which cannot fail to be highly valued by the sound Biblical scholar. The present notice of it might, however, appear imperfect if, from amongst the numerous letters received upon its publication, a few were not here presented to the reader.

FROM DANIEL WILSON,
(now Bishop of Calcutta.)

October 27th, (1830.)

* * * I may tell you how very much I have been gratified by the entire perusal. I wish you could go on to some other line of scriptural passages, on the same or some other kindred subject. The bishops of London and Salisbury * have expressed their warmest approbation.

FROM CHARLES SIMEON.

K. C., February 4th, 1831.

MY BELOVED FRIEND,

Not I only, but the whole Christian world are greatly indebted to you. How you ever found time for such research I cannot imagine. But God has given you industry,

* This was the late Bishop Burgess, from whom, as well as from the Bishop of London, and several others of the English bishops, Joseph John Gurney himself received testimonials of their high value of the work.

and what in such labours is of no less value, method; and by these you have accomplished what puts us ministers all to shame. I am quite delighted with the clearness of your statements, and with the temperance and candour with which you treat those from whom you differ. I think no one will henceforth hesitate to ascribe to its true author, the epistle to the Hebrews. For all your criticisms I thank you from my inmost soul, but most especially for that on Blayney's interpretation of Jer. xxiii, 6. I had exceedingly grudged him that text, and lamented that I was not able to rescue it from his grasp. And all who love our most adorable Saviour will bless you for the service you have in this instance rendered to the Church. Had I conceived that your powers were such as I now see them to be, I should never have dared to advise, as I did about nine years ago, that your productions should wait for the *nonum annum*. But I do not repent of my rashness, for time has not only matured, but greatly increased your researches, and enabled you to bring them forth to far greater advantage. May God of his infinite mercy long protract your life, that you may render yet greater and greater services to his cause. I am most thankful to have such books as that and your last, to recommend to the young students of the University.

And now, my beloved friend, let me say, that, whilst I admire, and honour, and love the talents with which God in his mercy has endowed you, I feel anxious that you should carefully bear in mind what line of labour that is. It is of immense use to the Church of God; but it may be followed too exclusively as it respects your own soul. Do not mistake me. I do not intend to intimate, in the slightest degree, that such pursuits *must* operate to the disadvantage of your soul in its devotional feelings, but only to suggest, with truly brotherly affection, that they *may*. *Vitam perdidi operosè nihil agendo*, was the dying complaint of a great critic; and therefore it will be well to bear in mind, that the species of research, which God has so wonderfully enabled you to prosecute, may, by *possibility*, become a snare, and rob the soul whilst it is furnishing the mind. It may doubtless be united, as I am well assured it is in you, with much devotional feeling, and be as great a blessing to yourself as it is to the world; but as there is a possibility of giving it too exclusive a place in your heart, I venture, with all humility and in tender love, to suggest the idea to your mind: and I the rather do this because, whilst others may be afraid of offering such a hint, I am no more afraid of your imputing it to me for evil, or feeling offended at it, than I am afraid of such a reception of it at the hands of my heavenly Father.* If you needed any proof, you would find in it a proof with what truly Christian regard I am

Your much edified disciple,
and your most affectionate brother in the Lord,
C. SIMEON.

FROM ABRAHAM RAWLINSON BARCLAY.

Leytonstone, 28th 1st mo., 1831.

* * * I have been reading at my ease thy last work, and have been much interested with some of the Essays, especially the critical parts, which form a very valuable addition, I think, to our Biblical criticisms. Number sixteen I have noted,† particularly the latter half, parts of which are beautifully striking. * * * With thy motto from Athanasius I have often finished off my reading; and again and again with deep profit.

FROM HENRY HUNTINGFORD.

Winchester, June 27th, 1832.

Though I have not the pleasure of your acquaintance, yet the perusal of your works on Christianity has made me feel for you something much more than respect,—a very great esteem. But my object in troubling you with this letter, is

* How much alive Joseph John Gurney was to these considerations his Journal bears ample testimony. But the faithfulness and love which this letter breathes, may surely be classed among the fruits of that "one Spirit" which circulates through the various members of the "one body" of Christ.

† On the Prophecies of Isaiah, in chap. vii, viii, and ix.

to mention to you that, had my beloved and revered relative, the late Bishop of Hereford, lived longer, you would have received a letter from him expressing the very great satisfaction he had derived from reading your two volumes;* the sentiments of which I have heard him often say, exactly corresponded with his own. He delighted in your strenuous support of Θεὸς ἐφανερώθη, and of the epistle to the Hebrews; and in the exalted notions you entertain of the divine nature and supreme and uncreated dignity of that blessed Saviour, in whose merits alone man can find refuge or hope. It was my dear relative's habit, not to thank any author for sending a work till he had read it through; which he had not had sufficient leisure to do with yours, till lately. He had half finished a letter to you, containing some remarks on various passages, when it pleased a merciful Providence to call him from this state of trial, into the presence of that Being, in whom, though he had not seen him, he so firmly believed, and so affectionately confided.

To return to the Journal:—

2nd mo., 6th. Some praises bestowed upon me in the Quarterly Review are mixed with abuse of the sect to which I belong. There is often to be observed a tendency in the world, to exalt individual Quakers, and utterly to trample on the principles which give birth to what little good may be found in them. May we be content to be accounted fools for our Redeemer's sake! And may we be increasingly delivered from everything in religion, which is not pure and simple Christianity!

2nd mo., 20th. A fortnight since I wrote. I find it difficult to catch time in its rapid flight. What a ceaseless stream is bearing me onwards to eternity! On sixth day the 11th, I went with my dear sister Fry, (who had been staying with us,) to Upton, reading the Chalmeriana as we journeyed. It was a privilege to enjoy her society quietly. In London

*The Essays on Christianity, and the Biblical Notes.

and its neighbourhood, many duties, some pain, and more pleasure, awaited me. An anti-slavery party at Buxton's, with a view of arranging his parliamentary proceedings, was a lively and interesting occasion. Present, Mackintosh, Lushington, Lord Calthorpe, Lord Nugent, Macaulay, (father and son,) Evans, Briscoe, Wood, Sykes, Weyland, (all M.P's.,) Daniel Wilson, Richard Watson, Burnet from Ireland, James Cropper, Samuel Hoare, my brother Samuel, and myself. I was glad to be enabled to give the discussion a turn in a way that helped Fowell, our leader and chief labourer.

2nd mo., 28th. My studies have been in some degree prospered; and the subject of the Sabbath, on which I am now writing, has become deeply interesting to me. Yesterday was a solemn sabbath indeed, especially at the morning meeting, in which the apostolic declaration that "whether we live or die, we are the Lord's," was treated of as a "two-edged sword," (Heb. iv.) for the alarm of the ungodly, and for the consolation of the afflicted. In our evening reading, also, the glories of the heavenly state were much before us. I earnestly pray, that the truth of these things may be brought home to my own spirit.

3rd mo., 20th. First day morning. What an amazing privilege for so poor and vile a creature as I am, to be permitted to hold intercourse with a being of perfect purity, and infinite power and glory. How could it be so, were it not for him who is the way? "Bless the Lord, O my soul, and all that is within me, bless his holy name!" * * Age is beginning to make perceptible inroads upon us all. May we be prepared for every change that can befall these short-lived bodies! It is cheering to believe, and certainly to *know* (on the sure evidence of God's promise) that if we live and die in Christ, we shall be made partakers of a glorious resurrection, and shall inhabit spiritual bodies, like unto the body of our Lord, glorious and incorruptible. Christ has abolished the whole law of death. "Thy dead men shall live," &c., Isa. xxvi, 19.

Afternoon. The morning meeting was to me unusually solemn, and I humbly hope the language of invitation and exhortation was not held out in vain. Yet I have feared lest in the flow of the gift, I should in any degree lose sight of *simplicity* and *humility*. How needful to abide in them, even as *the little child!*

Third day morning, (*3d mo., 22nd.*) Having felt a lively interest in the parliamentary reform question, I wrote a long letter on the subject to Lord Calthorpe, but have been this morning called home to my centre, and reminded that much of these matters is not my business. Rather let me leave all with prayer to the gracious care of my God and Saviour.

In the early part of this year he was closely engaged in preparing for the press his work upon the Sabbath.

"When the Biblical Notes were completed," he writes in his Autobiography, "I believed it right to direct my studies to a subordinate point of no small practical importance, the History, Authority, and Use of the Sabbath day. The investigation occupied the leisure of a full winter, and my little work on this subject was the result.*

"The Original Sabbath, the Sabbath under the Mosaic Law, and the Sabbath under the Gospel, are there severally examined with a good deal of pains and attention. The general conclusion in which the pursuit of this study fully confirmed me was, that the practice of setting apart one-seventh part of time, for the special purposes of rest and worship, belongs to that law of the Lord which changes not; that it is no affair of expediency, but clearly a duty which has received the divine sanction from the beginning. Yet, I think, there is abundant authority, under the Gospel, both for

* The title of the work is, Brief Remarks on the History, Authority, and Use of the Sabbath. The first edition was published in the spring of 1831, and numerous editions have been subsequently issued. It has been reprinted and largely circulated in the United States, with a preface and notes by the late Moses Stuart.

the relaxation of legal strictness in this matter, and for the change of day from the seventh, a day of death to the Saviour, to the first of the week; when he afresh displayed his glorious power by his resurrection from the dead. Of that most important event, the Christian Sabbath, held on the first day of each week, has been a living and effective, though silent witness, in each succeeding age of the church; and will, I doubt not, continue to be so, until she is finally glorified where the Sabbath never ceases."

"I wish it to be distinctly understood," he remarks on another occasion, "that in sometimes applying the term Sabbath to the first day of the week, as it is observed among Christians, I have had a view to the simple meaning of the Hebrew word, viz: 'cessation from labour.' And, while I am of the judgment that the setting apart of one day, after every recurring period of six days of labour, for the blessed purposes of rest and worship, is not to be regarded as a matter of mere expediency, but as a moral and religious duty, truly belonging to the law of our God; I fully unite in the sentiment expressed by Robert Barclay, and others of our early Friends, that no one portion of time ought to be regarded by Christians as in itself holier than another; that all our time is the Lord's, and that, ceasing from our own wicked works, and all the willing and running of the carnal mind, we must press forward after that glorious rest, (typified by the sabbath of the Jews,) of which a precious foretaste is bestowed even here; and which is perfected, for the people of God, in the world to come." *

FROM SIR FRANCIS PALGRAVE.

July 30th, 1831.

I cannot deny myself the pleasure of addressing you on the subject of your late little work. It is perhaps one of the most thoroughly argumentative and conclusive of any of the productions of a similar kind; and, under Providence, we may

* Letter to Stephen A. Chase, dated 7th mo., 26th, 1846.

hope that its utility will equal its merits. The seventh day cycle must have been adopted *simultaneously* (if such a term can be used) by all the different nations who adopt it, because they all seem to have had the same starting point. The first day of the Hindoos is the same actual first day as that of the Jews, or of the Teutonic nations. Had it been merely arbitrary, nations might have agreed in employing the same cycle, but their starting points would not necessarily have been uniform. * * In London the evil arising from Sunday papers is incalculable, though it is hopeless to attempt any legislative remedy.

In the Spring of this year he believed himself called into religious service in the West of England, particularly at Bristol and its neighbourhood. After alluding to the "deep conflict" into which his mind had been plunged in reference to this engagement, he says:—

O that I may be for ever delivered from my own willings and runnings, and have faith to follow the *clue* which is leading me, I trust, through the mazes of life to a joyful eternity.

Whilst absorbed in his labours at Bristol, one of his nephews, resident in the neighbourhood of London, was seized with a violent attack of illness.

"Were my engagements of a different kind," he writes to his sister Catherine, then in London, "it would be the greatest happiness that I could have, under the circumstances, to be with my dearest brother and sister; whose concerns you all know to be as near to me as almost anything in life, and I believe as life itself. But I dare not quit my work at present.* I never before, that I remember, set my hand to so weighty an engagement."

* This sentence is slightly transposed.

In his Autobiography he writes, in allusion to this period : —

About 270 visits were paid to the families of Friends ; many public and other meetings were held; and the conclusion was marked by great peace, and the general love and unity of my friends. I met with some interesting persons at Bristol besides Friends; among others, Conybeare, the geologist; and Dr. Prichard, the author of the Physical History of Man, &c. : persons in whose hands science, of prime order, comes in as the handmaid and supporter of religion. Among the meetings held at my request at Bristol, four were for the express purpose of instructing the younger part of the Society, in the evidences of the Christian religion, historical, prophetical, and internal; also the scriptural ground of the views which distinguish our own body. They were appointed under a direct apprehension of duty, then and there impressed; and, I may truly say, in as much of dependence on divine help as meetings of a higher character. Friends entered into the concern with cordiality, and it is not to be denied that the seal of solemnity was graciously permitted to rest upon these meetings, and to crown their termination. I had previously held meetings of this kind at Kendal; and have since held many of the same description in Manchester, Liverpool, Newcastle, London, &c.; always with the sanction of the Friends among whom my lot was cast. My view of the subject is, that there is to be known and used in the Church, the gift of teaching, as well as that of preaching; that both these gifts are from the Spirit of the Redeemer; but that the former allows of freer exercise of our natural powers than the latter. It ought, in my opinion, to have no place in our meetings for worship; but on other occasions, both public and private, may be rightly exercised in the fear of the Lord. We shall never thrive upon ignorance. Our Creator would have us cultivate our understandings in matters of a religious as well as civil nature. The great rule is, that all should be subordinate to the highest object, all "in the name of the Lord Jesus Christ," all "for the glory of God." While this rule is observed, there is no danger. When I speak of *teaching* as having no place in our meetings for worship, I refer to that lower gift, the exercise of which does not rise to the scale of gospel ministry; but in a wider sense of the term there will often be much of teaching in the public services of rightly qualified ministers. Like the apostles of old, they will "not cease to *teach* and to preach Jesus Christ." *

A letter to one of his children has already been introduced. His mode of communicating with them may be further illustrated by the following extracts from a letter to his son at school, written whilst at Melksham, on his way to Bristol.

Elm Grove, 4th mo., 8th, 1831.

Τῷ καιρῷ δουλεύοντες.

Rom. xii, 11. Griesbach's Text.

MY DEAR J—— H——,

I suppose thou hast observed the motto on my title-page, and I trust thou hast found no difficulty in translating it. "SERVING THE TIME." The more commonly

* Some idea of the general character of the addresses delivered at the meetings here referred to may be obtained from a little volume published in 1835, by Hamilton, Adams, and Co., under the title of Four Lectures on the Evidences of Christianity, delivered in Southwark, 1834, to the Junior Members of the Society of Friends, by J. J. Gurney, Esq. This volume, printed from short-hand notes, never received Joseph John Gurney's sanction, and abounds with inaccuracies obvious to every intelligent reader. With all these disadvantages, however, the excellent spirit that pervades the addresses, as here given, is very conspicuous; and many of the observations, especially in the third lecture, "On the Divinity of Christ;" and in the fourth, "On the Doctrine of the Holy Spirit," and its development in the principles and practices of Friends, are striking and appropriate, and throughout highly practical. Far indeed was it from his desire, to cherish the acquisition of knowledge, rather than that deep-searching heart-work which he knew, from his own experience, to be all-important.

received text is rendered, "Serving the Lord;" but there is a preponderating authority of ancient manuscripts and versions in favour of the words of my motto; and, whilst the whole Scripture is calculated to impress upon us the primary duty of serving the Lord, we may be content to derive from this particular passage a very useful though subordinate lesson. What is that lesson? It is, that we should be *always on the watch to make a good use of our time.* As the servant who waits well on his master is ever on the *qui vive* to know what will next be wanted, so are we to wait on the hours, and even on the moments, of each passing day, to know what duties they point out to us, or what employment they suggest for the improvement of our minds. There is nothing more astonishing, or more calculated to impress us with the glorious, incomprehensible nature of God, than the infinite magnitude and minuteness of nature. The wonders developed to us by the telescope are matched by those which the microscope reveals — and powerful as these instruments are become, through the devices of modern science, they each leave unperceived an infinity of marvels into which man cannot dive. Something after the same sort may be observed as it relates to time. Philosophers are sometimes heard to speak, not only of the eternal courses of ages and centuries, but of the endless divisibility of moments; and the best of all philosophy teaches us that with God "a thousand years are as one day;" and also, that "one day" is "as a thousand years." How watchful and diligent then ought we to be in applying even the shortest spaces of time to their right use! I do not mean to infer that we are always to be on the strain; far from it. We do not serve a hard Master. I mean only, that while we tread the course of life with a step at once steady and easy, we should never degenerate into indolence; but be quick to seize every passing opportunity, both for doing good to others and for the cultivation of our own minds. We should, in this respect, endeavour to form the habit of vigilance, and such a habit will be sure to yield us an abundant return both of pleasure and profit.

I have sometimes endeavoured to apply these principles to

travelling, in which a considerable portion of the time of many persons is almost unavoidably occupied. A call of duty or business may often carry us to places at a distance from our own homes. Is the time taken up by the *journey* to be one of mere indolence? Is the convenience of being conveyed from one place to another to be the only profit which it shall yield? Ought we not rather to make a point, on such occasions, of adding to our stock of knowledge, and of useful ideas, by reading, conversation, and reflection? Is there no object of interest which may be examined by the way? Is there no person of piety or talent with whom we may find a passing opportunity of communicating? Are the motions of the coach or the chariot so rapid that we cannot leave behind us, as we pass from place to place, important instruction, in the form of Bibles, Testaments, or Tracts? *Much* may not be required of us, but it is well, if on our arrival at the place of our destination, we can acknowledge that we have both received and communicated a *little* good in the course of our journey.

I propose to illustrate these remarks by some account of the incidents of the journey which thy dear mother and I have just been taking from Earlham to Elm Grove: not because we consider ourselves by any means so watchful over our time in travelling, as we ought to be; but because it so happened that this transit from Norfolk to Wiltshire, required as it was by the calls of affection and duty, has afforded us some unexpected opportunities both of pleasure and mental improvement. Had we not been in some degree on the watch for them, they might have passed by us, unnoticed and unimproved. Since, however, our route, for the most part, lay through an uninteresting country, I shall confine myself to some notice of an afternoon at Cambridge, and a morning at Oxford, for both these places were on our nearest road.

We left home last third day morning before breakfast, with dear little Anna for our companion, and arrived at Cambridge—sixty-three miles—by three o'clock in the afternoon. How grateful ought we to be for well trained horses, and well made roads, which of late years have been the means of so curiously compressing distances; so that, for example, the citizen of Norwich becomes the near neighbour of the citizen of Cambridge. Ere long, *steam* may probably bring us into yet closer proximity!

As we drove up to the Eagle Inn, we met our dear nephew, E— B—, a student of Trinity college, who was our faithful companion during the remainder of the day; and G— H— afterwards joined us. After ordering dinner we sallied forth for a walk; but first sent a note to our dear friend, Charles Simeon, the well-known fellow of King's College, to propose spending part of the evening with him. While we were absent from the inn, there arrived a small, characteristic note, hastily written by him in pencil—"Yes, yes, yes, come immediately and dine with me!" Simeon has the warm and eager manners of a foreigner, with an English heart beneath them. He is full of love towards all who love his Master, and a faithful, sympathizing friend to those who have the privilege of sharing his more intimate affections. To all around him, whether religious or worldly, he is kind and courteous: and by this means, as well as by the weight of his character, he has gradually won a popularity at Cambridge, which now seems to triumph over all prejudice and persecution. He is upwards of seventy years of age, but his eye is not dim, his joints not stiffened, his intellect not obscured. His mind, lips, eyes, and hands move along together in unison. And singularly pliable and rapid is he both in his mental and bodily movements; quick to utter what he feels, and to act what he utters. His conversation abounds in illustrations; and, while all his thoughts and words run in the channel of religion, he clothes them with brightness and entertainment; and men, women, and even children, are constrained to listen. * * *

We declined his invitation to dinner, and had no intention of intruding upon him before the evening; but as we were walking near King's College, we heard a loud halloo behind us, and presently saw our aged friend, forgetful of the gout, dancing over the lawn to meet us. Although the said lawn is forbidden ground, except to the fellows of the college, we had little hesitation in transgressing the law on such an occasion; and our hands were soon clasped in his with all the warmth of mutual friendship. He then became our guide, and led us through several of the colleges. * * *

Our venerable friend seemed to take great delight in showing us the beauties of his favourite Cambridge; and as we walked along, we conversed pleasantly together.

I was observing that age was not sufficiently reverenced in the present day.

SIMEON. "It is worthy of reverence when found in the way of *righteousness.*"

We were soon afterwards talking of the crude zeal of many persons, who lose their balance in religion, and seem inclined to drive up the church of Christ into a narrow corner. This led us to think of the wisdom which is without partiality.

SIMEON. "I have long pursued the study of Scripture with a desire to be *impartial.* I call myself neither a predestinarian nor an anti-predestinarian; but I commit myself to the teaching of the inspired writers, whatever complexion it may assume. In the beginning of my inquiries, I said to myself, one thing I know assuredly—that in religion, of myself, *I know nothing.* I do not therefore sit down to the perusal of Scripture in order to *impose* a sense on the inspired writers, but to *receive* one, as they give it me. I pretend not to *teach* them; I wish, like a child, to be taught *by* them. When I come to a text which speaks of election, I delight myself in the doctrine of election. When the apostles exhort me to repentance and obedience, and indicate the freedom of my will, I give myself up to that side of the question, and behold I am an Arminian! Don't you know, my dear brother, that the wheels of your watch move in opposite directions? Yet they are all tending to *one result.* Let two balls be projected from equal angles—I care not what angle it may be—against a third ball lying before them; and if the forces are even, it will move forward in a line perfectly straight. But if the ball on the right hand be alone projected against the central ball, the latter will fly off to the left. If the left hand ball is the only one which strikes it, away it rolls to the right. So it is in religion. Hope and fear are the strongest motives which actuate the mind of man. Here comes the doctrine of election, fraught with hope and consolation, and strikes the mind of the believer from one quarter. From the opposite quarter comes the doctrine of free-will and man's responsibility, calculated to excite our *fear*. They operate in true harmony, and the believer moves straight *forward*. Let him embrace the doctrine of election only, and off he goes to the left hand; or of free-will only, and away he flies to the right. Nothing will preserve him in a straight line, but the joint action of both motives, or, in other words, undivided Christianity. Why in Scotland, Sir, they will tell you that heaven itself is not large enough to hold John Wesley." We now reached the new hall of King's just as the college dinner was awaiting him. "You see I have taken leave of the gout," said he merrily, as he leaped up the steps.

In the evening we walked to Simeon's rooms, and met with the usual warm and courteous reception. Over the chimney piece, in his drawing room, hangs an interesting picture of Henry Martyn; once the *elève* of Simeon at Cambridge, and senior wrangler in his year; afterwards the devoted missionary of high talent and love unfeigned, who counted not his life dear unto himself, "that he might finish his course with joy, and the ministry which he had received of the Lord Jesus to testify the *gospel of the grace of God*."

SIMEON. "The picture was painted in India. When I went to the India House, in London, and saw the box opened, I started back with mixed emotions of sorrow and delight, when I beheld the countenance of my beloved Henry. As I retreated to the other end of the room, I heard the people saying—'That is his FATHER.'"

Whilst we were enjoying our cup of tea, our dear friend continued to converse in his own peculiar manner. * * *

SIMEON. "Perfect religion is to the soul what the soul is to the body. The soul animates the whole person. It sees through the eye—hears through the ear—tastes through the mouth—handles through the hands—talks through the tongue—reflects through the brain. The whole body is moved and regulated by an impulse from within. Let religion take full possession of the soul, and it will be found to actuate all its movements, and direct all its powers. There will be no violent efforts, no stiffness, no awkwardness. All will be natural and easy. An unseen and gentle influence will pervade the *whole mind*, and regulate the *whole conduct;* and thus the creature will gradually become conformed to the image of his Creator. This, my brother, is perfect religion."

We talked of spiritual *discernment*. I mentioned the declaration of Paul, that "the spiritual man judgeth all things (πάντα ανακρίνει) and is judged himself of no man."

SIMEON. "Yes, my brother, the spiritual man has a sense of his own; or rather, his natural vision is corrected, and rendered applicable to divine things, by an influence from above. I am told to look at the planets. I can see Jupiter and Venus; but there is the Georgium Sidus. I look again —I strain my eyes — I cannot see it. Here, take the telescope. O! yes, now I see it. How beautiful the star! how perspicuous the vision! You tell me to read that almanack. I am young and short sighted. The ball of my eye is too convex; the rays meet before they arrive at the *retina*. My brother, it is all confusion. I am old, my lens is flattened; the rays meet even *behind my head:* the retina is left untouched by them. Give the young man those spectacles with a concave glass. Now he sees! now he can read the book! now the rays meet precisely on his retina. Here, my *old* friend, take these convex glasses; they will rectify your fading vision. He sees! he reads! again the retina is touched and pencilled with nice precision. So it is with the Spirit. In whatever manner or degree the vision of the soul is disordered, the Spirit is always applicable—always a rectifier! The wordling is like the mariner of ancient times, who had nothing to guide him through the trackless deep but the sun, the moon, and the stars: when these were veiled, all was obscurity, guess work, and peril. But the religious man, however simple, is like the *modern* mariner, who has a compass on board, which will always guide him aright, however cloudy the atmosphere, however dark the night. The Christian has a compass WITHIN him — a faithful monitor — a clear director. If he consult his compass diligently, he will be sure to form a right decision on every moral question;

while the proud philosopher, who knows no such teacher, is tossed on the waves of doubt and confusion. And how is this? Why, my dear brother, 'he is renewed in the *spirit* of his mind.' It is because his *dispositions* are rectified, that his vision is restored."

The hour of the evening was advancing, and these beautiful remarks formed a happy conclusion to familiar conversation. His respectable elderly female servants were now called in, and I was requested to read the Scriptures. I chose the first half of the third of Lamentations, and the passage, as I read it, seemed to me to be full of marrow. A very precious solemnity ensued, during which the language of prayer and praise arose; I humbly hope with acceptance. I believe both my dear wife and myself were ready to acknowledge that we had seldom felt with any one more of the "*unity of the Spirit in the bond of peace.*" Under this feeling we took our leave.

We arrived at Oxford the following evening soon after dark. The next morning we rose early, and sallied forth, the weather being fine, for a stroll before breakfast. Anna accompanied us, and our walk was very agreeable.

Adorned as Cambridge is with new buildings, we were constrained to confess that in point of scale, and grandeur, and classic beauty, Oxford is far the superior. It is indeed a delightful city; rendered peculiary pleasant, by the intermixture of broad streets, noble buildings, and extensive gardens. We returned after breakfast to the Radcliffe Library, from the roof of which very handsome edifice there is quite an enchanting *coup d'œil*, which fully justifies this description. The inside of the Radcliffe Library furnishes some objects of great interest. It is a library of medicine and natural history; with the exception of a few theological books. Amongst these are two Bibles, well worthy of particular notice. The first is a highly finished and delicate manuscript of the Hebrew Scripture, exquisitely illuminated. The second is Dr. Kennicott's own manuscript, from which was published his Hebrew Bible, with collations. He is said to have collated upwards of 600 Hebrew MSS.; and this copy, from which his great work was printed, affords an evidence that order came to the assistance of his industry. A slip, containing a single verse of printed Hebrew, is pasted on the top of every blank space, and below those slips the Dr. has notified all the various readings with a neatness and beauty of penmanship which are quite uncommon. He is said to have been taught writing by his father, who was a merchant's clerk. From this work of elaborate assiduity, we turned to some of the ever varied, ever easy sports of nature,—a thousand admirable specimens, collected and arranged in beautiful order, of marbles, alabasters, gypsums, lavas, porphyries, agates, &c. The collection was made and presented to the University by Corsi, the Italian naturalist. The various beauty of these stones, which are all finely polished, almost overwhelms the mind with a sense of the profusion with which the Creator has scattered his ornaments even where they lie deeply hidden from the eye of man.

> "Full many a gem of purest ray serene
> The dark unfathomed caves of ocean bear;
> Full many a flower is born to blush unseen,
> And waste its sweetness on the desert air."

I now proposed to make a call on Dr. Macbride, the master of Magdalen Hall. He is a man who bears the character of much literary acquirement, as well as talent, and what is better, of decided piety. He has supported the Bible Society at Oxford with a noble spirit of independence. We found him at home, and, with his lady, he received us very courteously. I had sent him a copy of my Biblical Notes, which I was pleased to find had met his approbation, and we soon fell into conversation. He told me that the number of religious young men in the University was increasing, and that many of them bore the stamp of sober piety. One preacher at Oxford, known to both of us, flies high in doctrine, and holds out glowing expectations of the outward reign of the Messiah, even venturing to declare in *what year* he may be expected to appear.

MACBRIDE. "These new fancies are much to be regretted. Persons who occupy their speculative powers with calculations of the year of Christ's coming, may easily forget to *prepare themselves* for the event (whenever he may be pleased to come) by watchfulness and prayer. Such persons, instead of preaching the home truths of practical Christianity, convert religion into a sort of romance."

As we walked along to the New Press, we enjoyed some agreeable intercourse, and I soon found him to be an acute and well-informed, yet unaffected person. He told us that the Bodleian Library had now increased to a great extent, but that it was of no great use to the resident members of the University. Persons engaged in authorship often come from a distance, and obtain a free access to its almost innumerable treasures. The New Press, situated near the Observatory, and on the borders of the town, is an extensive and superb structure. The centre of the front is an imitation of the triumphal arch of Antoninus, and the Corinthian pillars are remarkably fine. Dr. Macbride pointed out to us a singular ornament which crowns each of their chapiters. It is the figure in stone of a small open Bible, with the University motto, (adopted at the time of the Reformation,) "DOMINUS ILLUMINATIO MEA." A truly appropriate device! On our entrance we found my old friend, Samuel Collingwood, conductor of the press; who first introduced us to the spacious apartment in which is carried on the miscellaneous printing. It is a curious and animating scene; very new to Anna, who seemed eager to take a lesson from one of the compositors, who was picking out his types with peculiarly rapid fingers. I was interested in observing the operation of the *roller*, which effects a far more even distribution of the ink than the old ball or puff; and we were delighted with the rapidity with which the pressmen were converting blank sheets of paper into the well printed pages of Dr. Burton's new edition of the Greek Testament with English notes. * *

Samuel Collingwood now led us to the other side of the house into the vast room where the Bibles are printed. A more interesting sight can hardly be imagined. To behold the mighty powers of the press directed exclusively and perpetually to one object, and that object the diffusion of the truths of Christianity, could not fail to excite many sensations of a very satisfactory as well as interesting kind. Nor does it appear that the business of this part of the University Press will be diminished even if the printing of Bibles (now restricted by law to the King's printer and the two Universities) should be thrown open; since the many advantages which they possess will enable them, according to their own account, to defy all competitors. Collingwood is, however, of opinion, that the measure would be a dangerous one, as giving an almost unlimited opportunity for the falsification of the sacred text. He says this has already taken place, to a dangerous extent, in Bibles printed with notes; such Bibles not being included in the restriction. Thus are we often driven in this world of variety and change, to a choice of evils; for the present restriction is certainly in some respects an *evil.*

MACBRIDE. "It is a singular circumstance, that the exclusive right of the Universities to print Bibles is grounded on no royal grant or charter given to us. It is merely implied in a few words of exception, contained in the charter of the King's Printer."

The Doctor now began to time the printers, and to calculate in what space of time all of them together could produce a whole Bible.

COLLINGWOOD. "I will save you the trouble of that calculation, as I have gone over the ground before you. Supposing all our presses to be in action, (as they often are,) and supposing the work to be distributed for the purpose, we should produce a complete Old Testament, New Testament, and Prayer Book every minute. This is the rate at which we pour forth religious knowledge into Great Britain."

While we walked up and down the apartment, we enjoyed some interesting converse. I was comparing the immense rapidity of production thus obtained, through the art of printing, with the life-long manual labour of the scribe who produced that exquisite manuscript of the Hebrew Scriptures which we had just been examining in the Radcliffe Library.

MACBRIDE. "Yet I sometimes think that the art of printing came before its time, was discovered before it was *wanted.* Many years elapsed before printed books were much circulated. Caxton's productions, for example, were kept in closets, and shown as curiosities."

Collingwood, who now joined us, recalled our attention to his own subjects. "The invention of stereotyping is so far good that it will enable us, with the same plates, to strike off about one hundred thousand copies of a book, but this is the extent. After this number the book becomes very shabby and indistinct. But standing types, composed in the usual way, and not forming one plate, are vastly more efficacious. With these we can print more than a million copies of a book with scarcely any perceptible deterioration. Not only can we rid ourselves, when we please, of a defective letter, but the manufacture of individual letters is far more successful than of stereotype plates. The article produced is very much stronger."

He now showed us the hydraulic presses, used in compressing the sheets after they are printed. The pressure is that of water, rising in a tube from below; and although the machine is not large, yet with a very small amount of manual labour it exerts a force equal to that of the weight of 250 tons of water. How admirable, how unquestionably useful is such an application of natural philosophy! And what a shame, my dear boy, that any of us should be ignorant of these things!

We were now led through the wetting room, where the quires of paper are dipped and sprinkled, and the moisture diffused by pressure through the whole mass; also through the drying room, where innumerable printed sheets are hung like linen on horizontal poles; and lastly we visited a sort of warehouse, where stacks of unbound printed Bibles and Prayer Books are seen rising on every side to various elevations.

Our time of leisure was now fully spent, we took a cordial leave of our benevolent and agreeable friends, and returned to our inn. As the clock struck twelve, our carriage came round to the door, and we soon found ourselves on the road to Melksham.

Of our diligence in general, or of the use which we make of our journeys, we freely confess that we have nothing to boast. But I wish thee to observe, that on the present occasion, a very little vigilance and activity enabled us to see much that was worth seeing, and to hear much that was worth hearing in a SHORT SPACE OF TIME.

CHAPTER XXIII.

1831—1832. ÆT. 43—45.

EXTRACTS FROM LETTERS AND JOURNALS; ESSAY ON THE MORAL CHARACTER OF CHRIST; CONTROVERSY IN THE BIBLE SOCIETY ON THE ADMISSION OF UNITARIANS; TERMS OF UNION; THE PORTABLE EVIDENCE OF CHRISTIANITY; RELIGIOUS VISITS TO BIRMINGHAM AND LANCASHIRE; MEETINGS IN THE OPEN AIR; ADDRESS TO THE MECHANICS OF MANCHESTER; DEATH OF JOSEPH KINGHORN; CONFERENCE IN LONDON ON THE REVISION OF THE "BOOK OF EXTRACTS."

TO JONATHAN HUTCHINSON.

Earlham, 6th mo., 26th, 1831.

* * I do love and hail that blessed principle of the Lord's own "anointing" which fits the weakest and poorest for his service, and "out of the mouths of babes and sucklings perfects praise." If our religious Society be preserved amidst the shakings of the day, it must be by our adhering firmly to this principle, not forgetting the foundation on which it stands, even "Christ crucified," our "resurrection and our life," our only "hope of glory."

Referring to the illness of one of his children, he writes in his journal:—

Third day morning, [*7th mo.*, 12*th.*] Yesterday was one of great anxiety respecting our dear boy. I have had a short time of religious communication with him this morning. I explained to him that as his medical attendants were physicians to his body, so Christ is the physician to his soul; that he made an atonement on the cross for our sins, and that when we are made to suffer we ought to remember him who suffered unutterably for us. I read to him some verses of evangelical consolation from 1 Peter ii, and, after a little silence, poured forth with him a few words of thanksgiving and prayer.

Sixth day morning. Since the last entry there has been gradual amendment, and to-day an evident appearance of convalescence. It is to me like a second edition of this precious gift of my Heavenly Father.

FROM JONATHAN HUTCHINSON.

Gedney, 7th mo., 16th, 1831.

I would that we always approached the writings of our early predecessors with caution and tenderness; treading lightly on the remains of the honourable dead. With the controversies of these ancient worthies, or their manner of conducting them according to the spirit of their age, we have now, I apprehend, little or nothing to do. Neither are we called upon to imitate or defend the occasional obscurity and tautology of their style. One thing it may be well for us to remember, that from these voluminous works may be extracted an essence of as pure and sublime truth as (if we except the Holy Scriptures,) ever, perhaps, fell from the lips or flowed from the pen of man; so that, on the whole, I am inclined to believe the best apology for the writings in question, if indeed they need one, would be an attentive and unprejudiced perusal of them, when they would themselves be found to be their best and, perhaps, altogether sufficient expositors.

7th mo., 31st. This morning we committed to the earth the mortal remains of poor ——, whom I have several times visited on his death-bed, and to whom I endeavoured to speak faithfully. He was one for whom I felt a regard, though the world spoke against him, and I have reason to believe that his illness was blessed to him, as the means of bringing him home to Christ as his only hope.

In the 8th and 9th months of this year Joseph John Gurney was engaged in the holding of various religious Meetings in his own county, and afterwards, as a member of the Yearly Meeting's Committee, in a visit to Friends in Suffolk.

TO JONATHAN HUTCHINSON.

Earlham, 8th mo., 17th, 1831.

* * * I sometimes think that the ministry of the gospel is the only thing I know which practice *never makes easy.* I believe I may say with truth that much engagement of this kind was never preceded in me, by a greater degree of conflict, than it has been during the present year. I doubt not that this very thing, though a source of suffering, is to be numbered among the tender mercies of our Lord. * * * How beautiful is the idea of "living, ever springing water!" An old Greek commentator remarks on John iv, that Paul had drunk of this water, when he said, "forgetting those things which are behind, and reaching forth unto those things which are before, I press towards the mark for the prize of the high calling of God in Christ Jesus." May this heavenly spring continue to refresh and nourish thee, my beloved friend, and may it yet make glad the whole heritage of the Lord!

9th mo., 25th. My dearest wife and I left home on sixth day afternoon, after a busy, clearing morning, the 9th of the 9th month. I held a good public meeting in the Methodist Meeting House, at Attleborough, that evening; and went up the next day to Upton, where we spent an interesting Sabbath. The death of our dear friend Eliza Masterman cast a deep and affecting solemnity over the day. I went down to Chelmsford on third day morning. There I met my brethren on the Suffolk committee, Peter Bedford, Joseph Marriage, and Richard Burlingham. The Essex Quarterly Meeting on third day was large; and, to my apprehension, a time of remarkable and dignified solemnity.

It is a confirming circumstance to me that, looking at the multitude of hours I have spent at Monthly and Quarterly Meetings, I have never found reason to believe that time so occupied is lost, or that it could be better spent. The Master often condescends to smile upon us at such times. I do believe he still graciously protects our little scattered Society; and sanctions our principles, as flowing from himself.

10th mo., 8th., Seventh day. The visit of the [Yearly Meeting's] committee in this county has been very acceptable. They have all been staying at Earlham, much to our pleasure and comfort, and we desire to be thankful for such society and intercourse.

First day. We have our friend Richard Cockin still with us. His bright and tender old age is very animating, and I hope his example and Christian deportment will long live in our recollection.

Second day. The Reform Bill, it seems, is thrown out by a large majority (41) of the Lords. I do not feel either grieved or anxious; yet it is to be feared that the event will cause considerable agitation. May the protecting hand of Divine Providence be over the nation, and with its head!

10th mo., 24th. Visits last week to Tivetshall and Harling, connected with the subject of tithe paying; in which some few in different parts of the county continue to be unfaithful. The importance of the testimony which Friends bear against the ecclesiastical system has been confirmed to me in the course of this little service.

After feelingly alluding to "the awful riots, conflagrations, and loss of life at Bristol," he continues his Journal a few days later:—

11th mo., 14th. The accounts of the cholera at Sunderland affecting and alarming; the whole prospect calculated to bring the mind into much seriousness. But I have felt the inexpressible privilege of having a "Rock" to flee to; and have been permitted, at times, the enjoyment of much precious quietness of mind.

First day morning, [*11th mo., 20th.*] A fire at one of our neighbour's farms; supposed to be the work of an incendiary; the frequently repeated acts of this description, and the apparently unsettled and ungodly state of the population are deeply affecting. The cholera at Sunderland appears to increase. It has been my prayer this morning, for all near and dear to me, that we may find our refuge in the Ark of God. May the great Head of the Church graciously condescend to bless this Sabbath day, to the quieting and comforting of many weak and sorrowful minds, to the calming of many fierce passions, and to the gathering in of many souls from the reign of darkness and sin, to the kingdom of our Lord and Saviour Jesus Christ!

12*th mo.*, 9*th.* We were favoured with a comforting meeting yesterday. I felt the oil flow in a way to which I have been of late much a stranger; and two of our women Friends were lively in the use of their gifts. How different from the confusion which appears to mark the wild notions of some worthy people in the present day! If there be gifts in the church, of which the exercise is spontaneous, and under the immediate influence of the Spirit, (in however low a degree,) silence is the only medium in which they can be exercised in order; and how abundantly good in itself is silence—the silence of the soul. May we increasingly know it to be in the *life!*

12*th mo.*, 11*th.* The accounts of the more rapid increase of the cholera at Sunderland, &c., are affecting and alarming. But let us remember that the scourge is sent in perfect wisdom and righteousness; I trust also in mercy, to call a wandering, sinful nation home to God. The unemployed and half-starving state of the poor has also been deeply trying to my feelings; and business has been fraught with considerable cares. O that I may have strength given to me, both to trust and to rejoice in the Lord my God!

12*th mo.*, 16*th.* My wife and I went to Tivetshall Monthly Meeting yesterday, being much interested about an appointment of overseers there. The meeting was a good one, and the appointment satisfactorily made; so that we returned home with a peaceful and satisfied feeling. I find that such a feeling peculiarly rests on any little service tending to build up or maintain our religious Society: which, I trust, amidst all discouragements, we may humbly receive as a token for good.

First day night, 12*th mo.*, 26*th.* This has been a peaceful and edifying day. I rose in good time, and wrote before breakfast, read Isaiah xxvi in Hebrew, and walked to Meeting. The working of truth in the mind of John Fothergill, as represented in his Journal, has been a source of instruction to me this afternoon. May the same "anointing" be in me and upon me; and may the Lord still graciously make a way for me, that I may be devoted to his service. This evening we have enjoyed the first two chapters of Luke. It is a blessed, delightful, soul-satisfying thing, to think of the unutterable gift of a Saviour. O that all men knew and loved him!

The year 1832 was one of much exertion. In the early part of it, Joseph John Gurney's intervals of leisure were closely occupied by several important literary undertakings, whilst other labours of various kinds continued rapidly to succeed one another. In the course of the preceding summer, he had written a brief Essay on the Moral Character of our Lord Jesus Christ; which was soon afterwards published. The following characteristic extract may properly find a place here:—

"In these days of much polemical discussion of various clashing opinions, and, I fear, of no little bitterness of spirit among the professed followers of Jesus, it is well for us all to remember that, in Scripture, his example is presented to us with an especial reference to love and union; humility and condescension; patience and forbearance. 'If I then, your Lord and Master, have washed your feet; ye ought also to wash one another's feet. For I have given you an example that ye should do as I have done to you.'* 'This is my commandment, that ye love one another as I have loved you.'† * * It is of the highest importance to the cause of true religion, that all who love the Lord Jesus Christ should keep the watch over their own spirits, and pray for

* John xiii, 14, 15. † John xv, 12.

ability to fulfil these injunctions. In order to this, let us cultivate a sense of our ignorance and weakness, and dwell in deep humility before God. Let us be more ready to cast the beam out of our own eye than to attempt to extract the mote out of the eye of a brother. And while we adhere with unalterable firmness to 'the truth as it is in Jesus,' let our religion be the religion of principle rather than of opinion, of the heart rather than of the head." *

With such views and feelings, it can excite no surprise that he looked with anxiety and sorrow upon the controversy that was now agitating the Bible Society, whether Unitarians should be allowed to continue in membership with it; whether some test should not be imposed which would insure their exclusion; and whether prayer should not be publicly offered at the various meetings of the institution. The object of the Bible Society having been, from the first, the circulation of the Holy Scriptures "*without note or comment,*" nothing sectarian had hitherto marked its character; and no other test of membership was required than the desire to co-operate in the circulation of the inspired volume.

"Like other old-fashioned friends of the cause," says Joseph John Gurney, "I was anxious to maintain the original principles of the Society; and in support of them I published a pamphlet entitled Terms of Union, of which many thousands were circulated. I trust it was beneficial as showing that the security of the Society lay not in the ineffectual bondage of a test; but in the purity and evangelical bearing of its object, and in that gracious protection of the great Head of the Church with which it had hitherto been

* From the Amethyst for 1832; reprinted in Joseph John Gurney's Minor Works, Vol. ii, 132—133.

favoured. In short, the strength and glory of the Bible Society consists in two things, the godliness of its design, and the simplicity of its constitution. Many there were of various denominations, who then rallied round the old standard; the Society weathered the storm and continues to flourish. Most wisely have its managers hitherto abstained from those public vocal offerings of prayer, which would have changed the true character of the meetings, and would almost certainly have become a source of difficulty and contention among the different denominations. Yet what true friend of this noble institution does not feel the importance of conducting all its concerns in the spirit of prayer; and in reverent dependence upon Him, without whose blessing all our exertions in his cause are less than nothing and vanity?"

The following extract from the Terms of Union, will illustrate his views upon a question of much practical importance.

"I have often thought that the grounds on which a serious Christian stands in connexion with other men, while he prosecutes his various objects in life, may be compared to the successive stories of a *pyramid.* When he is transacting the common business of the day, with men of all characters and conditions, he is surrounded by vast numbers of people, and stands on the broad basement story. Here, while he abstains from evil things, he is compelled to communicate with many evil persons; and he calls to mind the words of the Lord Jesus, 'I pray not that thou shouldest take them out of the world, but that thou shouldest keep them from the evil.' But now an hospital is to be built; he mounts to the second story, his ground is narrowed and his company lessens. The utterly selfish and dissolute disappear from his view; but he still finds himself in communication with the worldly as well as the religious; with the infidel as well as with the believer. Christian benevolence however has new services in store for him. A society is formed for distributing the Scriptures without note or comment. The object is one of undoubted excellence, and he heartily engages in the cause. Here he stands on the third section of the pyramid. Again the company is diminished; again the circumference is contracted. Yet it is large enough to comprehend all reflecting persons of every class who value the Bible and approve of its dissemination. Our philanthropist knows that the work is pure and good, and though he by no means agrees in sentiment with all who co-operate in it, the last thing he dreams of is to narrow the circle either of its friends or of its efficacy.

"But while in distributing the Bible he stands on a common level with all who approve that object, he well knows the importance of a sound interpretation of its contents; and on the next story of the pyramid he finds himself engaged with rather fewer companions, and within somewhat narrower boundaries in a Missionary Society, or in a sabbath-day school, formed for the express purpose of affording, to those who need it, *evangelical* instruction. The merely nominal Christian, and the Socinian subscriber to the Bible Society have now parted from him; yet he is still encompassed by many persons whose religious views, on secondary points, differ from his own. He ascends, therefore, when occasion requires it, to an area of still smaller dimensions, and there he joins the members of his own church, in distributing tracts written in defence of the sentiments or practices peculiar to themselves. Finally he has some solitary duty to perform, or some opinion, all his own, to maintain or develope; and behold, he stands alone on the top of the pyramid."

The Terms of Union had engaged his leisure in the early part of the year. Another work, of greater magnitude and importance, completed about the same time, had been in hand for a much longer period.

"Dr. Chalmers had much impressed me," he writes in the Autobiography, "with a sense of the value of the Portable Evidence of Christianity, as he called it, meaning that which every Christian carries about with him in his own mind and experience.* I subsequently gave up no inconsiderable portion both of mind and time to the thinking out of this subject; the result of which, after some delays, was the little volume published by me under that name. I am inclined to consider it the most useful of my works; and I hope it is calculated to lay hold of the heart, as well as to convince the head. This, at least, was my intention. It has sold largely in England; has been translated into French; and has been republished in America by Dr. Wayland, president of one of the colleges. The Searcher of hearts knows that I boast not of the performance. If there be any good in it, it is all of him; and as for myself, I can only wonder that such an one should be employed in any such service. Praised and for ever adored be his holy name! May it be glorified by me whether in life or in death." †

The Terms of Union and the Portable Evidence, were both of them published early in the Spring. They were hardly completed before he was called into another extensive field of labour. He left home in the beginning of the third month; and, after visiting the families of Friends at Birmingham and its neighbourhood, proceeded into Lancashire, where, especially at Liverpool and Manchester, and the adjacent manufacturing districts, he was largely engaged in preaching the gospel. From Liverpool he writes

TO JONATHAN HUTCHINSON.

5th mo., 7th, 1832.

MY DEAR FRIEND,

The constant flow of religious engagements (like wave after wave,) has prevented my earlier notice of thy

* See *supra*, p. 419.

† Besides being largely circulated through other channels, it has been published in a cheap form by the Religious Tract Society in London. It is reprinted in the first volume of Joseph John Gurney's Minor Works.

very acceptable and timely letter. The train of thought which it contains is just in correspondence with my own; for I have had to plead for immediate revelation, and for that ancient principle of our religious profession, the Lord's "anointing," or the Spirit of Christ in us, and upon us, without which we can do nothing well for his precious cause, or for our own soul's salvation. There are many dangers abroad in the present day. Some are for justifying themselves by their own works; and others, while they delight in the evangelical foundation, are too apt to disregard that superstructure which has been long precious to some of us, as to our forefathers in the truth. I cannot describe to thee the exercise of mind through which I have passed, especially in Manchester and at this place.

His labours in Lancashire were interrupted by the Yearly Meeting and an interval of rest at home.

Earlham, 6th mo., 17th. The Yearly Meeting was on the whole well attended, and appeared to me to be an improvement upon that of last year. Something like conflict of opinion was apparent; some being rather prone to clip the gospel, and others full enough inclined to omit a sufficient reference to the spiritual work, and the testimonies of Friends. For my own part, I felt deeply concerned on the one hand, that the glorious gospel should have free course, and Christ be set forth in all his gracious offices; and, on the other, that Friends might be called home to their ancient spiritual principles, and that we might be encouraged not to forsake any of our testimonies. I found it my duty to pay a visit to the women Friends, when the comparison of the word of God to a two-edged sword was deeply before me. The minister of Christ must cut down self-righteousness by the right hand stroke of his sword, and with the left hand stroke, self-indulgence. It was a deep and difficult exercise.

In allusion to various communications in the ministry, he remarks:—

I felt a desire to open my ear to what the Spirit might say to the churches through whatever instrument, under whatever complexion. We must still have our watchmen and watchwomen at different and even opposite doors: but O that it may please the Head of the Church to inspire more and more of unanimity as well as love, and preserve us in the unity of the Spirit and the bond of peace!

The epistle is weighty, Christian, and comprehensive. A large committee sat on the subject of the heathen, and some important principles were discussed, and I hope settled. It was an interesting circumstance, that we had at this Yearly Meeting the company of four American brethren. Jonathan Taylor, who, had he lived, would have been a fifth, died in Ireland last autumn; and left behind him a character of unusual purity, loveliness, and brightness.

First day night, 6th mo., 17th. I have to record a delightful Sabbath, rendered peculiarly instructive by the company of our dear friend Stephen Grellet. This evening, in a well-filled public meeting at Goat Lane, he preached on the new birth, in the fulness and clearness of the gospel. It was indeed a refreshing and satisfying occasion. May it sink deeply into many hearts, and lead to the production of much good fruit!

Second day morning. In my quiet sitting with my wife this morning, a view was opened to me of several distinct evil tendencies in my own mind. That view has been rather appalling, and reminds me of the absolute necessity of our endeavouring, through prayer and watchfulness, to have the work of sanctification applied to our particular failings,—to the sinfulness which actually besets us. In all this there is a large scope for the active and diligent co-operation of the believer with the grace of God.

7th mo., 2nd. The Quarterly Meeting last week was well attended, and was a time of renewed gracious visitation, chiefly through the instrumentality of our dear friend Charles Osborne, from Indiana. He passed two days under our roof. His simplicity, humility, and Christian piety, are very exemplary. Yesterday evening he held a large public meeting in the Gildencroft, in which the gospel was proclaimed with power, and which has left behind it a sweet savour on my mind.

7th mo., 22nd. We intend leaving home early to-morrow morning. Tidings of cholera from various quarters; but we desire to go forth trusting in the Lord. How sweet to know that we belong to our Lord Jesus Christ, who bought us with his blood, and who is supreme over all things, natural and spiritual, to his church. May he condescend to be our guide; to be with us every moment!

The young people's meeting last sixth day evening was very relieving. I again found much peace in explaining the principles of Friends.

The completion of his labours in Lancashire was his principal object in again leaving home. Referring to this visit, which occupied about five weeks, he writes:—

I believed it to be my duty to hold several meetings in the open air in some large places; particularly at Oldham and Middleton, where the population is at once very large and uncultivated. A waggon was prepared for me at both places; and, besides my dear wife, our friend Abigail Dockray and others were my companions. At Middleton, where about two thousand persons were present, I was exposed to peculiar difficulty in consequence of having nearly lost my voice; but we were favoured to get through pretty well. At Oldham, the assembly was also very large, and I have seldom attended a more solemn and satisfactory meeting. I wish we had more of that faith which dwelt so largely in our forefathers, and led them to proclaim the truth in the highways and market places. It is obvious to me, that more of this kind of aggressive warfare is wanted; it is almost impossible, by any other means, to have communication with a large, rough, irreligious population; such as still exists in Lancashire, notwithstanding the increasing diffusion of the truth.

But another service in which I was at this time engaged, was, if possible, still more exercising to my mind. Feeling a lively interest in the mechanics of Manchester, a hard-headed, ingenious set of men, and having in vain attempted to obtain the company of any large number of them at the public meetings for worship, I believed it right to give a lecture, at the Mechanics' Institution, "on the right use and application of knowledge." The advertisement of my intention, which met the approbation of the committee, was published a fortnight beforehand. In the meantime, I was daily and hourly occupied in ministerial labours, and utterly unable did I feel to direct my thoughts to the subject. Only, I believed, I had that blessed sanction, for proposing both the lecture and the subject, which I have ever found to be the seed of a happy result. So I went on with each day's work, in the humble hope that the Lord would be with me in the hour of need. When the day came I was very poorly, my voice almost entirely gone. As I lay resting on my bed during the morning, and reading a little of Beattie and some other writers, a very few thoughts only was I able to collect that bore on the subject, so that in the evening, I went to the appointed place with a weak body and unfurnished mind, yet with some degree of humble confidence in the Lord. When I entered, I took my station on the floor, and could not but enjoy the spectacle of more than 1200 mechanics, occupying the raised seats of the amphitheatre to a very considerable elevation. O how merciful was the Lord to his poor servant on that occasion! Many were, I believe, secretly praying for me; and their prayers were answered. After speaking for about ten minutes, I entirely recovered my voice. This might have been owing in part to the arrangement now alluded to, which constrained me to lift up the head and throw out the chest; but I, nevertheless, gratefully acknowledge it to have been a special favour from the hand of my Divine Master. Clearness of ideas and fluency of speech were also graciously bestowed; matter in abundance both presented and developed itself as I proceeded; the audience was extremely attentive; and I spoke for an hour and three quarters without difficulty, taking them by guile, and gently leading them from one point to another, until we ended with CHRIST.*

At once brief and comprehensive, popular and argumentative, the address is one eminently adapted for the class to whom it was delivered. None, perhaps, of Joseph John Gurney's published writings contain so many thoughts in so small a compass. The littleness of man; his ignorance and dependence contrasted with his exhaustless longings as an immortal being; the effect of all true knowledge in producing still deeper and deeper humility; the necessity of faith even in the ordinary transactions of life, and much more in our relation to the infinite Creator; the matchless wisdom, harmony, and love displayed in all the works of God, and, above all, in the great and glorious facts revealed in the Christian religion; the overwhelming amount of evidence in support of those facts; and the wondrous adaptation of the doctrines founded upon them to the wants, the capacities, and the otherwise unsatisfied desires of fallen man, are among the important topics which are here successively touched upon and enforced. One of his favourite illustrations may serve as a specimen of the whole.

"When a lock and key," he says, addressing his audience of mechanics, "are well fitted, a fair presumption arises, even though they be of a simple character, that they were made for each other. If they are complex in their form, that presumption is considerably strengthened. But if the lock is composed

* This address was soon afterwards published upon a penny sheet; and has been since widely circulated. It is reprinted in Joseph John Gurney's Minor Works, Vol. ii, pp. 169 to 199.

of such strange and curious parts as to baffle the skill even of a Manchester mechanic—if it is absolutely novel and peculiar, differing from everything which was ever before seen in the world—if no key in the universe will enter it, *except one*, and by that one it is so easily and exactly fitted, that a child may open it, then indeed are we absolutely certain, that the lock and the key were made by the same master-hand, and truly belong to each other. No less curiously diversified, no less hidden from the wisdom of man, no less novel and peculiar, are the prophecies contained in the Old Testament respecting Jesus Christ. No less easy, no less exact, is the manner in which they are fitted by the gospel history. Who then can doubt that God was the author of these predictions — of the events by which they were fulfilled — and of the religion with which they are both inseparately connected?"

FROM THE LATE BISHOP BURGESS.

Palace, Salisbury, October 23rd, 1832.

RESPECTED FRIEND,

I return you many thanks for the very interesting and valuable Address which you have had the kindness to send me. I should have thought it very improbable that a lecture to a meeting of mechanics could have given any one an opportunity of pressing upon their attention such a variety of intellectual, moral, and spiritual views. I cannot omit this occasion of saying how much I have been lately pleased with your beautiful compendium of Christian Evidences.

I am, with very sincere respect,

Your faithful servant,

T. SARUM.

FROM JONATHAN HUTCHINSON.

Gedney, 11th mo., 14th, 1832.

* * * Amidst the much that pleases me in this Address, there is one sentiment which I can most fully and cordially receive; it is that which supposes our humility to bear a considerable proportion to, if not to be dependent on, the *depth* of our knowledge, whether this knowledge be derived from

self-examination, philosophical research, religious inquiry, or the united influence of all these; a sentiment in support of which thou hast very appropriately introduced the name of one who, on account of his eminence both in science and lowliness of mind, has been justly denominated the child-like sage. As the true Christian would not desire a higher title, so perhaps he can scarcely propose to himself a brighter example than that of the pious philosopher, Isaac Newton.

First day, 9th mo., 12th. On our arrival at Norwich this morning, we were met by the affecting news of Joseph Kinghorn's death, which took place last night about nine o'clock, I have no doubt in peace. "Surely," have I said in my heart, "our brother rests with God." He was a man for whom I have long entertained a settled and deep esteem, and a true affection. Although not without his prejudices, he was distinguished by unbending integrity and true piety, great learning, and a very happy, cheerful disposition. His conversation has been often delightful to me. Very few minds are better stored than his was; and very few persons knew better how to bring forth from their treasury "things new and old." May the event quicken our footsteps towards that celestial city, of which I reverently believe he is now an inhabitant! His death has reminded me of that of my beloved uncle. I think they were two of the most thoroughly respectable and estimable men in Norwich; and neither of them has left his like behind.

9th mo., 17th. Catherine and I attended Joseph Kinghorn's funeral yesterday morning. After the service was over, I addressed a few sentences to the congregation, under a feeling of great solemnity, and bore testimony to my friend; but more especially to the grace and goodness of the Master whom he desired to serve.

9th mo., 21st., The day of the Bible Society meeting. We have abundant cause to be thankful for the aiding and preserving mercies of a most gracious God. I invited our Bible party to our Meeting at Goat Lane. It was a very solemn and interesting time.

In the eleventh month he attended a Conference of Friends in London, appointed to assist in a general review of the volume (then known as The Book of Extracts) containing the rules and advices of the Yearly Meeting, which more particularly relate to the internal government and discipline of the Society of Friends.

TO JONATHAN HUTCHINSON:

Earlham, 11th mo., 18th, 1832.

The revisal of The Book of Extracts brought before us, in succession, every subject of interest and importance to our Society; and some of the discussions were at once lively and weighty. We worked very hard: beginning at ten o'clock in the morning, and going on till half-past seven in the evening, allowing little more than an hour for dinner and about twenty minutes for tea, which was comfortably provided on the premises. This daily tea drinking appeared to me to be a sort of *love feast.* We were about eighty in number, and I think every sitting was begun and ended in a feeling of solemnity. The whole was concluded by a meeting for worship last fourth day morning at Gracechurch Street.*

Thus, my dear friend, it is evident that we are not forsaken of our great and glorious Head. May we trust him and serve him with all good fidelity, and we shall yet do well. I suppose thou hast heard of our friend Daniel Wheeler's prospect of visiting the Islands of the Pacific, Van Diemen's Land, and New South Wales. It was brought before the "Morning

* The results of the deliberations of the "Conference" here alluded to, after having been submitted to the approval of the Yearly Meeting of 1833, were, with a valuable explanatory preface, embodied in the volume, published in 1834, under the title of The Rules of Discipline and Advices of the Yearly Meeting; a volume which, as containing an authentic account of the discipline and usages of Friends, as well as for the Christian wisdom breathed throughout its pages, is well worthy the serious attention of members of other bodies of professing Christians.

Meeting" on second day; most of the "Conference Friends" being present; and, after serious deliberation, met with the full unity of the meeting. John and Martha Yeardley have a view to visiting Greece and the Islands of the Archipelago. Thus our "Missions" are going on apace!

First day afternoon, [11*th mo.*, 25*th.*] It is an unspeakable blessing to have our faith in the vast realities of the gospel enlivened and strengthened. The thought of many beloved ones now centred, I trust, with their Lord, is often very sweet to me. How joyful will be our re-union, where trouble, sorrow, and death will be no more! O Christianity, how great are thy treasures, and what rays of sunshine art thou the means of casting over a darkly clouded world!

Fourth day, [12*th mo.*, 11*th.*] Public affairs; the strife of party; the victories of the hot Tory partizans on the one side, and the brawlings of Radicals on the other; the absence of religious and even decently moral restraint, are subjects of deep lamentation to me, and I tremble lest the righteous cause of the Abolition of Slavery should still be frustrated. But I know there is One who surmounts the storm and rides on the wings of the wind.

[12*th mo.*, 26*th.*] I found it best to take the mail for Ipswich, on second day afternoon, with a view to the Quarterly Meeting held there yesterday. I returned this morning. The meeting in the morning was large and solemn, and in the evening the young people met me at the house of our dear friend Dykes Alexander; the party amounting to nearly ninety. The scriptural grounds of our various testimonies were unfolded. I trust the whole day was a time of favoured visitation to many, and I feel refreshed and comforted by the retrospect. What a mercy that one so weak and unworthy should be helped in time of need!

12*th mo.*, 31*st.* I feel the present a period of some critical importance in my life, and my soul has been brought into deep exercise and conflict, in the fear lest I should, in any respect, become a prey to the enemy. But I will not, I dare not, doubt the faithfulness of my God and Saviour.

CHAPTER XXIV.

1833. ÆT. 45.

ANTI-SLAVERY PROCEEDINGS; MEETING OF DELEGATES; PASSING OF EMANCIPATION ACT; ELECTION AT NORWICH; PETITION AGAINST BRIBERY; PROSPECT OF ENTERING PARLIAMENT; DOUBTS RESPECTING IT; ULTIMATE DECISION; COMMENCEMENT OF VISIT TO FRIENDS IN LONDON AND ITS NEIGHBOURHOOD; LETTER TO A YOUNG FRIEND; LETTER TO HIS CHILDREN; RACHEL FOWLER; GEORGE WITHY; WILLIAM WILBERFORCE.

THE important subject of Slavery, which had of late years given place to other questions of a more directly domestic and absorbing interest, was now again beginning to claim a large share of public attention. The efforts of the Abolitionists in 1823 and 1824, to which reference has been already made,* had spurred on the Government to some exertion; and for several of the following years no way had appeared open for more decided steps. But the opportunity afforded by the interval was not lost. The leading Abolitionists were diligently occupied in watching the progress and working of the remedial measures of the Government, and the disposition and conduct of both the planters and the slaves; and they failed not to take advantage of the openings that were presented for keeping alive

* See *supra*, pp. 253—255.

the attention of parliament and the public to the enormities and ruinous consequences attendant upon the system. A large mass of important evidence was accumulated. From tables, furnished by the Colonial authorities themselves, it was proved, in the most decisive manner, that the slave population was on the decline. The alarming fact was disclosed, that within the short space of twenty-three years, the number of slaves had diminished to the extent of 100,000. And yet, while ruin was thus following in the train of oppression, the planters had turned a deaf ear to the voice of warning. The golden opportunity had been frittered away unimproved. Not a step had been taken by any of the Colonial legislatures with a view to the extinction of slavery. The remedial propositions of the Government had been either wholly rejected or coldly received and studiously evaded. Meanwhile, public attention in England was more and more turned to the subject. And now that the great question of parliamentary reform was considered for the present settled, the abolition of Slavery became a leading topic of discussion; and soon ranked amongst the most popular questions of the day. The details of the movement are stated with so much clearness in the Memoirs of the late Sir Thos. Fowell Buxton,* that it is equally unnecessary as it would be out of place to repeat them here. The part taken by Joseph John Gurney in these efforts was necessarily subordinate, but his unabated interest in the cause requires that they should be briefly noticed. Whether the call was to cheer by encouragement, to aid by counsel, or to

* See particularly, chapters xvi to xx.

co-operate in a more active way, he was ever on the watch to assist his brother-in-law in the arduous struggle. In his Journal, towards the close of 1830, he describes himself as "closely engaged" with him "in arranging his parliamentary plan for the Abolition of Slavery." A few months later, offering to share his expenses in the contested election at Weymouth, he writes*:—

I am sure that whatsoever thou mayest find it necessary to spend will be spent virtuously. Thy return to parliament was never more important than it is now that thou hast, so satisfactorily to everybody, taken the lead in the Slavery question.

And when, in the beginning of the year 1833, he saw the near approach of what he felt persuaded would prove the final conflict, he was induced at the election for the county of Norfolk to make an exception to his general practice of non-interference; and his speech to the electors against Slavery, with that of another gentleman upon the same subject, being immediately published and widely circulated, had considerable influence in promoting the return of the Anti-Slavery candidate.

Early in the first session of the new parliament, the Government were prevailed upon to undertake the final settlement of this great question. They were anxious, however, that the Anti-Slavery party should accede to some arrangement which would include a plan for compensation to the slaveholder. This occasioned fresh difficulties. In 1824, the

* Under date 4th mo., 30th, 1831. See also Memoirs of Sir T. F. Buxton, pp. 188—189.

question of gradual emancipation had been connected in the minds of many of its advocates, (and Joseph John Gurney was one of this number,) with the idea, in a form more or less defined, of compensation to the planter. It was thought (whether rightly or wrongly this is not the place to inquire) that the state, which had vested in the master the *legal* right of property in the slave, could not, without sharing in the loss, honourably undo the wrong which it had itself occasioned. But *gradual* emancipation, as it had been before understood, was now abandoned as hopeless. Nothing, it was now felt, was practicable but the total and immediate extinction of Slavery. And with an increased acquaintance with the horrors of the system, and a growing detestation of its inherent evils, many of the warm friends of the cause, carried away by their anxiety to do justice to the Negro, deemed all concession to his owner a dereliction of principle; nor could they endure the idea of striking a bargain with the oppressor."

Notwithstanding these difficulties, "it was determined," to use the words of the Memoir already referred to, "that the idea of acquiescing in some system of compensation should be broached to the Anti-slavery Society at its approaching annual meeting. This meeting was held on the 2nd of April, Lord Suffield taking the chair; and Mr. Buxton undertook the delicate task of introducing the proposal. * * * He was ably followed by Dr. Lushington, Mr. Joseph John Gurney, and others; and their exertions appeared to be crowned with unexpected success. * * * But while the leaders of the Anti-slavery party made this concession to Government, they still deemed it necessary to rally all their forces, and render their victory complete. * * * A circular was addressed by the Committee to the friends of the cause in every considerable town, requesting them to appoint delegates, who were to meet in London on the 18th of the month, to represent in person the wishes of the nation. * * * The call was answered to an unexpected extent; and now the question arose, how, most prudently and effectually, to wield the force about to join them. Nor was the moment unattended with anxiety. It was very doubtful whether so many earnest advocates could be brought to act in concert. * * * They were not unlikely to mistake matters of expedience for matters of principle; and, in particular, to think that it would be a crime to give the planter compensation, however much the interests of the Negro might require concession. It was an occasion which called forth all Mr. Buxton's tact and powers of argument; but the delegates, strong and independent as their views were, placed a generous confidence in their leaders, and a sufficient degree of unanimity was at length obtained.

"It was necessary to frame an address to the Premier which should embody their sentiments. This difficult task fell to the lot of Mr. J. J. Gurney, and the paper which he prepared received a cordial assent. On the ensuing day they met again in Exeter Hall, and proceeded in a body to Downing Street." *

The result of these efforts is well known. The passing of the Act for the Abolition of Slavery before the close of the session, clogged though it was with the apprenticeship arrangement, could not but be hailed with satisfaction and gratitude; and, whatever diversity of opinion might exist as to compensation, there were few indeed who could not join in the thankful acknowledgment of William Wilberforce, that he had "lived to witness a day in which England was willing to give twenty millions sterling for the abolition of Slavery." Scarcely could

* Memoirs of Sir T. F. Buxton, pp. 313—317.

Joseph John Gurney have ventured to look for such a consummation of his wishes, when, in the early part of the year 1824, in a letter to his brother-in-law, an extract from which has been already given, after cheering him with the prospect of ultimate success, he had concluded with the inquiry, "Why should we expect to get the extinction of the monster into full train in less than *ten years?*"*

To return once more to his own more immediate course of labour. At the late election for the City of Norwich, — the first since the passing of the Reform Act — the Whig candidates, one of whom was his near relative, were defeated chiefly, as was generally believed, through the influence of bribery.

"As usual," writes Joseph John Gurney, "I took little or no part in the election; but when a petition was presented to Parliament against the returned members on the score of bribery, I imagined it to be my place to subscribe to the object; and wrote a letter in the Norwich newspapers stating the grounds of my so doing. Those grounds were in no degree personal, but simply moral and Christian.† But the

* See *supra*, p. 260.

† The following is a transcript of the letter in question: —

To the Editor of the Norfolk Chronicle.

While it is my earnest wish to promote good order and virtuous habits among the working classes of the community, and to assist in cutting off some of those temptations to evil by which they are surrounded, I have an utter abhorrence of party spirit; I know it is ever interfering with the quietness and welfare of our city, and am fully sensible how desirable it is, as a general rule, to avoid every measure calculated to excite its virulence or to prolong its reign. Under these feelings, it has been to me a subject of anxious consideration whether I ought, or ought not, to subscribe to the "appearance" of evil was not avoided. The measure was misconstrued into an act of political partizanship; and I evidently lost ground by it in my own true calling,—that of

expenses of the Petition, which is about to be presented to Parliament, against the election of our present members. The result has been a determination to support the object; and I hope thou wilt kindly allow me, through the medium of thy journal, a public opportunity of stating my reasons.

I have been long convinced that the whole system of Norwich electioneering is fraught with moral mischief; and I have carefully abstained, for many years past, from mixing myself up with the proceedings of either party, and especially from subscribing a single shilling to any of our elections, whether local or general. I am desirous of having this system fairly brought before Parliament, and, after much reflection on the subject, I think there are good grounds for hoping that it will receive an effectual remedy.

Our Ward Elections, and other contests of a merely local nature, have long been a scene of shameless bribery, licentiousness, and corruption. Thousands of pounds have been spent on both sides in the horrid work of depriving the poor voters of their best treasures: integrity and temperance. The colours of an idle ribbon have been substituted for principle; and without the smallest reserve has the motto been adopted, "Let us do evil that good may come."

In the meantime, the General Elections have been subject to some considerable degree of decency and restraint. Pure indeed they have never been in the view of the Christian moralist, nor by any means inoffensive in the eye of the law. For my own part, I consider the old practice of treating the voters in public-houses as a preparation for the election, and that of afterwards remunerating them with guineas or half-guineas, to be in a very high degree objectionable and improper. It is very probable that corruption may have gone somewhat farther on these occasions than I am aware of; but the full introduction of Ward Election iniquity into the election of members has unquestionably been reserved for our last contest. Entertainments were given at the public-houses on the day of the election itself, and direct bribery was practised to a very large extent. So many cases have, without my seeking them, come under my personal notice, that I am sure of the fact: it is indeed notorious and indisputable.

Now, although the opposite party appear to have met this

promoting simple Christianity among all classes. A more watchful endeavour to follow the only true guide in the application of the great principles of Christian truth to the common affairs of life,—I mean the immediate teaching of the Holy Spirit,—would, as I now believe, have preserved me from this course."

vigorous warfare with a comparatively dumb battery, I am perfectly aware that the violent partizans on either side are, in a moral point of view, equally blameable. The legal danger of bribery and corruption may indeed be different in the two cases, but the moral guilt is precisely the same, whether they be practised in an election for a senator or in one for a sheriff. But certainly it does appear to me, and I think it must be obvious to every one, that the notorious corruptions of our late General Election afford us an opportunity of bringing the whole subject before Parliament such as we have never had before. Had our local follies and miseries stood alone, we might in vain have solicited the aid of the legislature; but the wider and more important range which they have now taken, at once insures the attention of a committee of the House of Commons.

Whatever may be the result of the inquiry as it relates to the present members, the guilt and sorrow of our city will unquestionably be brought to light; and it is surely very reasonable to expect, as a consequence, such a re-arrangement of our municipal and elective system as will deliver us from all such evils for the future.

For these plain reasons, and without the smallest degree of ill will to any one, I am willing to subscribe to the object; and I certainly consider it worthy of general support. I cannot conclude without remarking, that among the various animosities which arise from the weakness and folly of mankind, there are two which appear to me to be pre-eminently absurd and vicious.

The first is, a cry for Reform going hand-in-hand with a lust for corruption.

The second is, a Conservative attempt to maintain the institutions of the country by undermining that foundation of religion and morals on which alone they can stand with safety.

Apologizing for the length of my letter, I remain thy sincere friend,

J. J. Gurney.

Earlham, 1st mo., 1st, 1833.

Another subject of great importance to himself was at this time occupying his mind. He thus alludes to it in a letter

TO JONATHAN HUTCHINSON.

Norwich, 2nd mo., 28th, 1833.

* * * The question which has pressed upon me day and night is this; whether I have a testimony to bear, I mean a quiet, patient, persevering testimony, to the cause of Christianity in the British Parliament? If this be indeed the Master's will, I fully believe it would not hinder or mar "the anointing" in ministry. I may confess that I have been utterly unable to escape from the consideration of the case. Of course thou wilt understand that it would be on a system of entire purity, and wholly independent of party.

The progress and final result of his deliberations will be seen in the following extracts from his Journal and Autobiography:—

1st mo., 6th, 1833. I cannot express the serious thought into which I have been introduced, in regard to a certain prospect of a public nature. Deep has been my conflict, for some time past, in the fear of the enemy's snares. I desire to be preserved in patience and simple dependence, resting assured that the Lord will not leave me without a light to follow: that he will make an opening in his providence for whatsoever is truly his own will concerning me; or, on the other hand, that he will graciously condescend to close every door through which his Spirit forbids an entrance. With him I leave it, and feel more than usually able to repose on his bosom.

"So strongly was my mind impressed with the subject," he writes in his Autobiography, "that in the prospect of an opening that was likely to occur, I communicated freely with a friend of mine, a gentleman of independent principles, and of the highest character, who fully agreed to unite with me as a candidate. Yet we fixed nothing, and in the meantime I went up to London to consult a few Friends on the subject. Solemn and interesting was the conference, and very close was our joint deliberation on the question whether a minister of the gospel could, consistently with our principles, occupy a seat in the British Parliament."

In his Journal, alluding to this conference, he says:—

1st mo., 19*th.* The subject of the incompatibility of such a prospect with the duties of the ministry was closely searched; and the dangers on all hands felt and examined. Three of the speakers were almost exclusively on the cautionary side, still committing it to the only safe test—Divine guidance. The remaining four seemed pretty fully prepared to close in with the prospect. ——'s testimony to his earnest wish to discourage it, but his entire inability so to do, was especially striking. Another Friend reminded us of the legislative functions of Friends, ministers as well as others, in Pennsylvania; and spoke on the diversity of gifts, even in one person, and the propriety of giving to each its proper scope. *All* acknowledged the preciousness of that liberty of the Spirit under which Friends have been accustomed to act, in reference to the pursuit of worldly duties, notwithstanding a call to the ministry; and I had to testify, that in my own experience, this simple principle of trusting all to "the anointing," has worked well. The result is, that I am fairly left at liberty. May I be rightly guided and governed in this most important and critical question!

Earlham; first day night, [*1st mo.*, 27*th.*] To-day has been one of some real solemnity; Daniel Wheeler's ministry lively and delightful. In the afternoon meeting he took his leave of us; and it was laid on me to commend him to our heavenly Father in prayer. He has just been addressing our large circle after our Scripture reading. Long shall we remember his influence and Christian example!

I have had many anxious thoughts as to my future lot and proceedings, and some conflict between opposite views of duty;

but I humbly believe that the Lord is graciously disposed to deal gently with me; to permit me time to try the fleece wet and dry; to go before me and to be my rearward. To him I commit my cause, but surely I am not worthy of the least of his regards.

Fourth day morning. I feel some capacity to say with an honest heart, "thy will be done:" and to recur to Christ as the ground of repose, and as the centre of action, is, amidst all, delightful to me. Life is flowing rapidly away; death, judgment, and eternity are approaching. The Lord grant that I may stand complete in all his will, by an abiding faith in his beloved Son.

3rd mo., 3rd. We are on the wing this morning for Bayswater; trusting that a time of quietness of mind, and, if it may be, some engagements in the Lord's service await me. In the meantime, I leave public interests to work in that way which a good Providence may see fit to direct, being clear that my own course must, at present, be one purely passive; and humbly trusting, that my divine and holy Master will not leave his unworthy servant without help and guidance.

3rd mo., 14th. I deeply feel that no mortal power either in myself or others, could have delivered my soul from these bonds. I went up to Bayswater, desiring in quietness and retirement, both outward and inward, to throw myself on the faithful love and guidance of my adorable Saviour. Up to the middle of last sixth day night, I could find no peace, except in resignation to the parliamentary prospect, *should the Lord clearly open the way for it;* but in that memorable midnight hour my mind became relieved; the prospect gradually disappeared, and, after the intense conflict which I have so long gone through on the subject, I am now, through the infinite condescension of my Divine Master, left without the shadow of a doubt. The whole of my experience in reference to this important question, and especially the concluding stage of it, has, as it were, brought me into contact with an unseen world. The dealings of God with me, and the direct impressions made upon my mind by his holy hand, have been as palpable and indubitable to me as things visible and material.

Upon learning his decision his intended colleague thus wrote to him:—

March 13th, 1833.

MY DEAR FRIEND,

Many thanks for your kind letter. So far from being grieved or hurt at the conclusion to which you have come, I cannot but entirely approve of it, and my wife begs to add, from her, that she congratulates you upon it. I always thought the *pros* and *cons*, humanly speaking, nicely balanced; and as you have taken counsel from One who never fails those who seek him, and the balance is cast into the negative scales, I am quite sure all is right. This also is quite clear to me; you never can repent the course you have now taken, inasmuch as it preserves you in your present obvious course of useful exertion; whereas, had you determined the other way, and found that your time was comparatively wasted in unavailing or abortive attempts to serve your country and mankind, you could scarcely have avoided feeling much regret and doubt as to the propriety of the course you had taken. I cannot, however, avoid feeling a little secret regret, that the impression which your appearance, language, and sentiments, would, as I believe, make upon a reformed House of Commons, is not likely to be realized.

"My present reflections on the whole matter," says Joseph John Gurney, a few years later in his Autobiography, "are, first, that the interference with the Norwich petition would have been better avoided; secondly, that the consideration of the Parliamentary question was permitted for some good purpose; and thirdly, that the conclusion was safe and sound, affording abundant cause for thankfulness: though I cannot fully agree to the position, that the entrance of a gospel minister on such a service would necessarily interfere with his higher calling. Such a position does not seem to me to consist with that glorious liberty of the Lord's Spirit for which we plead. Rare and peculiar, however, are the cases which would justify such a course."

TO JONATHAN HUTCHINSON.

Norwich, 3rd mo., 16th, 1833.

During my quiet sojourn at Bayswater, the prospect which has been long before my mind of paying a religious visit to Friends of London and Middlesex assumed a clear shape, and so obviously included an early visit to the families as entirely to supersede, and in the end to remove all prospect of an inferior nature. The Lord graciously heard my fervent prayers, stayed the restless efforts of the tempter, and broke all my bonds asunder. My soul is filled with praise and thanksgiving for his unmerited goodness towards one of the most unworthy of his children; and under such circumstances, it is no less than a delight to me to go forth again in the work of the ministry of the gospel. I am sure thou wilt rejoice with me, and offer up the *melody of the heart* on behalf of thy unworthy friend, thus graciously and mercifully dealt with.

After spending several months in London he writes in his Journal: —

Earlham, 7th mo., 18th. Four months have passed since my last entry in this journal, in various respects very differently from my anticipations.

In the first place I must remark, that even had I not been so graciously emancipated from the prospect of supposed public duties of a civil nature, the opening would have closed in Providence more painfully to me. It afterwards turned out, that no opportunity for such supposed duties was to occur. Under these circumstances, I am peculiarly thankful that the negative decision was arrived at so satisfactorily, independently of events.

From 3rd mo., 19th, for three weeks and upwards I was closely engaged in visiting the families of Devonshire House Monthly Meeting, and in holding various public meetings, with the young people, &c. I resided, during this work, with my beloved friend Peter Bedford; in much peace, and sweet harmony and unity, with him and his nephews. My ministry was often very close, yet I had to acknowledge that the Lord's gracious anointing was not withheld from me. When going from house to house in Spitalfields, I felt with gratitude, the safety of my allotment, compared with what it might have been in a far more secular, and at the same time, a more arduous employment. Peculiar strength, was, I believe, given to me in unfolding the principles of Friends to young people.

These engagements were followed, with some interruptions from illness, by others of a similar character, among Friends in the Monthly Meeting of Gracechurch Street.

TO A YOUNG FRIEND.

(On the contrast between *legal* and *gospel* obedience.)

Upton, 6th mo., 8th, 1833.

MY DEAR YOUNG FRIEND,

* * * * When we call to mind that we are by nature corrupt and sinful, and have actually sinned, (alas! how much and how often!) in thought, word, and deed, our hearts ought to overflow with gratitude to Him, who hath redeemed us with his precious blood. Under this feeling of gratitude to our Lord Jesus Christ, and of ardent love for God, we shall be constrained, by the most heart-cheering of motives, to take up our daily cross, to walk in the paths of Christian self-denial and to "follow the Lamb whithersoever he goeth."

Our motive then is *love* and the effect is *obedience.* Obedience to the pure law of God; as it is written in the page of Scripture, and as it is engraved with the finger of light on the tablets of the heart. This writing of the law on the heart is the work of the Holy Spirit, the Comforter, whom Jesus promised to his disciples; and who still illuminates their consciences, and guides them into all truth.

Now it requires great care that we distinguish between a cheerful obedience to this pure and heavenly guide, and that self-mortification, or "voluntary humility" as the apostle calls it, into which the Spirit does not truly lead; and by which, nevertheless, it is very natural for the anxious and troubled soul to seek to recommend itself to God. When we have long been walking in darkness, when desertion and secret sorrow have been our lot, we are prone to exchange the *gospel* for the *law;* and to seek out some peculiarly trying service or sacrifice, by which we may obtain the favour of the Lord. This is precisely the principle on which the Monks of La Trappe, and other Roman Catholics, have so long acted. Did they know the fulness of the love of Christ, were they more sensible that it is his blood alone which can cleanse from all sin, and his righteousness alone which can open for us the gates of heaven, they would be delivered from these bonds; and would no longer seek to obtain the favour of God by sacrifices which the *law of God* does not require.

That law is emphatically called the "Law of Liberty;" for while it binds down every unruly passion, and leads into true "simplicity and godly sincerity in all things," it encourages a noble freedom of action in the service of our Lord. The Spirit of Christ within us, is a Spirit of "love, and power, and of a sound mind."

Although these general observations are, I believe, worthy of thy attention, I by no means wish to apply them hastily to thy particular case. I would rather invite thee to ponder them before the Lord, that thou mayst know whether thou hast or hast not any part in them. With regard to plainness of dress, I heartily approve it; and, as thou art well aware, do not fail to recommend it. I think we cannot adopt a sounder view of the subject than that of Robert Barclay; who, after the example and on the authority of Paul and Peter, recommended a modest and decent attire, distinguished by true simplicity; and worn for use alone, not for *ornament.* At the same time he remarks, that, while we avoid all splendour and costliness, the materials of which our dress are composed, ought to be regulated by our circumstances in life.* If I mistake not, he mentions silk as proper for persons in a certain line of life; and since his day it has become a much cheaper and more common article.

Well, thou wilt perhaps answer, all these things are very

* See Barclay's Apology, Prop. xv., s. 2, p. 352—53, 1st English edition.

true and good, but must I not follow my own impressions of duty? Assuredly thou must, my dear young friend; but the Lord is no hard master. He would have us move on very gently and cautiously, especially when the impression on our minds does not appear to accord with a comprehensive and scriptural view of the law of our God. Give thyself a little time; be very patient; dwell near to Christ; pour forth thy heart in prayer; and he will in due season make his way clear before thee.

I well remember one occasion in which, during several months, I felt much bound in spirit to a particular sacrifice. It was in vain that some of my most intimate and judicious friends assured me that it was unreasonable, and would rather *mar* than *mend*. I could find no peace but in giving way to it, so far as to be entirely willing to leave myself respecting it in the Lord's hand. But in due season, the permitted temptation, for such I believe it was, was withdrawn; and I was left in sweet, peaceful liberty. Under such trials we cannot deliver ourselves, or put a force upon our consciences; but we can *leave ourselves to the Lord*, and in due season he will not fail to make a way for our help.

Commending thee in faith to the best and kindest of Friends and Masters, I am,

Thy affectionate friend and well-wisher,

J. J. GURNEY.

The increasing illness of his mother-in-law, Rachel Fowler, called Joseph John Gurney into the West of England in the course of the summer. Whilst there, he enjoyed the satisfaction of a parting interview with William Wilberforce, at Bath, about three weeks before his decease. Two days after the interview, he wrote from the house of his mother-in-law,

TO HIS CHILDREN.

Melksham, 7th mo., 13th, 1833.

MY DEAR J. H. AND A.

The longer we live the more we know, or ought to know, of the goodness of God; and the more the treasury of our heart and understanding may become stored with the good things of the kingdom of our Redeemer. It is the privilege of Christians, (O that it may always be yours!) to serve a prince of tender compassion; one who never fails to render his yoke easy, and even delightsome to his obedient children. And what shall we say of the wondrous *alchemy* with which Christianity converts all she touches into gold? Bright are the beams with which the religion of Jesus is sometimes known to gild the darkest gloom of the valley of tears. Behold, darkness becomes light; pain is changed into pleasure; sickness is the means of health; and life triumphs over death!

I have been led to these reflections, partly by watching the condition of your beloved grandmother. You know that she is suffering from a malignant disease, which in all human probability, must soon terminate in death. There was a time when the prospect of this particular visitation of the divine hand was the object of her terror, and occasioned her inexpressible conflict of spirit; but now *peace reigns;* and not only is she resigned, without a struggle or a murmur, to the will of her heavenly Father; but she seems to care but little by what means it may please him to close her mortal career. Rather does she rejoice in the hope graciously bestowed upon her, that she will so soon wing her way from all things temporal into regions of perfect felicity.

There shall she bathe her weary soul
In seas of endless rest;
And not a wave of trouble roll
Across her peaceful breast.

In this happy condition she has nothing to mar her cheerfulness and comfort, but mere bodily pain, which she endures with humble patience; and in the quietness of her spirit, finds alleviation for body as well as soul. Her Divine Master, whom it has been her delight to follow, and under whose gracious influence she has abounded in kindness to the poor and needy, is now accomplishing, in her experience, his gracious promise, "Blessed is he that considereth the poor; the Lord will deliver him in time of trouble. The Lord will preserve him and keep him alive. The Lord will strengthen him upon the bed of languishing: *thou wilt make all his bed in his sickness.*" Fully is this beloved sufferer aware, that to be translated into the more immediate presence of a perfectly holy God, and to stand, unclothed of mortality, before the judgment seat of the Searcher of hearts, is, of all things, the most solemn to all men; the most *terrible* to the impenitent sinner. But with this prospect before her, she is at *rest;* because she entertains a humble confidence, that through infinite mercy she is accepted in "the Beloved."

A few evenings ago, when a little company of intimate friends was surrounding her, she addressed them nearly as follows: "Although I am suffering from indisposition, and feel great weakness of mind as well as body, I think it right to acknowledge my feelings of fervent thankfulness to God, who has graciously supported me under all my sufferings and has permitted me to feel his holy arm to be underneath. I have known desertion, temptation, and trial; but when the enemy of souls has come in like a flood, the Lord has lifted up a standard against him. In the prospect of that awful change which awaits me, I am fully convinced that there is nothing for me to trust in but the atoning blood of a merciful Saviour. Having more experience from length of years, than any one present, I would exhort you all to be steadfast in the faith, and never to harbour a doubt in your minds respecting these great truths. We must know him to be our *Mediator*, our *Advocate*, our *Intercessor* with the Father during the present life; thus it is that our mortality will, in the end, be gloriously exchanged for immortality." On a subsequent occasion she exclaimed, "We can do nothing for ourselves to merit salvation; we must look for the MERCY of God in Christ Jesus. This, I may say, I believe I have unlimitedly obtained."

How can I witness such a scene, without feeling an earnest desire for you, my beloved children, that your views of Christian doctrine may, like hers, be clear as the noon day, and stable as the rock. Decided and settled Christianity may be said to make room for pure pleasure even of a temporal kind, while it is the means of qualifying us for the right performance of every duty. Who does not perceive that in its working on the human mind, and especially in its abounding consolations in sickness and in sorrow, we have a practical proof that God is the author of the religion of Jesus; and that this religion, imbibed in the heart by faith, is the pearl of great price! Let us each be willing to "sell all that we have;" or, in other words, to surrender our whole hearts to the Lord, that we may possess this pearl!

"There lives in this village another highly interesting person, a gifted minister of the Society of Friends, who has just completed the age of man. You have both heard of George Withy, a person remarkable for strong talent and native humour; but one who, during the last fifty years, has been grounded in the conviction that Christ is *all in all.* He was telling me this morning that during the whole of this period, his views of Christian truth have never varied. Like the veteran oak, which spreads its firm roots in every direction, and defies the blast, this experienced Christian is steadfast and immovable. No infidel cavils, no wind of false doctrine can shake him from the centre of his strength, and from the source of all his hope and comfort. He is a man of warm affections, and is fondly attached to his large family. Most of them were collected in his peaceful habitation to celebrate his seventieth anniversary. It was the Sabbath day —a day of delightful repose and solemnity—during which we felt the great privilege of the public worship of God. The silence which reigned in our little meeting, both morning and evening, was remarkable; and though broken, was not, I trust, marred by the ministry of the gospel. All seemed to be bound together in love; and all (I trust) were united in an ardent desire to be found *in Christ;* ready for health, or for sickness, for joy or for sorrow, for life or for death.

Our dear friend George Withy had risen early in the morning, and had occupied a few quiet hours in writing an address to his children. It was a very touching one, earnestly calling on them to press after the salvation of their immortal souls, and recommending to them their various social and religious duties. One thing, however, above all others, struck me in this address. It was the clear and oft-repeated declaration of this servant of Christ, that he had no trust whatsoever in his own righteousness; but that all his confidence was in the Lord; all his hopes of future happiness in the availing mediation and perfect righteousness of the Redeemer of men. His address, like the letters of Paul, was full of "Jesus Christ and him crucified." All boasting was excluded. Deep humiliation was the distinguishing mark of each passing sentence. Mercy, mercy was the theme; and God in Christ was exalted over all. Thus, out of the mouth of two experienced witnesses, has the gospel of life and salvation been confessed and confirmed in our hearing. And in both cases has the eye as well as the ear perceived its delightful efficacy, its gladdening, quickening influence. What indeed can be more lovely than the spectacle of advancing age softened, and ripened, and mellowed into sweetness, under the sunshine of genuine Christianity!

Both my mother-in-law and George Withy are persons of a marked natural character, and are rendered the more interesting by their peculiar traits. I never knew in any woman more of a quick feminine sensibility than in Rachel Fowler; nor in any man more of the spirit of bold and determined independence than in George Withy. But the former has become fearless as a lion, and the latter gentle as a lamb. The peculiar dispositions of each are sanctified without being annulled; and the besetting weaknesses of the two characters are counteracted by sovereign and all-sufficient grace. Such is the unvarying effect of the influence of God's Holy Spirit on the hearts and conduct of the believing and obedient. "Every valley shall be exalted, and every mountain and hill shall be brought low; and the crooked shall be made straight, and the rough places plain; and the glory of the Lord shall be revealed, and all flesh shall see it together." Both these cherished individuals are, as you know, attached and faithful members of our own society. They care not, indeed, for sect or party, but they have long been deliberately convinced, that the views and testimonies which distinguish

Friends, are built on Christ as their foundation, and truly belong to primitive Christianity. Nor are these views shaken by the nearer approach of death and judgment. They are still consistent advocates of what they conceive to be the entire spirituality of the gospel dispensation; still deeply solicitous that the young amongst us may adhere to that restricted course which they have themselves found to be a path of remarkable peace and safety.

I have, however, another witness to produce, who, though accustomed to a somewhat different administration, is descending towards the grave in the same essential and saving faith. This witness is the well known and long-beloved William Wilberforce. Long-beloved I may well call him, as regards myself; for I have now enjoyed a near friendship with him for nearly seventeen years, and I shall always consider my acquaintance with him as among the happiest circumstances of my life. I well remember his first visit to Earlham, (I think about the year 1816,) at the time of our Bible Society Meeting, when we were already crowded with guests. Wilberforce was the star and life of the party, and we all thought we had never seen a person more fraught with Christian love, or more overflowing with the praises of his Creator. He was then possessed of comparatively unimpaired powers. His eloquence was easy, lively, and captivating; and his cornucopia of thought and information rich and abundant. I never met with so discursive a mind, or with so interesting a companion. Many a roam have we enjoyed together over green fields and gardens; and very delightful has it been to me to draw out of his treasury things new and old. You have seen him, and cannot fail to recall his curved and diminutive person; his often illuminated countenance; his beaming smile of love; and the perpetual energy with which he flitted from one object of attention to another, like the bee gathering honey from every flower. I well remember that as he walked about the house he was generally humming the tune of a hymn or psalm, as if he could not contain his pleasurable feelings of thankfulness and devotion.

Wilberforce is now an old man — I think in his seventy-sixth year — and more than usually frail and infirm for his age. Since my first acquaintance with him, many sorrows and troubles have been his portion. His two daughters were his great delight:— the cold hand of death has smitten them both; and, in consequence of the imprudence of a near relation, he has been deprived, within the last two or three years, of by far the greater part of his property. Frequent illness has also visited him, and increasing years have occasioned some failure of his memory. Nevertheless, his eye is almost as lively as ever, his intellect lucid, and, above all, the sunshine of true religion continues to enlighten and cheer him on his way.

"What a gloomy, what a November evening prospect," said he to me in a letter describing the death of his elder daughter, "would now lie before me, were it not for the flood of light and of love which flows from the throne of God and of the Lamb!" This *flood of light and love* has been his chief delight since his twenty-second year, when an apparently accidental perusal of the New Testament, with a fellow traveller through France, was blessed as the means of his conversion; and now that his infirmities are gathered upon him, he has the same comfort, the same joy.

I called upon him the day before yesterday, on my way from Bristol to this place. I was introduced to an apartment up-stairs, where I found my beloved aged friend reclining on a sofa, with his feet wrapped in flannel, and his countenance bespeaking increased age, as well as much delicacy. He received me with warm affection, and seemed delighted by the unexpected sight of an old friend. I had scarcely taken my seat beside him before I felt that constraining influence of divine love, which seemed to draw us in secret towards the Lord under a canopy of silence; and I could not do otherwise than freely speak to him of the good and glorious things which, as I believe, assuredly await him in the kingdom of rest and peace. It seemed given me to remind him of the declaration of the Psalmist, "Although ye have lien among the pots, yet shall ye be as the wings of a dove covered with silver, and her feathers with yellow gold." The ministry flowed towards him in a stream which I dared not attempt to stay; and his countenance, in the meantime, was expressive of profound devotion and holy joy. Soon afterwards, he unfolded his own experience to me in an interesting manner. He told me that the text on which he was then most prone to dwell, and from which he was permitted to derive peculiar comfort, was a passage in Paul's Epistle to the Philippians: "Be careful for nothing; but in every thing by prayer and supplication, with thanksgiving, let your requests be made known unto God; and the peace of God, which passeth all understanding, shall keep your hearts and minds through Christ Jesus." Now that frail nature shakes, and the mortal tabernacle seems ready to be dissolved, this "*peace of God*" appears to be his blessed and abundant portion.

Wilberforce is a man of a polished and cultivated understanding; but he well knows that this jewel of divine peace transcends in value all merely intellectual riches; and that the human mind, in its own strength, (notwithstanding its vast resources,) is utterly unable even to comprehend it. It is the gift of God by his own Holy Spirit, and it stays the soul in deep and hidden reliance on him from whom it comes. The mention of this text immediately called forth one of his bright ideas, and led him to display, as in days of old, his natural versatility of mind. "How admirable," said he, "are the harmony and variety of St. Paul's smaller epistles! You might have given an argument upon it in your little work upon Evidence. The Epistle to the Galatians is a display of doctrine; that to the Colossians is a union of doctrine and precept, showing their mutual connexion and dependence; that to the Ephesians is *seraphic;* that to the Philippians is all LOVE. With regard to myself," he added with tears in his eyes, "I have nothing whatsoever to urge, but the poor publican's plea, God be merciful to me a sinner."

I well remember his own definition of mercy, "kindness to the criminal who deserves punishment." Ah, my dear children, if Wilberforce, who has been labouring for these fifty years, in the cause of virtue, religion, and humanity, can feel himself to be a poor criminal, with no hope of happiness but through the pardoning mercy of God in Christ Jesus, surely we ought all to be bowed down and broken under similar feelings! Such an example may solemnly remind us of the Apostle's question—"If the righteous scarcely be saved, where shall the ungodly and the sinner appear?"

Before we separated, he adverted to the loss of his fortune. "I am afraid of telling you what I feel about it," said he, "lest it should appear like affectation; but rest assured, that the event has given me no uneasiness—none whatsoever. In fact, it has only increased my happiness. I have, in consequence, been spending the whole winter with my son; the joyful witness of his gospel labours." In short, the world is under his feet, grace triumphs, and the Saviour whom he loves reigns over all, for this faithful believing servant. The covenant of his God with him is "ordered in all things and sure." Thus are we taught again and again, that "THIS is the victory which overcometh the world, even our FAITH." "Who is he that overcometh the world, but he that believeth that Jesus is the Son of God?"

And now, my dear children, store up these examples in your hearts, and keep this little memorial by you, for your father's sake, to remind you in days to come of that which he feels to be precious above all things—the redeeming love of God in Christ Jesus.

It would be easy to add to these instances of the happy work of true religion. What can account for this uniformity of Christian experience? *Truth, and truth alone.* May it be yours to know and to love "the truth as it is in Jesus;" and may it make us all free, entirely free from the bondage of this corrupt and evil world.

Now, therefore, "unto him who is able to keep you from falling, and to present you faultless before the presence of his glory with exceeding joy, to the only wise God our Saviour, be glory and majesty, dominion and power, both now and ever. Amen."

CHAPTER XXV.

ÆT. 45—46. 1833.

VISIT OF DR. CHALMERS AT EARLHAM; CONVERSATIONS WITH HIM; EXTRACTS FROM JOURNAL; FURTHER LABOURS IN THE NEIGHBOURHOOD OF LONDON; LETTERS; SERMON AT DEVONSHIRE HOUSE.

JOSEPH JOHN GURNEY'S labours in London and its neighbourhood, the commencement of which is noticed in the last chapter, were proceeded in very gradually. "I always believed," he writes to a friend, "and said when I asked for my certificate, that [the service] would come to me by degrees."

During a short recess at home after his return from Melksham, he enjoyed a visit from his friend, Dr. Chalmers, who had been spending a few weeks in London. In his letters to his family, Dr. Chalmers has thus recorded his impressions of Earlham and its inhabitants:—*

"*Friday*, 19*th*. Awoke after a night of delicious repose, and with the full consciousness of being embosomed in an abode of friendship and piety. Gave up the day to sauntering. A spacious and commodious house, with ample store both of bed and public rooms. My excellent friend, Mr. Bridges, left

* See Life of Dr. Chalmers, Vol. iii, pp. 398—400.

us at one o'clock; but not without leaving on my heart a profound sense of his Christian devotedness and worth. After he went out, Mrs. Francis Cunningham, the lady of one of our best English clergymen, came in, and has been an inmate during my abode at Earlham. She is sister to Mr. Gurney, and is really a very attractive person, for simplicity and Christian principle, and elegant accomplishment, and withal high intelligence and cultivation. But last of all, another lady, who dined and spent the night, now aged and in Quaker attire, which she had but recently put on, and who, in early life, was one of the most distinguished of our literary women; whose works, thirty years ago, I read with great delight; no less a person than the celebrated Mrs. Opie, authoress of the most exquisite feminine tales, for which I used to place her by the side of Miss Edgeworth. It was curious to myself that, though told by Mr. Gurney in the morning of her being to dine, I had forgot the circumstance, and the idea of the accomplished novelist and poet was never once suggested by the image of this plain-looking Quakeress, till it rushed upon me after dinner; when it suddenly and inconceivably augmented the interest I felt in her. We had much conversation, and drew greatly together; walking and talking together with each other on the beautiful lawn after dinner. She has had access into all kinds of society, and her conversation is all the more rich and interesting. * * * I felt my new acquaintance with her to be one of the great acquisitions of my present journey; and this union of rank, and opulence, and literature, and polish of mind, with plainness of manners, forms one of the great charms of the society in this house."

The following are extracted from Joseph John Gurney's reminiscences of this visit.

One morning we conversed on the subject of the great minds with which he had been brought into contact. I asked him who was the most talented person with whom he had associated, especially in power of conversation. He said,

"Robert Hall was the greatest proficient he had known as a converser;" and spoke in high terms of his talents and of his preaching. "But," said he, "I think Foster is of a higher order of intellect; he fetches his thoughts from a deeper spring; he is no great talker, and writes very slowly, but he moves along in a region far above the common intellectual level. There are passages in his Essays of amazing depth and beauty, especially in that on 'Popular Ignorance.'"

We called on the venerable bishop, now in his ninetieth year, and very delightful was our interview. The dear old man was in good heart and health, reading without spectacles, hearing without the smallest difficulty, and able to talk with his old vivacity. He was evidently much animated by seeing Dr. Chalmers.

BISHOP. "Dr. Chalmers, I am very glad to be introduced to you. I have just been reading your Bridgewater Essay, with great satisfaction; and am especially pleased that you have insisted so much on the views of Bishop Butler, whom I have always reckoned to be one of the best and wisest of writers."

I remarked that it was strange that a writer of so liberal and comprehensive a cast should be accused of popery.

BISHOP. "There is no ground for it; people will always call names."

They then conversed on Dr. Adam Smith's "Theory of Moral Sentiments."

BISHOP. "I am sorry to find from your work, that his splendid passage respecting the necessity of a mediator was omitted in the second edition."

CHALMERS. "The omission was probably owing to his intimacy with Hume."

I asked the bishop whether he had not himself been acquainted with Hume.

"O yes," he replied, "I used to meet him at the old Lord Bathurst's." He then repeated to us part of the passage from Dr. Adam Smith, with peculiar accuracy and feeling, telling us that it had been fixed in his memory from his early manhood. He afterwards drew a lively picture of the talented but hot-headed Atterbury, Bishop of Rochester, who was well known to his uncle, Lord Bathurst; and of the mighty Warburton with whom he was familiarly acquainted. He described him as a giant in conversation, and a fearless champion against Hume and other infidels.

I was glad to hear Chalmers and the bishop fully according in the praise of Warburton's "Julian," which surely contains important and specific, though somewhat indirect evidence of the truth as it is in Jesus. * * * *

One morning the Doctor and I walked down to a fir grove, at the extremity of the park, where a colony of herons have lately formed a settlement. He was as much interested and pleased as a schoolboy would have been, in watching the singular appearance, gestures, and sounds of these birds. His mind seemed quite occupied by the *fitness* between the length of their necks and that of their legs, and also by the circumstance, that as they swim not, but only *stand* in the waters, they do not, like other aquatic birds, require webs to their feet, and *therefore* have none! It is remarkably the habit of Dr. C——'s mind to see and feel God in *everything;* and what can be more desirable?

We talked of a correspondence respecting the Irish Education Bill, between himself and E. G. Stanley,* chief secretary for Ireland, who had written to Dr. Chalmers inquiring his opinion of the measure.

CHALMERS. "I expressed my disapprobation of the system. I think we ought to have a 'Bible Class' in every school instituted by national authority; and that it should be left to the parents of the children to decide whether they should attend that class, or not. A Roman Catholic child might avail himself of all the other parts of instruction afforded in the school, and might, nevertheless, withdraw from the Bible Class at the bidding of his parent. According to the present system, the Bible, not the Roman Catholic, is treated as the Dissenter. It is not that the Roman Catholic withdraws

* Now the Earl of Derby.

because he does not like the Bible; it is that the Bible withdraws because the Roman Catholic does not like *it*.

I observed, that the use of extracts from Scripture in schools appeared to me to be unobjectionable.

CHALMERS. "Very true: but in this case there is an objectionable principle—it is the omission of parts of Scripture *on the ground* that a certain class of men object to their being read."

I must confess that these remarks have considerable weight; and, considered in connexion with the eagerness displayed by the Roman Catholics in the adoption of the plan, have a good deal shaken my confidence in its advantages. * * *

We were talking of Fuller, the quaint historian of the Church of England. I remarked that he was fond of a dash of humor. "Yes," said Chalmers, "his book is dashed all over with it. Even so grave a subject as the death of a Bishop he cannot treat without humor."

One evening we were speaking of a certain class of persons who united to a great apparent gentleness and pliability, a peculiarly effective resistance to all reform in church or state.

FRANCIS CUNNINGHAM. "I have heard Wilberforce compare men of this description to sacks of wool lying before artillery; yielding, to all appearance, to the impulse of the cannon balls, yet effectually stopping their progress."

CHALMERS. "The great fear I entertain respecting the operation of the reform bill is, lest it should throw the legislative power into the hands of men of business, already full of all kinds of occupation,—to the exclusion of men who have *leisure* for deep study and reflection, and are therefore able to cope with great principles, on the various subjects of legislation. There is a fine passage in Ecclesiasticus, on the danger of entrusting with the arcana of government, men whose hearts and hands are full of the common business of life. * I wish we were more alive to the principles which are there unfolded. It is an alarming fact, that in order to effect a paltry saving of two or three thousand pounds per annum,

* See Ecclesiasticus, chap. xxxviii.

that great work, the trigonometrical survey of Great Britain, was on the point of being left incomplete. It was saved by a majority of only two votes, in a Committee of the House of Commons."

* * * * * *

Fifth day morning, [*7th mo., 25th.*] Dr. Chalmers left us yesterday morning. We parted with him the preceding night, after a time of Scripture reading, silent waiting, and prayer, in which I had fervently to commend him and his family to the grace of God. His visit has been memorable indeed.

FROM DR. CHALMERS.

Edinburgh, August 29th, 1833.

I arrived at home only yesterday, and this is the reason why you have been so long without hearing from me. I waited till I could apprise you of my safe arrival, and of the delivery of your kind letter and present to my children. They read it with the deepest interest; and I can assure you that they have all been inspired by you with the greatest desire to visit Earlham. Nothing could exceed the enjoyment I had under your roof; and if my own happiness was the only element included in the deliberation, I should not be long in re-appearing in the midst of you. * * *

I shall never forget your great kindness to me, so much beyond my deserts, and my powers of requital, in any way. Earlham holds out many temptations, but the most powerful of them all is, that the companionships there, are those that I most love; all its accompaniments, and chief of all, its society, are precious to me. May heaven's best blessings rest upon you and yours!

The quotation you refer to is from Cicero, though at present I am unable to state from what part of his writings.

8th mo., 2nd. My birthday; forty-five years completed in this mutable scene. Alas! what inexpressible and multiplied cause have I for humilitation! But when I call to mind the sparing mercy of my God, have I not equal cause for thankfulness?

3rd. This morning, in all probability, have the remains of my beloved friend William Wilberforce, been followed to their last home, in Westminster Abbey, by a large number of peers and commoners; a pomp which can have been nothing to him; but we may value a tribute paid to virtue, humanity, and religion.

First day. I woke very low this morning, but am not without a hope that the glorious "Master of Assemblies" will condescend to bless this Sabbath day to many souls. Oh that his church may be preserved in life, in love, and in oneness; and that more of his "anointing," which alone fully leads into these things, may be experienced by all who love his name.

8th mo., 20th. I returned home yesterday evening, after a week of mournful, yet peaceful interest. My dear wife and I left home on second day. On reaching London, the next afternoon, we received very alarming tidings of our dear mother, so that we thought it best to travel through most of the night, and we arrived at Melksham to breakfast on fourth day morning. We found her much reduced, but not dying. Her mind is bright and serene as ever, and she can assure us, with all confidence, that she has not followed "cunningly devised fables," in embracing for herself, and in making known to others, the power and coming of our Lord Jesus Christ. I took leave of her on sixth day night. It was difficult to tear myself from them, and my journey to London was rather mournful.

On arriving in London it was a great delight to meet Fowell and Hannah; the former greatly relieved by the happy termination of the Slave Question in Parliament. They went with me to Stoke Newington meeting; to which I had felt a particular pointing. It was a large meeting, chiefly of the young, and very solemn. I had to speak on the Lord's method of teaching his people, and boldly to uphold what I believe to be the genuine principles of Friends.

[*Earlham.*] *8th mo., 25th.* On fourth day arrived the bishop of Winchester, with his wife and four children; and our brother and sister Francis and Richenda Cunningham. C. Wodehouse and E. Edwards were with us at dinner. We passed a very pleasant afternoon, and I read the "Sketch of Wilberforce" to them in the evening. The bishop's courteous and gentle manner, and evident sweetness of mind, are very endearing. On sixth day morning he read to us, 1 John v, evidently under great and tender feeling. I took a private walk with him before we parted, and enjoyed the sweet savour of his Christian mind, converse, and demeanor.

9th mo., 12th. The [past] fortnight has been a memorable time to me. It was, I believe, well that I followed the secret impression of duty in leaving home, although at the time, it seemed rather contrary to evidence. In consequence, I had the satisfaction of attending my dear mother's dying bed, and of being with my beloved wife at a time of such deep and critical interest to her; a debt which I did, indeed, owe to so tender and devoted a companion. I arrived at Melksham on third day evening, and found my mother sinking into the arms of death; but she knew me, and seemed pleased with my coming. I do not think our beloved sufferer was devoid of consciousness; but the tabernacle was in too low and shattered a state to allow of her making that consciousness much known to those around her. This state of things, when almost nothing but the suffering, sinking body meets our perception, is affecting, and in some degree trying to the faith; but certainly there is no good reason why it should, in the smallest degree, affect our assurance of the immortality of the soul. This truth is no more disproved by half death, than by whole death: in fact, the life of the soul, and the dying and death of the body, are independent of each other. On one occasion she woke up in rather an extraordinary manner; and, in the recollection of a letter received about a fortnight before, gave us clearly to understand her wish, that money should be sent to the pious captain of a certain steam packet for the distribution of Bibles on the north coast of France. These were almost her last intelligible words. The funeral took place on the following fourth day morning; many Friends attended, and it was a peaceful and edifying occasion.

[*Earlham*,] *9th mo.*, *29th*. *First day night*. At meeting this afternoon, (after an interesting visit to the Bethel, and reading in three wards,) I was much engaged in ministry. "Faith is the substance of things hoped for, the evidence of things not seen." I afterwards rode round by the corner of Heigham Falgate, where I stopped my horse, and was soon surrounded by a congregation, to whom I preached for about a quarter of an hour.

Fourth day morning, [*10th mo.*, *30th*.] Yesterday morning we received the affecting tidings of the death of our beloved nephew, S. Hoare,* after about three months, illness; a rapid decline. He has long been conspicuously ranged on the Lord's side, and appears to have been wonderfully favoured with his sustaining power, both in illness and death. His last words were, "Lord, I am thine."

In the prospect of resuming, for a short time, his religious labours in London, Joseph John Gurney writes:—

11th mo., *20th*. I look to it with a degree of awe, knowing my unfitness. For about two weeks longer, I expect to be employed at home, chiefly on the revisal of my work on our Distinguishing Views. Thus Friends' principles are a good deal brought before me, and have not been weakened in my mind by further research and thought. I feel a sincere and earnest desire, that the "wisdom from above, without partiality," may be given to me, that all fear of man may be removed, and that wholesome, sound truth, may ever be upheld by me, in its purity and strength.

12th mo., *27th*. The annals of the three weeks, during which I have been absent from home, I know not how to

*The eldest son of the late Samuel and Louisa Hoare, of Hampstead.

enter into. Lynn Monthly Meeting; my dear sister Fry and Jonathan Hutchinson there. Journey to London. Call on Charles Simeon by the way. The religious visits at Stoke Newington gently continued during two weeks. Some of them close and searching, and many very comforting; much of the baptism of tears. The meetings on the three first days were of a very serious complexion. On the last of the three, we were much favoured; a blessed day we had, through the mercy of our God and Saviour.

During the preceding week, I held three young people's meetings; [the subjects before me being] the Evidences of Christianity, the Atonement and Divinity of Christ, the Doctrine of the Holy Spirit, and Friends' principles. These meetings made their way through unusually deep exercise of mind. The last was remarkably relieving. A display of this part of the great system was, as I have much reason to believe, required by the doubting, cavilling state of many minds. O that all may settle into truth and peace!

The Quarterly Meeting for London and Middlesex on second and third days, was a very favoured time. I spent the afternoon and evening of second day, with Elisha Bates, at Bromley; and enjoyed a *tête a tête* with this extraordinary man. May he be graciously, and in all respects, preserved!

I felt constrained in the men's meeting on third day, to give notice for a meeting, the next morning, of the Friends of the Quarterly Meeting. Deep was the conflict which I went through previously. I felt the ground difficult to tread on, and the responsibility great, but we were favoured with a noble meeting for which I felt very thankful. * * *

"The dangers of one-sidedness in religion," he writes to Jonathan Hutchinson, a few days afterwards, "and the essential importance of embracing and holding fast the whole truth, were points which, with some others, arose in array before me. When this mountain was passed over, I found the tie which bound me to London, cut, as it were, in a moment—I mean for the present—and I gladly hastened home by mail that evening.

I believe there is a fine work of grace going on amongst many of our younger friends. Oh that they may be kept *watchful, humble, impartial, obedient!* Each of these epithets has a meaning of much importance.

TO ———

Norwich, 12th mo., 28th, 1833.

MY DEAR FRIEND,

I am best satisfied to express the love and interest I feel for thee under thy present circumstances;—new and surprising to me, I may truly call them. I can easily understand how persons who have been educated in our Society, but who have never been properly instructed in the true nature and scriptural grounds of our religious principles, sometimes find a place which they apprehend to suit them better, in other departments of the church; but that those who have undergone the process of *convincement* (which I had before suppposed to have been thy case,) should turn their backs upon us, is, in my view, much more remarkable.

Thou knowest, my dear friend, that words have a variety of bearings; and that if we use the same phrases in different meanings, we are not likely to understand each other.

The doctrine of "universal and saving light" I apprehend to be identical with that which the Wesleyans call the doctrine of "universal grace." It is simply that the moral law of God is written by his Spirit, (through the mediation of Jesus Christ,) on the hearts of all men; and that every man, born into the world, has his day of visitation. This doctrine is held not merely by Friends, but by a large proportion of other Christians, especially the Methodists, of which thou wilt find ample proof in the first vol. of Dr. Adam Clarke's life. The late William Wilberforce decidedly embraced it. He twice told me that he fully believed "that an effective offer of salvation is made to every man born into the world." How could such an offer be made but by the Holy Spirit. The poet Cowper has an admirable passage on the subject, I think in his Truth.

"Let heathen worthies, whose exalted mind
Left sensuality and dross behind,
Possess for me, their undisputed lot,
And take, unenvied, the reward they sought.
But still, in virtue of a Saviour's plea,
Not blind by choice, but destined not to see,
Their fortitude and wisdom were a flame
Celestial, though they knew not whence it came;
Derived from the same source of light and grace
That guides the Christian in his swifter race.
* * * * * *
But let not him that shares a *brighter day*,
Traduce the splendour of a noontide ray,
Prefer the twilight of a darker time,
And deem his base stupidity no crime."

These are my sentiments, and they have always been those of our Society. Had we been half an hour together, I think I could show thee clear proof of them in the Scriptures. By that test, like all other doctrines, they must stand or fall.

To speculate on the eternal prospects of the heathen, I do not apprehend to be our business. We may rest assured that God will deal with all the rational workmanship of his hands, after a law of perfect equity. The only duty which we have to look to in reference to them, is to promote, by every means in our power, the diffusion of gospel light amongst them. There cannot be a moment's question that it is our plain duty to communicate to them the superior blessings which we enjoy ourselves. No persons were clearer on this point than some of the early Friends, especially George Fox. Hast thou really ever given an attentive perusal to his deeply interesting journal?*

From what I have now said, thou canst not fail to perceive in what sense Friends, (as well as others,) deem the work of the Spirit to be "independent of the Holy Scriptures." Thou wilt surely not venture to deny that the Spirit graciously acted on the hearts of men, long before the

* See also George Fox's Epistles, pp. 205—208, 257, &c. of the Second Edition of Samuel Tuke's Selection.

Scriptures existed, and that, had it not been for the "independent" operation of the Spirit, the Scriptures themselves could never have been a divinely authorized record. But, my dear friend, with us, the work of the Spirit, and the precious gift of the Holy Scriptures are in close connexion. Friends have always asserted just as strongly as other Christians, (and I apprehend more frequently,) that it is our bounden duty, diligently to read the Holy Scriptures, and that it is in the use and not in the disuse of them, that we are to expect the guidance and government of the Holy Spirit. Canst thou point out any one doctrine in Scripture more plainly or emphatically stated than that the Spirit is bestowed on those who truly believe in Jesus, as a Cleanser, as a Governor, and as a Guide into all truth; that they need not that any *man* teach them; but that "the anointing" will teach them all things, and is truth and no lie; that the Spirit will take of the things of Christ, and show them to our souls?

Woe will be to those, whether Friends or others, who let down this Christian doctrine; who refuse obedience to that Holy, inward Teacher, who guides the children of God, by that safe and narrow way which alone leads to life everlasting. I own I feel an extreme fear lest an unwillingness to take up our cross and follow Jesus, should be at the bottom of the objections which some make to the testimonies of Friends. I do not say it is thy case. I hope not; but thou canst not too closely scrutinize thy motives, or too fervently and honestly ask counsel of God.

Is it possible that thou canst seriously imagine that Friends, in pleading for their peculiar testimonies, make their appeals to the inward Guide alone, exclusively of the Scriptures? Such seems to me to be the import of thy letter. Such an appeal would be utterly at variance with their genuine principles. We assert that our testimonies respecting baptism, the supper, silent worship, women's ministry, &c., are not founded on any mere impressions made on our own minds, but *on plain and simple Scripture.* Thou mayest, perhaps, differ from us in opinion, but it is surely a mistake on thy part, to ascribe an origin to those testimonies, which we ourselves entirely disavow, and which our forefathers as distinctly disavowed before us. The early Friends were always ready to accept the Holy Scriptures as the only proper test, by which all their doctrines and opinions were to be tried. Every dogma, however specious, which goes *beyond* Scripture, or *takes away* from, or (above all) *contradicts* Scripture, they always professed their willingness to reject as a mere delusion; and we make the same profession now.

I have not time to go into the particulars alluded to by thee; but never did I more clearly see that our *true* views, (not the exaggerated ones falsely imputed to us,) on these several subjects are absolutely and entirely scriptural. As such, and as such only, I hold them as a part of that superstructure which the Lord himself would have us to build on the glorious, broad foundation of Jesus Christ and him crucified.

From what I have now stated, thou wilt understand the sense in which alone we declare the Spirit to be "superior to the Scriptures." Who will deny that the fountain is superior to the stream? And the omnipotent, all-wise producer to that which he is pleased to produce? But supposing a person to say, "I have such and such impressions which I take to be from the Spirit of the Lord," and suppose that the Scriptures should contradict these impressions, dost thou really suppose that any true and sound Quaker would take the impression so made on his mind as a guide of superior authority to the Holy Scriptures? If such be thy idea of our principles, I must say that it is utterly false and unfounded. Certainly we should still hold the Holy Spirit to be superior to his own written word; but we regard the Scriptures as an infallible standard, and the contradiction in question would afford us an unanswerable evidence that the impressions so made on the mind were not from the Spirit, but were a mere delusion of human imagination. * * * *

Frequent as are the notices of Joseph John Gurney's ministerial labours contained in the extracts from his Journal, they are not of a nature to enable the reader to form a correct idea of the general tone and character of his preaching. A lengthened extract from notes, soon afterwards published,* of a sermon which he preached at the Quarterly Meeting of Friends of London and Middlesex, in the spring of this year, will convey a more distinct and lively impression of his ministry than any laboured description. This extract may properly close the present chapter. It should be borne in mind by those who are but little acquainted with the usages of Friends, that what is spoken on such an occasion is not the result of previous preparation. The whole assembly sits down in silence. There is no preconcerted appointment or arrangement as to the services in the ministry. Indeed it is not known whether any such services may be called for, or offered. Each waits in silence, and they who desire to be true worshippers, seek to have their hearts turned to the Lord. According to the belief of Friends, Christ is the "one Mediator," and none other is needed either to lead the worship, or to present the prayers of the people unto God. In their persuasion the true worship of him who "searcheth the heart" is not confined to that which is seen or heard. It may be without words as well as with them. And if words are spoken, it should be under a deep

*It should be stated that these notes were taken down and published altogether without Joseph John Gurney's knowledge or permission. The excellence of the matter contained in them, has prevailed over the hesitation felt by the Editor as to their insertion. He would much regret appearing to give a general sanction to the practice of taking down such communications. See note by the late John Barclay, in the note at p. 275 of his Memoirs of William Dewsbury.

sense of individual duty; and of a call and qualification renewed for the occasion.

After referring to the declaration of the Apostle Paul, "As in Adam all die, even so in Christ shall all be made alive;"* Joseph John Gurney proceeded:—

I wish we were all sensible how worthy we are of death. I wish we might remember, that even when the mourners go about the streets; when we lose the joy of our hearts, and the delight of our eyes; when our own strength withers, and we descend to the chambers of darkness, that these are tokens, these are proofs, that we are a fallen sinful race. But there is a death of a deeper kind; there is a darkness more impenetrable than that of the grave; there is a destruction infinitely more formidable than that of the body; there is the death of that which in one sense can never die; the separation of the soul from the source and spring of life. And *we* are dead, my brethren, we are "by nature the children of wrath even as others." We are separated from our God, not by the sin of Adam, not by the imputation of the fault of another, but by the awful consequences of the sin of our first parent, traced, as it is, in the depravity and corruption of our nature, and finding its way into our own selves. I wish we were more alive to this truth; for many of us conduct ourselves very differently from condemned criminals, dependent on the pure mercy of our Sovereign Lord God. And what is mercy, my dear brethren? There are those who have very meagre apprehensions of the meaning of this word. They mistake it for kindness and love in a general point of view. But mercy is the love which acquits the *criminal;* mercy is the love which obliterates all our transgressions, through the blood of the everlasting covenant; mercy is the love which delivers us from the bitter pains of eternal death, and bestows upon us, in great loving-kindness, the glorious gift of everlasting life.

* 1 Cor. xv. 22.

Where then is our humiliation before the Lord? Where are our mouths in the dust? Where is our contrition? Where is the breaking to pieces of the rock work of our hearts? I believe that we stand in peculiar need of coming under the immediate influence of that Word from heaven which is "quick and powerful, sharper than any two-edged sword, and piercing asunder;" for there are many among us who are taking up a false rest; moving on the surface of things; well satisfied with the system in which they have been educated; and all the while, while they are making a pretty good profession, they are slumbering the slumbers of death, they are sleeping the sleep of the grave. Alas for such a condition! "I know thy works, that thou hast a name that thou livest, and art dead. Be watchful, and strengthen the things which remain that are ready to die; for I have not found thy works perfect before God." *

Beloved young friends, ye who have been favoured with a guarded and religious education; ye who have some fleeting desires in your minds after holiness and heaven, do not deceive yourselves, I beseech you. Whilst you continue in your unregenerate nature you are "dead in trespasses and sins;" you are, with all your amiability, and all your steadiness, "the children of wrath even as others." I dare not flatter you. I love you too dearly. I long, I pray for your salvation. I want you to be humbled, broken to pieces, brought into the valley of tears, made sensible of your loss; of your liability to ruin by nature; of your sinfulness; of your death. Let no one suppose that we would depreciate a guarded education, a moral or steady life. Oh! no, we can rejoice in your moral, and amiable, and steady conversation. We believe that you have often been visited by "the dayspring from on high;" we believe that the Lord is at work in your hearts; but you are not regenerate; you cannot be born again until you make the unconditional surrender. It is no time for any of you to delay and trifle with eternal things; much less to play with edged tools; or to throw yourselves in

* Rev. iii. 1, 2.

the way of temptation. Now is your time to become decided in your religious course; now is your time to give up all for Christ; now is your time to surrender without conditions, that the Lord may make of you what he pleases, that you may be born again of the Spirit, and live everlastingly.

There are more than a few, I greatly fear, even in this assembly, who have followed the devices and desires of their own hearts, until they have become the very slaves of Satan; and how have they fallen? O the deep instructiveness of their history. First they have given way in some very little things; they have grieved the unflattering witness for the truth in their own bosoms, respecting some of those things which the world calls matters of indifference; and thus a small aperture has been made in the wall round about them, and the enemy has made it by degrees larger and larger. First there was room for "the little foxes" just to pass through the aperture and "spoil the tender grapes,"* and now there is room for the ravenous, and deadly, and noisome beasts of the forest to pass and repass just as they please.

And there are sins of the intellect which have done desperate mischief within our borders. We do not distinguish things aright, we misapply our powers, we are ever prone, under the influence of the corruption of our hearts, to call good evil; and evil good; to put sweet for bitter, and bitter for sweet. Let not my beloved young friends suppose for a moment that some of us who are anxious for their welfare would discourage them in their intellectual pursuits. Oh! no. We delight in their forming a refined and virtuous taste; we rejoice in their zeal for the acquirement of useful knowledge; we know the plain principle of our holy religion, that it is our bounden duty to make the very best of all our powers for the glory of God, and for the welfare of man; and woe unto those who, under the false pretence of their inability, are wrapping their talent in a napkin, and burying it in the earth. But are there not those who think that they can obtain

* Solomon's Song, ii, 15.

divine knowledge by the mere application of their natural powers? are there not those who are prone to make themselves wise above that which is written, and to build systems of their own contrivance, like those builders in days of old, hoping to scale the heavens by the strength of their own wisdom?—and it will end in their eternal confusion. Yes, my dear friends, the intellect and reason of man have their proper province, even in religion; let us never depreciate their value. It is our duty to bring them to bear, and for the highest of purposes. Would to God that the patient, deliberate, pious, and careful examination of the holy Scriptures more abounded among us; that we might be more like those noble Bereans, who searched the Scriptures, that they might know whether these things are so, yea or nay. And let me tell my dear young friends, that, whether we plead for the great fundamental doctrines of the Gospel, or for those Christian testimonies which we believe to rest upon them, we are bold, as our forefathers were before us, to make our honest appeal to the inspired records, and we are willing that our sentiments and our practice should stand or fall by this test. But, beloved friends, when we bring our natural powers into their right office, in daily reading and meditating on Holy Writ, are we to forget, shall we for a moment forget, that the very ground, and spring, and root of the authority of Scripture is immediately from revelation? Shall we for a moment forget, that it is "the Lion of the tribe of Judah," who alone holds "the key of David," and "openeth and no man shutteth, and shutteth and no man openeth?" Ah! my friends, let us endeavour to gather our minds into deep dependence on the power of a risen Saviour, and on the guidance of his Holy Spirit; that the Spirit of truth himself may take of the things of Christ, and open them to our understandings, and apply them to our hearts. There is the animal faculty and there is the rational faculty in man, and woe unto those in whom the animal faculty rebels even against the plainest dictates of common reason; and, above the rational faculty, there is the light of heaven, and woe unto those in whom the rational faculty is not subject to the light of heaven; light, and life, my dear brethren, going hand in hand, and being inseparable companions.

"In Him,"—in Jesus, in our Saviour,—"was light, and the light was the life of men." I have feared that there are some among us, who would not only discard what may be called the outside of our system, but that which belongs to the very root and ground of our religious profession—immediate revelation. And I am bold to assert that mankind would for ever have groped in the darkness of the chambers of death, had it not been for immediate revelation. What! friends, shall we, a poor, corrupt, sinful people; shall we think lightly of the gospel of Christ? shall we clip it; shall we narrow it by any system of our own; shall we circumscribe God's glorious plan of redemption? Oh! no, friends, let us have the gospel in its length, and breadth, and height, and depth, in all its fulness, as that light from heaven which will manifest to us our own darkness, and our own sinfulness. Then we shall see the perfect fitness of the Saviour to the sinner; and "as in Adam all died, so in Christ shall all be made alive."

There is but one way for any of us to experience "the redemption [even] the forgiveness of sins," and that is through the atoning blood of our Lord Jesus Christ, who is "the propitiation for our sins, and not for ours only but also for the sins of the whole world." Now the word "propitiation" is synonymous, in the common acceptation of it, with the word "atonement;" and those who are accustomed to the reading of the original text, are well aware that what is called the doctrine of the atonement is plainly stated in Scripture, in terms that cannot be mistaken, under the word "propitiation." Yes, friends, he came from heaven in his infinite mercy and humbled himself, and became obedient unto death, and bore the burden of all our sins; and, by this most important of all facts, God has displayed for our instruction his own immutable holiness, and his boundless mercy, to a lost and sinful world. And I beseech you, for ever to discard all dependence on your own works as the ground of the favour of God; even your best works, even those which you may humbly hope you perform under the influence of his good Spirit. Do not mistake the superstructure for the foundation—"other foundation can no man lay than that is laid, which is Christ Jesus." The veil is rent for you; God hath consecrated for you a new and living way through the veil; that is to say through the flesh of Jesus Christ, which was broken for you on the cross; and I beseech you not to attempt to enter into the pastures of life by any other way. Believe in the Lord Jesus; humble yourselves at his feet; wash your garments by faith in his blood; it is the ground of your acceptance, the foundation of your hope, the rock on which your peace is built for ever.

Remember how it was with our honorable elder, George Fox, when he was brought under sore conflicts; when he was laid low as a young man before the Lord. Would to God that many of our young men could be brought into this condition! They could be if they would. Would that we might see that day! Would that we might be delivered from our superficial walk. Would that we might be baptized; that the Lord's hand might be laid with power on our vanity, our folly, and our pride! I believe that if we were better acquainted with the experience of our forefathers in the truth, we should have a greater value for those testimonies which they were led to bear, in the sight of the world, to the perfect spirituality of the gospel. And how was it with this young man, after he had been baptized with the baptism of suffering in so remarkable a manner? He became instructed in the lessons of heavenly wisdom; and there was no lesson so near his heart at that time, as the lesson of the exceeding preciousness of the atoning blood of Jesus; so that when the priest of the parish inquired of him what was the meaning of our Lord's suffering and agony in the garden of Gethsemane, and of his words on the cross—"My God, my God, why hast thou forsaken me," he plainly answered "that the Saviour of men was then bearing on himself the weight of the sins of all mankind." * Let none then pretend to say that this honored elder was not deeply sensible of the practical

* See George Fox's Journal, under the year 1645.

bearing of the Christian doctrine of the atonement. Now it is on the heart that these things are intended to bear: it is on the heart that the blood of Christ must be sprinkled; we must be filled with the Saviour's love. I call upon you, my beloved brethren and sisters, for the surrender of your hearts, to that Lord, who, in his infinite compassion has bought you with his blood; and you will soon understand that the sacrifice of our Lord Jesus Christ without the gates of Jerusalem, is no matter of cold speculation, no matter of religious theory alone, but that it is, of all things, the most practical and the most influential on the heart of fallen, wandering, and benighted man. And how are you to prove your love? How are you to develope your gratitude? What is to be the fruit? O friends, here comes the part from which human nature shrinks. We know who could say in the days of old, "I am crucified with Christ." Are you crucified with Christ? There is the vital question. Are you made comformable to his death? Do you follow him to Calvary's mount? Are you willing that your pride and your vanity, and your systems, should be slain on his cross? Will you be buried with him in baptism? Will you go down with him into the depths of the grave. O the depth, my friends, of true Christian experience!

And some of you who have thrown off the restraints of your youth, let a plain man ask you a plain question: Was it the love of a Saviour that constrained you to choose that course? Or was it the delusion of the world? Was it the unmortified pride of your own hearts? Was it your conformity to the god of this world, who would lead you first one little step in the downward path, and then another—and then another—and then another—and then another, and you go down—and down—and down, till nothing can arrest your progress. I trust there are many of you who will be arrested in your progress towards the world. I do not desire to speak hardly of any one. There are varieties in our circumstances and in our conditions, great varieties; and God looketh not at the outward appearance, he searcheth the heart. But I am bold to express my conviction that as a religious Society we shall never gain strength by turning our back on our Christian testimonies. I long that all these may be borne in the light of truth; not in dry morality, not in hypocritical profession, but under the influence of the love of Christ. I believe pure truth is diffusing itself in the world, and oh that we may not be left in the rear. I wish I could convey to my younger brethren and sisters the deep settled conviction of my spirit, that though we be a poor, scattered people in the estimation of some, they never will gain anything by seeking out another way for themselves. No, friends, let us have the glorious gospel in our borders; let us cherish it; let us give it room to circulate; let it have its free course; let the truth, the very truth, the whole truth "as it is in Jesus," circulate among us and reign over all.

And, my beloved friends, one thing more before I venture to take my seat. We know that immediate revelation is the very root and ground of the Scriptures themselves. It is the preparatory work also of the Holy Spirit which can alone bring us to Christ. All other ways, however they may appear in the sight of human wisdom, must end in confusion. But, friends, when we are thus brought to Christ, does the Spirit cease from his office? Does he suspend his holy teaching? Does he then fail to guide the Lord's children? Is there an end of his work? Is this Christianity? Is it not the very compact of the new covenant, and the peculiar privilege of all true believers that the law of their God is "written on their hearts," and "put into their inward parts," and that they need not say every man to his neighbour, Know the Lord? O, my dear friends, my soul is exercised on your account. "I am tired," says one of my younger brethren, "I am wearied of these prolonged silences. I go from meeting to meeting; I repeat my attendance three times a week; I scarcely hear a word, I want to have a little more teaching, I long for a little more ministry." And I hope the day is coming, friends, if you will have patience, when there will be more of a truly anointed ministry amongst us, and I shall hail that day. It was so in the early days of our Society, and I believe it will be so again. But, my dear young friends, forget not the peculiar privilege of true Christians, "All thy children shall be taught of the Lord, and great shall be the peace of thy children." There was the promise of the old covenant, and there is the promise of the new covenant; the promise of the old covenant was Christ, and the promise of the new covenant is the Spirit. It is specifically declared to be the Father's promise in the new covenant; and Christ hath promised that he will send the Comforter to us, even the Spirit of truth, who shall bring to our remembrance whatsoever he hath said unto us, and guide us into all truth. Do you believe it, friends? yea or nay. It was the profession of our ancestors, and God forbid that it should ever cease from being our profession. We shall never prosper if we go seeking after words. We shall never prosper if we place our dependence on anything less perfect than the Lord's own anointing. I deeply feel the importance of the subject. I am not one of those, you will believe me, my dear friends, who think lightly of the gospel labours of such as are not of our religious denomination. I believe that they have often flowed from a right zeal, and are often blessed with fruit by the giver of all grace; but of one thing I am well persuaded, that our security and prosperity as a religious body, is intimately and inseparably connected with our maintaining our own place in the universal church of Christ; not in the form, not in the system, not in the prejudices of man, not in the bitterness and narrowness of mere sectarian views; but in the light of immortal truth, in the beauty and strength of primitive Christianity, in the spirituality of the gospel of Christ, the old, the unchanging path.

O my beloved friends, I hope you will bear with a poor unworthy brother, as I feel constrained to say, in the first place, that I never felt my spirit more entirely bound to the whole of the glorious gospel of our Saviour, and the doctrine of a crucified Immanuel, than I do at this moment; and on the other hand, I never have been more constrained in my spirit to confess that I am a Quaker. I would not lightly use the words, but I do believe it is my bounden duty to maintain our profession inviolate. I wish I could do it better; I know my own weakness; but I beseech you, as you value your immortal souls, and your standing as a religious body, make free room for the gospel to circulate—let us have it without clipping, without constraint, without restriction; in its fulness, in its unsearchable riches. Let us have the glorious ocean of light and love, overflowing the ocean of death and darkness: but let us not be beguiled by any of the temptations of the enemy, into a forsaking of our own standing, of our own duty, of our own belief. Let us "be steadfast, immoveable, always abounding in the work of the Lord, forasmuch as ye know that your labour shall not be in vain in the Lord.*

* See a little volume entitled Sermons, by Messrs. Allen, Bates, Gurney, Tuke, and other ministers of the Society of Friends. London: Hamilton, Adams and Co., 1834.

CHAPTER XXVI.

1834—1835. ÆT. 46—47.

FURTHER LABOURS IN LONDON; INTERVIEW WITH EARL GREY AND EDWARD G. STANLEY; EXTRACTS FROM LETTERS AND JOURNAL; VISIT TO ACKWORTH; ESSAY ON LOVE TO GOD; CONCLUSION OF LABOURS IN LONDON; DEATH OF JONATHAN HUTCHINSON.

After a short interval at home, at the beginning of the year 1834, Joseph John Gurney again returned to his labours amongst Friends in London; which were continued, with some intermission, until the sixth month. "Two things have I desired," he writes, in closing his Journal for the year 1833, "the first that I may be enabled to abstain from my own works in religion; the second, that I may be clear of the blood of all men. God alone can do the work for me."

His Journal describes, in some detail, his engagements at Tottenham, Ratcliff, and Plaistow, in the course of the second and third months. He afterwards writes:—

4th mo., 5th. I forgot to mention, in my account of my late engagements in London, an interesting interview with Lords Grey and Calthorpe, and Edward G. Stanley, on the subject of the Norwich and Norfolk labouring poor. They gave me a full opportunity of stating the case, as it relates to the evil of the popular election of our municipal officers in Norwich; and as it regards the degraded and demoralized state of the agricultural labourers. The causes stated:—beer houses, as an accelerating cause; the poor-law system, as a primary one; the want of Christian education. The remedy, in the opposites:—abolition of beer houses; permissive abolition of poor law, on Dr. Chalmers' plan; pervasive system of Christian education; commodious cottages for the poor, a preventive of immorality as well as distress; small allotments of land, a good antidote against pauperism. I spoke very plainly on the utter uselessness of teaching the poor to read and write, unless they be imbued with the principles of Christianity. The Scriptures must be the groundwork; and in this, one would hope, most denominations in this country might unite. On parting with them, I expressed my belief, that nothing but the goodness of divine Providence can save the country, especially as regards its labouring population; and my desire that he might guide their counsels. I have since received a kind letter from Lord Grey.

Whilst in London he received the following

FROM JONATHAN HUTCHINSON.

Gedney, 3rd mo., 1st, 1834.

Thou hast expressed a desire for my sympathetic remembrances in the prosecution of thy arduous engagements in London and its vicinity. These thou hast, I believe, daily. If ever my heart be enabled to ascend by living aspirations to the throne of grace, I desire to bear thee upon it; and that thy true interests of every kind may be inseparably connected with every breathing and every cry for myself and others. * *

As I often find it easier to copy than to compose, I purpose occupying a part of the present sheet by the following extract from Henry Martyn:—"It has been well observed by one,*

* Pascal.

who took a profound view of human nature, that there are three very different orbits in which great men move and shine, and that each sphere of greatness has its respective admirers. There are those who, as heroes, fill the world with their exploits; they are greeted with the acclamations of the multitude: they are ennobled whilst living, and their names descend with lustre to posterity. Others there are who, by the brilliance of their imagination, or the vigour of their intellect, attain to honour of a purer and a higher kind. The fame of these is confined to a more select number; all have not a discriminating sense of their merit. A third description there is, distinct from both the others, and far more exalted than either, whose excellence consists in a renunciation of themselves, and a compassionate love for mankind. In this order the Saviour of the world was pleased to appear, and those obtain the highest rank in it who, by his grace, are enabled most closely to follow his example."

I very much admire the correctness of these views, particularly as regards the last, which I think the climax of human excellence. In the class thus defined, I desire not only that thou, my dear friend, mayest ever be found, but that all thy labours, by word or writing, may have an uniform tendency to produce and to cherish such true disciples of Christ, of which the world has much need. And whilst it is admitted that such characters must not seek great things for themselves, and that they need not expect the distinctions of earthly grandeur or fame, either on a throne, in the academy, or in the senate; but, on the contrary, in following their despised and dishonoured Master, may occasionally have to appear as "spectacles to the world, and to angels, and to men;" still I must maintain the sublime and superior nature, both of their present reward and of their future prospects, which are no less than a foretaste of heavenly peace, even in this world, and in that which is to come, life everlasting. In endeavouring to secure these, is it not worth while to make some sacrifices, and even, if it must be so, to suffer persecution, by being accounted as "the filth of the earth, and the offscouring of all things?"

TO LORD SUFFIELD.*

Norwich, 4th mo., 10th, 1834.

MY DEAR FRIEND,

* * * I cannot express what I think of the value of those religious convictions which are hinted at in thy letter. I consider them to be beyond all price, because they are the work, not of man, but of God. I should conceive that it must have been through much mental conflict that thou hast come at them, for I have long found occasion to believe that we must be made in some measure partakers of the sufferings of Christ, before we can enjoy the privileges of true religion: "Are ye willing to drink of the cup that I drink of?" &c. The whole of Christianity seems to me to be comprehended in two things: first, the forgiveness of sin, through faith in the atoning blood of Christ; and secondly, deliverance from sin, through the power of the Holy Spirit.

That thou and I, and all that are near and dear to us, may fully experience these two things, and that we may meet in heaven at last, is the fervent prayer of thy affectionate friend,

J. J. GURNEY.

TO ANNA GURNEY AND SARAH M. BUXTON.

Earlham, 4th mo., 19th, 1834.

* * * I have been much longing to see you; but after a break of nearly four weeks, which have been, I hope, well spent at home, I am now about to return to the field of labour at Southwark. There is some cross to myself in exchanging the moral and natural sweets of Earlham for scenes so different; but I ought to consider it a high privilege to be in any measure useful in helping any poor soul on the journey towards heaven.

* See the Memoirs of Lord Suffield, by Richard Mackenzie Bacon, pp. 461—462.

6th mo., 22nd. I have but a broken account to give of the last two months. Nearly the whole of this period has been occupied by Southwark Monthly Meeting and the Yearly Meeting. Soon after entering on the work I was thrown out of a gig in Southwark; and although I received no blow except in the hand and wrist, the nerves of the head were shaken, so that I have since been a good deal troubled with uncomfortable sensations of pressure and confusion; and have been compelled to go on with my work gently, not to say rather languidly. During the six weeks so employed, I do not think I had more than 220 private sittings; four young people's meetings, all largely attended, and very favoured times especially the last, held last week, on the Doctrine of the Holy Spirit; and four public meetings at Southwark, Deptford, Wandsworth, and Peckham; the last, in Dr. Collyer's chapel, a time of eminent feeling and outpouring; of which many testimonies have since reached me.

I had gone some way towards appointing a public meeting for the handicraft workmen in Southwark, in the open air, but was prevented from confirming the appointment by the state of my head; an effort made in Exeter Hall, at the Bible meeting, having convinced me of my inability for a great exertion of voice. I afterwards looked to the Methodist chapel, but was again prevented, and am at length returned home without holding it. Perhaps the way may yet open in due season.

Twice I attended the Monthly Meeting of———, and had to speak very plainly on the true intent of our discipline. I have been sometimes tried with indications of the hand which cuts off, or repels, and by the want of a more seeking, loving, gathering spirit; yet Friends in London are placed, in these respects, under peculiar difficulties. One sixth day morning was delightfully spent at the Croydon school, in a three hours' examination of the children; many Friends present. It was greatly to our satisfaction, and very precious was the influence over us, especially in prayer, at the close; no unsuitable conclusion to our labours in those parts. The Yearly Meeting was to some Friends a time of mental distress, but all seemed to allow that the power and love of Christ were over all, still holding us together in bonds not soon broken. There certainly exist extremes of rather a painful nature, and each is haunted by an unduly coloured picture of its opposite. May nothing occur to occasion the stumbling of the young, who are, many of them, earnestly inquiring after the truth.

Writing to Jonathan Hutchinson, in allusion to a Friend lately deceased, he says, under date 7th mo., 5th:—

She dearly loved the truth, and was loved by her friends, though one of the simple, little ones. How satisfactory in the view of death is this description of the Christian character. May I live, saith my soul, to be a little child.

7th mo., 20th. Last second day I joined a large party of the friends of the London Missionary Society, [at Norwich,] after their breakfast at the Swan Inn,—probably two or three hundred present,—and spoke to them on several points which were interesting to my own mind, particularly the reign of Christ, and the desirableness of avoiding party politics.

27th, First day. We have passed a comfortable solemn day, a description particularly applicable to both our meetings, and to the reading this evening. Much remembrance of the dead, and much sweet feeling of their "living to God." My wife and I are intending to set off on our journey to Ackworth, early to-morrow morning. O gracious Lord, be pleased to be with those who go, and those who stay, preserving us from danger and temptation, keeping us always as in the hollow of thy hand! May we part, may we meet again in Thee!

Having returned from Ackworth, he writes:—

8th mo., 8th. The prayer with which the last entry concluded has been mercifully answered; as I may acknowledge with humble gratitude. The dear party whom we left behind appear to have been, in every sense of the word, preserved unhurt, and we have been truly favoured and blessed in our journey. It has indeed brought its close mental exercises with it, but every item in it has been marked with the loving-kindness of our Lord.

The first of the eighth month in this year, the day on which, by the Emancipation Act, Slavery was to cease throughout the British dominions, was made a day of innocent enjoyment at Ackworth School. Medals commemorating the event were presented to all the children, and they, on their part, joined in a subscription for the Negro Schools. In the evening coffee was provided for them in the open air, and the day closed with the reading of the 58th chapter of Isaiah, followed by an address from Joseph John Gurney, and a prayer of much feeling and solemnity from Mary Gurney.

The day was also distinguished in their family circle by the marriage of his long loved niece, Priscilla Buxton, with Andrew Johnston, of Renny Hill, then M.P. for St. Andrews.

TO HIS SISTER HANNAH BUXTON.

Ackworth, 7th mo., 31st, 1834.

My beloved Sister,

Perhaps a few lines from me of tender love and sympathy, may be as acceptable on the day after your great event as on the day itself; when a crowd of objects partly bright and partly solemn will be before thee, and sorrow and joy a little confused together. I hope that on the comparatively quiet day when this letter will reach thee, thou wilt be enjoying what I have heard called "peaceful poverty." If poverty of spirit, and a low estate of mind be thy experience, and if outwardly thou art deprived for a season of one of thy constant objects of pleasure and care, there will be, I trust, that feeling of *peace at the bottom*, on which thy soul may repose and be at rest in the Lord. "In quietness and in confidence shall be your strength."

10*th mo.*, 22*nd*. On fifth day, we, with dear Anna, went to Northrepps, where we passed some happy, highly favoured days. We have never been more united with the families of Buxton and Hoare, and the dear inmates of the cottage. The maintenance of an intimacy with Fowell has been especially delightful. He and I dined at Gunton, (Lord Suffield's,) there I slept and ministered to the large household yesterday morning, from 1 Peter ii. Much pleasant and interesting conversation with Lord Suffield.

FROM THE LATE LORD SUFFIELD.

Gunton Park, Wednesday Night.

MY DEAR FRIEND,

I cannot deny myself the pleasure of acquainting you with the excellent reception of your address yesterday morning, by my household. I need not say that *I* felt gratitude for one so applicable to each and all of us, that it would be our own faults if we were not the better for it; yet I confess I doubted how far prejudices in my family, (among those at least, in a subordinate capacity,) might operate to darken their perceptions. To my great satisfaction, (and I have taken pains to ascertain the fact,) the effect produced both upon the minds and hearts of *all* your hearers was exactly that which you would most desire. I am assured that a deep and I would hope a lasting impression was made upon the whole establishment. How thankful should you be, my dear friend, to Him who has given you such powers, with the disposition to use them in his service! I could not withhold this.

In haste, sincerely yours,

SUFFIELD.

The work to which Joseph John Gurney had been lately devoting much of his leisure, was published early in the autumn of this year, under the title of an Essay on the Habitual Exercise of Love to God, considered as a preparation for Heaven. "I hope," he writes in his Journal in allusion to it, under date 8th mo., 8th, "I feel a little warranted in the undertaking. May the 'anointing' be with me, for without it, all my thoughts and words on religion must, of necessity, be dry and unprofitable."

It was warmly received and met with a rapid sale. The first edition of 500 copies, printed "as an experiment," was taken up in about eleven days; a second and larger edition was, in like manner, soon exhausted, which was quickly followed by a third. The work has been since many times reprinted, both in England and in America; and has been translated into French, Spanish, and German. It may be, perhaps, not improperly regarded as the first, and not the least important portion of the work, the remaining part of which appeared several years later under the title of Thoughts on Habit and Discipline.

"At the earnest request," says Joseph John Gurney, "of my friend Richard Phillips, of Wandsworth,* I had for some time been devoting my leisure hours to the composition of a work on Habit and Moral Discipline: first the philosophy of the subject, next its practical application to the purposes of this life; but above all the great work of preparing for eternity. I had made considerable progress in this undertaking, when

* Richard Phillips was an acknowledged minister amongst Friends, and an early and efficient labourer in the cause of the Bible Society.

my mind was more peculiarly directed, partly by my own feelings, and partly under the same pressing influence from without, to the crowning point of the whole matter, "Love to God, considered as a preparation for heaven." Seeing no prospect of completing the whole design, I gave up my literary leisure to this specific object; and with the help of Richard Phillips, who was frequently writing to me letters full of quotations and suggestions, I produced the little volume under the above title which has since been widely circulated. "We love him because he first loved us." The composition of this work was a source of great interest and pleasure to myself, not the less so for its having cost me a great deal of thinking. I am inclined to consider it the best written of my works; though there were a few passages in the first edition which I afterwards thought it right to modify, and the third edition was considerably enlarged. The subject is infinitely important. Never have I written anything which has occasioned me so much of the feeling of the difference between what one says, and what one is."

Towards the close of the year, Joseph John Gurney was again engaged in religious labours amongst Friends, in the neighbourhood of London.

TO JONATHAN HUTCHINSON.

Earlham, 1st mo., 3rd, 1835.

My Beloved Friend,

I am very desirous of again hearing from or of thee, for it seems long since we have received any tidings of thy health or spirits. May the year 1835 be replete with rich blessings to thee, both in body and soul! "The God of hope fill thee with all joy and peace in believing, that thou mayest abound in hope through the power of the Holy Ghost!" Many, various and deep, as have been thy conflicts of mind, and painful as are the proofs yet permitted thee, that the enemy has not forgotten the art of tormenting the Lord's children, mv belief is, that, through all, thou canst acknowledge the immutable firmness of the rock underneath. That foundation will never fail thee; and all the winds shall blow, all the waves beat in vain.

The little book, which I sent thee some time since, has been well received both by Friends and others, and as it relates to divine love, a theme so sweet and dear to thee, I trust it may have afforded thee some comfort in thy quiet, secluded hours. I feel assured that thy love to him who "first loved us," burns in a flame, which, although it may not always appear bright to thyself, will never, never, be extinguished, Blessed be the name of that adorable Redeemer, whose blood alone cleanseth from all sin.

My dearest Mary and I have passed a very interesting, and, on the whole, encouraging time, since I last wrote. About five weeks were taken up by the various meetings and families of Kingston and Longford Monthly Meetings; and it was a great comfort to us to be permitted to labour together. I ventured to convene many public meetings, which cost me, as thou mayest believe, much feeling and sometimes conflict. One of them, at Uxbridge, was attended by Joseph Bonaparte, the ex-king of Spain, and brother to Napoleon; and another at Jordans, by William Penn, an amiable young man, the great grandson of our venerable Penn, who once attended that meeting, and now lies buried in the adjoining ground. It is a romantic and beautiful spot. We afterwards called on William's father, Granville Penn, of Stoke Park, a literary, invalided, old gentleman; and were much pleased with him, his house, and his family. I have since supplied his young people with a few religious books, and William promised me that he would read the No Cross, no Crown.

FROM ROBERT WALPOLE.

London, January 12th, 1835.

MY DEAR GURNEY.

I could not return you thanks before for your letter and for your kind present of your works, because I wished to read some of them attentively. I have now looked sufficiently at them to see how much there is in them, for which I ought to thank you; and mean to go through the whole with great care. The alterations in the new edition of that very sound work in defence of the Deity of Christ, (the Biblical Notes,) are considerable, and they are improvements. The subject I am well acquainted with, having formerly collected large materials for a history of Unitarianism, both ancient and modern. There are some curious passages in Eusebius, particularly in the account of Paul of Samosata. In a future letter I shall have something to say on part of your work. It is a most valuable arrangement of the critical evidence on the subject; nothing can be more unexceptionable than the controversial part of it; the whole is marked with a most candid and Christian spirit.

The Portable Evidence of Christianity, is an admirable summary of that particular evidence which is the subject of the work. The fourth and fifth sections are the parts with which I was particularly pleased. The elaborate volume on the religious principles of the Friends requires to be very attentively perused; and I mean at the same time to go through Barclay's Apology. The introductory part, to which you drew my attention, is a most able statement of the prominent principle in the creed of your society. I have no doubt that Milton at one period of his life approximated to it.

I do not say anything about politics, as I mix myself in no degree with them. We are living in a most critical period; the popular feeling, from obvious causes, (such as the alteration of the constituency, the spirit of inquiry, more extended reading, &c.,) is getting great weight. What the result will be none of us can tell; it will be seen in a generation or two.

I turned with the greatest pleasure the other day to a reperusal of one of Robert Hall's finest efforts, "on the death of the Princess Charlotte." It is delightful to refresh oneself with such reading, such pure English, the channel of such sentiments and Christian feeling. He was in his line one of the most gifted men of modern times.

Joseph John Gurney's labours amongst Friends

in London were now brought to a conclusion by a visit to the Friends of Westminster, in which he was accompanied by his wife who had been lately "acknowledged" as a minister. On his return from this engagement he writes:—

3rd mo., 3rd. No words can express the relief, (not without a most undeserved portion of real internal quiet and peace,) of having quite finished London and Middlesex. Of my beloved wife I may say, she has been a helper indeed. We have laboured in close and uninterrupted unity and harmony from house to house.

3rd mo., 25th. My quiet retirement at home to-day is rendered the more agreeable by an improved state of health, and by the absence of any particular pressure of care. Earnest are my desires that grace may always be near to keep down "the enemies of my own household." I endeavour from day to day to cast myself in faith on the infinite compassions of God in Christ Jesus. Here alone is my hope. The trials, sorrows, and iniquities which abound on every side, are often the means of bringing me low, and of mantling me as in a dark shroud; but when I reflect on the display of the love and holiness of God, in the incarnation and death of his Son, I am cheered and comforted. That glorious dispensation contains in itself a sufficient and satisfying proof of his infinite goodness; and, when to this proof is added the precious evidence of that divine influence, which calms, gladdens, cleanses, anoints, and still directs the Lord's children as to a hair's breadth, we have, indeed, abundant reason to bow before the Lord, in cheerful, believing acquiescence, under all his dispensations, and cordially to bless his holy name.

FROM JONATHAN HUTCHINSON.

Gedney, 1st mo., 29th, 1835.

* * I am at present favoured with a considerable degree of relief from mental suffering; yet former experience con-

vinces me that I ought to "rejoice with trembling;" and, if I express my feelings at all, that it should be in the subdued and chastened voice of deep humiliation; seeing that I am still in the body, attended by wants and infirmities, and surrounded by the combined operation of causes, both physical and mental, which, but for the exercise of unmerited mercy and almighty power, must long since have sunk me to rise no more, and which, but for a continuance of the same power and mercy, may yet conduct my "grey head, by the path of sorrow, to the grave."

On a comparison of intellectual, or even religious characters, we perceive a surprising variety; and if thou wert to place thy two aged friends, the late William Wilberforce, and the one who is now addressing thee, side by side, I suppose the contrast would appear striking; but need this offend or alarm us? Is not harmony itself composed of different parts appropriately sustained? So that if every bird is but true and faithful to its own note, perhaps it shall not matter much, whether it be that of the plaintive dove, or the more melodious nightingale.

I have been comforted, and almost delighted, by the second section of thy little volume on love to God. Of the first few pages I have been a little doubtful, as to how far a meetness or preparation for the enjoyment of heaven, may not be insisted on, in a way and to an extent, rather discouraging to the eleventh-hour sinner, or the death-bed penitent—two descriptions of persons, who, I am persuaded, are so interesting to each of us, that we should be sorry to put them in too much fear of losing the blessed and high privilege promised even to a late repentance, by the "forgiveness of sins." The poor prodigal, Mary Magdalene, the thief on the cross, Rochester, Buckingham, and similar instances suit my own case so well, and have been so much and so long the subjects of my meditation, that I may possibly have acquired too strong a bias in favour of gratuitous mercy, as containing in itself a grand preparative, by inspiring, sometimes very late and very suddenly, the important sentiments and feelings of deep self-abasement, on the one hand, and, on the other, the most exalted love and gratitude to God; dispositions in which, whatever else may be granted, I desire, more than I can express, that we, my beloved friend, may, with the innumerable company of redeemed souls, who reach that haven of rest and peace, spend a joyful eternity in thanksgiving and praise."

A few weeks later, after alluding to a severe attack of illness, Jonathan Hutchinson writes, under date 2nd mo., 26th:—

Though I believe myself convalescent, it would be presumptuous to be sanguine. I shall at present only add that goodness and mercy attend me. Praised be the Lord!

These were the last lines received by Joseph John Gurney from his long loved and honoured friend. He peacefully expired, after a very short illness, on the 1st of the 4th mo., 1835.

"It was on a beautiful bright day of sunshine, when his favourite 'green Gedney' looked greener than usual," says Joseph John Gurney in a tribute to his memory written two years later, "that my dear wife and myself attended the funeral of my beloved friend and father in the truth, Jonathan Hutchinson. Many Friends were convened from different parts, and the villagers of the place and neighbourhood flocked in large numbers, and in their most decent dresses, to pay their last token of respect to the best man of Gedney. 'So the best man in Gedney is gone,' said one poor labourer to another. 'What!' said the other, 'is Mr. Hutchinson dead?' His remains were deposited in a little family burying ground, not far from his house, where his respectable, though not wealthy predecessors, had been laid in their turns during several generations, and which he had taken the pains to plant with considerable taste. Indeed it was truly remarkable, with what skill this ardent, and almost poetic lover of nature, had contrived to adorn, by judicious planting, the small estate of rich pasture land, which he inherited from his ancestors; who had possessed and occupied the same little farm as he did for the period, as I understand, of about 200 years, never rising above or falling below the rank of respectable yeomen; and since the rise of Friends, members of that religious Society. Nothing can be said of the picturesque appearance of low Lincolnshire: but to this general remark, his little domain, cultivated and adorned as it was, by its late beloved owner, forms a striking exception.

"To revert to the funeral; it was an occasion of precious, comforting solemnity. The meeting-house is at the distance of a mile from the place of interment; but the assembled company followed the train of Friends and relations, first to the meeting, and afterwards to the grave, in the most orderly manner. The meeting afforded a full opportunity for reverent waiting upon the Lord, and for the preaching of the glorious gospel of our holy Redeemer; and at the grave, the thickening circle of Friends and neighbours were again addressed; all seemed united, not only in a sense of their own great loss, but in some view and apprehension of his blessedness,—the blessedness of one who had lived and died in the Lord. The striking mark of affection and respect, which was shown on that day, by the inhabitants of rather an extensive district, was obviously the result of the influence which is gradually obtained over a surrounding population by the weight of sound, practical, but unostentatious Christianity. The good man was gone; the meek, kind, humble, generous neighbour was no more; and many were they, of every description, who seemed ready to rally round his grave in the remembrance of his virtues.

"A painful disease, I believe in the heart, carried him off very suddenly. The unexpected attack came on in the course of the night, after he had retired to rest considerably better than usual. The pain was violent, though short; and death ensued without the opportunity of any expression except a very short prayer, and, I may add, without a struggle. Surely this beloved friend, this humble devoted Christian, rests in Jesus; surely 'when Christ, who is our life, shall appear,' he also shall 'appear with him in glory.'" *

* Colossians iii. 4.

APPENDIX.

TO J. J. GURNEY.

Tottenham, 10th mo., 14th, 1815.

MY VERY DEAR FRIEND,

I fear thou wilt hardly give me credit for much sincerity, if, after so many weeks' delay, I now tell thee, that on the receipt of thy last affectionate and acceptable communication, such were the feelings of sympathy and gratitude, and, (if I may venture to use the term,) of Christian fellowship, that it excited in my heart, that I determined on attempting something in the shape of a reply, as soon as I was able; but just at that time, I was so fully occupied, that I had scarcely more leisure than was necessary for retirement and rest; and after my return home, though the same feeling of brotherly love and friendly interest followed me from day to day, yet I was easily content with making thee my mental companion, without discharging a debt, which I think I am sure would not have had the effect of discharging thee from my best remembrance—no: I think it could not have been so; for I feel, that something has been at work, so to rivet thee on my heart, that almost every day I think of thee, I wish to hear about thee—to know how it fares with thee, and I will not say, that if I really know what it is to pray, that I do not remember thee in my feeble attempts to look towards the throne of grace; but yet I wish I had written before, for in the first place, I might have written to better purpose, and in the next, I might by this time have hoped to hear from thee again.

I wish I knew how to tell thee all I have thought, and felt, in reference to thy biblical researches, and how much I am interested in the result. I was really glad, that thou hadst given up thy time and attention to the subject, particularly so, because I was aware, that thou wast impressed with its importance, and I did not doubt but thou might be able to throw some light upon passages of Scripture which may have been too much overlooked, especially those in the Old Testament. I think thou wilt not be offended with me, nor attribute it altogether to the workings of a weak mind, if I say that I felt so much the awfulness of the engagement, that I could not but desire, in secret aspiration to the Source of help, that grace might be granted, adequate to the exigencies of the occasion. Nor could I doubt, but He, who knew thy desire to promote his glory, would vouchsafe the aid of his Spirit, so that at least thy own faith might be strengthened, whilst thou wast endeavouring to do what thou could for the confirmation of thy fellow-believers. I am the better pleased with the thought of thy observations being made public, under the consideration that they will wear an appearance, doctrinal or critical, rather than controversial: the latter has been so much the case with most of the Anti-Socinian tracts that I have met with; and it is so difficult to manage that kind of writing, in a truly Christian temper, that I fear our adversaries have had a little cause for triumph on that head. I am clearly of the mind, that thou need not trouble thyself about the morning meeting in the business, as its principal concern is to inspect manuscripts, relating to our own peculiar doctrines and principles. The doctrine of the eternal divinity of the Lord Jesus, has obtained much of my most serious thoughtfulness, since I last saw thee. I feel it, awful as it may be, for any of his disciples, however experienced, to speak, write, or think upon the subject, to be one of infinite importance; I am more and more convinced of its truth, and regard it more than ever as the key-stone of our holy religion; take that away, and the grand combination of truth in the mystery of redemption, will soon fall into confusion; therefore, I should value it as a privilege to be allowed to look over thy manuscript; but as my learning extends but little beyond my mother tongue, thou must be aware, that there is much to which I should feel myself incompetent. I think I could highly enjoy a few evenings' conversation with thee upon some of these topics, and others of the leading doctrines of the gospel. Oh! how I love to dwell upon the mercies of God in Christ Jesus; how it humbles the pride of man into the very dust of his unworthiness; and, when applied under the animating influence of the Spirit, how it raises the soul in hope of an inheritance incorruptible in the heavens! no room for the creature, its own works, its own merits, or its own excellencies; there every crown is cast down at the footstool of the Redeemer, and Christ within, and Christ without, becomes our hope of glory; not one without the other, but both in blessed union exalting his own praise.

Let me beg to hear from thee before I leave home. I generally sink very low, and I think a letter from thee would help to cheer me. Try to think of me in thy retirements, and if thou canst do no more, to wish me increase of faith, but above all, an increase in humility.

I am thy very affectionate friend,

W. Forster, Jun.

FROM WILLIAM FORSTER,

[Then on a religious visit to the United States of America.]

New Hampshire, 10th mo., 1st, 1822.

My dearest Joseph—

Scarcely a day has passed for many weeks, but I have wished it were in my power to tell thee of the very near and intimate fellowship, the brotherly love and affectionate sympathy with which I have cherished the remembrance of thee; and how much I have desired to be given up to feel with thee in thy depths of sorrow. * * * The many trials, and sore privations thou hast been permitted to endure, must have brought thee sensibly to feel, to what degree we are pilgrims on earth; and prayer, which has been so much thy resting-place, in happier and more prosperous days, I cannot doubt has often proved thy refuge and thy hiding-place—so that when the blast of the terrible one has been as a storm against the wall, thou hast found the Lord thy Redeemer to be present with thee, and by the clear shining of the light of his heavenly countenance, quickening and strengthening thy soul to a steadfast hope in the continuance of his protection. Surely He, whom thou hast acknowledged as thy Lord and Saviour—He who has been made "precious" to thee, as our High Priest—touched with the feeling of our infirmities—He who having borne our griefs, and carried our sorrows, is continually thy Mediator at the throne of grace—will never suffer thee to be moved from that patient, filial confidence, to which He himself has brought thee, even though thou shouldst be allowed to sink into very humbling feelings of the unworthiness and insufficiency of the creature; I make myself sure, that when reduced to the last extremity, when the floods may seem ready to overwhelm, and thou mayest be scarcely able so much as to say, "Lord, save me," that in the constancy of that love, with which He is ever watching over his dependent and believing disciples, his hand will be stretched forth for thy help, and as in days that are past, thy faith will be renewed and confirmed in his divine omnipotence; and thus it is firmly my trust, that through the power of his grace, it will be given thee again, upon the banks of deliverance, to praise his holy name. I take great comfort in the persuasion, that under thy afflictions (sanctified as I humbly trust they are, by the blessing of the Lord richly resting upon thee) that he is enlarging thy experience, and preparing thee more fully for his service upon earth, and for an inheritance incorruptible in the heavens. My dearest brother, if the present should be a day of gloominess and clouds, if those aboundings in joy and spiritual consolation, with which thou hast been so eminently sustained, should subside for a small moment, if thy heart and thy flesh should fail thee, if thy lips should be closed, and all capacity withdrawn, for uttering a word to the praise of him who is thy strength and thy Redeemer; may it be given thee to possess thy soul in patience and in quietness; to wait the breaking forth of that light, which has often been to thee "a morning without clouds;" and if in this light, thy path be opened to a more extended sphere of religious usefulness, I cannot say to what degree my heart is engaged in desire for thy faithfulness, thy entire devotedness to God; if he hath separated thee to himself, for his own service, (and surely we must not, cannot doubt it,) we may reverently trust, that in the riches of his love, he will fulfil the many gracious promises in thy experience; in *blessing thee, make thee a blessing*, and in his own love and power, render thee instrumental to the confirmation and comfort of his heritage. This has been much the impression of my mind respecting thee, my dear friend, for some time past; it may seem almost out of season to allude to it now, but some months since (and I ought to have told thee of it sooner) thou wast brought before me with a peculiarly sweet and solemn feeling of what I take to be the heavenly unction, in association with Jer. xxvi. 2, "Stand in the court of the Lord's house, and speak unto all the cities of Judah which come to worship in the Lord's house, *all* the words which I command thee to speak unto them; *diminish not a word.*"

*   *   *   *   *

I trust thou wilt feel for me, when I say, that I have not been able to discover a door open for my release as soon as my beloved wife, and my many dear friends, may probably expect my return. I wish to stand constantly on the watch, ready to accept the very first intimation that may be granted me; and very earnestly do I crave an interest in the prayers of all who can feel with me, that I may be endued with patient resignation to the Divine will, and entire devotedness to the service of the Lord, until in the same love and power in which he made me willing to forsake all for his name's sake, He may be pleased to lead me back again to the enjoyment of my many social and domestic comforts.

Farewell, my beloved friend, in the love and fellowship of the Gospel of our Lord and Saviour Jesus Christ, believe me as ever, most truly thine, WILLIAM FORSTER.

FROM WILLIAM FORSTER.

Earlham, 2d mo., 12th, 1836.

MY DEAREST JOSEPH,

* * * * * * By a letter from K. F. we learn that thou hast concluded to stay over First day in their neighbourhood. I am sure we ought not to regret thy tarriance at Upton, as I dare say thy presence is most valuable and important to them; but I know thou wilt allow us to say that we really *long* to see thee back again. Thou canst hardly think what Earlham is without thee! Our little party is going on most smoothly; our boys are gone to Norwich as usual—they are regular and industrious with Kidd, and in every respect much as thou wouldst wish them to be. * * * * * * I hope thou art not going to pass by "*Truth Vindicated*," without some refutation of the sceptical notions which it is so much calculated to insinuate. * * * The quietness and retiredness of Earlham is not at all uncongenial to my taste at the present moment. I spend much of my time in the *study*, reading, &c., and have been a good deal cast down, perhaps unduly so, by poor dear ———'s secession. I really feel for him, both in sympathy and pity, though I dare say he does not think his case calls for it. It does go hard with me to give him up; and I am earnest and rather anxious in desire that Friends and the Church at large may be made fully aware that he was under no necessity to withdraw from us, because there is not amongst us an ear to hear and a heart to receive *pure gospel truth*—for, so far as my experience and information go, there is no department of the great Christian community in which the gospel of Christ, in all its parts and in all its fulness, (when it comes in the freshness and freedom of the divine anointing,) is either more precious or more effectual

than it is among Friends at the present day. I shall greatly value some free and intimate communication with thee on thy return. I need not tell thee what thorough, deep-rooted unity I have with thee in thy exercises, and how much I can and do rejoice when *thou* art honoured in the work and service of the Lord, though at the same time *I* may be abased, and laid very low. And when I can believe, as I often do, that thou art lifted up from thy depths of sorrow and spiritual conflict, and enlarged and strengthened by our Saviour to declare that blessed message of redemption and pardon through the blood of the everlasting covenant with which I do believe that God himself has commissioned thee, I cannot say how much it is my concern that thou mayest never be straitened in *thyself*, and that neither we nor the church may ever straiten thee, but that thou mayst be kept unfettered and at liberty to go, at the bidding of thy Lord, whithersoever he may be pleased to send thee; and that working while it is day, thou mayst finish thy course with joy, (*but not just yet*,) and the ministry thou hast received of the Lord Jesus to testify the gospel of the grace of God. * * * *

I have a pleasant and refreshing remembrance of the true, unrestricted fellowship in Christ, which was so great a comfort to me whilst we were together in Lancashire, and which has been so often renewed and strengthened during our long visit at Earlham Hall. * *

Thine most affectionately,

WILLIAM FORSTER.

END OF THE FIRST VOLUME.

www.ingramcontent.com/pod-product-compliance
Lightning Source LLC
LaVergne TN
LVHW021240110826
845150LV00002B/371

* 9 7 8 1 4 2 5 5 6 2 0 5 2 *